The *Ultimate*
SPANISH VERB
Review and Practice

The *Ultimate* SPANISH VERB
Review and Practice

Second Edition

Ronni L. Gordon, PhD, and David M. Stillman, PhD

New York Chicago San Francisco Lisbon London Madrid Mexico City
Milan New Delhi San Juan Seoul Singapore Sydney Toronto

3 4 5 6 7 8 9 10   QVS/QVS   19 18 17 16 15

ISBN   978-0-07-179783-2
MHID   0-07-179783-1

e-ISBN 978-0-07-179784-9
e-MHID   0-07-179784-X

Library of Congress Control Number 2012942569

Online Audio Exercises
Recordings for the Oral Exercises for each chapter (see pages 281–292) are available
at www.audiostudyplayer.com.

McGraw-Hill products are available at special quantity discounts to use as premiums
and sales promotions or for use in corporate training programs. To contact a
representative, please e-mail us at bulksales@mcgraw-hill.com.

This book is printed on acid-free paper.

Contents

Preface

> The Verb was the storm-center. This discovery made plain the right
> and wise course to pursue in order to acquire certainty and exactness
> in understanding the statements which the newspaper was daily
> endeavoring to convey to me: I must catch a Verb and tame it.
>
> —Mark Twain, "Italian With Grammar"

The Ultimate Spanish Verb Review and Practice: Mastering Verbs and Sentence Building for Confident Communication, Second Edition is designed to provide advanced beginners through advanced learners of Spanish with a powerful tool for reviewing and mastering Spanish verb forms and turning these forms into the building blocks of meaningful sentences. We present the forms of Spanish verbs through verb paradigms in the seven simple tenses and seven compound tenses, and the progressive tenses, and proceed to show how these verb forms function in phrases, clauses, and sentences. This highly productive sentence-building feature, unique to our book, moves the learner effectively from verb forms to communication.

We use a contrastive approach in presenting grammar, comparing Spanish verb tenses and structures to the usage of their English counterparts. Grammar explanations of verb formation and usage are clear, concise, and well-organized. Copious examples, many presented in dialogue format, reflect authentic, everyday language usage. Charts and tables are clear and easy to read. Verb lists are presented in structural and semantic groupings and include the latest additions to the lexicon, as in the case of verbs related to the computer and technology.

All Spanish tenses and moods are presented in the 15 efficiently organized chapters of **The Ultimate Spanish Verb Review and Practice, Second Edition**. Each chapter treats one or more tenses, such as the preterit, or type of verb, such as stem-changing or irregular verbs. Following the presentation of verb paradigms and tenses is a section called *Building Sentences,* in which the chapter material is functionally expanded. As learners master each tense, they learn to expand the forms of that tense into real sentences that can be used for communication through the addition of different elements, such as other verbs, objects, and subordinate clauses, and the transformation of statements into questions. The flexible organization of the chapters permits the learner to study them in any order.

The Ultimate Spanish Verb Review and Practice, Second Edition provides a large number of varied exercises that are designed to facilitate the learner's mastery of the Spanish verb system and sentence building. Exercise types include writing verb forms and dialogue exchanges, translation into Spanish and English, building sentences, replacement, expansion, and identifying types of sentences and verb endings. Useful current vocabulary is incorporated in the exercises. Some exercises provide helpful hints marked ¡Ojo! that aid the learner in proceeding correctly and efficiently. The Answer Key at the end of the book allows learners to monitor their progress as they work through the exercises.

Several chapters have *language boxes* that present information about interesting lexical, historical, and cultural aspects of the Spanish language. These brief language notes are designed to enhance the learner's knowledge and appreciation of the language by presenting etymology, borrowing, punctuation, verb and tense formation, and other features.

In this second edition, we have added an oral component to help learners make the crucial leap from written practice to oral control of forms and patterns. Recorded by native speakers of Spanish, the oral exercises to be practiced in each chapter are based on topics and material presented in the chapter. These structures, the building blocks of communication, will help learners progress to the next level of language skills development—listening and speaking. Many of the exercises are contextual, offering the learner practice in authentic settings, such as home and office. Instruction lines and *Modelos* for the oral exercises can be found on pages 281–292, and responses can be found on pages 317–337 of the Answer Key; to make these pages easy to find, a gray band is printed on their outer edges. The audio material is easily accessible on McGraw-Hill's website (www.audiostudy player.com).

Our acclaimed grammar review and workbook, **The Ultimate Spanish Review and Practice: Mastering Spanish Grammar for Confident Communication**, provides learners with a highly effective tool for review and progress in the Spanish language. We use the same successful pedagogy in **The Ultimate Spanish Verb Review and Practice, Second Edition,** with the knowledge that learners will benefit measurably from its application. This book is ideal for learners working on their own and as an ancillary for students using a textbook in a classroom setting.

We have every confidence that with **The Ultimate Spanish Verb Review and Practice, Second Edition,** you too will be able to catch a Verb and tame it!

∿

We want to express our deepest gratitude to Christopher Brown, our editor and publisher par excellence, for sharing our pedagogical vision and making it a reality in this book and all the others we have written for McGraw-Hill. We are fortunate to have him not only as an expert guide and professional supporter, but also as a most cherished friend.

We dedicate this book to our children, Alex and Mimi, whose brilliance, love, and laughter inspire every word we write.

Ronni L. Gordon, PhD
David M. Stillman, PhD

Introduction

Verbs are presented in conjugation paradigms that summarize the forms of a verb in each tense. Spanish verbs change their form for person and number. Verbs are said to have three persons: the speaker, the person spoken to, and the third person, referring neither to the speaker nor the person spoken to. Spanish, like English, has two numbers: singular and plural.

Here are the persons of the verb and their corresponding subject pronouns in English.

	SINGULAR	PLURAL
FIRST PERSON	*I*	*we*
SECOND PERSON	*you*	*you*
THIRD PERSON	*he, she, it*	*they*

Here are the persons of the verb and their corresponding subject pronouns in Spanish.

	SINGULAR	PLURAL
FIRST PERSON	yo	nosotros/nosotras
SECOND PERSON	tú	vosotros/vosotras
THIRD PERSON	él/ella	ellos/ellas
THIRD PERSON (*you*)	usted	ustedes

Differences Between English and Spanish

- In English, subject pronouns are required to show who the subject of the verb is, since verbs have only two forms in the present tense. In Spanish, however, verb forms are complete in themselves. Subject pronouns are added for emphasis or contrast.

  Ella pregunta y **él** contesta.   *She asks and he answers.*
  Ellos empiezan a trabajar cuando   *They start to work when we finish.*
    nosotros terminamos.

- English has only one form for *you*; Spanish has four. **Tú** is a singular form and is informal. The **tú** form of the verb is used to address one person with whom you have an informal relationship: a family member, a close friend, a fellow student, etc. In Spain, **vosotros** is the plural of **tú**. The **vosotros** form of the verb is used to address two or more people with whom you have an informal relationship.

  tú, vosotros (INFORMAL ADDRESS)

  Esteban, ¿cuándo regresas?   *Esteban, when are you coming back?*
  Mamá, papá, ¿cuándo regresáis?   *Mom, Dad, when are you coming back?*

Usted is used to address one person with whom you have a formal relationship: a stranger, a customer, a superior at work, etc. **Ustedes** is the plural of **usted**. It is used to address two or more people with whom you have a formal relationship. **Usted** is used with the third-person singular forms of the verb. **Ustedes** is used with the third-person plural forms of the verb. **Usted** and **ustedes** are often abbreviated **Ud.** and **Uds. Vd.** and **Vds.** are also used as abbreviations.

usted, ustedes (FORMAL ADDRESS)

Usted puede esperar aquí, señor.	*You can wait here, sir.*
Ustedes pueden esperar aquí, señores.	*You can wait here, gentlemen / ladies and gentlemen.*

In Spain, four forms of *you* are used: **tú, Ud., vosotros,** and **Uds.** In Spanish America, **vosotros** is not used. It is replaced by **ustedes**. Thus, in Spanish America, **ustedes** is also the plural of **tú** and is used to address all groups consisting of two or more people, whether the relationship is formal or informal.

Mamá, papá, ¿cuándo regresan?	*Mom, Dad, when are you coming back?*

- Spanish has no subject pronoun for *it*. All nouns, whether animate or inanimate, are referred to as either **él** or **ella**. Thus, masculine nouns such as **el muchacho** and **el lápiz** are referred to as **él**, while feminine nouns such as **la mujer** and **la ciudad** are referred to as **ella**.

- Spanish makes a gender distinction in the third-person plural. (Note that English *they* does not.) **Ellos** refers to masculine plural nouns, while **ellas** refers to feminine plural nouns. **Ellos** also refers to groups of males and females, while **ellas** refers to groups consisting of females only.

—¿Quiénes son esas personas? ¿Lucas y Anita?	*"Who are those people? Lucas and Anita?"*
—No, no son **ellos**. Son Alejandro y Miriam.	*"No, it's not they. It's Alejandro and Miriam."*
—¿Rebeca y Luisa están ya?	*"Are Rebeca and Luisa here already?"*
—No, **ellas** no, pero están Julia y Marta.	*"No, they're not. But Julia and Marta are here."*

- The Spanish pronouns **nosotros** and **vosotros** also show gender distinctions. **Nosotros** and **vosotros**, like **ellos**, refer to groups of males and females, while **nosotras** and **vosotras** refer to groups consisting of females only.

—Carlos y Diana, **vosotros** sois hermanos, ¿verdad?	*"Carlos and Diana, you're brother and sister, aren't you?"*
—No, **nosotros** somos primos.	*"No, we're cousins."*
—Pilar y Sara, **vosotras** sois hermanas, ¿verdad?	*"Pilar and Sara, you're sisters, aren't you?"*
—No, **nosotras** somos primas.	*"No, we're cousins."*

The Present Tense of Regular Verbs

Subject + verb, subject + verb + direct object
Negative sentences

All Spanish verbs belong to one of three different classes, or *conjugations*. The ending of the infinitive tells which conjugation a verb belongs to: **-ar**, **-er**, or **-ir**.

INFINITIVE

The infinitive is a form of the verb unmarked for person or tense. English infinitives have the word *to* before the verb: *to speak, to eat, to live.*

Spanish infinitives end in **-ar**, **-er**, or **-ir**. When you remove the infinitive ending, you are left with the *stem* of the verb.

Conjugation of -ar Verbs

Spanish verbs of the first conjugation have infinitives ending in **-ar**. **-Ar** verbs are conjugated as follows.

hablar (STEM **habl-**) *to speak*

(yo)	habl**o**	(nosotros/nosotras)	habl**amos**
(tú)	habl**as**	(vosotros/vosotras)	habl**áis**
(él/ella/usted)	habl**a**	(ellos/ellas/ustedes)	habl**an**

NOTES

1 · The vowel **a** is present in all the endings of the present tense of **-ar** verbs except the **yo** form.

2 · The forms of the singular (**hablo, hablas, habla**) and the third-person plural form (**hablan**) are stressed on the stem, as indicated by the underlined vowel. The **nosotros** and **vosotros** forms are stressed on the ending: **hablamos, habláis**.

Common -ar verbs

acabar *to finish*	**ahorrar** *to save*
aceptar *to accept*	**alcanzar** *to reach, overtake*
acompañar *to go with, accompany*	**almacenar** *to store*
aconsejar *to advise*	**alquilar** *to rent*
aguantar *to put up with, stand, tolerate*	**analizar** *to analyze*

apagar *to turn off, shut off*
aparcar *to park*
aprovechar *to take advantage of*
archivar *to file*
armar *to set up, put together*
arrastrar *to drag*
arreglar *to arrange, fix up*
aumentar *to increase*
averiguar *to find out*
avisar *to let know, tell, notify*
ayudar *to help*
bailar *to dance*
bajar *to go down; to lower, turn down;*
   to download
besar *to kiss*
borrar *to erase*
brindar *to drink a toast (to); to toast*
buscar *to look for*
calcular *to calculate, work out*
cambiar *to change*
caminar *to walk*
cantar *to sing*
cargar *to load; to upload*
celebrar *to celebrate*
cenar *to have dinner*
charlar *to chat*
cocinar *to cook*
colocar *to put, place*
comprar *to buy*
contestar *to answer*
cortar *to cut*
crear *to create*
cruzar *to cross*
cursar *to study, take (a course on)*
dejar *to let, leave*
desarrollar *to develop*
desayunar *to have breakfast*
descansar *to rest*
descargar *to download*
desear *to want*
dibujar *to draw*
diseñar *to design*
disfrutar *to enjoy*
doblar *to turn* (change direction);
   to dub (film)
durar *to last*
echar *to throw*

empujar *to push*
ensayar *to test, try out; to rehearse*
enseñar *to teach; to show*
entrar *to go/come in, enter; to input*
entregar *to hand in/over*
escuchar *to listen to*
esperar *to wait, hope, expect*
estacionar *to park*
estornudar *to sneeze*
estudiar *to study*
explicar *to explain*
felicitar *to congratulate*
firmar *to sign*
funcionar *to work, function* (machine)
ganar *to earn, win*
gastar *to spend, waste*
grabar *to record*
gritar *to shout*
guardar *to keep; to put away; to save*
   (computer file)
hablar *to speak*
instalar *to install*
invitar *to invite*
llamar *to call*
llegar *to arrive*
llevar *to carry; to wear*
llorar *to cry*
luchar *to fight, struggle*
mandar *to send, order*
manejar *to drive*
marcar *to dial; to mark*
mascar *to chew*
mirar *to look at*
nadar *to swim*
navegar *to surf* (the Web, Internet)
necesitar *to need*
pagar *to pay*
parar *to stop*
pasar *to spend* (time); *to pass*
patinar *to skate*
pegar *to stick, glue; to hit*
pintar *to paint*
pisar *to stand on, step on*
practicar *to practice; to go in for,*
   play (as a sport)
preguntar *to ask* (a question)
preparar *to prepare*

presentar *to present, introduce*	**terminar** *to finish, end*
programar *to program*	**tirar** *to throw*
pulsar *to press, push* (button)	**tocar** *to play a musical instrument;*
quitar *to take away, remove*	*to touch*
regresar *to come back, return*	**tomar** *to take; to drink*
reparar *to repair, fix*	**trabajar** *to work*
repasar *to review*	**trotar** *to jog*
sacar *to take out; to remove*	**usar** *to use; to wear*
saludar *to greet, say hello to*	**utilizar** *to use, utilize*
tardar *to take/be a long time*	**viajar** *to travel*
telecargar *to load, upload*	**visitar** *to visit*
telefonear *to telephone*	

A *Practice the forms of regular -ar verbs by completing each sentence with the correct form of the verb in parentheses.*

1. (mandar) Yo _mande_ el correo electrónico ahora.
2. (estudiar) Alejandro _estudio_ administración de empresas.
3. (tomar) Nosotros _tomamos_ el tren de las nueve.
4. (entrar) Uds. _entran_ en la sala de exposición.
5. (escuchar) Tú _escuchas_ unos discos compactos.
6. (hablar) Vosotros _hablamos_ por teléfono celular.
7. (tocar) Miriam _toca_ la flauta.
8. (llevar) Yo _llevo_ mi computadora portátil.
9. (navegar) Ellos _navega_ en la Red.
10. (regresar) ¿A qué hora _regresa_ Verónica y David?
11. (alquilar) Ud. _alquilar_ videos los fines de semana.
12. (mirar) Tú y yo _miramos_ la televisión.
13. (llegar) Mis amigos no _llegan_ hasta el miércoles.
14. (trabajar) ¿Ud. _trabajas_ en una empresa multinacional?
15. (guardar) Tú _guardars_ los datos.
16. (viajar) Nosotras _viajamos_ a España en junio.
17. (enseñar) ¿La profesora Alonso _enseñar_ ingeniería informática?
18. (estacionar) Uds. _estacionaron_ el coche en el parqueo, ¿verdad?
19. (esperar) ¿Vosotras _esperan_ delante del cine?
20. (charlar) Los colegas _charlan_ en el cibercafé.
21. (pasar) Yo _paso_ todo el día en el museo.

22. (cambiar)   El turista español _cambia_ los euros por dólares.

23. (entregar)   ¿Cuándo _entregas_ Jaime su informe?

24. (doblar)   Tú _doblas_ a la derecha.

25. (funcionar)   La máquina no _funciona_ bien.

26. (durar)   ¿La película _dura_ dos horas?

27. (desayunar)   Nosotros no _desayunamos_ fuerte.

28. (necesitar)   Ud. _necesitas_ unas tarjetas de memoria.

B   Answer the questions, using the following strings of elements. Include subject pronouns in your responses.

MODELO   ¿Qué toman?

tú / un taxi   _Tú tomas un taxi._

ellos / un café   _Ellos toman un café._

yo / historia   _Yo tomo historia._

1. ¿Qué buscan?
   a. nosotros / las llaves   _Nosotros buscamos las llaves._
   b. él / su teléfono móvil   _El busca su teléfono móvil_
   c. Uds. / la tienda de ropa   _Uds. buscan la tienda de ropa._

2. ¿Qué compran?
   a. yo / unos libros de texto   _yo compro unos libros de texto_
   b. vosotros / un condominio   _vosotros compramos un condominio_
   c. Ud. / zapatos de tenis   _Ud. compras zapatos de tenis_

3. ¿Qué estudian?
   a. tú / informática   _Tu estudias informatica_
   b. ella / programación   _ella estudia programación_
   c. tú y yo / mercadeo   _Tu y o estudiamos mercadeo_

4. ¿Qué graban?
   a. Uds. / una película   _Uds graban una película_
   b. ellas / un programa de televisión   _Ellos graban un programa de televisión_
   c. él / una canción francesa   _el graba canción francesa_
   graba

5. ¿Qué hablan?
   a. Ud. / inglés   _Usted hablas ingles._
   b. vosotras / italiano   _Vosotras hablamos italiano_
   c. ellos / chino   _Ellos hablan chino._

6. ¿Qué llevan?

   a. tú / una maleta _Tu llevas una maleta._

   b. yo / mi portafolio _Yo llevo mi portafolio_

   c. Uds. / el equipaje _Ustedes llevan el equipaje_

C   *Rewrite each of the following sentences, changing the subject to the plural. You are in Spain, where the plural form of informal **tú** is **vosotros** and the plural form of formal **Ud.** is **Uds.***

   MODELOS   Hablas inglés. _Habláis inglés._

               Habla inglés. _Hablan inglés._

1. Alquilas un coche. _Alquiláis un coche._
2. Escucha las noticias. _Escucháis las noticias._
3. Tomas café en Starbucks. _Tomáis café en Sta_
4. Telecarga los documentos. _Telecargáis los docum_
5. Estacionas detrás del banco. _Estacionáis de_
6. Cambia de opinión. _Cambiás_
7. Averigua la información. _Averiguáis_
8. Mandas el correo electrónico. _Mandáis_
9. Pulsa el botón. _Pulsáis_
10. Llegas a las siete. _llegáis a las 7._

D   *Rewrite each of the following sentences, changing the subject to the plural. You are in Spanish America, where both the plural form of informal **tú** and the plural form of formal **Ud.** are **Uds.***

   MODELOS   Hablas inglés. _Hablan inglés._

               Habla inglés. _Hablan inglés._

1. Crea un sitio Web. _Crean un sitio Web._
2. Regresas al anochecer. _Regresan_
3. Ganas una beca. _Ganan_
4. Aprovecha la oferta. _aprovechan_
5. Arrastra el ratón. _arrastran_
6. Compras jeans. _Compran_
7. Trabajas en el centro. _Trabajan_
8. Prepara los sándwiches. _Preparan_
9. Lleva una computadora portátil. _Llevan_
10. Desarrollas un plan. _Desarrollan un plan._

E *Complete each sentence with the correct form of the verb in parentheses, omitting the subject pronoun.*

MODELO   (ellos/caminar) <u>*Caminan*</u> por la zona histórica.

1. (él/aceptar) <u>acepta</u> la pasantía (*internship, assistantship*).
2. (nosotros/averiguar) <u>averiguamos</u> los detalles.
3. (yo/sacar) <u>saqee</u> los billetes.
4. (Uds./practicar) <u>practican</u> el béisbol.
5. (tú/firmar) ¿No <u>firmaste</u> los documentos?
6. (vosotros/preparar) ¿Qué <u>preperamos</u>?
7. (ella/escuchar) <u>Escucha</u> la radio.
8. (Ud./descargar) ¿~~Descargaste~~ los ficheros? Descargadoa
9. (Juan/marcar) <u>marca</u> el número de teléfono.
10. (ellas/crear) ¿<u>crearon</u> una base de datos?
11. (ella/celebrar) <u>celebraron</u> su cumpleaños.
12. (él y yo/bailar) <u>bailamos</u> salsa en la discoteca.
13. (tú/contestar) <u>contestas</u> las preguntas.
14. (ellos/trotar) <u>trotaroos</u> todas las tardes.
15. (Uds./llevar) <u>llevan</u> una mochila.

F *Identify the subject(s) of each sentence by writing the correct subject pronoun(s). Write all possibilities.*

1. Disfrutamos la vida. <u>Nosotros, ~~nosotros~~</u>
2. Acaban la novela. <u>ellos, ellas</u>
3. Dejo un recado. <u>Ella, el</u>
4. ¿Paga las cuentas? <u>Ella</u>
5. Cocinas muy bien. <u>Usted, tu</u>
6. ¿Usa anteojos? <u>Usted</u>
7. Ahorráis mucho dinero. <u>Vosotros</u>
8. Echan la basura. <u>Ellas</u>
9. Apago la luz. <u>Ella, el</u>
10. ¿Por qué lloras? <u>Tu</u>
11. Telecarga los programas. <u>Ella, el</u>
12. Estacionamos frente al cine. <u>Nosotros</u>
13. Toco el clarinete. <u>Ella, el</u>

14. Alquiláis un apartamento. _Vosotros_

15. ¿Qué deseas? _Tú, usted_

Conjugation of **-er** and **-ir** Verbs

In the present tense, second-conjugation **-er** verbs and third-conjugation **-ir** verbs are conjugated alike, except for a difference in the vowel of the **nosotros** and **vosotros** endings. **-Er** and **-ir** verbs are conjugated as follows.

comer (STEM **com-**) *to eat*

(yo)	com**o**	(nosotros/nosotras)	com**emos**
(tú)	com**es**	(vosotros/vosotras)	com**éis**
(él/ella/usted)	com**e**	(ellos/ellas/ustedes)	com**en**

vivir (STEM **viv-**) *to live*

(yo)	viv**o**	(nosotros/nosotras)	viv**imos**
(tú)	viv**es**	(vosotros/vosotras)	viv**ís**
(él/ella/usted)	viv**e**	(ellos/ellas/ustedes)	viv**en**

NOTES

1 · Stress is a very important feature of the Spanish verbal system. The forms of **-er** and **-ir** verbs, like those of **-ar** verbs, are stressed on the stem in the singular and the third-person plural (**ellos/ellas/ustedes**) forms, and on the ending in the **nosotros** and **vosotros** forms. Examine the following forms, in which the stressed vowel is underlined.

(yo)	c_o_mo	(nosotros/nosotras)	com_e_mos
(tú)	c_o_mes	(vosotros/vosotras)	com_é_is
(él/ella/usted)	c_o_me	(ellos/ellas/ustedes)	c_o_men

(yo)	v_i_vo	(nosotros/nosotras)	viv_i_mos
(tú)	v_i_ves	(vosotros/vosotras)	viv_í_s
(él/ella/usted)	v_i_ve	(ellos/ellas/ustedes)	v_i_ven

2 · The vowel of the infinitive of **-ir** verbs (**i**) appears only in those forms where the ending is stressed (viv**i**mos, viv**í**s). With the exception of the **yo** form, the vowel **e** appears in all other present tense endings of **-ir** verbs.

3 · The **yo** form ending is **-o** in all three conjugations.

Common **-er** verbs

aprender *to learn*	**comprender** *to understand*
beber *to drink*	**correr** *to run*
comer *to eat*	**coser** *to sew*

creer *to believe, think*
deber *ought, must, to be supposed to;*
   to owe
leer *to read*
meter *to put in, insert*

prender *to turn on*
romper *to break*
toser *to cough*
vender *to sell*

Common -ir verbs

abrir *to open*
añadir *to add*
aplaudir *to applaud*
asistir a *to attend*
compartir *to share*
cumplir *to fulfill, carry out; to keep one's*
   word; to turn _____ years old
describir *to describe*
difundir *to publicize, broadcast, spread*
discutir *to discuss, argue*
escribir *to write*

imprimir *to print*
insistir (en) *to insist (on)*
interrumpir *to interrupt*
ocurrir *to happen*
permitir *to permit, allow*
recibir *to receive*
resistir *to resist, stand, endure*
subir *to go up, raise; to upload*
sufrir *to suffer*
transmitir *to transmit, broadcast*
vivir *to live*

G *Practice the forms of regular -er and -ir verbs by completing each sentence with the correct form of the verb in parentheses.*

1. (comer)   Ellos _____ en un restaurante hoy.
2. (leer)   Yo _____ un libro de historia inglesa.
3. (asistir)   Nosotros _____ a un concierto esta noche.
4. (imprimir)   ¿Jaime _____ su informe?
5. (meter)   Tú _____ tantas cosas en el maletín.
6. (discutir)   Uds. _____ sobre política.
7. (vender)   Carmen _____ su coche.
8. (escribir)   Ud. _____ poesía, ¿verdad?
9. (correr)   Vosotros _____ en la carrera.
10. (compartir) Las chicas _____ un apartamento.
11. (toser)   ¿Quién _____?
12. (beber)   Los invitados _____ vino de California.
13. (vivir)   Yo _____ en el centro.
14. (aprender) Nosotros _____ a esquiar.
15. (subir)   Vosotras _____ al tercer piso.
16. (comprender) ¿Daniel y Elisa _____ chino?
17. (recibir)   Ud. _____ muchos paquetes.
18. (ocurrir)   ¿Qué _____ aquí?

19. (creer) ¿Uds. _____ eso?

20. (interrumpir) ¡Cuánto _____ esos niños!

21. (insistir) ¿Por qué _____ tú en ese punto?

22. (deber) Tú _____ un dineral (*fortune*).

23. (transmitir) Esta estación de televisión _____ a toda hora.

24. (resistir) Marco Antonio no _____ el calor.

25. (abrir) El centro comercial _____ a las nueve y media.

H *Identify the subject(s) of each sentence by writing the correct subject pronoun(s). Write all possibilities.*

1. ¿Qué crees? _____

2. Añade sal y pimienta. _____

3. No permitimos esto. _____

4. Comparto sus ideas. _____

5. Cosen un botón. _____

6. ¿Por qué rompéis la cita? _____

7. No comprendemos su motivo. _____

8. ¿Todavía sufre de dolor de cabeza? _____

9. ¿Dónde vivís? _____

10. Imprimen el informe en su nueva impresora. _____

11. Corro en la carrera. _____

12. Escribes mensajes electrónicos. _____

13. Subimos en el ascensor. _____

14. ¿Bebes vino tinto o blanco? _____

15. Come demasiado. _____

I *Write sentences using the following strings of elements. Omit the subject.*

MODELO   nosotros / correr / en la pista universitaria

Corremos en la pista universitaria.

1. yo / discutir / la idea con ellos _____

2. ellas / vivir / en esta vecindad _____

3. Roberto / vender / cosas en eBay _____

4. nosotros / abrir / las maletas _____

5. vosotros / beber / vino con la carne _____

6. Ud./aprender/latín y griego _____

7. Paloma y Esteban/subir/en la escalera mecánica

   _____

8. tú/no comprender/la teoría _____

9. Uds./compartir/una pizza _____

10. ella/deber/una fuerte cantidad de dinero

    _____

11. Miguel y yo/comer/de todo _____

12. ¿vosotras/asistir/al partido de fútbol? _____

13. nosotras/leer/varias revistas electrónicas

    _____

14. tu hermana/prender/las luces _____

15. tú/escribir/un artículo para el periódico

    _____

Verbs with Spelling Changes

Verbs Ending in **-ger** and **-gir**

For verbs ending in **-ger** and **-gir**, **g** changes to **j** before **a** and **o**. In the present tense, the change occurs only in the first-person singular (**yo**) form.

coger *to take, grasp, catch*

(yo)	cojo	(nosotros/nosotras)	cogemos
(tú)	coges	(vosotros/vosotras)	cogéis
(él/ella/usted)	coge	(ellos/ellas/ustedes)	cogen

fingir *to pretend*

(yo)	finjo	(nosotros/nosotras)	fingimos
(tú)	finges	(vosotros/vosotras)	fingís
(él/ella/usted)	finge	(ellos/ellas/ustedes)	fingen

Verbs ending in **-ger**

acoger *to welcome, receive* (someone)   **proteger** *to protect*
coger[1] *to take, grasp, catch*   **recoger** *to collect, gather; to pick up*
encoger *to shrink*   **sobrecoger** *to surprise*
escoger *to choose*

---

[1]This verb is taboo in much of South America; **tomar** and **agarrar** are used instead.

Verbs ending in -gir

afligir *to afflict*	**restringir** *to restrict*
corregir[2] *to correct*	**resurgir** *to rise up again; to reappear*
dirigir *to direct; to lead, conduct; to address*	**rugir** *to roar; to bellow; to shout*
	sumergir *to submerge*
elegir[2] *to choose, elect*	**surgir** *to arise, come out, spring up; to appear, emerge*
exigir *to demand*	
fingir *to feign, pretend*	**teledirigir** *to direct by remote control*
infligir *to inflict*	**transigir** *to compromise, give in*
infringir *to infringe*	**ungir** *to anoint*
refulgir *to shine, glitter*	**urgir** *to be urgent/pressing*
regir[2] *to govern, manage*	

In the verb lists and vocabulary of this book, verbs that have this spelling change will be marked as follows.

escoger (g > j/o,a)
fingir (g > j/o,a)

Verbs Ending in -guir

For verbs ending in **-guir**, **-gu** changes to **-g** before **a** and **o**. In the present tense, the change occurs only in the first-person singular (**yo**) form.

distinguir *to distinguish*

(yo)	disting**o**	(nosotros/nosotras)	distinguimos
(tú)	distingues	(vosotros/vosotras)	distinguís
(él/ella/usted)	distingue	(ellos/ellas/ustedes)	distinguen

conseguir[3] *to get; to manage*	**perseguir**[3] *to pursue*
distinguir *to distinguish*	**proseguir**[3] *to pursue, proceed, continue with*
extinguir *to extinguish*	**seguir**[3] *to follow*

Verbs Ending in -uir

Verbs ending in **-uir** (but not **-guir**) insert **y** between the stem and those present tense endings that are unstressed (all forms except **nosotros** and **vosotros**). Note that this spelling change reflects the pronunciation of these verbs. The **y** is clearly sounded where it appears.

construir *to build*

(yo)	construyo	(nosotros/nosotras)	construimos
(tú)	construyes	(vosotros/vosotras)	construís
(él/ella/usted)	construye	(ellos/ellas/ustedes)	construyen

---

[2]The vowel of the stem changes from **e** to **i** in the singular and the third-person plural. You will see other verbs with this change in Chapter 2.

[3]The vowel of the stem changes from **e** to **i** in the singular and the third-person plural. You will see other verbs with this change in Chapter 2.

atribuir *to attribute*   **huir** *to flee*
concluir *to conclude*   **incluir** *to include*
contribuir *to contribute*   **influir** *to influence*
destruir *to destroy*   **instituir** *to institute*
diluir *to dissolve; to dilute*   **instruir** *to instruct*
distribuir *to distribute*   **sustituir** *to substitute*

J *Complete each sentence with the correct form of the verb in parentheses.
All verbs end in -ger, -gir, -guir, or -uir.*

1. (seguir)   ¿Por qué no _____ (tú) nuestros consejos?

2. (escoger)   Yo _____ un regalo para la cumpleañera.

3. (exigir)   Yo no _____ demasiado, ¿verdad?

4. (construir)   Se _____ un centro comercial en la carretera.

5. (recoger)   Yo _____ el equipaje en la aduana.

6. (huir)   Ellos _____ del huracán.

7. (conseguir)   Uds. no _____ convencernos.

8. (corregir)   Felipe _____ sus faltas.

9. (coger)   Vosotros _____ un taxi en la esquina.

10. (elegir)   ¿Cuál marca _____ Ud.?

11. (destruir)   La humedad _____ la madera.

12. (proteger)   ¿Cómo se _____ el medio ambiente?

13. (extinguir)   Nosotros _____ el fuego de campamento.

14. (perseguir)   ¿Paloma _____ sus objetivos?

15. (dirigir)   Un director norteamericano _____ la compañía.

16. (acoger)   Nosotros _____ a nuestros amigos con mucho cariño.

17. (surgir)   ¿Por qué _____ tantos conflictos?

18. (distinguir)   Yo no _____ el perfil (*skyline*) de la ciudad por la niebla.

19. (diluir)   Tú _____ la pólvora en el agua.

20. (urgir)   Este asunto _____.

Uses of the Present Tense

The Spanish present tense is used to express general actions or states.

—¿Dónde trabaja tu hermana?   *"Where does your sister work?"*
—Enseña matemáticas en una   *"She teaches math at a university."*
   universidad.

It can also express actions going on at the present time, a function for which English usually prefers the present progressive tense (see Chapter 14).

—¿Los chicos **trotan**?	*"Are the kids jogging?"*
—No, ahora **navegan** en la Red.	*"No, now they're surfing the Web."*

Note that Spanish has no equivalent for the English auxiliary *do, does* in questions or negative sentences.

—¿Qué idioma **estudias**? ¿El alemán?	*"What language do you study? German?"*
—No, **no estudio** alemán. Curso francés.	*"No, I don't study German. I take French."*

The present tense can be used to ask for instructions.

¿**Nos reunimos** el viernes?	*Shall we get together on Friday?*
¿**Mando** un e-mail?	*Shall I send an e-mail?*

Spanish can use the present tense to express future time when another element of the sentence makes it clear that the verb is referring to the future. Note that English often uses the present progressive to express the future.

—¿A qué hora **llegan** mañana?	*"What time are you arriving tomorrow?"*
—**Llegamos** a las diez. Y al llegar, te **llamamos**.	*"We're arriving at ten. And when we arrive, we'll call you."*

The present tense can be used to express past actions once the conversation makes clear that the past is being referred to. This may occur in both speech and writing, and it has parallels in English. This use of the present to refer to the past is called the *historical present*.

No te puedes imaginar lo que pasó anoche. **Entro** en el teatro, **busco** mi asiento, **me siento** y **levanto** la vista. Y ¿a quién **veo** sentado a mi lado? A Fernando mi ex-novio. ¡Y acompañado de mi mejor amiga!	*You can't imagine what happened last night. I go into the theater, I look for my seat, I sit down and look up. And whom do I see sitting next to me? Fernando, my ex-boyfriend. And he was with my best friend!*

Spanish uses the present tense to refer to actions that began in the past but are continuing into the present. English uses a *have/has been doing something* construction for this function. The Spanish construction consists of the following elements.

- ¿**cuánto tiempo hace que** + verb in present tense?

  This construction is used to ask a question about how long something has been going on. The word **tiempo** can be omitted in the question.

¿**Cuánto hace que** Ud. vive en este barrio?	*How long have you been living in this neighborhood?*

- **hace** + time expression + **que** + verb in present tense OR verb in present tense + **hace** + time expression

  These constructions are used to tell how long something has been going on.

—¿**Cuánto tiempo hace que** Ud. vive en este barrio?	*"How long have you been living in this neighborhood?"*
—**Hace un año que vivo** aquí.	*"I've been living here for a year."*
—**Vivo** aquí **hace un año**.	*"I've been living here for a year."*

- **Desde** is added to specify the starting point of an action that began in the past and continues into the present.

—¿**Desde cuándo** vives al lado de los Vega?	*"**Since when** have you been living next door to the Vegas?"*
—Somos vecinos **desde** septiembre.	*"We've been neighbors **since** September."*

- When the verb is *to be*, Spanish often prefers to use the verb **llevar** to express *have/has been* with expressions of time.

—¿Cuánto tiempo **llevas** aquí?	*"How long **have you been** here?"*
—**Llevo un año** en Madrid.	*"I've been in Madrid **for one year**."*
—**Llevamos más de dos años** en esta universidad.	*"We've been at this university **for more than two years**."*

- **Tener** can also be used with this meaning, especially in Spanish America.

¿**Tienes mucho tiempo** con esta empresa?	*Have you been with this company **for a long time**?*
Tienen dos años en Nueva York.	*They've been in New York **for two years**.*

K   *How long has this been going on?* Form a question from the elements given, and then answer it in two ways.

MODELO   Ud./esperar el tren (quince minutos)

  ¿Cuánto tiempo hace que Ud. espera el tren?

  Hace quince minutos que espero el tren.

  Espero el tren hace quince minutos.

1. Carolina/navegar en la Red (dos horas)

   _____

   _____

   _____

2. tú/estudiar administración de empresas (un año)

   _____

   _____

   _____

3. Uds./vivir en Londres (cuatro años)

   _____

   _____

   _____

4. los Soriano / viajan por Europa (seis semanas)

_____

_____

_____

5. vosotros / asistir a estas conferencias (un par de meses)

_____

_____

_____

6. Ud. / descargar los documentos (media hora)

_____

_____

_____

7. nosotros / discutir los trámites (*steps, procedures*) (una semana)

_____

_____

_____

8. yo / exigir la colaboración de todos (varios días)

_____

_____

_____

L **Translation.** *Express the following dialogues in Spanish.* **¡Ojo!** *There might be more than one way to express an answer.*

1. *Are you (tú) working in the office tomorrow?*

_____

2. *No, I'm spending the day at home.*

_____

3. *Are you (Ud.) attending the concert tonight?*

_____

4. *Yes, and before that I'm having dinner with some friends.*

_____

5. *How long have you (Uds.) been building the house?*

_____

6. *We've been building the house for a year.*

   _____

7. *How long have they been in the United States?*

   _____

8. *They've been here for fifteen years.*

   _____

9. *Since when have you (Ud.) been pursuing your studies?*

   _____

10. *I've been taking engineering courses since January.*

    _____

BUILDING SENTENCES | **Subject + verb, subject + verb + direct object**

The subject is the element of the sentence that determines the ending of the verb. In the following sentences, **Juan** and **los chicos** are subjects.

Juan navega en la Red.

Los chicos nadan en la piscina.

In many Spanish sentences, the subject is not expressed, but is indicated solely by the ending of the verb.

Siempre **tomo** café por la mañana.	*I always **have** coffee in the morning.*
¿A qué hora **comes**?	*At what time **do you eat**?*
Asistimos a todos los conciertos.	*We **attend** all the concerts.*

In the third person, the subject is omitted when context clarifies who or what it is.

—¿Dónde están los asesores?	*"Where are the consultants?"*
—Creo que **llegan** pronto.	*"I think **they're arriving** soon."*
—¿Por qué no llevas tu reloj?	*"Why aren't you wearing your watch?"*
—**No funciona.**	*"**It doesn't work.**"*

A complete Spanish sentence may consist of a verb form by itself.

—¿Qué haces?	*"What are you doing?"*
—**Leo.**	*"**I'm reading.**"*
—Mañana estáis ocupados, ¿verdad?	*"Tomorrow you're busy, right?"*
—Sí. **Trabajamos.**	*"Yes, we are. **We're working.**"*

The idea or action expressed by the verb may affect or be directed at a person or thing. That person or thing is the object of the verb. Spanish treats objects that refer to animate beings differently from objects referring to things. If a noun is not the subject of a sentence and it both refers to an inanimate object and follows the verb directly without a preposition, it is called a *direct object*. In the sentences below, the direct objects are in boldface.

Queremos modernizar **nuestra cocina**.	*We want to modernize **our kitchen**.*
Necesito comprar **sellos**.	*I need to buy **stamps**.*
¿Lavas **el carro**?	*Are you washing **the car**?*

Transitive and Intransitive Verbs

Spanish verbs that take a direct object are called *transitive verbs*. In most cases these verbs *must* appear with a direct object. In the verb lists in this book, transitive verbs that take an inanimate direct object (an object that is a thing) are followed by **algo**.

preparar algo *to prepare something*
romper algo *to break something*
ver algo *to see something*

Spanish verbs that cannot be followed by a direct object are called *intransitive verbs*. Most verbs of motion fall into this category.

Mis amigos **salen**.	*My friends **are going out**.*
Regresan a la una para almorzar.	*They're **coming back** at one to have lunch.*
Por la tarde **van** al cibercafé.	*In the afternoon **they're going** to the Internet café.*

Some verbs can be used either intransitively or transitively.

Sube al quinto piso. (INTRANSITIVE)	*He's going up to the fifth floor.*
Sube el equipaje. (TRANSITIVE)	*He's bringing the luggage up.*
Los precios bajan en verano. (INTRANSITIVE)	*Prices fall in the summer.*
Bajan los cuadros. (TRANSITIVE)	*They're taking the paintings down.*
Corro todos los días. (INTRANSITIVE)	*I run every day.*
Corro la milla en quince minutos. (TRANSITIVE)	*I run the mile in fifteen minutes.*

THE VERB regresar

In American Spanish, the verb **regresar** can be used as a transitive verb as well as an intransitive one.

Regresamos a fines del mes.	*We're coming back at the end of the month.*
Regresamos el coche lo antes posible.	*We're returning the car as soon as possible.*

Sometimes transitive verbs appear without an expressed direct object, but have an implied direct object that is understood from context.

Abrimos (la tienda) a las nueve.   ***We open** (the store) at nine o'clock.*

Here are some transitive verbs in Spanish that do not take a direct object in English, but do take an inanimate direct object in Spanish. Note that the English verbs have a preposition (*of, for, about, in, at, on, to,* or *into*).

aprobar (o > ue) algo *to approve of something*

No apruebo su conducta.   *I don't approve of his conduct.*

aprovechar algo *to take advantage of something*

Debemos aprovechar las instalaciones   *We should take advantage of the sports*
deportivas del hotel.   *facilities of the hotel.*

buscar algo *to look for something*

Él busca un apartamento.   *He's looking for an apartment.*

comentar algo *to comment on something*

Todos comentan el acontecimiento.   *Everyone is talking about the event.*

escuchar algo *to listen to something*

Escucho las noticias por la mañana.   *I listen to the news in the morning.*

esperar algo *to wait for something*

Espero el autobús en la esquina.   *I wait for the bus at the corner.*

mirar algo *to look at something*

Siempre miro los anuncios del diario.   *I always look at the newspaper ads.*

pagar algo *to pay for something*

¿Quién paga la comida?   *Who's paying for the meal?*

pedir (e > i) algo *to ask for something*

Ella siempre me pide dinero.   *She always asks me for money.*

pisar algo *to step on something*

No pisar el césped. (*sign*)   *Don't step on the grass.*

profundizar algo *to go into, study something in depth, delve deeply into*

El profesor profundiza el tema.   *The professor goes into the subject in depth.*

solicitar algo *to apply for something*

¿Solicitas aquel puesto?   *Are you applying for that job?*

There are also English transitive verbs whose cognates or equivalents do not take a direct object in Spanish. These verbs have a preposition (typically **a** or **de**, depending on the verb) linking them to their objects.

asistir a algo *to attend something*

Asistimos a muchos conciertos.   *We attend a lot of concerts.*

entrar a/en *to enter*

Entramos al café / en el café.   *We enter the café.*

NOTE: **Entrar** is also used as a transitive verb with a direct object in the expression **entrar datos** *to enter/input data.*

jugar (u > ue) a + the definite article (name of sport or game)
  to play (a sport or game)

En verano jugamos al béisbol. *In the summer we play baseball.*

NOTE: Some speakers omit the preposition **a** and the definite article before the name of the game: **En verano jugamos béisbol.**

renunciar a algo *to give up something, resign from / quit something*

Mi hermano renuncia a su puesto. *My brother is quitting his job.*

salir de (un lugar) *to leave (a place)*

Los empleados salen de la oficina a las cinco. *The employees leave the office at five.*

M *Identify each sentence as having a transitive or intransitive verb.*

	TRANSITIVE	INTRANSITIVE
1. Firma los cheques.	☐	☐
2. Bajan al patio.	☐	☐
3. Recojo las hojas.	☐	☐
4. Descargan los documentos.	☐	☐
5. Diseñas ropa muy elegante.	☐	☐
6. Camináis hacia el metro.	☐	☐
7. Almacenamos la información.	☐	☐
8. Maneja con cuidado.	☐	☐
9. ¿Compras un nuevo teléfono?	☐	☐
10. Sustituyen este teclado por otro.	☐	☐
11. Busco su dirección electrónica.	☐	☐
12. ¿Él sube a la azotea (*roof*)?	☐	☐
13. Transmiten las noticias a las seis.	☐	☐
14. Creamos una base de datos.	☐	☐
15. Llegáis para las once.	☐	☐

N ***Subject + verb.*** *Write sentences using the intransitive verbs and other elements given in the following strings.*

MODELO   Rodrigo y yo / cenar / a las ocho

  Rodrigo y yo cenamos a las ocho.

1. tú / cantar / afinadamente (*in tune*)

_____

2. los atletas / correr / en la carrera

_____

3. Pablo / toser / mucho

_____

4. ¿Uds. / vivir / en las afueras?

_____

5. yo / regresar / la semana entrante

_____

6. el programa / funcionar / bien

_____

7. nosotros / subir / al tercer piso

_____

8. los habitantes / huir / del terremoto (*earthquake*)

_____

9. yo / trotar / por el parque

_____

10. el gerente / trabajar / de lunes a viernes

_____

11. ¿vosotros / llegar / en tren?

_____

12. tú / viajar / por el sudoeste del país

_____

13. ¿Mercedes y Sofía / estornudar / por su alergia?

_____

14. un conflicto / surgir / entre los socios

_____

15. Ud. / bajar / por la escalera

_____

16. nosotros / participar / en el foro de debate

_____

17. ¿qué / opinar (Uds.) / de la facultad de educación?

_____

O *Subject* + *verb* + *direct object.* Write sentences using the transitive verbs and direct objects given in the following strings.

MODELO   Clara / romper / los papeles
           Clara rompe los papeles.

1. Roberto y yo / ahorrar / dinero

   _____

2. yo / regir / la empresa

   _____

3. los jefes / concluir / su conversación

   _____

4. ¿Ud. / conseguir / sus billetes electrónicos (*e-tickets*)?

   _____

5. tú / guardar / el secreto

   _____

6. Uds. / comprar / una cámara digital

   _____

7. vosotros / imprimir / el informe

   _____

8. Beatriz y Alicia / compartir / la computadora

   _____

9. Ud. / leer / la página Web

   _____

10. nosotras / crear / unas carpetas

    _____

11. Marco Antonio / aprender / las fechas de memoria

    _____

12. ¿vosotros / marcar / el número de teléfono?

    _____

13. yo / conseguir / los boletos

    _____

14. los programadores / instalar / un programa de gráficas

    _____

15. tú / recibir / revistas de informática

_____

16. el director de la junta / interrumpir / la reunión

_____

P *Write sentences using the following strings of elements, adding prepositions as needed.*

MODELOS   yo / pagar / la cuenta
          *Yo pago la cuenta.*_____

          yo / entrar / la librería
          *Yo entro a/en la librería.*_____

1. Alberto y Daniela / esperar / un taxi

_____

2. ¿Ud. / asistir / el congreso?

_____

3. tú y yo / escuchar / estos discos compactos

_____

4. la jefa / renunciar / su puesto

_____

5. el ingeniero / entrar / los datos

_____

6. vosotras / mirar / los sitios Web

_____

7. Uds. / salir / el hotel

_____

8. los jugadores / pisar / el césped

_____

9. Rafael y yo / jugar / fútbol

_____

10. yo / entrar / el centro comercial

_____

11. mi hermana / subir / su ropa al dormitorio

_____

12. los vecinos / comentar / las noticias del barrio

_____

13. los turistas / visitar / los monumentos

_____

14. ¿vosotros / aprobar / el plan económico?

_____

15. ¿tú / buscar / las llaves?

_____

Ｏ **Translation.** *Express the following sentences in Spanish.*

1. *I'm applying for this job.* _____

2. *Virginia is looking at her e-mail.* _____

3. *Are you (tú) taking advantage of the sales?* _____

4. *We're attending that concert.* _____

5. *They're entering the bookstore.* _____

6. *You (Ud.) are entering data.* _____

7. *Esteban is giving up the project.* _____

8. *What are you (Uds.) looking for?* _____

BUILDING SENTENCES | **Negative sentences**

Sentences are made negative in Spanish by placing the word **no** before the verb. Both declarative sentences and questions may be made negative.

Comen ahora.	*They're eating now.*
No comen ahora.	*They're not eating now.*
¿Escribes el informe?	*Are you writing the report?*
¿**No escribes** el informe?	*Aren't you writing the report?*

Note in the response below that a negative answer to a question may begin with two occurrences of the word **no**. The first is the opposite of **sí** *yes*. The second is the word **no** that negates the verb.

—¿**Llegan** el viernes?	*"Are they arriving on Friday?"*
—**No, no llegan** el viernes.	*"No, they're not arriving on Friday."*

The words **nunca** and **jamás** mean *never*. When they follow the verb, **no** precedes it. For some speakers, **jamás** is more formal or more emphatic than **nunca**.

—¿Nadas **a veces**?	*"Do you sometimes swim?"*
—**No, no nado nunca.**	*"No, I never swim."*
—¿Asisten Uds. **mucho** a los conciertos?	*"Do you attend concerts a lot?"*
—**No, no asistimos jamás** a los conciertos.	*"No, we never attend concerts."*
—¿Trasnocháis **siempre**?	*"Do you always stay up late?"*
—**No, no trasnochamos nunca.**	*"No, we never stay up late."*

The words **nunca** and **jamás** may appear before the verb. In this case, **no** is not used before the verb.

—¿Nadas **a veces**?	*"Do you sometimes swim?"*
—**No, nunca nado.**	*"No, I never swim."*
—¿Asisten Uds. **mucho** a los conciertos?	*"Do you attend concerts a lot?"*
—**No, jamás asistimos** a los conciertos.	*"No, we never attend concerts."*
—¿Trasnocháis **siempre**?	*"Do you always stay up late?"*
—**No, nunca trasnochamos.**	*"No, we never stay up late."*

The phrase **ya no** means *not anymore* and precedes the verb. It can be used as a short response.

—¿Los señores Alba viven al lado?	*"Do the Albas live next door?"*
—**No, ya no viven** al lado.	*"No, they don't live next door anymore."*
—**Ya no.**	*"Not anymore."*

The phrase **todavía no** means *not yet* and precedes the verb. It can be used as a short response.

—Necesito ver al jefe.	*"I have to see the boss."*
—**Todavía no está.**	*"He isn't in yet."*
—¿Uds. firman el contrato?	*"Are you signing the contract?"*
—**Todavía no.**	*"Not yet."*

Nada means *nothing* and usually follows the verb. **No** precedes the verb.

—¿Buscan **algo**?	*"Are you looking for something?"*
—No, **no buscamos nada.**	*"No, we're not looking for anything."*
—¿Compran **algo**?	*"Are they buying anything?"*
—No, **no compran nada.**	*"No, they're not buying anything."*

Nadie means *no one* and often precedes the verb when it is the subject of the sentence. **No** is not used when **nadie** precedes the verb.

—¿Los invitados comen?	*"Are the guests eating?"*
—No, **nadie come.**	*"No, no one is eating."*

Nadie as subject may follow the verb (and often does). In this case, the word **no** is used before the verb.

—¿Los invitados comen?	*"Are the guests eating?"*
—No, **no come nadie.**	*"No, no one is eating."*

Nadie and **alguien** as direct objects of the verb are presented in Chapter 2 (see p. 39).

At the top of the next page is a summary of the most common negative words and their affirmative counterparts.

NEGATIVE WORDS AND EXPRESSIONS	AFFIRMATIVE WORDS AND EXPRESSIONS

nunca, jamás *never* {

alguna vez *sometime*
algunas veces, a veces *sometimes*
muchas veces, a menudo *often*
mucho *a lot, often*
siempre *always*

nada *nothing*

algo *something*

nadie *no one, nobody* (as subject)

alguien *someone, somebody* (as subject)

a nadie *no one, nobody*
  (as direct object)

a alguien *someone, somebody*
  (as direct object)

R *Answer each question in the negative.*

MODELO   ¿Ud. patina sobre hielo?

  No, no patino sobre hielo.

1. ¿Uds. usan una calculadora de bolsillo?

  _____

2. ¿Daniel habla por teléfono celular?

  _____

3. ¿Echáis las cartas al buzón?

  _____

4. ¿Prendes el ordenador (*computer,* Spain)?

  _____

5. ¿Tú y tus amigos comparten los gastos?

  _____

6. ¿Ellos transmiten el documental esta noche?

  _____

7. ¿Ud. corrige las faltas en el manuscrito?

  _____

8. ¿Carmen renuncia a su puesto de contable (*accountant*)?

  _____

9. ¿Los campistas extinguen el fuego de campamento?

  _____

10. ¿Uds. influyen en la decisión?

  _____

S *Answer each question, using the negative words and expressions that correspond to their affirmative counterparts. ¡Ojo! There might be more than one way to express your answers.*

MODELO   ¿Dibujas animales a veces?

No, no dibujo animales nunca/jamás. / No, nunca/jamás dibujo animales.

1. ¿Uds. solicitan algo?

_____

2. ¿Alguien grita?

_____

3. ¿Los novios salen a bailar muchas veces?

_____

4. ¿Exiges algo?

_____

5. ¿Ud. espera a alguien?

_____

6. ¿Los niños lloran mucho?

_____

7. ¿Laura siempre llega puntualmente?

_____

8. ¿Montáis a caballo a menudo?

_____

9. ¿Tus amigos trasnochan algunas veces?

_____

10. ¿Pablo llega tarde alguna vez?

_____

T **Translation.** *Express the following sentences in Spanish.*

1. *Don't you (tú) stay up late anymore?*

_____

2. *We don't repair the computer often.*

_____

3. *Jaime isn't saving the files yet.*

_____

4. *You (Uds.) never have dinner before eight o'clock.*

_____

5. *They're not looking at anything.*

   _____

6. *No one is taking advantage of the opportunity.*

   _____

7. *Nothing is happening.*

   _____

8. *I'm not choosing anything.*

   _____

9. *We often surf the Web.*

   _____

10. *Sometimes they watch baseball games on the computer.*

    _____

11. *Someone is looking for you* (tú).

    _____

12. *She never interrupts anyone.*

    _____

2

Stem-Changing Verbs; Special Verbs Ending in **-iar** and **-uar**

BUILDING SENTENCES

Verb + infinitive construction
Personal a

Stem-Changing **-ar** and **-er** Verbs

Many Spanish verbs change the vowel of the stem in the present tense in those forms where the vowel of the stem is stressed. For **-ar** and **-er** verbs, the changes that occur are **e** > **ie** and **o** > **ue**.

In the present tense, the change in the vowel of the stem takes place only in those forms where the stress falls on the stem. There is *no* change in the vowel of the stem in those forms where the stress falls on the ending (the infinitive and the **nosotros** and **vosotros** forms).

Study the present tense forms of **pensar** *to think*, **querer** *to want*, **contar** *to count, to tell*, and **volver** *to return*.

pensar (e > ie) *to think*	
pienso	pensamos
piensas	pensáis
piensa	piensan

querer (e > ie) *to want*	
quiero	queremos
quieres	queréis
quiere	quieren

contar (o > ue) *to count; to tell*	
cuento	contamos
cuentas	contáis
cuenta	cuentan

volver (o > ue) *to return*	
vuelvo	volvemos
vuelves	volvéis
vuelve	vuelven

Common verbs that pattern like **pensar** and **querer** (e > ie)

acertar *to be on target, guess right*
apretar *to squeeze, be tight; to grip*
ascender *to go up, rise; to promote, be promoted*
atravesar *to cross*
cerrar *to close*
comenzar *to begin*

confesar *to confess, admit*
defender *to defend*
descender *to go down*
despertar(se) *to wake up*
empezar *to begin*
encender *to light, turn on* (appliance)
encerrar *to lock in; to contain*

entender *to understand*
gobernar *to govern, manage, direct*
helar[1] *to freeze*
merendar *to have an afternoon snack*
nevar[1] *to snow*

perder *to lose; to miss* (train, etc.)
quebrar *to break*
recomendar *to recommend*
sentar(se) *to seat, sit down*

Common verbs that pattern like contar and volver (o > ue)

acordarse *to remember*
acostar(se) *to put to bed, go to bed*
almorzar *to have lunch*
conmover *to move* (emotionally)
costar *to cost*
demostrar *to show*
devolver *to return (something),*
    give (something) back
doler *to hurt, ache*
encontrar *to find*
envolver *to wrap up*
jugar (u > ue) *to play*
llover[2] *to rain*

mostrar *to show, display*
oler (o > hue) *to smell*
poder *can, be able*
probar(se) *to try, taste; to try on*
recordar *to remember; to remind*
resolver *to solve, resolve, decide*
rodar *to roll; to film, shoot a film*
rogar *to ask, request; to beg, plead*
soler *to usually do something,*
    be accustomed to doing something
tronar[2] *to thunder*
volar *to fly*

A *Practice the forms of stem-changing verbs that pattern like* **pensar** *and* **querer (e > ie)** *by completing each sentence with the correct form of the verb in parentheses.*

1. (querer)   Yo _____ una computadora portátil.

2. (pensar)   Nosotros _____ mucho en el futuro.

3. (comenzar)   La película _____ a las diez de la noche.

4. (entender)   Tú no _____ mi genial idea.

5. (recomendar) ¿Ud. _____ esta marca?

6. (perder)   Ellos _____ el tren a menudo.

7. (encender)   Vosotros _____ las luces.

8. (gobernar)   El presidente _____ el país muy hábilmente.

9. (descender)   Tú _____ en ascensor.

10. (empezar)   Yo _____ a navegar en la Red.

11. (cerrar)   ¿Estas farmacias nunca _____?

12. (nevar)   _____ casi todos los días en invierno.

13. (atravesar) Nosotros _____ la calle en la esquina.

14. (defender)   Los soldados _____ la frontera.

---

[1]Impersonal verb conjugated only in the third-person singular: **hiela, nieva**.
[2]Impersonal verb conjugated only in the third-person singular: **llueve, truena**.

15. (ascender)   La temperatura _____ rápidamente.

16. (helar)   El frío _____ el agua del lago.

17. (despertar)   Nadie se _____ temprano los fines de semana.

18. (sentar)   Los invitados se _____ en la sala.

B *Practice the forms of stem-changing verbs that pattern like* **contar** *and* **volver** *(**o** > **ue**) by completing each sentence with the correct form of the verb in parentheses.*

1. (volver)   Ellos _____ de vacaciones el sábado.

2. (encontrar)   Yo no _____ las tarjetas de memoria.

3. (envolver)   Pilar y yo _____ los regalos.

4. (almorzar)   ¿Tú _____ en la cafetería hoy?

5. (devolver)   Ud. nos _____ el coche mañana.

6. (costar)   Este televisor de plasma _____ una fortuna.

7. (merendar)   Vosotros _____ a las cuatro.

8. (demostrar)   Marco Antonio _____ interés en la inteligencia artificial.

9. (llover)   Siempre _____ por aquí en abril.

10. (poder)   ¿Ud. _____ terminar el informe para el lunes?

11. (probar)   Nosotras _____ muchos platos exóticos.

12. (recordar)   Ellas no _____ nada del acontecimiento.

13. (oler)   Algo _____ mal en la cocina.

14. (resolver)   Yo _____ todos los problemas.

15. (volar)   Estas aves _____ al sur de Estados Unidos.

16. (mostrar)   La agencia _____ unas casas amuebladas.

17. (acostar)   Tú te _____ demasiado tarde.

18. (acordar)   ¿Vosotros no os _____ de la fecha?

The verb **jugar** *to play* is anomalous in that it changes the stem vowel **u** to **ue** in the present tense. The **u** remains in the **nosotros** and **vosotros** forms.

jugar (u > ue) *to play*

j**ue**go	jugamos
j**ue**gas	jugáis
j**ue**ga	j**ue**gan

LA LENGUA ESPAÑOLA jugar

The reason for the apparently anomalous change **u** > **ue** in this verb is its medieval form. **Jugar** was pronounced **jogar** in Medieval and early Renaissance Spanish. Thus, the original pattern **jogar** > **juego** was not irregular at all.

NOTES

1 · **Jugar** is used with the preposition **a** and the definite article to indicate the game or sport played.

> **jugar al tenis** *to play tennis*
> **jugar al baloncesto** *to play basketball*
> **jugar a las cartas** *to play cards*
> **jugar al escondite** *to play hide-and-seek*

> —¿A qué juegan?   *"What are they playing?"*
> —Juegan al béisbol.   *"They are playing baseball."*

Some speakers omit the preposition **a** and the definite article before the name of the game: **jugar béisbol, jugar tenis, jugar baloncesto, jugar cartas**, etc.

2 · The verb **tocar**, not **jugar**, is used for *to play a musical instrument.*

> tocar el piano, la flauta, el violin,   *to play the piano, the flute, the violin,*
>   el saxofón, el clarinete, la guitarra   *the saxophone, the clarinet, the guitar*

3 · **Jugar** also means *to gamble, bet.* The noun **el juego** *game* also means *gambling.* **Perder su dinero en el juego** means *to gamble one's money away.*

C *Write sentences using the verb* **jugar** *and the following strings of elements.*

> MODELO   Paco / jugar / golf *Paco juega (al) golf.*

1. Uds. / jugar / béisbol _____

2. yo / jugar / en un equipo de tenis

   _____

3. los jugadores / jugar / limpio (*play fairly*) _____

4. él / jugar / sucio (*play dirty/foul*) _____

5. tú / jugar / baloncesto _____

6. nosotros / jugar / fútbol americano / en otoño

   _____

7. vosotros / jugar / juegos electrónicos

   _____

8. los campeones / jugar / el partido / el sábado

   _____

Stem-Changing -ir Verbs

In addition to the stem changes **e > ie** and **o > ue**, some **-ir** verbs have a third change: **e > i**. Here are the present tense forms of **sentir** *to regret, to feel,* **pedir** *to ask for, order,* and **dormir** *to sleep.* **Pedir** changes **e** to **i** in those forms of the present tense where the stress falls on the stem.

sentir (e > ie) *to regret; to feel*

siento	sentimos
sientes	sentís
siente	sienten

pedir (e > i) *to ask for, order*

pido	pedimos
pides	pedís
pide	piden

dormir (o > ue) *to sleep*

duermo	dormimos
duermes	dormís
duerme	duermen

The verb **morir** *to die* is conjugated like **dormir**.

Common verbs that pattern like sentir (e > ie)

advertir *to notify, warn, inform, point out*	**hervir** *to boil*
convertir *to convert*	**mentir** *to lie*
convertirse en *to become*	**preferir** *to prefer*
divertirse *to have a good time*	**referirse (a)** *to refer (to)*

Common verbs that pattern like pedir (e > i)

conseguir[1] *to get, obtain*	**reír(se)** *to laugh*
despedir *to fire*	**reñir** *to quarrel; to scold*
despedirse (de) *to say good-bye*	**repetir** *to repeat; to have a second helping*
gemir *to groan, moan*	**seguir**[1] *to follow, continue*
impedir *to prevent*	**servir** *to serve*
medir *to measure*	**sonreír(se)** *to smile*
perseguir[1] *to pursue, chase, aim for, go after*	**vestir(se)** *to dress*
proseguir[1] *to pursue, proceed, carry on with*	

Note that **reír** *to laugh* and **sonreír** *to smile* have **í** as the stem vowel in the singular and the third-person plural.

reír *to laugh*

río	reímos
ríes	reís
ríe	ríen

sonreír *to smile*

sonrío	sonreímos
sonríes	sonreís
sonríe	sonríen

---

[1]Verbs ending in **-guir** such as **seguir, conseguir, perseguir,** and **proseguir** drop the letter **u** in writing before the first-person singular ending **-o: sigo, consigo, persigo, prosigo.**

NOTES

1 · You cannot predict from the infinitive which verbs will have a stem change and which will not. For instance, **volver** has a stem change (**vuelvo**, etc.) but **comer** does not (**como**, etc.). It is therefore necessary to memorize which verbs have a stem change.

2 · In the verb lists and vocabulary of this book, stem-changing verbs will be marked as follows.

    pedir (e > i)
    pensar (e > ie)
    volver (o > ue)

D   *Complete each sentence with the correct form of the stem-changing -ir verb that patterns like* **sentir (e > ie)**.

1. (sentir)   Yo lo _____ mucho.

2. (preferir)   ¿Tú _____ los aretes (*earrings*) de oro o los de plata?

3. (divertir)   Ellos se _____ mucho en la fiesta.

4. (referir)   Ella no se _____ a nada.

5. (hervir)   El agua no _____ todavía.

6. (mentir)   Nosotros nunca _____.

7. (convertir)   La ciudad se _____ en una importante capital cosmopolita.

8. (advertir)   Ellos _____ en la radio que hay embotellamientos.

E   *Complete each sentence with the correct form of the stem-changing -ir verb that patterns like* **pedir (e > i)**.

1. (pedir)   Uds. _____ mucho dinero por la casa de campo.

2. (servir)   ¿Ella _____ pescado o pollo?

3. (vestir)   Sara y Laura se _____ de azul.

4. (despedir)   Yo me _____ de mis colegas.

5. (seguir)   Tú _____ por la avenida hasta llegar al semáforo.

6. (reír)   Nosotros nos _____ de sus chistes.

7. (impedir)   Vosotros _____ el progreso del equipo.

8. (sonreír)   El bebé _____ mucho.

9. (repetir)   Él _____ las palabras dos veces.

10. (medir)   Nosotros _____ la foto con una regla.

11. (conseguir)   Yo _____ los billetes en la taquilla.

12. (perseguir)   Uds. _____ el doctorado en ingeniería mecánica.

F *Complete each sentence with the correct form of* **dormir (o > ue)**.

1. Yo _____ mucho los fines de semana.

2. ¿Tú no _____ bien en este dormitorio?

3. Ellos _____ entre siete y ocho horas.

4. Nosotros _____ la siesta hoy.

5. Uds. _____ profundamente.

6. Elena _____ en casa de sus abuelos.

7. ¿Ud. _____ en un colchón suave (*soft mattress*)?

8. Pablo _____ como un tronco (*like a log*).

Special Verbs Ending in -iar and -uar

Some verbs ending in **-iar** and almost all verbs ending in **-uar** stress the vowel before the **a** of the infinitive in the singular and the third-person plural. An accent mark is written over the **i** and **u** in those forms.

enviar *to send*	
envío	enviamos
envías	enviáis
envía	envían

continuar *to continue*	
continúo	continuamos
continúas	continuáis
continúa	continúan

Verbs that pattern like enviar

confiar (en) *to trust, rely on*	**guiar** *to guide, lead, drive*
criar *to raise, bring up*	**resfriarse** *to catch a cold*
desafiar *to challenge, dare, defy*	**rociar** *to sprinkle, spray, water*
espiar *to spy on, keep watch*	**vaciar** *to empty*
esquiar *to ski*	**variar** *to vary*
fiarse (de) *to trust*	

Verbs that pattern like continuar

acentuar *to accent, stress, emphasize*	**evaluar** *to evaluate, assess*
actuar *to act, perform, behave*	**graduarse** *to graduate*
efectuar *to effect, carry out, do, execute*	**insinuar** *to hint*

You cannot tell from the infinitive which verbs have stressed **i** or **u** in the singular and third-person plural and which do not. The verbs **enviar, esquiar, actuar,** and **graduarse** *do* have these respective changes, while verbs such as **estudiar, iniciar, limpiar,** and **averiguar** do not.

In the verb lists and vocabulary of this book, verbs that have stressed **i** or **u** will be marked as follows.

efectuar (efectúo)
resfriarse (me resfrío)

G *Complete each sentence with the correct form of the special verb ending in -iar or -uar.*

1. (confiar)   Nosotros _____ en su buena voluntad.

2. (enviar)   Uds. _____ unos mensajes electrónicos.

3. (continuar)   ¿Tú _____ con el proyecto?

4. (graduar)   Yo me _____ el año próximo.

5. (variar)   Ellos nunca _____ su rutina.

6. (resfriar)   Ud. se _____ todos los años.

7. (insinuar)   ¿Vosotros _____ algo?

8. (fiar)   Ella se _____ de sus amigos.

9. (evaluar)   Nosotros _____ bien la situación.

10. (guiar)   El guía _____ a los turistas por el museo.

11. (efectuar)   Los gerentes _____ muchos cambios.

12. (esquiar)   Yo _____ en las Montañas Rocosas.

13. (acentuar)   Tú siempre _____ lo más interesante.

14. (vaciar)   ¿Uds. _____ las cajas?

15. (actuar)   Ella _____ en una comedia musical.

16. (espiar)   Los espías _____ a sus enemigos.

17. (criar)   Vosotros _____ ganado en la hacienda.

18. (rociar)   El jardinero _____ las flores.

BUILDING SENTENCES   **Verb + infinitive construction**

Some Spanish verbs can be followed directly by an infinitive to form a verb + infinitive construction. In the following list, **hacer algo** represents any infinitive.

> **conseguir (e > i) hacer algo** *to succeed in doing something,*
>   *manage to do something*
> **creer hacer algo** *to think/believe something done*
> **deber hacer algo** *ought to do something, should do something*
> **decidir hacer algo** *to decide to do something*
> **dejar hacer algo** *to let/allow to do something*
> **desear hacer algo** *to want to do something*
> **elegir (e > i) hacer algo** *to choose to do something*
> **escoger (escojo) hacer algo** *to choose to do something*
> **esperar hacer algo** *to hope to do something*
> **evitar hacer algo** *to avoid doing something*
> **fingir (finjo) hacer algo** *to pretend to do something*
> **hacer (irreg.) hacer algo** *to make do something, to have something done*

impedir (e > i) hacer algo *to prevent from doing something*
intentar hacer algo *to try to do something*
lamentar hacer algo *to regret doing something*
lograr hacer algo *to succeed in doing something, manage to do something*
mandar hacer algo *to order to do something*
merecer (merezco) hacer algo *to deserve to do something*
necesitar hacer algo *to need to do something*
ofrecer (ofrezco) hacer algo *to offer to do something*
oír (irreg.) **hacer algo** *to hear something done*
olvidar hacer algo *to forget to do something*
ordenar hacer algo *to order to do something*
parecer (parezco) hacer algo *to seem to do something*
pedir (e > i) hacer algo *to ask to do something*
pensar (e > ie) hacer algo *to intend/plan to do something*
permitir hacer algo *to allow to do something*
poder (o > ue) hacer algo *to be able to do something, can do something*
preferir (e > ie) hacer algo *to prefer to do something*
pretender hacer algo *to claim/try to do something*
procurar hacer algo *to try to do something*
prohibir (prohíbo) hacer algo *to prohibit from doing something*
prometer hacer algo *to promise to do something*
querer (e > ie) hacer algo *to want to do something*
recordar (o > ue) hacer algo *to remember to do something*
resolver (o > ue) hacer algo *to resolve to do something*
saber (irreg.) **hacer algo** *to know how to do something*
sentir (e > ie) hacer algo *to be sorry for / regret doing something*
soler (o > ue) hacer algo *to usually do something, be accustomed to doing something*
temer hacer algo *to be afraid to do something*
ver hacer algo *to see something done*

—¿**Sabe Ud. reparar** esta máquina?	*"Do you know how to repair this machine?"*
—Lo siento pero **no puedo ayudarle.**	*"I'm sorry, but I can't help you."*
—¿**Logran terminar** el informe para la fecha tope?	*"Can they manage to finish the report by the deadline?"*
—**Procuran terminarlo** pero **temen no poder respetar** el plazo fijado.	*"They're trying to finish it, but they're afraid they can't meet the deadline."*
—**Espero verte** en la tertulia.	*"I hope to see you at the get-together."*
—**Quiero ir,** pero no sé si puedo.	*"I want to go, but I don't know if I can."*
—¿**Piensas venir** a la oficina hoy?	*"Do you intend to come to the office today?"*
—No, **prefiero trabajar** en casa.	*"No, I prefer to work at home."*
—**Siento molestarla,** señora.	*"I'm sorry to bother you, ma'am."*
—No es ninguna molestia. **Necesito hablar** con Ud.	*"It's no bother. I need to speak with you."*

H **Sentence expansion.** *Practice the* verb + infinitive *construction, expanding each sentence with the verb in parentheses.*

MODELO   Archivan los documentos. (necesitar)

Necesitan archivar los documentos.

1. Ahorramos mucho dinero. (lograr)

   _____

2. No averiguan nada. (poder)

   _____

3. Interrumpo su conversación. (sentir)

   _____

4. Llueve por aquí en abril. (soler)

   _____

5. Escribe el informe en un solo día. (conseguir)

   _____

6. Construyen unos rascacielos. (hacer)

   _____

7. ¿Manejáis en la autopista? (temer)

   _____

8. Vuelves lo antes posible. (procurar)

   _____

9. Compro un organizador personal. (querer)

   _____

10. No pierde el tren. (esperar)

    _____

11. No mienten más. (prometer)

    _____

12. Aprovecho las rebajas navideñas. (pensar)

    _____

13. ¿Bebes el vino tinto o el blanco? (preferir)

    _____

14. Pide los billetes electrónicos. (olvidar)

    _____

15. No encienden el lavaplatos. (recordar)

_____

16. Aparcan en esta zona en hora punta (*rush hour*). (prohibir)

_____

17. Corremos en el maratón. (decidir)

_____

18. Ese carro cuesta una fortuna. (deber)

_____

19. ¿Creáis sitios Web? (saber)

_____

20. Envío el paquete por el FedEx. (escoger)

_____

I **Translation.** *Express the following sentences in Spanish.*

1. *I want to surf the Web.*

_____

2. *We hope to begin the project next week.*

_____

3. *He can read his e-mail at the Internet café.*

_____

4. *Do you (Uds.) intend to travel by plane or by train?*

_____

5. *They usually spend the weekends in New York.*

_____

6. *You (tú) shouldn't interrupt the meeting.*

_____

7. *She prefers to buy clothing in department stores.*

_____

8. *Do you (vosotros) know how to download music?*

_____

BUILDING SENTENCES   **Personal a**

You have seen that direct object nouns that refer to things, not people, directly follow the verb without a preposition.

Nosotros resolvemos **el problema**.	*We are solving **the problem**.*
Hacen reparar **la computadora**.	*They have **the computer** repaired.*
¿Cuándo envías **los paquetes**?	*When are you sending **the packages**?*
Repito **las palabras** interminablemente.	*I repeat **the words** ad nauseam.*

However, when the direct object noun refers to a specific, definite animate being (a person or a higher animal), it is linked to the verb by **a**. This function of **a** is called *personal a*. An animate direct object noun is considered definite if it is preceded by the definite article (**el, la, los, las**), a demonstrative adjective (forms of **este, ese, aquel**), or a possessive adjective (forms of **mi, tu, su, nuestro, vuestro**).

No comprendemos **a la profesora**.	*We don't understand **the professor**.*
Los abuelos cuidan **a los niños**.	*The grandparents are looking after **the children**.*
¿Conoces **a aquel señor**?	*Do you know **that man**?*
Baño **a mi perro** todos los días.	*I bathe **my dog** every day.*

NOTE

The personal **a** contracts with the definite article **el** to form the contraction **al**.

Buscamos **al** profesor Estrada.	*We're looking for Professor Estrada.*
No veo **al** dependiente.	*I don't see the salesperson.*

Proper names of people are also considered definite and are preceded by personal **a** when they function as direct objects.

Quiero ver **a Juan**.	*I want to see **Juan**.*
¿Recuerdas **a Laura Martínez**?	*Do you remember **Laura Martínez**?*

When **quién** is the direct object of the verb, it is also preceded by **a**. Personal **a** is required before **alguien** and **nadie**, and before **alguno, ninguno (ningun-), cualquiera (cualquier)**, and **¿cuántos?** when they modify a noun referring to people or are used as pronouns referring to people.

—¿**A quién** buscas?	*"**Whom** are you looking for?"*
—No busco **a nadie**.	*"I'm not looking for **anyone**."*
—¿Esperan **a alguien**?	*"Are they waiting for **somebody**?"*
—No, no esperan **a nadie**.	*"No, they're not waiting for **anybody**."*
—Sí, esperan **a algunos colegas**.	*"Yes, they're waiting for **a few colleagues**."*
—¿Ud. conoce **a algunos** de los gerentes?	*"Do you know **any** of the managers?"*
—No, no conozco **a ninguno**.	*"No, I don't know **any**."*
—No, no conozco **a ningún gerente**.	*"No, I don't know **any (managers)**."*
—¿Puedo llevar **a cualquier amigo**?	*"May I bring **any friend**?"*
—Claro, puedes invitar **a cualquiera**.	*"Of course, you may invite **anyone**."*

—¿**A cuántas personas** debemos llamar?   *"**How many people** should we call?"*
—Debéis llamar **a veinte personas**.   *"You should call **twenty people**."*

—¿**A cuántos candidatos** eligen este año?   *"**How many candidates** are they electing
                                                  this year?"*

—Eligen **a siete**.   *"They're electing **seven**."*

When a direct object animate noun is preceded by the indefinite article (**un, una, unos, unas**), it is usually not preceded by a personal **a**.

Necesitamos **un abogado**.   *We need **a lawyer**.*
El autobús recoge **unos turistas** delante   *The bus picks up **some tourists** in front
   del museo.   of the museum.*

However, personal **a** is sometimes used before an animate noun preceded by the indefinite article in order to indicate that the person referred to is a known individual.

Cuando queremos vender propiedades,   *When we want to sell property, we call
   llamamos **a un agente**.   an agent.*

The above sentence implies the identity of the agent is known. Compare it with the following sentence.

Para vender propiedades es mejor llamar   *To sell property it's better to call an agent.*
   un agente.

J   *Complete each sentence by adding personal **a** where necessary. If none is needed
in the sentence, write an X in the blank. ¡**Ojo!** Don't forget to use the contraction **al**.*

1. Pienso comprar _____ una nueva impresora.

2. ¿_____ quién llevas al cine?

3. Felipe intenta solicitar _____ ese puesto.

4. Esperamos ver _____ nuestros familiares el domingo.

5. Encuentras _____ el arquitecto en su oficina.

6. No conocen _____ ningún programador.

7. Necesitan buscar _____ unos consultores.

8. ¿_____ cuántos empleados despiden este año?

9. Deciden no visitar _____ nadie este fin de semana.

10. ¿No deseáis probar _____ el helado de coco?

11. ¿Buscáis _____ alguien?

12. Invito _____ Sofía al concierto.

13. Suelen escuchar _____ las noticias en el canal tres.

14. ¿No entiendes _____ la profesora?

15. Prefiero ver _____ una película policíaca.

16. Llevan _____ los turistas por el barrio histórico.

17. Los señores Martínez crían _____ sus hijos muy bien.

18. Debemos saludar _____ los recién llegados.

19. Resuelven no variar _____ el horario.

20. Puedes contratar _____ cualquiera de las traductoras.

21. Traigo _____ algunos informes.

22. Los policías persiguen _____ el ladrón.

K **Translation.** *Express the following sentences in Spanish.*

1. *Whom do you (tú) want to invite to the dance?*

   _____

2. *They plan to see the (male) engineer.*

   _____

3. *Isabel doesn't help anybody.*

   _____

4. *I'm waiting for someone.*

   _____

5. *The firm should hire programmers.*

   _____

6. *Do you (Uds.) know Roberto Murillo?*

   _____

7. *We're looking for our dog.*

   _____

8. *The restaurant needs a (male) chef.*

   _____

9. *How many soccer players do you (Ud.) know?*

   _____

10. *I don't know any (soccer players).*

    _____

11. *Sir, are you looking for me?*

    _____

12. *No, Miss, I'm not looking for you.*

    _____

Irregular Verbs (Part I)

Many Spanish verbs do not follow the conjugation patterns presented in Chapters 1 and 2. These are called *irregular verbs*. It should be noted, however, that there are patterns even among the irregular verbs. Many irregular verbs are irregular only in the first-person singular (**yo**) form of the present tense. The other five present-tense forms of such verbs are regular.

Verbs with Irregular Stems in -g-

A common irregularity is the appearance of a **g** before the **-o** ending of the first-person singular. We call these verbs *g verbs*. The verb **hacer** *to do, make* is typical of this category of irregular verbs.

hacer *to do, make*

ha**go**	hacemos
haces	hacéis
hace	hacen

Compounds of **hacer**, such as **deshacer** *to undo* and **rehacer** *to redo*, are conjugated like **hacer**.

Expressions with hacer

hacer un viaje / una excursión *to take/go on a trip*
hacer las maletas *to pack*
hacer cola *to line up, stand in line*
hacer planes *to make plans*
hacer ejercicio to *exercise*
hacer el desayuno / el almuerzo / la cena *to make breakfast/lunch/dinner*
hacer la compra *to do the shopping*
hacer una pregunta *to ask a question*
hacer el papel de *to play the part/role of*
hacer algo pedazos *to break/smash/tear something to pieces*
hacer (un) clic al / en el botón / en el enlace / en el icono *to click on the button / on the link / on the icon* (computer)
hacer un login / un logon / un logoff *to log in / log on / log off*
hacer investigaciones *to do research*
hacer una lista *to make a list*

Weather expressions with hacer (used only in the third-person singular)

¿Qué tiempo hace? *What's the weather like?*
Hace buen/mal tiempo. *The weather's good/bad.*
Hace (mucho) calor/frío/fresco. *It's (very) warm/cold/cool.*
Hace (poco) sol/viento. *It's (not very) sunny/windy.*
¿Qué temperatura hace? *What's the temperature?*
Hace 70 grados. *It's seventy degrees.*

Here are some other verbs that have a **g** before the **-o** ending of the first-person singular. Note that their conjugations may have stem changes in other persons.

caer *to fall*

cai**go**	caemos
caes	caéis
cae	caen

Compounds of **caer**, such as **decaer** *to decline, weaken, deteriorate* and **recaer** *to fall again, backslide, relapse,* are conjugated like **caer**.

Expressions with caer

caer en un error *to make a mistake*
caer en una trampa *to fall into a trap*
caer enfermo *to fall ill*

Mi cumpleaños cae en sábado. *My birthday falls on a Saturday.*
Cae por la casa sin llamar. *She drops by without calling.*
El sol cae. *The sun is setting.*
La noche cae. *It's nightfall.*
La lluvia/nieve cae. *The rain/snow is falling.*
Las manzanas caen del árbol. *The apples fall from the tree.*

decir *to say, tell*

digo	decimos
dices	decís
dice	dicen

Expressions with decir

decir la verdad / una mentira *to tell the truth / a lie*
decir algo sin querer *to say something without meaning to*
decir que sí/no *to say yes/no*
decirle cuatro verdades *to tell someone off*

Compounds of **decir**, such as **desdecir** *to fall short of, not live up to,* **maldecir** *to curse,* and **predecir** *to predict,* are conjugated like **decir**.

oír *to hear*

oigo	oímos
oyes	oís
oye	oyen

Note that in **oímos** an accent mark is added to indicate that the **i** represents a full syllable and not the second part of the diphthong **oi**.

Expressions with oír

oír un ruido *to hear a noise*
oír música *to listen to music*
oír hablar de *to hear of*
oír decir que *to hear that*
oír mal *to misunderstand, be hard of hearing*

poner *to put*

pongo	ponemos
pones	ponéis
pone	ponen

Compounds of **poner**, such as **componer** *to compose, fix,* **descomponer** *to break, make malfunction,* **disponer** *to dispose,* **imponer** *to impose,* **oponer** *to oppose,* **posponer** *to postpone,* **proponer** *to propose,* **reponerse** *to get well, recover,* and **suponer** *to suppose,* are conjugated like **poner**.

Expressions with poner

poner al día *to bring up to date*
poner la mesa *to set the table*
poner una película *to show a film*
poner la televisión *to turn on the television*
poner fin a algo *to put an end to something*
poner a alguien por las nubes *to praise someone highly / to the skies*

salir *to go out, leave*

salgo	salimos
sales	salís
sale	salen

Expressions with salir

salir al cine *to go out to the movies*
salir a comer *to go out to eat*
salir a pasear / de paseo *to go out for a walk*
salir de viaje *to go on a trip, leave on a trip*
salir bien/mal *to turn out well/badly, work out well/badly*
salir para un lugar *to leave for a place*

salir ganando/perdiendo *to win/lose, wind up winning/losing*
salir a alguien *to take after / resemble someone*

tener *to have*

tengo	tenemos
tienes	tenéis
tiene	tienen

Compounds of **tener**, such as **contener** *to contain,* **detener** *to stop, arrest, detain,* **mantener** *to maintain, keep, support* (economically), **obtener** *to obtain, get,* **retener** *to retain,* and **sostener** *to support,* are conjugated like **tener**.

Expressions with tener

tener (mucha) hambre / (mucha) sed *to be (very) hungry / (very) thirsty*
tener (mucho) calor / (mucho) frío *to be (very) warm / (very) cold*
tener éxito *to be successful*
tener confianza en *to have confidence in*
tener (mucha) prisa *to be in a (big) hurry*
tener sueño *to be sleepy*
tener (poca) paciencia *to (not) be patient*
tener (muchos) celos *to be (very) jealous*
tener ganas de *to feel like doing something*
tener miedo *to be afraid*
tener razón *to be right*
tener suerte *to be lucky*
¿Cuántos años tienes? *How old are you?*
tener _____ años *to be _____ years old*
tener lugar *to take place*
tener que + infinitive *to have to do something*
tener que ver con *to have to do with*
tener cuidado *to be careful*
tener la culpa *to be at fault*
tener mala cara *to look bad*
tener vergüenza de *to be ashamed of*

traer *to bring*

traigo	traemos
traes	traéis
trae	traen

Compounds of **traer**, such as **atraer** *to attract,* **contraer** *to contract,* and **distraer** *to distract, amuse, entertain,* are conjugated like **traer**.

Expressions with traer

traer noticias *to bring news*
traer flores *to bring flowers*
traer buena/mala suerte *to bring good/bad luck*

valer *to be worth*

val**go**	valemos
vales	valéis
vale	valen

Expressions with **valer**

valer mucho/poco *to be worth a lot/little*
valer un mundo / un ojo de la cara *to be worth a fortune*
(no) valer para ese trabajo *(not) to be suitable for / good at that work/job*
¿Cuánto vale? *How much does it cost?*
valer la pena *to be worth it, worth the trouble*
más vale ir *it's better to go*

venir *to come*

ven**go**	venimos
vienes	venís
viene	**vie**nen

Compounds of **venir**, such as **convenir** *to agree, be convenient or fitting,* **devenir** *to happen, become,* **prevenir** *to prevent, warn,* and **provenir** *to come, arise, originate from,* are conjugated like **venir**.

Expressions with **venir**

venir temprano/tarde *to come early/late*
venir en coche / en taxi *to come by car/taxi*
venir cansado/entusiasmado *to arrive tired/excited*
venir con cuentos *to tell tall stories / gossip / fibs*

A *Complete each dialogue exchange with the correct forms of the verbs in parentheses.*

1. —Teodoro y yo _____ al cine esta noche. (salir)

   —¿Ah sí? ¿Qué película _____? (poner)

2. —¿Sabes que _____ 90 grados? (hacer)

   —Por eso nosotros _____ tanto calor. (tener)

3. —La nieve _____ todo el día. (caer)

   —Y _____ mucho frío y viento. (hacer)

4. —¿Tú _____ la música? (oír)

   —No, yo no _____ nada por el ruido del tráfico. (oír)

5. —Yo _____ hambre. (tener)

   —Yo también. Ahora yo _____ el almuerzo. (hacer)

6. —¿Cuándo _____ Sara y Manuel a la casa? (venir)

   —¿Quién sabe? Seguro que _____ por la casa como de costumbre. (caer)

7. —¿Uds. _____ lo que yo _____? (oír, decir)

   —Sí, nosotros _____ lo que tú _____. (oír, decir)

8. —¿Tú me _____ al día? (poner)

   —Sí, te _____ todas las noticias. (traer)

9. —Vosotros _____ muy cansados. (venir)

   —Es verdad que _____ mucho sueño. (tener)

10. —Marisol siempre _____ ganando. (salir)

    —Es que la chica _____ mucha suerte. (tener)

11. —¿Qué (ellos) _____ del tiempo? (decir)

    —Según el parte meteorológico, _____ muy buen tiempo. (hacer)

12. —¿Tu cumpleaños _____ en viernes? (caer)

    —Sí, esa noche yo _____ a bailar en una discoteca. (salir)

13. —Javier _____ mucho éxito en los negocios. (tener)

    —En efecto. Y sus colegas lo _____ por las nubes. (poner)

14. —¿Nosotros _____ la tele ahora? (poner)

    —No quiero. Más _____ salir al teatro. (valer)

15. —Yo _____ la mesa si tú _____ la comida. (poner, hacer)

    —¡Yo no _____ para ese trabajo! (valer)

B *Write sentences using the following strings of elements.*

MODELO   nosotros / decir / que no   *Decimos que no.*

1. yo / oír / hablar del nuevo centro comercial

   _____

2. Uds. / venir / en taxi _____

3. él / tener / veintiséis años _____

4. yo / posponer / la reunión un par de días

   _____

5. nosotros / traer / dos botellas de vino a la fiesta

   _____

6. ¿quién / decir / tal cosa? _____

7. yo / salir / para la oficina / temprano _____

8. en otoño / las hojas / caer / de los árboles

   _____

9. ¿tú / salir / al cine esta noche? _____

10. yo / no valer / para esas cosas _____

11. yo / hacer / clic / al botón _____

12. ¿Ud. / oír / las noticias? _____

C *Complete each sentence by selecting the correct verb from the two given,
and writing its correct form.*

1. (poner | caer)   Cada vez que Cristóbal viaja en avión, _____ enfermo.

2. (hacer | traer)   Yo _____ cola para sacar los billetes.

3. (oír | venir)   Tú siempre _____ con cuentos. ¡Basta ya!

4. (decir | poner)   ¿Cuándo _____ Uds. fin a los chismes?

5. (tener | salir)   Su pregunta no _____ nada que ver con el tema.

6. (valer | decir)   ¿Cómo se _____ eso en español?

7. (oír | caer)   Nosotros _____ unos ruidos muy desagradables.

8. (traer | salir)   ¿Con quiénes (vosotros) _____ a pasear?

9. (traer | poner)   Por desgracia yo no _____ dinero.

10. (valer | poner)   Su sortija _____ un ojo de la cara.

11. (hacer | tener)   Carmen _____ poca paciencia.

12. (venir | hacer)   ¿Qué actor _____ el papel de don Juan?

Verbs Ending in -cer

Verbs that end in a vowel + **-cer** have **zc** in the **yo** form. The rest of the conjugation is
regular.

conocer *to know*	
cono**zc**o	conocemos
conoces	conocéis
conoce	conocen

The verbs **desconocer** *to not know, be unaware or ignorant of* and **reconocer** *to recognize*
are conjugated like **conocer**.

NOTE

See Chapter 4 (p. 60) for the uses of **conocer** vs. **saber**, two verbs that mean *to know*.

merecer *to deserve*		**parecer** *to seem*	
merezco	merecemos	parezco	parecemos
mereces	merecéis	pareces	parecéis
merece	merecen	parece	parecen

Verbs conjugated like **merecer** and **parecer**

aborrecer *to hate*	**envejecer** *to grow old*
agradecer *to thank, be grateful*	**establecer** *to establish*
amanecer *to wake up in the morning*	**estremecer** *to shake, startle*
aparecer *to appear*	**fallecer** *to die* (formal)
carecer *to lack*	**favorecer** *to favor, flatter*
compadecer *to feel sympathy, feel sorry for*	**fortalecer** *to fortify, make strong*
convalecer *to convalesce*	**humedecer** *to dampen, moisten*
crecer *to grow*	**obedecer** *to obey*
desaparecer *to disappear*	**ofrecer** *to offer*
desobedecer *to disobey*	**padecer** *to suffer, endure, bear*
embellecer *to beautify, embellish*	**palidecer** *to turn pale*
enflaquecer *to lose weight, get thinner*	**perecer** *to perish*
enfurecer *to make furious, infuriate*	**permanecer** *to remain, stay*
enloquecer *to drive crazy or mad*	**pertenecer** *to belong*
enriquecer *to make rich or wealthy*	**prevalecer** *to prevail, take root*
enternecer *to soften, make tender, touch*	**resplandecer** *to shine, blaze, glow*
entristecer *to make sad*	**restablecer** *to reestablish, restore*

In the verb lists and vocabulary of this book, verbs that have **zc** in the **yo** form will be marked as follows.

merecer (yo merezco)

Verbs that end in **-cer** preceded by a consonant do *not* have **zc** in the **yo** form. However, the final **c** of the stem changes to **z** in this form.

torcer (o > ue) *to twist*	
tuer**zo**	torcemos
tuerces	torcéis
tuerce	**tue**rcen

The verb **retorcer** *to twist, wring* is conjugated like **torcer**.

vencer *to defeat, beat*	
ven**zo**	vencemos
vences	vencéis
vence	vencen

The verbs **convencer** *to convince* and **ejercer** *to exercise, practice, be in practice* (profession) are conjugated like **vencer**.

The verbs **mecer** *to rock* (a child), *to swing* (in a swing) and **cocer (o > ue)** *to cook* have **z**, not **zc**, in the first-person singular.

mecer *to rock* (a child), *to swing* (in a swing)

mezo	mecemos
meces	mecéis
mece	mecen

cocer (o > ue) *to cook*

cuezo	cocemos
cueces	cocéis
cuece	cuecen

Verbs ending in **-ucir** have **zc** in the **yo** form. The rest of the conjugation is regular.

conducir *to drive*

conduzco	conducimos
conduces	conducís
conduce	conducen

lucir *to shine; to seem (look); to sport (wear)*

luzco	lucimos
luces	lucís
luce	lucen

traducir *to translate*

traduzco	traducimos
traduces	traducís
traduce	traducen

Verbs conjugated like conducir, lucir, and traducir

deducir *to deduce, infer, deduct*
inducir *to lead, induce*
introducir *to introduce, show in, cause*
producir *to produce*
reducir *to reduce*
relucir *to shine, glitter, gleam*
reproducir *to reproduce*
seducir *to seduce, tempt, attract*

D *Complete each sentence with the correct form of the verb in parentheses.*

1. (conocer) Yo _____ a ese locutor.

2. (torcer) La patinadora se _____ el tobillo patinando.

3. (vencer) Los campeones _____ fácilmente a los otros equipos.

4. (permanecer) Nosotros _____ en Chicago todo el mes.

5. (introducir) Yo _____ datos en la base de datos.

6. (favorecer) El color rojo te _____ mucho.

7. (cocer)   Yo _____ la carne a fuego lento (*on low heat, slowly*).

8. (conducir)   Tú _____ muy rápidamente.

9. (obedecer)   Esos niños malcriados no _____ a sus papás.

10. (amanecer)   ¿A qué hora vosotras _____ los días de trabajo?

11. (ofrecer)   Yo les _____ mi amistad.

12. (producir)   La compañía _____ fibra óptica.

13. (agradecer)   Yo le _____ sus atenciones.

14. (aparecer)   Blanca, tu nombre no _____ en la lista.

15. (reducir)   Yo _____ mis gastos poco a poco.

16. (traducir)   Yo _____ los documentos del español al inglés.

17. (ejercer)   Arturo es ingeniero pero ya no _____.

18. (resplandecer)   Sus pendientes de oro _____.

19. (reproducir)   Yo _____ el documento en blanco y negro (*black and white*).

20. (establecer)   La cadena _____ una sucursal en las afueras.

BUILDING SENTENCES   **Questions**

Yes/No Questions

Yes/no questions expect either *yes* or *no* as an answer. They do not begin with an interrogative word. The most common way to form *yes/no questions* in Spanish is to change the intonation of the sentence so that your voice rises abruptly at the end, rather than falls as it does in statements.

In writing, this is shown by the addition of a pair of question marks, an inverted question mark at the beginning of the question and a traditional one at the end.

¿Tienes hambre?	*Are you hungry?*
¿Luz y Paco salen de viaje?	*Are Luz and Paco leaving on a trip?*
¿Este país produce acero?	*Does this country produce steel?*

The subject may also be placed after the verb, either before the direct object or after it. To focus on the subject, place it at the end of the sentence, since in Spanish the element that comes last in a sentence is emphasized. The subject is in boldface in each of the following questions.

¿Mece **la madre** a su hijo?	*Does the mother rock her child?*
¿Conducen **Uds.** un coche deportivo?	*Do you drive a sports car?*
¿Reproduce bien los colores **aquella cámara digital**?	*Does that digital camera reproduce colors well?*
¿Tiene mucho trabajo **María Elena**?	*Does María Elena have a lot of work?*

SIGNOS DE PUNTUACIÓN

The Spanish custom of placing an inverted question mark (¿) at the beginning of questions and an inverted exclamation point (¡) at the beginning of exclamations can be seen as parallel to other punctuation that affects an entire phrase or sentence, such as quotation marks, which appear both at the beginning and end of the material quoted.

E *Translate the English yes/no questions into Spanish. The underlined words are emphasized.* **¡Ojo!** *Think about word order.*

1. *Does <u>Miriam</u> play the flute?* _____

2. *Are they <u>translating the reports</u>?* _____

3. *Are <u>Raquel and Daniel</u> making dinner?*

   _____

4. *Are you (Uds.) listening to <u>classical music</u>?*

   _____

5. *Are <u>you</u> (tú) coming in a taxi?* _____

6. *Am <u>I</u> setting the table?* _____

7. *Is Jorge driving <u>a sports car</u>?* _____

8. *Are <u>you</u> (Ud.) asking a question?* _____

9. *Are <u>Julia and I</u> bringing the cake?* _____

10. *Does Miguel's birthday fall on <u>Friday</u>?*

    _____

Spanish adds phrases such as **¿no?, ¿verdad?, ¿no es verdad?,** and **¿no es cierto?** to statements to turn them into questions. These phrases are called *tags. Tag questions* signal that the speaker expects the answer *yes.* If the statement is negative, only **¿verdad?** can be used as a tag. Similarly, English uses tags such as *isn't it?* and *are you?* to turn statements into questions.

Hace calor hoy, ¿no es cierto?   *It's warm today, isn't it?*
Uds. no tienen prisa, ¿verdad?   *You're not in a hurry, are you?*

F *Write tag questions, using the following strings of elements.*

MODELO   todos / venir / en taxi / ¿no es verdad?
          Todos vienen en taxi, ¿no es verdad?

1. Miguel / buscar / un sitio para aparcar (*parking space*) / ¿no es cierto?

   _____

2. Uds. / hacer / una excursión el domingo / ¿no?

   _____

3. tú / no conocer / nuestro barrio / ¿verdad?

   _____

4. Pilar / tener / confianza en sí misma / ¿no es verdad?

   _____

5. aquellos terrenos / pertenecer / a tu familia / ¿no?

   _____

6. yo / no necesitar / pagar con contante (*cash*) / ¿verdad?

   _____

7. nosotros / deber / digitalizar (*digitize*) los documentos / ¿no es cierto?

   _____

8. Ud. / no conseguir convencerlo / ¿verdad?

   _____

Information Questions

Information questions begin with an interrogative word and ask for a piece of information.

Common interrogative words

¿Qué? *What?*	**¿Dónde?** *Where?*
¿Quién? *Who?* (singular)	**¿Adónde?** *Where?* (= to what place)
¿Quiénes? *Who?* (plural)	**¿De dónde?** *From where?*
¿A quién? *Whom?* (singular)	**¿Cuándo?** *When?*
¿A quiénes? *Whom?* (plural)	**¿A qué hora?** *At what time?*
¿De quién? *Whose?* (singular)	**¿Cómo?** *How?*
¿De quiénes? *Whose?* (plural)	**¿Cuánto?, ¿Cuánta?** *How much?*
¿Cuál?, ¿Cuáles? *Which one(s)?*	**¿Cuántos?, ¿Cuántas?** *How many?*
	¿Por qué? *Why?*
	¿Para qué? *Why?, For what purpose?*

Note that all question words have a written accent.

In information questions, the subject usually follows the verb.

¿Cuántos días por semana **trabaja Juan**?	*How many days a week does Juan work?*
¿Por qué **no vienen tus amigos**?	*Why aren't your friends coming?*

Some of the interrogative words are used differently from their English equivalents.

NOTES

1 · **¿Cómo?**, in addition to its meaning of *how*, is used to ask for repetition when you don't hear what someone says or to express surprise at what you just heard. Its English equivalent in these cases is *what?*

¿Cómo dices?	*What are you saying?*
¿Cómo?	*What?*

2 · Before a noun, **¿qué?** is usually used for *which.*

    ¿Qué libro quieres?   *Which book do you want?*

However, in parts of Latin America, **¿cuál?**, **¿cuáles?** may be used before nouns.

    ¿Cuál libro quieres?   *Which book do you want?*
    ¿Cuáles libros quieres?   *Which books do you want?*

3 · Spanish makes a distinction between **¿qué?** and **¿cuál?** that does not exist in English.

   ¿Cuál? asks for identification or selection.

¿Cuál es la importancia de este artículo?	*What is the importance of this article?*
¿Cuál es la capital de Chile?	*What is the capital of Chile?*
¿Cuál es la marca de computadora que piensa comprar?	*What is the brand of computer that you intend to buy?*
¿Cuál es la fecha de hoy?	*What is today's date?*
¿Cuál es la diferencia entre estas calculadoras?	*What is the difference between these calculators?*

   ¿Qué? asks for a definition.

¿Qué es la informática?	*What is computer science?*
¿Qué es un nanosegundo?	*What is a nanosecond?*

4 · **¿Dónde?** asks about location. **¿Adónde?** asks direction and is used with verbs of motion.

¿Dónde viven tus primos?	*Where do your cousins live?*
¿Adónde van los empleados?	*Where are the employees going?*

Many speakers, however, use **¿dónde?** with both meanings.

5 · In questions with **¿de quién(es)?**, the subject is placed after the verb. The resulting word order is thus different from English.

    ¿De quién es este teléfono celular?   *Whose cell phone is this?*

6 · Spanish speakers use **quiénes** instead of **quién** when they are certain the reference is plural.

    ¿Quiénes salen al cine? ¿Inés y Raúl?   *Who's going out to the movies? Inés and Raúl?*

7 · A preposition used with an interrogative word in Spanish always precedes it: **¿con quién?**, **¿para dónde?**, **¿en qué?**, etc. It cannot be placed at the end of a question as in English.

¿Con quién sale Gabriel?	*Whom is Gabriel going out with?*
¿Para dónde camináis?	*Where are you walking / headed toward?*
¿En qué calle viven?	*What street do they live on?*
¿Sobre qué van a hablar Uds.?	*What are you going to talk about?*

G *Create information questions based on the statements.* **¡Ojo!** *Some items may have more than one possible question.*

1. Viven en San Francisco.

   _____

2. Tengo dos hijos.

   _____

3. San Juan es la capital de Puerto Rico.

   _____

4. Van al centro comercial.

   _____

5. Leo este libro.

   _____

6. La ofimática es la informática aplicada a la oficina.

   _____

7. Conocemos a su hermano.

   _____

8. Las cosas salen bien.

   _____

9. Salen para el campo.

   _____

10. Camina por el parque.

    _____

11. El comercio electrónico son las transacciones comerciales por Internet.

    _____

12. Esta cámara digital cuesta quinientos dólares.

    _____

13. Llegan Iván y Lucía.

    _____

14. Las tarjetas de memoria son de Carlos.

    _____

15. Vuelvo a las cuatro y media.

    _____

16. Hoy es el veintidós de febrero.

    _____

17. Nicolás quiere bailar con Sofía.

    _____

18. No vamos a la playa porque llueve.

    _____

19. El cibercafé está en la avenida Sur.

    _____

20. Expresan sus ideas muy lógicamente.

    _____

21. Juan Ramón estudia justicia criminal.

    _____

22. Compran tres tarjetas telefónicas.

    _____

    _____

H _Write a question that would elicit each of the following responses in instant messaging (**mensaje instantáneo**) with your friend. You will use the **tú** form. **¡Ojo!** There are both information and yes/no questions._

1. La reunión tiene lugar el jueves.

    _____

2. Necesito comprar una computadora personal.

    _____

3. Prefiero la marca Apple.

    _____

4. Voy al teatro esta noche.

    _____

5. Elena estudia enfermería.

    _____

6. Voy a la fiesta con Teodoro.

    _____

7. No, no trabajo el viernes.

    _____

8. Sí, hago ejercicio ahora.

    _____

9. Sí, mañana salimos de paseo.

    _____

10. Sí, conduzco yo.

_____

11. Debemos ir a eso de la una.

_____

12. Sí, vamos a estar de vuelta para las seis.

_____

I **Translation.** *Express the following questions in Spanish.*

1. *Where are they coming from?*

_____

2. *What is the capital of Spain?*

_____

3. *Whom are you (tú) making plans with?*

_____

4. *In what month are you (Uds.) leaving on a trip?*

_____

5. *What's the weather like?*

_____

6. *Is it sunny?*

_____

7. *Is it worth it?*

_____

8. *Why is he in such a hurry?*

_____

9. *What is "telemarketing" (el telemercadeo)?*

_____

10. *Shall I click on the link?*

_____

Irregular Verbs (Part II)

4

BUILDING SENTENCES

Verb + connector + infinitive construction

Ir, ver, and dar

The verb **ir** *to go* is irregular.

ir *to go*	
voy	vamos
vas	vais
va	van

Expressions with **ir**

ir a México *to go to Mexico*
ir a pie / a caballo / en bicicleta *to go on foot / on horseback / by bicycle*
ir al médico / al dentista *to go to the doctor / to the dentist*
ir a + infinitive *to be going to do something*
ir al grano *to get straight to the point*
ir bien/mal *to go well/badly*
ir de compras *to go shopping*
ir de mal en peor *to go from bad to worse*
ir de vacaciones *to go on vacation*
ir de viaje *to go on a trip*
ir en carro/tren/avión/lancha/barco/taxi/metro *to go by car/train/plane/rowboat/ boat/taxi/subway*
ir por algo *to go get something*

The verb **ver** *to see* is irregular in the **yo** form. Its stem in the remaining forms consists solely of the letter **v-**.

ver *to see*	
veo	vemos
ves	veis
ve	ven

The verb **dar** *to give* is irregular in the **yo** form. Its stem in the remaining forms consists solely of the letter **d-**.

dar *to give*

doy	damos
das	dais
da	dan

Note that the **vosotros** forms of **ir**, **ver**, and **dar** have no written accent marks: **vais**, **veis**, **dais**.

Expressions with **ver**

ver televisión/tele *to watch TV*
ver los documentos *to look at the documents*
no ver ni jota *to be as blind as a bat*
no ver por qué *not to see why, not to understand why*
no ver más allá de sus narices *not to be able to see further than the end of one's nose*

Expressions with **dar**

dar al mar / a las montañas *to face the ocean / the mountains*
dar (un) clic al botón / en el enlace / en el icono *to click on the button / on the link / on the icon*
dar con *to find, run across, bump into*
dar consejos *to give advice*
dar la bienvenida *to welcome*
dar las gracias *to thank*
dar mucho trabajo *to give/make a lot of work*
dar un concierto *to give a concert*
dar un paseo / una vuelta *to take a walk/ride*
dar una película *to show a film*

—¿Ves a Carlota a menudo?   *"Do you see Carlota often?"*
—Si, siempre **doy con ella** en el centro.   *"Yes, I always run into her downtown."*

—**No veo por qué ellos dan tantos consejos.**   *"I don't see why they give so much advice."*
—Yo tampoco. No saben nada. **No ven más allá de sus narices.**   *"I don't either. They don't know anything. They aren't able to see further than the end of their noses."*

—¿**Das un paseo** con nosotros?   *"Will you take a walk with us?"*
—No, hoy **veo tele.** Quiero ver el partido.   *"No, today I'm watching TV. I want to see the game."*

Caber *and* haber

The verb **caber** *to fit* is irregular in the **yo** form.

caber *to fit*

quepo	cabemos
cabes	cabéis
cabe	caben

The verb **haber,** literally *to have,* is used almost exclusively as an auxiliary verb to form the compound tenses (see Chapters 8, 10, and 12).

haber *to have*	
he	hemos
has	habéis
ha	han

Hay, a modified form of **ha,** means *there is, there are.* **Hay** may be followed by either a singular or a plural noun.

Hay un concierto hoy a las ocho.	*There is a concert today at eight o'clock.*
No hay necesidad de comprar más.	*There is no need to buy any more.*
Hay muchas razones por no hacer eso.	*There are many reasons not to do that.*
No hay suficientes aulas.	*There are not enough classrooms.*

The expression **hay que** means *one must / you must do something, it is necessary to do something.* It is always followed by an infinitive.

Hay que hacer una copia de seguridad.	*One must / It's necessary to make a backup copy.*
Hay que seguir una dieta equilibrada.	*You have to follow a balanced diet.*

Haber is used as a conjugated verb in one expression, **haber de** + infinitive *to have to do something.*

Hemos de terminar el proyecto.	*We have to finish the project.*
Has de oír lo que quieren.	*You have to hear what they want.*
Han de salir hoy.	*They have to leave today.*

Sometimes **haber de** is used as a substitute for the future tense. This is common in Mexican usage.

Ha de regresar a las once.	*He will return at eleven.*

Saber and conocer

The verb **saber** *to know* is irregular in the **yo** form. The other persons are formed regularly from the stem **sab-.**

saber *to know*	
sé	sabemos
sabes	sabéis
sabe	saben

Expressions with saber

saber algo de memoria *to know something by heart*
saber algo de sobra *to know something all too well*
saber dónde vive Daniel *to know where Daniel lives*
saber inglés y español *to know English and Spanish*

> **saber lo del accidente** *to know about the accident*
> **saber para quién trabaja Alicia** *to know for whom Alicia works*
> **saber** + infinitive *to know how to do something*
> **no saber lo que pasa** *not to know what's happening / what's wrong*
> **no saber nada de nada** *not to know anything at all*
> **no saber ni jota / ni papa de algo** *not to have a clue about something*

The verb **conocer** also means *to know*. It is conjugated like verbs ending in **-cer** (see p. 48).

conocer *to know*

conozco	conocemos
conoces	conocéis
conoce	conocen

Expressions with **conocer**

conocer a alguien de vista *to know someone by sight*
conocer un lugar como la palma de la mano *to know a place like the back of one's hand*

Saber means to know facts, to know something you can state or repeat. It is used before nouns and clauses.

No sé su dirección electrónica.	*I don't know his e-mail address.*
¿Sabes dónde viven?	*Do you know where they live?*
¿Sabe Ud. a qué hora llega el avión?	*Do you know at what time the plane is arriving?*
No sabemos por qué lo dicen.	*We don't know why they say that.*
Sé que Felipe trabaja por aquí.	*I know that Felipe works around here.*

Conocer means to be familiar with a person or place. It is used before nouns, and if the noun refers to people, it is preceded by the personal **a**.

¿Conocen Uds. al director?	*Do you know the director?*
Conocen a Isabel Montero.	*They know Isabel Montero.*
¿A quién conoce Ud. en Barcelona?	*Whom do you know in Barcelona?*
No conozco a nadie en esta ciudad.	*I don't know anyone in this city.*
Conocemos muy bien Buenos Aires.	*We know Buenos Aires very well.*
No conozco Perú.	*I've never been to Peru.*

A *Complete each sentence with the correct form of one of the following verbs: **ir**, **dar**, **ver**, **saber**, **caber**. Then write the infinitive of each verb on the line in parentheses.*

1. Esteban _____ de Filadelfia a Nueva York en tren. (_____)

2. Nosotros _____ televisión por cable. (_____)

3. Yo les _____ las gracias por sus atenciones. (_____)

4. No _____ ni una sola cosa más en esta cajita. (_____)

5. ¿Uds. _____ las fechas de memoria? (_____)

6. Yo _____ a la tienda de deportes. (_____)

7. Aurelia no _____ ni jota de la tecnología informacional. (_____)

8. Somos tantos pasajeros que yo no _____ en el taxi. (_____)

9. Antonio no _____ más allá de sus narices. (_____)

10. Nuestro hotel _____ a la playa. (_____)

11. _____ una película inglesa en el cine Multiplex. (_____)

12. Yo _____ los contratos detenidamente. (_____)

13. Vosotros _____ clic sobre la imagen. (_____)

14. ¿Tú _____ por la pizza? (_____)

15. ¿Vosotros no _____ mis llaves por aquí? (_____)

16. Yo no _____ su código postal. (_____)

17. Vosotras nos _____ buenos consejos. (_____)

18. ¿Vosotros _____ de vacaciones a mediados de mayo? (_____)

19. Jaime y yo no _____ hacer funcionar este aparato. (_____)

20. Tú _____ qué pasa con tus propios ojos. (_____)

21. ¿Nosotros _____ al museo el sábado? (_____)

22. _____ trescientas personas en la sala de conciertos. (_____)

B   *Complete each dialogue with the correct forms of* **saber** *and* **conocer**.
   ¡Ojo! *Remember the different meanings and uses of the two verbs.*

1. —¿Ud. _____ una buena tienda de cómputo?

   —Yo _____ que hay una supertienda en el centro.

2. —¿Tú _____ a los miembros del equipo?

   —Yo _____ a algunos de vista.

3. —¿Ud. _____ por qué Alberto no llama?

   —No, no _____ el motivo.

4. —¿Tú _____ al nuevo consultor?

   —No, no lo _____ pero _____ quién es.

5. —Uds. _____ Nueva York, ¿verdad?

   —No, ni _____ a nadie en la ciudad.

6. —¿Vosotros _____ que yo trabajo para una empresa multinacional?

   —Sí, nosotros _____ la compañía.

7. —¿Lorenzo _____ crear páginas Web?

   —No, no _____ ni jota.

8. —¿Tomás e Isabel _____ italiano?

—Sí, _____ hablarlo con soltura (*fluently*).

C *Write sentences using* **hay** *with the following strings of elements.*
¡Ojo! Remember to use **que** *when necessary.*

1. hay / una función (*performance*) el sábado a las dos

   _____

2. hay / hacer clic en el icono

   _____

3. hay / ser un buen ciudadano

   _____

4. no hay / necesidad de quedarse

   _____

5. hay / conferencias en la feria del libro (*book fair*)

   _____

6. hay / una megatienda tecnológica en esta carretera

   _____

7. hay / pasar por la aduana (*customs*)

   _____

8. ¿hay / alguna dificultad en realizar el proyecto?

   _____

9. hay / invertir en varias industrias

   _____

10. hay / entrevistar a los candidatos

    _____

BUILDING SENTENCES **Verb + connector + infinitive construction**

In Chapter 2 you learned that many Spanish verbs are followed directly by the infinitive
to form the verb + infinitive construction.

No puedo salir hoy.	*I can't go out today.*
¿Qué **piensan Uds. hacer** mañana?	*What do you plan to do tomorrow?*
Queremos viajar por Europa este verano.	*We want to travel around Europe this summer.*
Ud. debe cobrar su cheque.	*You should cash your check.*
Necesitas arrastrar y **soltar** en este ejercicio.	*You need to drag and drop in this exercise.*

Remember that the verb **saber** is followed directly by the infinitive with the meaning *to know how to do something*.

¿**Sabe Ud. programar** la computadora?	*Do you know how to program the computer?*
Todos los chicos **saben nadar.**	*All the children know how to swim.*

Verb + *a, de, en, con, por, que* + Infinitive

Some verbs, however, require a *connector* to link them to a following infinitive. The most common connectors are the prepositions **a** and **de**. In the following examples, **hacer algo** represents any infinitive.

Verbs connected by *a* to a following infinitive

acostumbrarse a hacer algo *to be accustomed to doing something*
animar a uno a hacer algo *to encourage someone to do something*
aprender a hacer algo *to learn to do something*
atreverse a hacer algo *to dare to do something*
ayudar a uno a hacer algo *to help someone do something*
comenzar (e > ie) a hacer algo *to begin to do something*
decidirse a hacer algo *to decide to do something*
dedicarse a hacer algo *to devote oneself to doing something*
disponerse a hacer algo *to get ready to do something*
echar(se) a hacer algo *to begin to do something*
empezar (e > ie) a hacer algo *to begin to do something*
enseñar a hacer algo *to teach/show how to do something*
invitar a uno a hacer algo *to invite someone to do something*
ir a hacer algo *to be going to do something*
llegar a hacer algo *to succeed in doing something, manage to do something*
llevar a hacer algo *to be led to do something*
meterse a hacer algo *to start to do something*
negarse (e > ie) a hacer algo *to refuse to do something*
obligar a uno a hacer algo *to force/compel someone to do something*
persuadir a uno a hacer algo *to persuade someone to do something*
ponerse a hacer algo *to begin to do something*
prepararse a hacer algo *to prepare to do something*
renunciar a hacer algo *to renounce/give up doing something*
volver (o > ue) a hacer algo *to do something again*

Verbs of motion connected by *a* to a following infinitive

bajar a hacer algo *to go downstairs to do something*
correr a hacer algo *to run to do something*
entrar a hacer algo *to go in(side) to do something*
pasar a hacer algo *to stop by to do something*
regresar a hacer algo *to go/come back to do something*
salir a hacer algo *to go out(side) to do something*
subir a hacer algo *to go upstairs to do something*
venir a hacer algo *to come to do something*

—**Vuelvo a recordarte** que no tenemos más pasta de dientes en casa.	*"I'm reminding you again that we don't have any more toothpaste in the house."*
—**Salgo a comprarla** ahora mismo.	*"I'm going out to buy it right now."*
—¿Qué hacemos si Rodolfo **viene a pedir** un préstamo?	*"What will we do if Rodolfo comes to ask for a loan?"*
—Lo **animamos a buscar** trabajo.	*"We'll encourage him to look for work."*
—Oye, ¿me **ayudas a instalar** el equipo físico?	*"Hey, will you help me install the hardware?"*
—Está bien. ¿Pero cuándo **aprendes a hacerlo** tú?	*"Okay. But when are you going to learn to do it yourself?"*
—**Empiezo a tener** hambre.	*I'm beginning to get hungry.*
—Ven. Te **invito a comer**.	*Come. I'll treat you (invite you to eat).*

Ir a + infinitive is often a substitute for the future tense, much like English *going to*.

—No sé lo que **vamos a hacer**.	*"I don't know what we will do."*
—No te preocupes. La situación **va a mejorar**.	*"Don't worry. The situation is going to improve."*
—¿Adónde **vas a ir**?	*"Where will you go?"*
—**Voy a estudiar** en Londres.	*"I'm going to study in London."*

Verbs connected by **de** to a following infinitive

acabar de hacer algo *to have just done something*
acordarse (o > ue) de hacer algo *to remember to do something*
alegrarse de hacer algo *to be glad to do something*
arrepentirse (e > ie) de hacer algo *to regret doing something*
avergonzarse (o > üe) de hacer algo *to be ashamed to do something*
cansarse de hacer algo *to get tired of doing something*
dejar de hacer algo *to stop doing something*
desesperar de hacer algo *to despair / lose hope of doing something*
encargarse de hacer algo *to take charge of doing something*
hartarse de hacer algo *to get fed up with / have enough of doing something*
jactarse de hacer algo *to boast about doing something*
olvidarse de hacer algo *to forget to do something*
presumir de hacer algo *to presume to do something*
terminar de hacer algo *to finish doing something*
tratar de hacer algo *to try to do something*

—**Desespero de encontrar** al perro.	*"I am giving up hope of finding the dog."*
—Pero yo **acabo de verlo** en el jardín.	*"But I have just seen him in the garden."*
—Este mes **dejo de fumar**.	*"This month I'm going to stop smoking."*
—Yo también **trato de no fumar**.	*"I'm also trying not to smoke."*
—¿**Te cansas de escribir** tu informe?	*"Are you getting tired of writing your report?"*
—**Acabo de terminarlo**.	*"I have just finished it."*

Verbs connected by **en** to a following infinitive

consentir (e > ie) en hacer algo *to consent/agree to do something*
consistir en hacer algo *to consist of doing something*
demorar en hacer algo *to delay/put off/take long in doing something*
dudar en hacer algo *to hesitate/be hesitant to do something*
empeñarse en hacer algo *to insist on doing something, be determined to do something*
esforzarse (o > ue) en hacer algo *to strive to do something*
insistir en hacer algo *to insist on doing something*
interesarse en hacer algo *to be interested in doing something*
quedar en hacer algo *to agree to do something*
tardar en hacer algo *to take time/delay/take long in doing something*
vacilar en hacer algo *to hesitate to do something*

—Juan **insiste en hablar** con nosotros.   *"Juan insists on talking with us."*
—Debemos **quedar en verlo** mañana.   *"We should agree to see him tomorrow."*

—¿El puesto que te ofrecieron **consiste**   *"Does the job they offered you consist*
en redactar** muchos informes?   *of writing a lot of reports?"*
—Sí, por eso **dudo en aceptarlo.**   *"Yes, that's why I'm hesitant to accept it."*

Verbs connected by **con** to a following infinitive

amenazar con hacer algo *to threaten to do something*
contar (o > ue) con hacer algo *to count on/rely on doing something*
soñar (o > ue) con hacer algo *to dream of/about doing something*

—Luis no se concentra en la clase. **Sueña**   *"Luis is not concentrating in class. He's*
con ver el partido de baloncesto.   *dreaming of seeing the basketball game."*
—Por eso el profesor **amenaza con**   *"That's why the teacher is threatening*
suspenderlo.   *to fail him."*

Verbs connected by **por** to a following infinitive

empezar (e > ie) por hacer algo *to begin by doing something*
esforzarse (o > ue) por hacer algo *to strive/work hard to do something*
interesarse por hacer algo *to be interested in doing something*
optar por hacer algo *to opt/choose to do something*
votar por hacer algo *to vote to do something*

—**Optó por renunciar** a su puesto.   *"He chose to quit his job."*
—Es que su jefe nunca consintió en   *"The fact is that the boss never agreed*
ascenderlo.   *to promote him."*

—Siempre **se interesaba por ser** cirujana.   *"She was always interested in being*
                                                                    a surgeon."

—Ahora **se esfuerza por terminar** su   *"Now she's working hard to finish her*
residencia en cirugía.   *residency in surgery."*

There are two verbs that use **que** as the connector to a following infinitive.

tener que hacer algo *to have to do something*
hay que hacer algo *one must do something*

—¿Qué **tienes que hacer** hoy?	*"What do you have to do today?"*
—**Tengo que llevar** mi coche al taller.	*"I have to take my car to the mechanic's."*

Hay que is not conjugated. It expresses a general obligation, not a personal one. Sometimes the English passive voice best translates **hay que hacer algo**.

—**Hay que trabajar** mucho hoy.	*"We have / One has to work hard today."*
—Sí, **hay que terminarlo** todo.	*"Yes, everything has to be finished."*

Verb + Preposition + Noun

Many of the verbs listed above take the same preposition before a noun that they require before an infinitive complement.

Ella **se dedica a enseñar**.	*She devotes herself to teaching.*
Ella **se dedica a su familia**.	*She devotes herself to her family.*
Cuento con recibir tu apoyo.	*I'm counting on receiving your support.*
Cuento con tu apoyo.	*I'm counting on your support.*
Votaron por presentar la moción.	*They voted to table the motion.*
Votaron por el otro partido.	*They voted for the other party.*
Se interesa en diseñar.	*He's interested in designing.*
Se interesa en el diseño gráfico.	*He's interested in graphic design.*
Me harto de oírla quejándose.	*I get fed up with hearing her complain.*
Me harto de sus quejas.	*I get fed up with her complaints.*

SPANISH VERBS CORRESPONDING TO ENGLISH ADVERBS

English speakers should remember to use **acabar de hacer algo** *to have just done something* and **volver a hacer algo** *to do something again*. These constructions in Spanish are very different from their English equivalents. There is another construction where the equivalent of an English adverb is a verb in Spanish (see p. 252).

seguir trabajando *to still be working*
seguir enfermo *to still be sick*

D *Complete each sentence with the correct connector. Choose* **a, de, en, con, por,** *or* **que**.

1. Emilia acaba _____ graduarse en el instituto de arte culinario.

2. Cuento _____ verlos en la reunión.

3. Hay _____ almacenar los datos.

4. Vuelvo _____ enviar el mensaje electrónico.

5. Samuel insiste _____ dejar la propina.

6. Salgo _____ jugar tenis.

7. Quedan _____ reunirse en el cibercafé.

8. Comienza _____ llover.

9. Victoria sueña _____ realizar sus ambiciones.

10. Terminan _____ hacer un curso a distancia.

11. Tienen _____ ir al supermercado.

12. Gabriel no deja _____ decir tonterías.

13. ¿Te ayudamos _____ subir los paquetes?

14. El proyecto me va _____ quitar mucho tiempo.

15. ¿Vaciláis _____ comprar la casa por el precio?

16. Le enseñan _____ programar.

17. El puesto consiste _____ hacer investigaciones.

18. ¿Por qué tardan _____ regresar del aeropuerto?

19. Magdalena se esfuerza _____ triunfar en la vida.

20. Ellos se encargan _____ la campaña publicitaria.

21. Votan _____ suspender (*adjourn*) la reunión.

22. Se arrepiente _____ portarse tan mal.

E *Complete each sentence with the correct connector in those sentences that require them. If none is needed in a sentence, write an X in the blank.*

1. Quiero _____ darles la bienvenida.

2. Consienten _____ compartir los gastos.

3. Ricardo puede _____ ganar una beca.

4. ¿Aprendes _____ esquiar?

5. Dudamos _____ ponernos en contacto con ellos.

6. Suelo _____ leer las novelas policíacas.

7. ¿Qué tratáis _____ hacer?

8. Sé _____ patinar sobre hielo.

9. Susana empieza _____ estudiar contabilidad.

10. Esperan _____ terminar su maestría este año.

11. ¿Adónde piensas _____ viajar este verano?

12. El jefe amenaza _____ despedirlo.

13. Opta _____ quedarse unos días más.

14. Se empeña _____ tener una firma exitosa.

15. Se avergüenzan _____ contar chismes.

16. Nos acostumbramos _____ vivir en un rancho.

17. Teme _____ subir en el ascensor de la torre.

18. El avión demora _____ despegar.

19. Ese tipo se jacta _____ ser más inteligente que nadie.

20. Al llegar a la oficina me pongo _____ trabajar.

F **Translation.** *Express the following sentences in Spanish.*

1. *There's a cell phone on the table.*

   _____

2. *It is necessary to know English in the world market.*

   _____

3. *They've just gone out to have dinner.*

   _____

4. *Sergio is calling again.*

   _____

5. *Are you (Ud.) beginning to write the report?*

   _____

6. *I don't know the new (male) programmer.*

   _____

7. *Do they know her telephone number?*

   _____

8. *I know how to download the files.*

   _____

9. *We agree to go by car.*

   _____

10. *Ana is counting on seeing Federico at the party.*

    _____

11. *You (tú) are striving to be successful in life.*

    _____

12. *I'm glad to see them.*

    _____

Ser and Estar

Spanish has two verbs that mean *to be*, **ser** and **estar**. Both are irregular.

ser *to be*		estar *to be*	
soy	somos	estoy	estamos
eres	sois	estás	estáis
es	son	está	están

Note that the forms of **estar** are all stressed on the endings. The **vosotros** form of **ser**, **sois**, has no accent mark. Compare **vais** (**ir**), **dais** (**dar**), and **veis** (**ver**).

Although **ser** and **estar** both mean *to be* in English, they are not interchangeable. In most cases, the choice between **ser** and **estar** depends on structural factors.

Uses of *ser*

Ser is used to connect nouns and/or pronouns.

Álvaro Domínguez **es** profesor de informática.	*Álvaro Domínguez is a professor of computer science.*
El culpable **es** él.	*He is the guilty one (party).*
Es un edificio muy moderno.	*It's a very modern building.*
Uds. **son** los responsables del lío.	*You are the ones responsible for the mess.*
Tú **eres** el siguiente.	*You're next / the next one.*
Las víctimas **somos** nosotros.	*We're the victims.*

When the predicate of **ser** is plural, **son** is used even when the subject is singular.

El mayor problema **son** los gastos.	*The biggest problem is the expenses.*
Lo importante **son** nuestros planes.	*The important thing is our plans.*
Su felicidad **son** sus hijos.	*Her happiness is her children.*
Nuestro equipo favorito **son** los Medias Rojas.	*Our favorite team is the Red Sox.*

Ser is used with subject pronouns to express *It's me*, etc.

Soy yo.	*It's I.* (colloquial, *It's me.*)
Eres tú.	*It's you.*
Es él/ella/Ud.	*It's he/she/you.* (colloquial, *It's him/her.*)
Somos nosotros/nosotras.	*It's we.* (colloquial, *It's us.*)
Sois vosotros/vosotras.	*It's you.*
Son ellos/ellas/Uds.	*It's they/you.* (colloquial, *It's them.*)

Ser is used with phrases beginning with **de** to express possession, origin, or the material something is made of.

- **Possession**

Aquella finca **es de** mis tíos.	*That farm belongs to my aunt and uncle.*
Los carros **son de** los estudiantes.	*The cars are the students'.*

Ser is also used before long-form possessive adjectives.

Aquella computadora **es mía**.	*That computer is mine.*
Esas maletas negras no **son nuestras**.	*Those black suitcases aren't ours.*

- **Origin**

Los estudiantes **son de** los Estados Unidos.	*The students are from the United States.*
Somos de Puerto Rico.	*We're from Puerto Rico.*
Estas joyas **son de** Sudáfrica.	*These jewels are from South Africa.*
Soy de origen irlandés.	*I'm of Irish background/descent.*

- **Material**

El edificio **es de** betún armado.	*The building is (made of) reinforced concrete.*
Su reloj **es de** oro y plata.	*His watch is (made of) gold and silver.*
Las cajas **son de** cartón.	*The boxes are (made out of) cardboard.*
Estas camisas **son de** algodón y ésas **son de** seda.	*These shirts are (made of) cotton and those are (made of) silk.*

Ser is used to express clock time, days of the week, and dates.

¿Qué hora **es**?	*What time is it?*
Ahora **es** la una.	*It's one o'clock now.*
Son las dos y cuarto.	*It's a quarter after two.*
Son las diez cuarenta y cinco.	*It's ten forty-five.*
Mañana **es** martes.	*Tomorrow is Tuesday.*
—¿Cuál **es** la fecha de hoy?	*"What is today's date?"*
—**Es** el veintidós de enero.	*"It's January twenty-second."*
—¿Qué día **es** hoy?	*"What day is today?"*
—**Es** viernes.	*"It's Friday."*

¿Qué horas son? is commonly used in Spanish America for *What time is it?*

Ser is used to indicate the place where an event takes place.

—¿La boda **es** en el Club Miami?	*"Is the wedding at the Miami Club?"*
—No, **es** en el Hotel Internacional.	*"No, it's at the International Hotel."*

Ser is used with adjectives that describe a condition that the speaker sees as objective, inherent, or unchanging.

Mis vecinos **son** españoles.	*My neighbors are Spanish.*
Nuestro carro **es** rojo.	*Our car is red.*
Esta ciudad **es** muy grande.	*This city is very big.*
Yo **soy** muy idealista.	*I'm very idealistic.*

Somos profesores.	*We're teachers.*
¿**Eres** católico o protestante?	*Are you Catholic or Protestant?*
Jorge **es** republicano y Juan **es** demócrata.	*Jorge is a Republican and Juan is a Democrat.*
Fernando **es** casado con Paloma.	*Fernando is married to Paloma.*
Marta **es** divorciada.	*Marta is divorced.*
Elena **es** viuda.	*Elena is a widow.*

The verb **estar** may also be used with **casado** and **divorciado**: **Fernando está casado. Marta está divorciada.**

Ser answers the questions ¿**Cómo es?** *What is he/she like?, What does he/she look like?* and ¿**Cómo son?** *What are they like?, What do they look like?*

—¿**Cómo es** la novia de Carlos?	*"What is Carlos's girlfriend like?"*
—**Es inteligente, simpática y muy bonita.**	*"She's intelligent, nice, and very pretty."*
—¿**Cómo son** los dependientes?	*"What are the salespeople like?"*
—**Son serviciales** y **amables.**	*"They're helpful and pleasant."*

Spanish doesn't use an indefinite article before a predicate noun for a profession the way English does.

Alicia es abogada.	*Alicia is a lawyer.*
Marcos es hombre de negocios.	*Marcos is a businessman.*
Diego es cantante.	*Diego is a singer.*
Soy actriz.	*I'm an actress.*

Uses of estar

Estar is used to express the location of people or physical objects.

Mis amigos **están en Costa Rica.**	*My friends are in Costa Rica.*
—¿**Estás en casa** ahora?	*"Are you at home now?"*
—No, **estoy en la oficina.**	*"No, I'm at the office."*
—¿**Dónde está** el museo de ciencias?	*"Where is the science museum?"*
—**Está en la calle del Conde frente a la plaza.**	*"It's on Conde Street, across from the square."*

However, **ser** is used to express the location of events.

La conferencia **es** en aquella aula.	*The lecture is in that classroom.*
La fiesta **es** en un restaurante.	*The party is at a restaurant.*
La reunión **va a ser** en la oficina del jefe.	*The meeting will be in the boss's office.*

When **estar** is used by itself with a person as subject, it means *to be in, to be home, to be available.*

—Busco al señor Acevedo.	*"I'm looking for Mr. Acevedo."*
—Lo siento, pero **no está** en este momento.	*"I'm sorry, but he's not here right now."*

Estar and **ser** contrast only before adjectives. **Ser** is used for conditions that the speaker sees as inherent, objective, or unchanging. **Estar**, however, is used for conditions that the speaker sees as resulting from a change, or conveys the idea that the adjective expresses the speaker's subjective impression.

Compare the following uses of **ser** and **estar**.

Pedro Gómez tiene 90 años. **Es viejo.**	*Pedro Gómez is 90. He's old.*
María ha trabajado duro y ha criado ocho hijos. Ahora, a los 42 años, **está vieja.**	*María has worked hard and raised eight children. Now, at 42, she is/looks/seems/ acts old.*
Laura **es guapa.**	*Laura is good looking. (= is a good-looking woman)*
Marisa tiene un nuevo peinado. ¡Qué **guapa está!**	*Marisa has a new hairdo. How nice she looks!*
El yogur **es bueno** para la salud.	*Yogurt is good for your health.*
Este yogur **está malo.**	*This yogurt is spoiled.*
Luis Mario **es nervioso.**	*Luis Mario is a nervous person.*
Estamos nerviosos porque hoy hay examen.	*We're nervous because there's a test today.*

Only **estar** can be used with the adjective **contento** *happy, glad, satisfied.* **Ser** is used with **feliz** *happy,* although in Spanish America **estar** is common with **feliz** as well. Both **ser** and **estar** occur with **alegre,** though with a slight difference in meaning.

Paula **es alegre.**	*Paula is a cheerful person.*
Veo que **estás** muy **alegre** hoy.	*I see you're very cheerful today.*

Estar can be used before certain adverbs to express conditions of health or well-being.

Estoy bien.	*I'm feeling fine.*
Estás mal.	*You're feeling ill.*
Estamos perfectamente.	*We're doing fine. / We feel terrific.*
En este momento **están muy mal.**	*At this time they're not doing well.*

Estar is used to answer the question **¿Cómo estás/está/estáis/están?** *How are you?*

—**¿Cómo está Ud. hoy?**	*"How are you today?"*
—**Estoy regular. Estoy un poco acatarrado.**	*"I'm so-so. I have a slight cold."*

Adjectives and Expressions with **ser** and **estar**

Some adjectives have different English translations depending on whether they are used with **ser** or **estar.**

ser aburrido *to be boring*	**estar aburrido** *to be bored*
ser bueno *to be good*	**estar bueno** *to be tasty; to be funny* (of a joke)
ser interesado *to be self-interested*	**estar interesado** *to be interested*
ser listo *to be sharp/clever*	**estar listo** *to be ready*
ser malo *to be bad*	**estar malo** *to be sick*
ser preocupado *to be caring*	**estar preocupado** *to be worried*
ser rico *to be rich*	**estar rico** *to be delicious*
ser verde *to be green; to be risqué*	**estar verde** *to be unripe*
ser vivo *to be sharp/clever/shrewd*	**estar vivo** *to be alive*

Both **ser** and **estar** are used as auxiliary verbs. **Ser** is used to form the passive voice (see Chapter 15), and **estar** is used to form the progressive tenses (see Chapter 14).

Some common expressions with ser

¿De qué color es?	*What color is it?*
¿De qué es la camiseta?	*What is the T-shirt made of?*
¿De quién es la mochila?	*Whose backpack is it?*
¿Para quién es la carta?	*Whom is the letter for?*
Si no fuera por ti,…	*If it weren't for you, . . .*
Érase una vez…	*Once upon a time . . .*
¿Cuál es su nacionalidad?	*What is your nationality?*
¿Cuál es su profesión?	*What is your profession?*
¿De dónde eres?	*Where are you from?*
¿De qué origen es Ud.?	*What is your origin/background?*
¿Cuál es su fecha de nacimiento?	*What is your date of birth?*

Some common expressions with estar

estar de vacaciones	*to be on vacation*
estar reunido	*to be at a meeting*
estar de acuerdo con	*to agree with*
estar comprometido para hacer algo	*to be obliged to do something*
Maya está prometida con Octavio.	*Maya is engaged to Octavio.*
Los prometidos están enamorados.	*The fiancés (engaged couple) are in love.*
Estamos en primavera/verano/otoño/ invierno.	*It's spring/summer/fall/winter.*
estar hecho una sopa	*to be soaked through and through*
estar en la luna	*to be out of it, have one's head in the clouds*
No estoy para quejas.	*I'm not in the mood for complaints.*
Chicos, ¡esténse quietos!	*Kids, don't move around so much! (Stay still!)*
—**¿A cuánto está el peso hoy?**	*"What's the exchange rate of the peso today?"*
—**El peso está a cincuenta centavos de dólar.**	*"The peso is at fifty cents to the dollar."*

LA LENGUA ESPAÑOLA   ser and estar

Spanish has two verbs for *to be* because it absorbed two different Latin verbs, **essere** *to be* and **stare** *to stand,* and distributed the functions of *to be* between them. These original meanings explain things such as the use of **ser** for essential, unchanging conditions and the use of **estar** for location. There are examples as early as the fourth century of **stare** encroaching upon the domain of **essere**, so the distribution of the meanings of *to be* between two verbs goes back to Late Latin. It is a feature Spanish shares with Portuguese and Italian, especially southern Italian dialects (although the distribution of functions varies).

A   *Complete each sentence with the correct form of the verb **ser** to describe these people.*

1. Ud. _____ honesto y responsable.

2. Mario y Virginia _____ arquitectos.

3. Yo _____ optimista.

4. Uds. _____ judíos.

5. Nosotros _____ republicanos.

6. Guillermo _____ gracioso.

7. Tú _____ delgado y rubio.

8. Claudia _____ encantadora.

9. Vosotros _____ artísticos.

10. Los jugadores de baloncesto _____ altísimos.

B   *Create sentences using the verb **ser** with the following strings of elements to tell the nationality and origin of these people.*

MODELO   Carlos / México / español

     Carlos es de México. Es de origen español.

1. yo / los Estados Unidos / inglés

   _____

2. Matías / Polonia / francés

   _____

3. tú / España / italiano

   _____

4. nosotros / Taiwán / chino

   _____

5. Ud. / la India / ruso

   _____

6. Jacobo y Sara / Israel / ruso

   _____

7. Uds. / Vietnám / tailandés

   _____

8. vosotros / Australia / coreano

   _____

9. María Luisa / Chile / alemán

_____

10. los Madero / Francia / kosovano

_____

C *Complete each sentence with the correct form of the verb* **estar** *to tell where these people are.*

1. Tú _____ en el centro comercial.

2. Álvaro _____ en el gimnasio.

3. Los usuarios _____ en línea.

4. Yo _____ en Chicago.

5. Uds. _____ en un cibercafé.

6. Nosotros _____ en el aeropuerto.

7. El profesor Pastor _____ en el laboratorio.

8. Carolina y Daniel _____ en Escocia.

9. Vosotras _____ en la peluquería.

10. Ud. _____ en la facultad de ciencias políticas.

D *Create sentences using the verb* **estar** *with the following strings of elements to tell where these places and things are.*

MODELO   el restaurante japonés / lejos de aquí

   El restaurante japonés está lejos de aquí.

1. los grandes almacenes / a la vuelta de la esquina

_____

2. el club de jazz / por esta avenida

_____

3. el parqueo / detrás del teatro

_____

4. los hoteles más lujosos / en frente del jardín público

_____

5. la piscina del condominio de tiempo compartido (*time share*) / en el patio

_____

6. la estación de tren / en la zona oeste de la ciudad

_____

7. los sillones / delante de la ventana

_____

8. los dormitorios / en el segundo piso

_____

9. la librería técnica / a dos cuadras de aquí

_____

10. los monumentos históricos / en la ciudad vieja

_____

11. la farmacia / al lado de una pizzería

_____

12. los centros comerciales / en las afueras

_____

E *Complete each sentence with the correct form of either* **ser** *or* **estar**.

1. Isabel _____ de Inglaterra.

2. Todos nosotros _____ perfectamente.

3. El quemador de CD _____ mío.

4. Los muebles de patio _____ de madera y plástico.

5. Los directores _____ reunidos en la sala de conferencias.

6. Cristóbal _____ emprendedor e inteligente.

7. Ud. _____ comprometido para entregar el informe.

8. Los pantalones grises _____ de lana.

9. Yo no _____ de acuerdo con su estrategia.

10. ¡Vosotros _____ hechos una sopa!

11. Nosotros _____ de origen francés.

12. Yo _____ profesora de diseño gráfico.

13. ¿Tú _____ listo para salir?

14. Vosotros _____ los más aplicados.

15. Tú _____ de Santiago, ¿verdad?

16. Marisol _____ enamorada de Adán.

17. Todos nosotros _____ estadounidenses.

18. ¿A cuánto _____ el dólar hoy?

19. _____ las once y media.

20. La fiesta de cumpleaños va a _____ en la casa.

21. Ellos _____ republicanos.

22. Alejandro _____ gracioso y encantador.

23. ¿De quiénes _____ estas maletas?

24. Vais a _____ de vacaciones, ¿verdad?

25. Tú _____ muy contento.

26. ¿Uds. _____ acatarrados?

Yes/No Questions with **ser** or **estar** + Adjective

Statements that consist of a subject, **ser** or **estar**, and an adjective are usually made into *yes/no questions* by placing the subject at the end of the sentence, unlike English, which places it after the verb.

El condominio es caro.	The condominium is expensive.
¿Es caro el condominio?	Is the condominium expensive?
Estos consumidores son ahorrativos.	These consumers are thrifty.
¿Son ahorrativos estos consumidores?	Are these consumers thrifty?
Su hija es traviesa.	Their daughter is mischievous.
¿Es traviesa su hija?	Is their daughter mischievous?
Las tiendas están abiertas.	The stores are open.
¿Están abiertas las tiendas?	Are the stores open?

F *Create statements using the correct form of* **ser** *or* **estar** *and the following strings of elements. Then create information questions that ask for that same information.*

MODELO   el traje / azul

El traje es azul.

¿De qué color es el traje?

1. yo / ingeniero genético

   _____

   _____

2. las siete y media de la mañana

   _____

   _____

3. el Cine Mediaplex / al lado de un bar

   _____

   _____

4. los mensajes electrónicos / para Eva

_____

_____

5. los aficionados de béisbol / entusiasmados y nerviosos

_____

_____

6. hoy / el veintitrés de junio

_____

_____

7. estas llaves de coche / de Marcelo

_____

_____

8. el euro / a noventa centavos de dólar

_____

_____

9. los gemelos de Hugo y Silvia / consentidos y malcriados

_____

_____

10. nosotros / de Canadá

_____

_____

G *Create statements using the correct form of* **ser** *or* **estar** *and the following strings of elements. Then create yes/no questions that ask for that same information.* **¡Ojo!** *Remember the differences between* **ser** *and* **estar**.

MODELO   la aspiradora / barata

     La aspiradora es barata.

     ¿Es barata la aspiradora?

1. el coche / descompuesto

_____

_____

2. su ropa / elegante

_____

_____

3. estos platos de comida fusión / ricos (*delicious*)

_____

_____

4. las clases de finanzas / fáciles

_____

_____

5. los analistas / superinteligentes

_____

_____

6. su nuevo abrigo / azul marino

_____

_____

7. el museo de arte / abierto

_____

_____

8. los meseros / ocupados

_____

_____

9. la chica / simpática

_____

_____

10. las tiendas / cerradas

_____

_____

11. aquellos hoteles / lujosos

_____

_____

12. los directores / reunidos

_____

_____

13. su buzón de correo electrónico / lleno

_____

_____

Translation. *Express the following sentences in Spanish.* **¡Ojo!** *Review the differences between* **ser** *and* **estar**.

1. Esteban is a programmer.

   _____

2. They're on vacation at this time.

   _____

3. It's nine fifteen.

   _____

4. The premiere (el estreno) of the film will be in New York.

   _____

5. Alicia is worried and tired.

   _____

6. The program is boring and the TV viewers (los televidentes) are bored.

   _____

7. The most interesting part of the exhibit is the paintings.

   _____

8. Julia is married to Miguel. Her sister is divorced.

   _____

9. Are the windows broken?

   _____

10. What are your (tú) neighbors like?

    _____

11. How are you (Uds.)?

    _____

12. They are of English descent.

    _____

13. The peaches are not ripe yet.

    _____

14. All these T-shirts are cotton.

    _____

15. I'm from the Southwest.

    _____

| BUILDING SENTENCES | Sentences with direct object pronouns |

First- and Second-Person Object Pronouns

Direct object pronouns replace direct object nouns. In the first and second persons the direct object pronouns are as follows (the corresponding subject pronoun appears in parentheses).

me (yo)   **nos** (nosotros/nosotras)
te (tú)   **os** (vosotros/vosotras)

In Spanish, direct object pronouns are placed before the conjugated verb.

—¿Cuándo **me** llamas?   *"When will you call me?"*
—**Te** llamo mañana, sin falta.   *"I'll call you tomorrow without fail."*

—¿**Nos** necesitan Uds.?   *"Do you need us?"*
—Sí, Uds. siempre **nos** ayudan mucho.   *"Yes, you always help us a lot."*

In verb + infinitive constructions, direct object pronouns may either precede the first verb or follow the infinitive. When they follow the infinitive, they are attached to it in writing.

—¿**Me quieres** ayudar?   *"Do you want to help me?"*
—Sí, quiero, pero no sé si puedo   *"Yes, I do, but I don't know if I can help*
  ayudarte.   *you."*

—Uds. **nos deben** visitar.   *"You should visit us."*
—¿Y cuándo piensan Uds. **invitarnos**?   *"And when do you plan to invite us?"*

In many verb + connector + infinitive constructions, direct object pronouns may either precede the first verb or follow the infinitive.

—Paso por tu casa. **Tengo que verte.**   *"I'm coming by your house. I have to see*
                                              you."
—¿A qué hora **me vienes a ver**?   *"What time are you coming to see me?"*

Third-Person Object Pronouns

In the third person, the direct object pronouns are more complicated. Spanish third-person object pronouns refer to people and things, unlike English, where *him/her* are distinguished from *it*. Spanish pronouns reflect the gender and number of the nouns they replace and they refer to both people and things.

MASCULINE SINGULAR NOUNS   MASCULINE PLURAL NOUNS
lo   **los**

FEMININE SINGULAR NOUNS   FEMININE PLURAL NOUNS
la   **las**

—¿Conoces **el centro de la ciudad**?   *"Do you know the downtown area?"*
—No, no **lo** conozco.   *"No, I don't know **it**." (I haven't been*
                                              there.)

—¿Conoces **a Juan Meléndez**?	*"Do you know Juan Meléndez?"*
—No, no **lo** conozco.	*"No, I don't know **him**."*
—¿Buscas **la nueva revista**?	*"Are you looking for the new magazine?"*
—Sí, necesito ver**la**. (OR **la** necesito ver)	*"Yes, I need to see **it**."*
—¿Buscas **a la profesora Mora**?	*"Are you looking for Professor Mora?"*
—Sí, necesito ver**la**. (OR **la** necesito ver)	*"Yes, I need to see **her**."*
—¿Oyen Uds. **esos anuncios**?	*"Do you hear those announcements?"*
—No, no **los** oímos.	*"No, we don't hear **them**."*
—¿Oyen Uds. **a los niños**?	*"Do you hear the children?"*
—Sí, **los** oímos.	*"Yes, we hear **them**."*
—¿Adónde lleva Ud. **esas cajas**?	*"Where are you carrying those boxes to?"*
—**Las** llevo a la oficina.	*"I'm taking **them** to the office."*
—¿Adónde lleva Ud. **a esas programadoras**?	*"Where are you taking those programmers to?"*
—**Las** llevo a la oficina.	*"I'm taking **them** to the office."*

Third-person object pronouns, like first- and second-person object pronouns, precede the conjugated verb. In both the verb + infinitive and the verb + connector + infinitive constructions, they may either precede the first verb or follow the infinitive, in which case they are attached to it in writing.

¿Me prestas el periódico? **Lo** quiero leer. OR Quiero leer**lo**.	*Will you lend me the newspaper? I want to read it.*
Tengo que hablar con Felisa. **La** voy a llamar esta tarde. OR Voy a llamar**la** esta tarde.	*I have to talk with Felisa. I'm going to call her this afternoon.*

A direct object noun can be moved to the front of the sentence for emphasis or focus. When it is moved, the direct object pronoun must be used along with it. (See "Building Sentences: Word order in Spanish," p. 259.)

Veo a Pablo. No veo a Gloria. **A Pablo lo** veo, a Gloria, no.	*I see Pablo. I don't see Gloria. I see Pablo, but not Gloria.*
El pescado lo compro en la pescadería, pero **la carne la compro** en el supermercado.	*I buy fish in the fish store, but I buy meat in the supermarket.*

The Neuter Pronoun lo

The object pronoun **lo** can also serve as a neuter pronoun. It can replace sentences and clauses.

—¿Sabes dónde trabaja Luis Pedro?	*"Do you know where Luis Pedro works?"*
—No, no **lo** sé. (**lo** = dónde trabaja Luis Pedro)	*"No, I don't."*

The neuter pronoun **lo** is mandatory with **ser** and **estar** to replace predicate nouns and adjectives. It does *not* vary for gender and number.

—¿Luisa es una buena estudiante?	*"Is Luisa a good student?"*
—Sí, **lo** es.	*"Yes, she is."*
—¿Esos hombres son astronautas?	*"Are those men astronauts?"*
—Sí, **lo** son.	*"Yes, they are."*
—¿Los chicos están emocionados?	*"Are the kids excited?"*
—Sí, **lo** están.	*"Yes, they are."*

In central Spain, the object pronoun **le** (an indirect object pronoun; see p. 104) replaces **lo** as the direct object of a verb when referring to a person. Thus, the examples given on pp. 82–83 would appear as follows.

—¿Conoces **el centro de la ciudad**?	*"Do you know the downtown area?"*
—No, no **lo** conozco.	*"No, I don't know **it**." (I haven't been there.)*
—¿Conoces **a Juan Meléndez**?	*"Do you know Juan Meléndez?"*
—No, no **le** conozco.	*"No, I don't know **him**."*

In contemporary usage, however, **lo** seems to be encroaching on this use of **le**.

I   *Answer the following questions in the affirmative, changing direct object nouns to pronouns in your responses.*

    MODELO   ¿Pagas las cuentas? _Sí, las pago._

1. ¿Ud. usa anteojos? _____
2. ¿Haces la compra? _____
3. ¿Tere toma cursos de tecnología informacional? _____
4. Paco y Tito reparan sus bicicletas? _____
5. ¿Los navegantes leen estas revistas electrónicas? _____
6. ¿Entráis los datos? _____
7. ¿Uds. conocen al nuevo empleado? _____
8. ¿Ud. aprovecha esta ocasión (*opportunity*)? _____
9. ¿Agustín busca su gorro? _____
10. ¿Los invitados felicitan a la cumpleañera? _____
11. ¿Esperas a las dentistas? _____
12. ¿Traéis el vino? _____
13. ¿Ellos imprimen los papeles? _____
14. ¿Oyes a los cantantes? _____
15. ¿Conduces la furgoneta (*van*)? _____

J *Rewrite each sentence, changing the direct object nouns to pronouns. Write each sentence in two ways, according to the model.*

MODELO   El pintor empieza a pintar la naturaleza muerta (*still life*).

El pintor empieza a pintarla.

El pintor la empieza a pintar.

1. Quiero comprar el coche todo terreno (*SUV*).

   _____

   _____

2. ¿Acabas de grabar la telenovela?

   _____

   _____

3. Vamos a analizar los problemas.

   _____

   _____

4. Ud. debe conocer a la directora de la empresa.

   _____

   _____

5. ¿Comienzas a comprender mis ideas?

   _____

   _____

6. Los aficionados piensan ver el partido.

   _____

   _____

7. Los usuarios no saben utilizar las herramientas.

   _____

   _____

8. Ramón corre a buscar a los policías.

   _____

   _____

9. Aprendo a tocar el piano.

   _____

   _____

10. Tratamos de ganar la beca.

_____

_____

K *Translation.* *Express the following dialogues in Spanish.*

1. *Are you (tú) ordering the meat dish as usual?*

_____

2. *Yes, if I find it on the menu.*

_____

3. *Are you (tú) going to wait for me?*

_____

4. *Yes, I'll see you after the lecture.*

_____

5. *Do you (Uds.) want to listen to these songs?*

_____

6. *No, we've just listened to them.*

_____

7. *Is Daniela the best dancer?*

_____

8. *Yes, she is.*

_____

9. *Where are you (Ud.) taking the (male and female) consultants?*

_____

10. *I'm taking them to meet the (female) boss.*

_____

11. *I see Mauricio over there. Do you (tú) see him?*

_____

12. *I see Laura, but I don't see Mauricio.*

_____

The Preterit

The preterit tense in Spanish is used to express past actions that are seen as completed in the past or as having happened once.

Regular Verbs in the Preterit

The preterit tense of regular verbs has its own set of endings. All of these endings are added to the stem of the verb and are stressed. Study the endings of the preterit tense of regular -**ar** verbs.

comprar *to buy*

compr**é**	compr**amos**
compr**aste**	compr**asteis**
compr**ó**	compr**aron**

-**Er** and -**ir** verbs share the same set of endings in the preterit. They differ from the preterit of -**ar** verbs in having **i** rather than **a** as the characteristic vowel.

comer *to eat*

com**í**	com**imos**
com**iste**	com**isteis**
com**ió**	com**ieron**

vivir *to live*

viv**í**	viv**imos**
viv**iste**	viv**isteis**
viv**ió**	viv**ieron**

Note that the **nosotros** forms of -**ar** and -**ir** verbs are the same in the present and the preterit.

compramos (present OR preterit) *we buy* OR *we bought*

Compramos un coche todo terreno. *We're buying an SUV.*
Compramos un coche todo terreno *We bought an SUV last year.*
el año pasado.

vivimos (present OR preterit)   *we live* OR *we lived*

    Vivimos en Boston.   *We live in Boston.*

    Vivimos en Boston hasta el año pasado.   *We lived in Boston until last year.*

Context clarifies which one is meant. Compare English verbs such as *put, hit,* and *cut,* which have no past tense marker in certain persons.

Yesterday we put the car in the garage.
We always put the car in the garage.

I hit a home run in last night's game.
I hit a home run in every game I play.

They cut themselves shaving this morning.
They cut themselves shaving every morning.

The **nosotros** forms of **-er** verbs are distinct in the present and the preterit.

comemos (present)   *we eat*
comimos (preterit)   *we ate*

bebemos (present)   *we drink*
bebimos (preterit)   *we drank*

A *Identify the subject(s) of each verb in the preterit, and write the correct subject pronoun(s). Then write the infinitive of each verb on the line in parentheses.*

1. _____ vendió (_____)

2. _____ celebré (_____)

3. _____ imprimimos (_____)

4. _____ aprendieron (_____)

5. _____ patinó (_____)

6. _____ vivisteis (_____)

7. _____ corrimos (_____)

8. _____ ahorraron (_____)

9. _____ aprendí (_____)

10. _____ insististe (_____)

11. _____ bebisteis (_____)

12. _____ saludasteis (_____)

13. _____ compartió (_____)

14. _____ disfrutamos (_____)

15. _____ escribí (_____)

16. _____ hablaste (_____)

17. _____ rompiste (_____)

18. _____ transmitieron (_____)

19. _____ utilizó (_____)

20. _____ añadí (_____)

B *Practice the forms of the preterit of regular verbs by completing each sentence with the correct form of the verb in parentheses.*

1. (regresar)   Tú _____ lo antes posible.

2. (asistir)   Yo _____ al concierto de música contemporánea.

3. (correr)   Nosotros _____ a coger el tren.

4. (transmitir)   Los locutores _____ el reportaje del terremoto (*earthquake*).

5. (aceptar)   Cristóbal _____ el puesto de gerente de ventas.

6. (recibir)   ¿Vosotros _____ los mensajes electrónicos?

7. (aprender)   Tú _____ japonés.

8. (discutir)   Mis colegas y yo _____ el asunto.

9. (toser)   Ud. _____ toda la noche sin parar.

10. (viajar)   Uds. _____ por el sudoeste del país.

11. (abrir)   Yo _____ una cuenta bancaria.

12. (tomar)   Verónica y Andrés _____ algo en el bar.

13. (vender)   ¿Uds. ya _____ su casa de campo?

14. (insistir)   Octavio _____ en participar en el equipo.

15. (alquilar)   Yo _____ un carro.

16. (beber)   Los aficionados _____ cerveza durante el partido.

17. (romper)   Magda _____ con su novio.

18. (vivir)   Tú _____ en Santa Fe.

19. (comprar)   ¿Ud. _____ todo lo necesario?

20. (grabar)   Nosotros _____ el documental histórico.

21. (dibujar)   Vosotras _____ un hermoso paisaje.

22. (compartir)   Uds. _____ las ganancias.

23. (comer)   Ud. _____ como un rey.

24. (prender)   Daniel _____ la televisión.

Verbs with Stem Changes in the Preterit

Stem-changing -**ar** and -**er** verbs do not have any stem changes in the preterit because the stem is not stressed in any of the forms. Study the preterit of **pensar** *to think.*

pensar	
pensé	pensamos
pensaste	pensasteis
pensó	pensaron

Compare the preterit of **pensar** with its present tense.

pienso	pensamos
piensas	pensáis
piensa	piensan

Here is the preterit of **volver** *to return.*

volver	
volví	volvimos
volviste	volvisteis
volvió	volvieron

Compare the preterit of **volver** with its present tense.

vuelvo	volvemos
vuelves	volvéis
vuelve	vuelven

NOTE

See Chapter 2 to review verbs that pattern like **pensar** and **volver**.

-**Ir** verbs having a stem change in the present tense *do* have stem changes in two forms of the preterit tense, the **él/ella/Ud.** form (third-person singular) and the **ellos/ellas/Uds.** form (third-person plural). The verbs **dormir** *to sleep* and **morir** *to die* change **o** to **u** in these forms.

dormir		morir	
dormí	dormimos	morí	morimos
dormiste	dormisteis	moriste	moristeis
durmió	durmieron	murió	murieron

Verbs having the stem changes **e** > **i** or **e** > **ie** in the present tense change **e** to **i** in the **él/ella/Ud.** form (third-person singular) and the **ellos/ellas/Uds.** form (third-person plural) of the preterit. Compare the present and preterit forms of **sentir** *to feel* and **pedir** *to ask for.*

sentir (present tense)		**sentir** (preterit tense)	
siento	sentimos	sentí	sentimos
sientes	sentís	sentiste	sentisteis
siente	sienten	sintió	sintieron

pedir (present tense)		**pedir** (preterit tense)	
pido	pedimos	pedí	pedimos
pides	pedís	pediste	pedisteis
pide	piden	pidió	pidieron

Note that these are some of the few stem changes in Spanish verbs that occur when the stem is *not* stressed.

Verbs conjugated like **sentir** in the present and preterit

advertir *to warn*
convertir *to convert, change*
divertirse *to have a good time, have fun, enjoy oneself*

hervir *to boil*
mentir *to lie (tell a falsehood)*
preferir *to prefer*
referirse (a) *to refer (to)*

Verbs conjugated like **pedir** in the present and preterit

conseguir *to get, obtain*
derretirse *to melt*
despedir *to fire*
despedirse (de) *to say good-bye (to)*
gemir *to groan, moan*
impedir *to prevent*
medir *to measure*
perseguir *to pursue, chase, aim for, go after*
proseguir *to pursue, proceed, carry on with*

reír(se) *to laugh*
reñir[1] *to quarrel, scold*
repetir *to repeat*
seguir *to follow*
servir *to serve*
sonreír(se) *to laugh*
teñir[1] *to dye*
vestir(se) *to dress*

C *Rewrite the verb in each sentence, changing it from present tense to preterit.*

1. Vuelven en el vuelo de las ocho.

   _____

2. Pienso visitarlos en Mallorca.

   _____

---

[1]**Reñir** and **teñir** differ from **pedir** in the third-person singular and plural. They have the expected **i** as the stem vowel, but they lose the **i** of the preterit endings **-ió, -ieron** in these forms: **riñó/riñeron, tiñó/tiñeron**. These verbs are also treated in the section on spelling changes below.

3. Nos divertimos mucho en la fiesta.

_____

4. Moisés pierde el tren.

_____

5. ¿Encuentras tu ordenador (*computer*, Spain) portátil?

_____

6. Ud. prueba la comida tailandesa.

_____

7. Uds. piden un préstamo.

_____

8. Servís unos platos muy sabrosos.

_____

9. Nieva mucho en esta región.

_____

10. Entiendo exactamente lo que pasó.

_____

11. Raquel se viste de buen gusto.

_____

12. Truena fuerte todo el día.

_____

13. Cierran las fronteras.

_____

14. No llueve mucho este año.

_____

15. Los padres riñen a su hijo malcriado.

_____

16. Medís la alfombra persiana.

_____

17. El joven se convierte en un hombre hecho y derecho (*a real man*).

_____

18. ¿Uds. siguen mis consejos?

_____

19. Ella no siente el calor.

_____

20. El hielo se derrite.

_____

21. El agua hierve.

_____

22. Prefieren usar la cámara digital mía.

_____

23. Ese chico nunca miente.

_____

24. El fuego de campamento muere.

_____

25. Los niños duermen la siesta.

_____

Verbs with Spelling Changes in the Preterit

Most verbs with spelling changes are regular in speech. The rules of Spanish spelling, however, cause changes in their written forms.

Spelling Changes with c, g, z

-Ar verbs whose stems end in **c**, **g**, and **z** have the following spelling changes in the **yo** form of the preterit.

c > qu
g > gu
z > c

Compare the spelling of some of these spelling change verbs in the **yo** form of the present and the preterit.

INFINITIVE	PRESENT TENSE	PRETERIT
buscar	busco	busqué
sacar	saco	saqué
llegar	llego	llegué
pagar	pago	pagué
comenzar	comienzo	comencé
alcanzar	alcanzo	alcancé

The reason for this change is that Spanish spells the sounds /k/, /g/, /s/ (spelled **z**) differently before **e** and **i**. Study the spelling of these sounds before the five vowels.

/k/	ca, **que**, **qui**, co, cu
/g/	ga, **gue**, **gui**, go, gu
/s/ (spelled **z**)	za, **ce**, **ci**, zo, zu

Verbs like buscar

acercarse *to approach*
aparcar *to park*
arrancar *to pull/root out; to start up*
   (vehicle)
atacar *to attack*
calificar *to grade, give a grade to*
chocar *to crash, collide with*
colocar *to put, place*
criticar *to criticize*
dedicar *to devote*
desbancar *to supplant, replace*
educar *to educate, bring up, rear, train*
embarcarse *to embark, go on board*
equivocarse *to be mistaken*
explicar *to explain*

fabricar *to make, manufacture*
identificar *to identify*
indicar *to indicate*
justificar *to justify*
marcar *to dial; to mark*
mascar *to chew*
masticar *to chew*
pescar *to fish*
practicar *to practice*
publicar *to publish*
roncar *to snore*
sacar *to take out*
secar *to dry*
tocar *to touch; to play* (a musical instrument)
volcar (o > ue) *to tip, knock over, upset*

Verbs like llegar

agregar *to add*
ahogarse *to drown*
apagar *to put out, extinguish*
cargar *to load*
castigar *to punish*
colgar (o > ue) *to hang*
conjugar *to conjugate*
despegar *to take off* (airplane)
encargar *to put in charge, entrust;*
   to order
entregar *to hand in/over*
fregar (e > ie) *to scrub, rub*
interrogar *to question, interrogate*

investigar *to investigate*
jugar (u > ue) *to play* (a sport)
juzgar *to judge*
madrugar *to get up early*
navegar *to navigate; to surf* (the Web)
negar (e > ie) *to deny*
pagar *to pay*
pegar *to stick; to beat*
regar (e > ie) *to water*
rogar (o > ue) *to beg, ask*
tragar *to swallow*
vengar *to avenge*

Verbs like comenzar

abrazar *to hug, embrace*
actualizar *to bring up to date*
adelgazar *to get thin*
alcanzar *to reach, overtake*
almorzar (o > ue) *to have lunch*
alzar *to raise*
amenazar *to threaten*
analizar *to analyze*
aplazar *to postpone*
bautizar *to baptize*
bostezar *to yawn*
cruzar *to cross*
deslizarse *to slip*
destrozar *to destroy, ruin*

empezar (e > ie) *to begin*
enlazar *to tie together, link; to embrace*
gozar *to enjoy*
hipnotizar *to hypnotize*
lanzar *to throw*
organizar *to organize*
popularizar *to popularize*
realizar *to fulfill*
rechazar *to reject*
rezar *to pray*
tranquilizarse *to calm down*
trazar *to draw, sketch, outline, trace*
tropezar (e > ie) *to trip, stumble*

D Answer the questions, using the **yo** form of the preterit. Change direct object nouns to pronouns in your responses. **¡Ojo!** Be sure to write the correct spelling changes.

MODELO   ¿Vas a pagar la cuenta? *Ya la pagué.*

1. ¿Vas a marcar el número de teléfono? _____

2. ¿Quieres jugar al béisbol? _____

3. ¿Tiene ganas de almorzar? _____

4. ¿Piensa navegar en la Red? _____

5. ¿Puede aparcar el carro? _____

6. ¿Piensas aplazar la reunión? _____

7. ¿Debe conjugar los verbos en pretérito? _____

8. ¿Quieres explicar tu idea? _____

9. ¿Esperas realizar tu proyecto? _____

10. ¿Procuras entregar la tesis? _____

11. ¿Esperas adelgazar? _____

12. ¿Te animan a tocar el piano? _____

13. ¿Va a practicar el español? _____

14. ¿Debes fregar las cacerolas? _____

15. ¿Va a actualizar los datos? _____

16. ¿Piensa organizar los papeles? _____

17. ¿Quiere colgar los cuadros? _____

18. ¿Va a agregar cilantro (*coriander*) a la carne? _____

19. ¿Puedes arrancar la mala hierba (*weeds*)? _____

20. ¿Tienes que apagar las luces? _____

An **-ir** verb whose stem ends in **ñ** drops the **i** of the third-person preterit endings **-ió** and **-ieron**.

INFINITIVE	THIRD-PERSON SINGULAR PRETERIT	THIRD-PERSON PLURAL PRETERIT
gruñir *to grunt, growl*	gruñó	gruñeron
heñir *to knead*	hiñó	hiñeron
reñir *to quarrel*	riñó	riñeron
teñir *to dye*	tiñó	tiñeron

Note that **heñir, reñir,** and **teñir** are stem-changing verbs (**e** > **i**).

Spelling Changes in **-er** and **-ir** Verbs Whose Stems End in a Vowel

In the preterit, **-er** and **-ir** verbs that have a vowel immediately preceding the preterit ending change **-ió** to **-yó** in the third-person singular and **-ieron** to **-yeron** in the third-person plural. This is not just a spelling convention: The **y** is actually pronounced in these forms. These verbs also add a written accent to the **i** of the **tú**, **nosotros**, and **vosotros** endings.

leer *to read*		**oír** *to hear*	
leí	leímos	oí	oímos
leíste	leísteis	oíste	oísteis
leyó	le**yeron**	oyó	o**yeron**

Verbs like **leer** and **oír**

caer *to fall*
creer *to believe, think*
poseer *to have, possess*

Traer, which has an irregular preterit, as well as verbs with prefixes added to **traer,** are exceptions to this pattern.

Verbs ending in **-uir** also change **i** to **y** in the third-person preterit endings, but do not add a written accent on the **i** of the **tú**, **nosotros**, and **vosotros** forms of the preterit.

construir *to build*	
construí	construimos
construiste	construisteis
constru**yó**	constru**yeron**

Verbs like **construir**

atribuir *to attribute, credit*	**incluir** *to include*
concluir *to conclude*	**instruir** *to educate, teach, instruct, train*
contribuir *to contribute*	**intuir** *to have a sense of, feel*
destruir *to destroy*	**obstruir** *to obstruct, hinder, impede*
disminuir *to diminish*	**reconstruir** *to rebuild*
distribuir *to distribute*	**sustituir** *to substitute*
huir *to flee*	

For verbs ending in **-guir,** such as **seguir** and **distinguir,** the **u** is not a pronounced vowel but merely a spelling feature. Such verbs are not conjugated like **construir** in the preterit.

seguir *to follow*		**distinguir** *to distinguish*	
seguí	seguimos	distinguí	distinguimos
seguiste	seguisteis	distinguiste	distinguisteis
siguió	**siguieron**	**distinguió**	**distinguieron**

E *Create sentences from the following strings of elements, using the preterit tense.* **¡Ojo!** *Be sure to write spelling changes.*

MODELO el perro / gruñir *El perro gruñó.*

1. los muchachos / teñir / las camisetas de rojo

   _____

2. la guerra / destruir / el país

   _____

3. los consumidores / no distinguir / entre los dos productos

   _____

4. Ana / conseguir / la maestría en salud pública

   _____

5. unas empresas / reconstruir / los barrios bajos

   _____

6. ¿Ud. / oír / la noticia?

   _____

7. el soldado / caer / en la batalla

   _____

8. los usuarios / leer / las páginas Web

   _____

9. los habitantes oprimidos / huir / de la dictadura

   _____

10. ¿por qué / (Uds.) reñir / todo el día?

    _____

11. Uds. / seguir / por la autopista

    _____

12. los hombres de negocios / concluir / la negociación del contrato

    _____

13. la pastelera / heñir / la masa (*dough*)

    _____

14. todo el mundo / creer / sus relatos

    _____

Irregular Preterits

Irregular preterits in Spanish have two features: an irregular stem and a special set of endings. The endings for these verbs are **-e, -iste, -o, -imos, -isteis, -ieron**. Note that the **yo** and **él** forms are stressed on the stem, not on the ending.

Some of these irregular preterits have stems with the vowel **i**.

decir *to say, tell*		**hacer** *to do, make*	
dije	dijimos	hice	hicimos
dijiste	dijisteis	hiciste	hicisteis
dijo	dijeron	hizo	hicieron

querer *to want*		**venir** *to come*	
quise	quisimos	vine	vinimos
quisiste	quisisteis	viniste	vinisteis
quiso	quisieron	vino	vinieron

NOTES

There are two important irregularities in the verbs above.

1 · The **él/ella/Ud.** form of **hacer** is spelled with a **z** (**hizo**), not a **c** as in the other forms. The spelling change **c > z** before **o** retains the /s/.

2 · The **ellos/ellas/Uds.** form of **decir** loses the **i** of the **-ieron** ending.

Other irregular preterits have stems with the vowel **u**.

andar *to walk, go*		**caber** *to fit*	
anduve	anduvimos	cupe	cupimos
anduviste	anduvisteis	cupiste	cupisteis
anduvo	anduvieron	cupo	cupieron

estar *to be*		**poder** *to be able to, can*	
estuve	estuvimos	pude	pudimos
estuviste	estuvisteis	pudiste	pudisteis
estuvo	estuvieron	pudo	pudieron

poner *to put*		**saber** *to know*	
puse	pusimos	supe	supimos
pusiste	pusisteis	supiste	supisteis
puso	pusieron	supo	supieron

tener *to have*	
tuve	tuvimos
tuviste	tuvisteis
tuvo	tuvieron

All verbs ending in **-ducir** have a preterit stem with the vowel **u**.

producir *to produce*

produje	**produjimos**
produjiste	**produjisteis**
produjo	**produjeron**

The verb **traer** has **a** in the stem of the preterit.

traer *to bring*

traje	**trajimos**
trajiste	**trajisteis**
trajo	**trajeron**

NOTES

1 · All preterit stems ending in **j** lose the **i** of the -**ieron** ending, as you saw in the preterit of the verb **decir**: **dijeron**.

2 · The verbs **conducir** *to drive* and **traducir** *to translate* are conjugated in the preterit like **producir**.

3 · Compounds of the verbs above show the same irregular stems in the preterit.

hacer

> **rehacer** *to do over, do again*: **rehice**
> **satisfacer** *to satisfy*: **satisfice**

poner

> **componer** *to fix, compose*: **compuse**
> **proponer** *to propose*: **propuse**

tener

> **detener** *to stop*: **detuve**
> **mantener** *to keep, support*: **mantuve**
> **sostener** *to support*: **sostuve**

traer

> **atraer** *to attract*: **atraje**
> **distraer** *to distract*: **distraje**

venir

> **convenir** *to be suitable*: **convine**
> **intervenir** *to intervene*: **intervine**
> **prevenir** *to notify, warn*: **previne**

4 · The preterit of **hay** (*there is, there are*) is **hubo**.

There are several other irregular verbs in the preterit.

Dar takes the endings of regular -**er** and -**ir** verbs in the preterit.

dar *to give*	
di	**dimos**
diste	**disteis**
dio	**dieron**

Ser and **ir** have the same conjugation in the preterit. Context clarifies whether *to be* or *to go* is meant.

ser *to be* / **ir** *to go*	
fui	**fuimos**
fuiste	**fuisteis**
fue	**fueron**

Note that the **yo** and **él/ella/Ud.** forms of **dar** and **ser/ir** are also written without accent marks: **di**, **dio**, **fui**, **fue**. This is because they are forms of one syllable. **Ver** is regular in the preterit, but the **yo** and **él/ella/Ud.** forms are written without accent marks.

ver *to see*	
vi	**vimos**
viste	**visteis**
vio	**vieron**

 Identify the subject(s) of each verb in the preterit, and write the correct subject pronoun(s). Then write the infinitive of each verb on the line in parentheses.

1. _____ hizo (_____)

2. _____ pudieron (_____)

3. _____ fue (_____)

4. _____ dijiste (_____)

5. _____ estuve (_____)

6. _____ supimos (_____)

7. _____ produjeron (_____)

8. _____ vi (_____)

9. _____ anduvisteis (_____)

10. _____ vine (_____)

11. _____ quisimos (_____)

12. _____ fui (_____)

13. _____ tuviste (_____)

14. _____ cupieron (_____)

15. _____ trajo (_____)

16. _____ di (_____)

G *Rewrite each sentence, changing the verb from present tense to preterit.*

MODELO   Andan muy de prisa.

   Anduvieron muy de prisa. _____

1. Pones fin a la discusión.

   _____

2. Tienen mucho éxito con su compañía.

   _____

3. Hago clic al botón.

   _____

4. ¿Ud. viene en taxi?

   _____

5. No decimos nada.

   _____

6. ¿Cómo lo sabes?

   _____

7. No puedo entender su actitud.

   _____

8. Queremos salir a comer.

   _____

9. Nos traen unos regalos.

   _____

10. Soy la directora del equipo.

   _____

11. Ve a Verónica en el cibercafé.

   _____

12. Hay grandes ofertas en las tiendas.

   _____

13. El compositor compone una canción.

   _____

14. Me dan las gracias.

   _____

15. Voy de compras.

   _____

16. ¿Por qué intervienen en el conflicto?

   _____

17. Conduzco a setenta millas por hora.

   _____

18. ¿Qué les atrae?

   _____

19. Traducimos los documentos al inglés.

   _____

20. No cabe nadie más en el aula.

   _____

Some Important Uses of the Preterit

■ The preterit is used to show that an event or action was completed in the past or that it happened once in the past.

Carla **salió** a las ocho.	*Carla left at eight.*
El mecánico **reparó** el coche.	*The mechanic repaired the car.*
Yo **terminé** mi trabajo.	*I finished my work.*
¿**Viste** la película?	*Did you see the movie?*

■ A series of preterits tells the events of a story.

Salí a comprar comida, **regresé** a casa, **preparé** la cena, **puse** la mesa, **comí**, **lavé** los platos y luego **fui** a casa de mi amigo para ver el partido de fútbol americano.	*I went out to buy food, came back home, prepared dinner, set the table, ate, washed the dishes, and then went to my friend's house to see the football game.*

■ Some verbs take on a different meaning when they are used in the preterit. The distinction in meaning will be especially important when you study the difference between the preterit tense and the imperfect tense, which are two aspects of (or ways of looking at) past time. When the verbs listed below are used in the preterit, the focus is on the beginning or completion of an action. For example, **conocí** means *I began to know someone*, that is, *I met someone*.

VERB	SPANISH	ENGLISH
saber *to know*	Supe la fecha hoy.	*I found out the date today.*
conocer *to know*	Conocimos a Carmen ayer.	*We met Carmen yesterday.*
tener *to have*	Tuvo una idea.	*He got an idea.*
poder *to be able to, can*	No pudieron salir.	*They didn't (manage to) go out.*
querer *to want*	No quisiste trotar.	*You refused to jog.*

H **Translation.** *Express the following sentences in Spanish.*

1. *Who set the table?*

   _____

2. *I set it.*

   _____

3. *What did you (Ud.) do yesterday?*

   _____

4. *I played tennis and then took a walk.*

   _____

5. *Where did you (tú) go last night?*

   _____

6. *I went to the movies.*

   _____

7. *Did you (tú) see our friends?*

   _____

8. *No, I arrived late and I couldn't (didn't manage to) find them.*

   _____

9. *Do you (Ud.) know Susana's e-mail address?*

   _____

10. *Yes, I found it out last week.*

    _____

BUILDING SENTENCES	**Sentences with indirect objects**

Remember that inanimate direct objects in Spanish are linked to the verb without a preposition.

—¿María trajo **las flores**?   *"Did Maria bring the flowers?"*
—Sí, compró **un ramillete de tulipanes**.   *"Yes, she bought a bouquet of tulips."*

However, when the direct object is a specific person (or an individualized animal), then the direct object is connected to the verb by personal **a**.

—¿Conociste **a Elena Sánchez**?   *"Did you meet Elena Sánchez?"*
—No, pero conocí **a su prima Marcia**.   *"No, but I met her cousin Marcia."*

—¿Paseaste **al perro** hoy?   *"Did you walk the dog today?"*
—Sí, llevé **al perro** al parque.   *"Yes, I took the dog to the park."*

Indirect objects are usually animate nouns, not things. They are connected to the verb by the preposition **a**. Indirect object nouns are usually accompanied by the corresponding third-person indirect object pronoun (**le** for singular nouns and **les** for plural nouns).

—Juan siempre **les** escribe **a sus padres.**	*"Juan always writes to his parents."*
—¿De veras? Yo prefiero llamar **a mi familia.**	*"Really? I prefer to call my family."*

Note that both object nouns in the sentences above are connected to the verb by **a**. However, **sus padres** is an indirect object because of the obligatory presence of **les**. The noun **mi familia** is a direct object because **le** cannot be used with it.

We can represent the underlying structure of the verbs **escribir** and **llamar** as follows. The word **uno** in these formulas represents any animate noun.

> **escribirle a uno** *to write to someone*
> **llamar a uno** *to call someone*

The presence of **le** in the above formula **escribirle a uno** tells you that **escribir** takes an indirect object of the person. The absence of **le** in **llamar a uno** indicates that **llamar** takes a direct object. The **a** of the two patterns is different. In **escribirle a uno**, the **a** is a preposition, roughly the equivalent of English *to*. In **llamar a uno**, the **a** is the personal **a**, the marker of an animate direct object.

Most verbs that take an indirect object of the person (an animate indirect object) also take an inanimate direct object. The verb **escribir** can be used both with or without an inanimate direct object.

—¿**Le** escriben Uds. mucho **a Paula?**	*"Do you write to Paula a lot?"*
—Sí, **le** escribimos **muchos correos electrónicos.**	*"Yes, we write many e-mails to her."*
—¿Qué **les** dieron sus amigos?	*"What did your friends give you?"*
—**Nos** trajeron **flores** y **bombones.**	*"They brought us flowers and candy."*
—¿Raúl **le** explicó **el problema a Carlos?**	*"Did Raúl explain the problem to Carlos?"*
—Sí, pero no **le** dijo **la verdad.**	*"Yes, but he didn't tell him the truth."*
—¿**Te** sirvieron **pescado?**	*"Did they serve you fish?"*
—Sí, y **me** ofrecieron **un bistec** también.	*"Yes, and they offered me steak too."*

Here is a table of all of the Spanish indirect object pronouns.

me	nos
te	os
le	les

Common Verbs Used with an Indirect Object of the Person and an Inanimate Direct Object

contarle algo a uno *to relate/recount something to someone*
darle algo a uno *to give something to someone*
decirle algo a uno *to tell/say something to someone*

devolverle algo a uno *to return something to someone*
enseñarle algo a uno *to show something to someone*
entregarle algo a uno *to hand over something to someone*
enviarle algo a uno *to send something to someone*
escribirle algo a uno *to write something to someone*
explicarle algo a uno *to explain something to someone*
mandarle algo a uno *to send something to someone*
mostrarle algo a uno *to show something to someone*
ofrecerle algo a uno *to offer something to someone*
pedirle algo a uno *to ask someone for something*
prestarle algo a uno *to lend something to someone*
recetarle algo a uno *to prescribe something for someone*
recordarle algo a uno *to remind someone of something*
regalarle algo a uno *to give something to someone as a gift*
servirle algo a uno *to serve something to someone*
traerle algo a uno *to bring something to someone*
venderle algo a uno *to sell something to someone*

The indirect object is the equivalent of English *from* with verbs that mean *to take away, steal, remove,* etc.

arrancarle algo a uno *to snatch/grab something from someone*
arrebatarle algo a uno *to snatch/grab something from someone*
comprarle algo a uno *to buy something from someone*
esconderle algo a uno *to hide something from someone*
exigirle algo a uno *to demand something of someone*
ganarle algo a uno *to win something from someone*
ocultarle algo a uno *to hide something from someone*
pedirle algo a uno *to ask something of someone*
pedirle prestado algo a uno *to borrow something from someone*
quitarle algo a uno *to take something away from someone*
robarle algo a uno *to steal something from someone*
sacarle algo a uno *to get something out of someone*
solicitarle algo a uno *to ask/request something of someone*
suspenderle algo a uno *to revoke/cancel something of someone's*

—**Al extranjero le** exigieron **los documentos.**
"*They demanded the foreigner's papers from him.*"
—Sí, y **le** quitaron **el pasaporte.**
"*Yes, and they took away his passport.*"

—¿Quién **le** compró **el coche a Mónica?**
"*Who bought Mónica's car from her?*"
—Pablo. **Le** pidió prestado **el dinero a su padre.**
"*Pablo. He borrowed the money from his father.*"

Verbs That Can Take Both **le** and **lo** with a Difference in Meaning

Some verbs are used with both **le** and **lo** as direct objects. There is usually a slight difference in meaning. **Le** usually refers to a person, **lo** to a thing. Usage of **le** as a direct object referring to people is not limited to Spain, but is found in Spanish America too.

Nadie **le cree** porque miente mucho. *No one believes him because he lies a lot.*
Eso es un cuento. Yo no **lo creo**. *That's gossip (a lie). I don't believe it.*

Al hijo menor **le llaman Benjamín**. *They call the youngest son Benjamín.*
Siempre **lo llamo** los domingos. *I always call him (phone him) on Sundays.*

Al asesino **le pegaron**. *They beat the murderer.*
Encontré los sellos y **los pegué** en el *I found the stamps and pasted them on*
 sobre. *the envelope.*

I *Using the following strings of elements, write sentences that have a preterit tense verb and an indirect object pronoun.*

MODELO Pedro / traer / un disco compacto / a ella

 Pedro le trajo un disco compacto.

1. tú / mostrar / tu iPod / a tus colegas

   _____

2. Uds. / enviar / un e-mail / a mí

   _____

3. Carolina / pedir / un favor / a él

   _____

4. yo / explicar / el concepto / a Uds.

   _____

5. ellos / hacer / una buena comida / a vosotros

   _____

6. nosotros / decir / el motivo / a Ud.

   _____

7. Ud. / leer / las instrucciones / a ellos

   _____

8. vosotros / vender / el coche / a nosotros

   _____

9. Carlos Manuel / recordar / la fecha de la conferencia / a ti

   _____

10. yo / entregar / los papeles / a ellas

    _____

11. Juan e Isabel / esconder / los regalos de cumpleaños / a su hijo

    _____

12. tú / ocultar / tu desilusión (*disappointment*) / a todos

    _____

J *Using the following strings of elements, write sentences that have a preterit verb, an indirect object noun, and a corresponding indirect object pronoun.*

MODELO   yo / enseñar / los carteles / a mi compañero de cuarto

Yo le enseñé los carteles a mi compañero de cuarto.

1. tú / escribir / unos mensajes electrónicos / a los directores

2. él / contar / el argumento (*plot*) de la película / a su amigo

3. Uds. / enviar / unos paquetes / a los soldados

4. nosotros / comprar / el quitanieves (*snow plow*) / al vecino

5. la anfitriona (*hostess*) / servir / comida italiana / a los invitados

6. Ud. / devolver / la calculadora de bolsillo / a su amiga

7. los jefes / ofrecer / el puesto / al programador

8. nuestro equipo / ganar / el partido / al equipo suyo

9. la niña / quitar / los cubos (*blocks*) / a los otros niños

10. yo / mostrar / mis maletas / al guardia de seguridad

K **Translation.** *Express the following sentences in English.*

1. Busqué a los programadores por todas partes.

2. Los Medias Rojas les ganaron la Serie Mundial a los Cardenales.

3. Le devolvimos los videos al empleado de la tienda.

4. La madre les contó un cuento de hadas (*fairy tale*) a sus hijitos.

5. ¿Le enviaste un correo electrónico a Pedro o lo llamaste?

_____

6. Martita paseó a su perro en el parque. Allí un perro grande le quitó los juguetes a su perro.

_____

_____

L *Translation.* *Express the following dialogues in Spanish.*

1. *I handed the report in to my boss.*

_____

2. *My boss requested the other report from me.*

_____

3. *Adrián asked Jaime to borrow the car.*

_____

4. *Jaime said yes to him.*

_____

5. *The thief stole the man's gold watch from him.*

_____

6. *The man grabbed the watch from the thief.*

_____

7. *We brought the children apples and grapes.*

_____

8. *They thanked us.*

_____

9. *Did you (tú) show your new dress to Claudia?*

_____

10. *Yes, and I showed the dress to my other friends too.*

_____

11. *The waitress served the (male) customer the chocolate cake.*

_____

12. *The customer asked the waitress for a fork.*

_____

The Imperfect; The Imperfect vs. the Preterit

The Imperfect Tense

The imperfect tense is used to describe background actions or situations in the past rather than events. Its formation is simple. Only three verbs are irregular. The endings of the imperfect tense for **-ar** verbs have **-aba-** in all forms. The endings for **-er** and **-ir** verbs have **-ía-** in all forms.

hablar *to speak*

habl**aba**	habl**ábamos**
habl**abas**	habl**abais**
habl**aba**	habl**aban**

vender *to sell*

vend**ía**	vend**íamos**
vend**ías**	vend**íais**
vend**ía**	vend**ían**

abrir *to open*

abr**ía**	abr**íamos**
abr**ías**	abr**íais**
abr**ía**	abr**ían**

NOTES

1 · The first- and third-person singular forms are identical for all verbs in the imperfect: **hablaba, vendía, abría**.

2 · In the imperfect of **-ar** verbs, the **nosotros** form is the only one with a written accent.

3 · In the imperfect of **-er** and **-ir** verbs, all forms have a written accent over the **i**.

4 · The imperfect of **hay** is **había** (*there was, there were*).

The verbs **ser**, **ir**, and **ver** are irregular in the imperfect.

ser *to be*

era	**éramos**
eras	**erais**
era	**eran**

ir *to go*

iba	**íbamos**
ibas	**ibais**
iba	**iban**

ver *to see*

veía	**veíamos**
veías	**veíais**
veía	**veían**

A *Identify the subject(s) of the following verbs in the imperfect, and write the correct subject pronoun(s).*

1. _____ hablaba
2. _____ creían
3. _____ empezábamos
4. _____ asistía
5. _____ compraban
6. _____ compartíamos
7. _____ preparabais
8. _____ eras
9. _____ seguíais

10. _____ iba
11. _____ merendabas
12. _____ cosías
13. _____ veían
14. _____ prendía
15. _____ éramos
16. _____ estaban
17. _____ atravesábamos
18. _____ ibais

B *Complete each sentence with the correct imperfect tense form of the verb in parentheses.*

1. (trabajar)   Marcos y Eduardo _____ en una tienda de deportes.
2. (leer)   Nosotros _____ la enciclopedia en línea.
3. (vivir)   Los Lapesa _____ en las afueras.
4. (correr)   Yo _____ a coger el tren.
5. (jugar)   Uds. _____ al golf los sábados.
6. (subir)   Los precios no _____.
7. (estar)   Nosotros _____ muy contentos.
8. (decir)   ¿Vosotros les _____ algo?
9. (poner)   Tú nos _____ al día.
10. (esperar)   Yo los _____ en el aeropuerto.
11. (rodar)   El director _____ un film en Las Vegas.
12. (tener)   Ud. _____ razón.
13. (abrir)   Yo _____ las cajas.
14. (hacer)   Uds. _____ investigaciones.
15. (tomar)   Vosotros _____ clases de cinematografía.
16. (ser)   Yo _____ el líder del grupo.
17. (aprender)   Alejandra _____ a patinar sobre ruedas.
18. (escribir)   Tú les _____ mensajes de texto a tus amigos.
19. (hablar)   Se _____ italiano en casa.
20. (preferir)   Uds. _____ invitarnos personalmente.
21. (beber)   Vosotras _____ jugo de naranja.

22. (salir)   Nosotros _____ a las ocho de la mañana.
23. (ir)   Yo _____ de vacaciones.
24. (ver)   ¿Uds. _____ televisión?
25. (nevar)   _____ toda la noche.
26. (funcionar) La lavadora y la secadora no _____.

C *Rewrite each sentence, changing the verb from present tense to imperfect.*

1. Quiero acompañarlos.

   _____

2. Envuelven los paquetes.

   _____

3. ¿Qué dicen Uds.?

   _____

4. Suele nevar en enero.

   _____

5. Te diviertes muchísimo.

   _____

6. Algo huele mal.

   _____

7. Pide los billetes electrónicos por computadora.

   _____

8. Vamos a caballo en la hacienda.

   _____

9. Comienza a estudiar.

   _____

10. Vuelven para las diez de la noche.

    _____

11. Les doy la bienvenida.

    _____

12. Se despiertan tarde los fines de semana.

    _____

13. ¿Sirves carne o pescado?

    _____

14. Sueñan con ser millonarios.

    _____

15. Finjo no entender el chiste.

_____

16. Cuenta con el apoyo de su familia.

_____

17. No pueden tranquilizarse.

_____

18. No entiendo el por qué.

_____

19. Son muy serios.

_____

20. Uds. se visten muy bien.

_____

21. Concluyen la presentación.

_____

22. Tiene mucho interés en el proyecto.

_____

Uses of the Imperfect

The imperfect tense is used to tell what time it was and to describe conditions existing in the past or past actions seen as backgrounds rather than events, actions that help set the scene. Therefore, the imperfect is usually used for descriptions in the past. Here are some specific examples of how the imperfect is used.

Time

The imperfect is used in clauses that tell the time at which something happened in the past. This includes not only clock time, but also time words such as **tarde** and **temprano**.

¿Qué hora **era**?	*What time was it?*
Ya **eran** las diez cuando volvimos.	*It was already ten o'clock when we came back.*
Ya **era** tarde cuando terminó la reunión.	*It was already late when the meeting ended.*

Weather

The imperfect is usually (but not always) used to describe weather conditions existing in the past.

Llovía cuando salimos.	*It was raining when we went out.*
No hacía mucho sol cuando estábamos en la playa.	*It wasn't very sunny when we were at the beach.*

D ***Time and weather.*** *Rewrite each sentence, changing background verbs from the present tense to the imperfect and verbs telling what happened to the preterit.*

MODELO   Es la una cuando regresan.

Era la una cuando regresaron.

1. Son las diez y media cuando llego a la oficina.

_____

2. Hace sol cuando comienza el partido.

_____

3. Es mediodía ya cuando vienen.

_____

4. Nieva cuando salgo para la pista de esquí.

_____

5. Son las siete treinta cuando despega el avión.

_____

6. Truena y hay relámpagos cuando aterrizamos.

_____

7. Es la madrugada cuando suena mi teléfono celular.

_____

8. Llueve a cántaros (*cats and dogs*) cuando los novios van a la iglesia.

_____

9. Hace muy buen tiempo cuando los recién casados salen de la iglesia.

_____

10. Hay montones de nieve en el parque cuando saco a mi perro a retozar (*romp, jump around*).

_____

_____

11. Hay tormenta cuando le devuelven el coche de alquiler al agente.

_____

12. Es ya tardísimo cuando los jóvenes se duermen.

_____

13. Está nublado y hace viento cuando llegamos a la cumbre (*top, peak*) de la montaña.

_____

14. Son las dos en punto cuando empieza la función de la tarde (*matinee*).

_____

Conditions

The imperfect is used to describe conditions in the past.

No fue fácil regresar a casa porque todos los autobuses **estaban** atestados.

It wasn't easy to return home, because all the buses were crowded.

Comimos en casa porque la mayor parte de los restaurantes **estaban** cerrados ese día.

We ate at home because most restaurants were closed that day.

Mis maletas **pesaban** tanto que tuve que llamar al cargador.

My suitcases weighed so much that I had to call the porter.

En esa época **venían** muchos inmigrantes al país. **Buscaban** la oportunidad de mejorar su vida. La población del país **subía** rápidamente.

In that period, many immigrants were coming to the country. They were seeking the opportunity to improve their lives. The population of the country was rising rapidly.

Description

The imperfect is used to describe in the past.

Su casa **era** muy grande. **Tenía** un jardín muy bonito.

His house was very big. It had a very pretty garden.

Los estudiantes **estaban** nerviosos porque sus cursos **eran** muy difíciles.

The students were nervous because their courses were very difficult.

Aquella señora **se llamaba** Laura Delgado. **Era** argentina, y **trabajaba** en el Ministerio de la Defensa.

That woman's name was Laura Delgado. She was Argentine, and she was working in the Ministry of Defense.

Mi abuela **era** una mujer sencilla que **se dedicaba** a su hogar y a sus cinco hijos. **Salía** poco porque **tenía** tantos quehaceres domésticos.

My grandmother was a simple woman who devoted herself to her home and her five children. She didn't go out much, because she had so many household chores.

Repeated Actions

The imperfect is used to label repeated actions in the past when the focus is on the actions themselves and not on when the actions began or ended. Adverbs and adverbial phrases such as **siempre, nunca, todos los veranos/días/domingos, cada vez, muchas veces, a menudo, generalmente, de costumbre**, etc. indicate repeated actions.

Cuando yo **era** joven, mi familia y yo **íbamos** al mar todos los veranos.

When I was young, my family and I used to go to the seashore every summer.

Él siempre me **telefoneaba** y me **hacía** preguntas.

He would always call me and ask me questions.

Ella nunca **recordaba** lo que yo le **decía**.

She never used to remember what I would tell her.

Cada vez que **venía** a mi casa, **se quedaba** a comer.

Every time he would come to my house, he would stay for dinner.

E ***Repeated actions in the imperfect.*** *Rewrite each sentence in the imperfect, using the adverbs and adverbial phrases of frequency in parentheses.*

MODELO   Lola me envía mensajes electrónicos. (todos los días)
Lola me enviaba mensajes electrónicos todos los días.

1. Les traigo bombones a los abuelos. (siempre)
   _____

2. Al terminar el trabajo los compañeros toman una copa. (de costumbre)
   _____

3. Daniela sale con Federico a bailar. (todos los sábados)
   _____

4. Paco le pide prestado el coche a su hermano. (a menudo)
   _____

5. Nadas en la piscina del gimnasio universitario. (cada semana)
   _____

6. Vamos a la sierra de Guadarrama para esquiar. (todos los inviernos)
   _____

7. Los chicos llegan hambrientos (*starved*) a la casa. (generalmente)
   _____

8. Pasamos un par de horas en el centro comercial. (muchas veces)
   _____

9. Ven a sus primos italianos. (todos los veranos)
   _____

10. ¿Hacéis un viaje de negocios? (todos los meses)
    _____

The Imperfect in Reported Speech

The imperfect usually replaces the present tense in reported speech (indirect discourse) when the main verb of the sentence is in a past tense. English works similarly. Compare the following pairs of sentences.

Dice que lo **sabe**.   *He says that he knows (it).*
Dijo que lo **sabía**.   *He said that he knew (it).*

Me escribe que **no viene**.   *She writes to me that she isn't coming.*
Me escribió que **no venía**.   *She wrote to me that she wasn't coming.*

Siempre **insisten** en que **pueden** hacerlo.   *They always insist that they can do it.*
Siempre **insistían** en que **podían** hacerlo.   *They always insisted that they could do it.*

F *Rewrite each sentence, showing reported speech in the past by replacing the present tense verb in the first clause with the preterit and replacing the present tense verb in the second clause with the imperfect.*

MODELO   Ellos nos dicen que quieren visitarnos.

Ellos nos dijeron que querían visitarnos.

1. Ignacio les informa que busca trabajo.

2. Laura anuncia que va a casarse.

3. Ellos insisten en que saben hacerlo.

4. Les escribo que hago un viaje en mayo.

5. Nos avisan que no pueden llegar puntual a la cita.

6. Me advierten que el ordenador está descompuesto.

7. Los jefes notifican que despiden a muchos empleados.

8. Pedro y Consuelo me cuentan que son felices.

The Imperfect and Preterit Contrasted

The imperfect and preterit both refer to past time, but express different ways of looking at past actions and events. The imperfect tense designates an action as going on in the past without any reference to its beginning or end. The preterit tense designates an action that the speaker sees as completed in the past or as having happened once.

Cuando yo estaba en Panamá, **hablaba** español.	*When I was in Panama, **I spoke** Spanish.*
Ayer **hablé** español con Diego.	*Yesterday **I spoke** Spanish with Diego.*

Spanish speakers must select one of these two aspects of past time—imperfect or preterit—for every past action they refer to. English often does not distinguish between these two aspects of past time.

Completed Action

The preterit implies that an action was completed in the past. It also may imply that the action happened once.

Llamaron a la puerta.	*There was a knock at the door.*
De repente, **se abrió** la puerta.	*Suddenly, the door opened.*
El avión **llegó** tarde.	*The plane arrived late.*
Estalló la bomba.	*The bomb exploded.*

Continuous or Repeated Action

The imperfect is used for actions that the speaker sees as going on in the past without reference to the beginning or the end of the action. The imperfect may convey that the action happened repeatedly.

El barrio **se hacía** cada vez más ruidoso.	*The neighborhood was getting noisier and noisier.*
Los chicos **estudiaban** en la biblioteca.	*The kids used to study in the library.*
Tú siempre **te acostabas** temprano.	*You always went to bed early.*

Description in the Past

A series of imperfects may be used to describe what was going on in the past.

Eran las seis de la mañana. La gente **dormía**. En la calle **pasaban** pocos coches. Algunos transeúntes **caminaban** hacia la parada de autobús y **esperaban**. El sol **salía**. **Era** un día como cualquiera.	*It was six in the morning. People were asleep. In the street, few cars were going by. Some pedestrians were walking to the bus stop and were waiting. The sun was coming out. It was a day like any other.*

For a Spanish speaker, the logical question to ask after hearing the above paragraph is **¿Qué pasó?** because in the imperfect, nothing really happens—the narration is not advanced at all. To make the above paragraph part of a narration, a preterit has to be added.

Eran las seis de la mañana. La gente **dormía**. En la calle **pasaban** pocos coches. Algunos transeúntes **caminaban** hacia la parada de autobús y **esperaban**. El sol **salía**. **Era** un día como cualquiera. De repente **se oyó** el ruido fuerte de una explosión.	*It was six in the morning. People were asleep. In the street, few cars were going by. Some pedestrians were walking to the bus stop and were waiting. The sun was coming out. It was a day like any other. Suddenly the loud noise of an explosion was heard.*

Background for Past Actions or Events

The imperfect often provides the background for past actions or events that are expressed in the preterit.

Paula **leía** cuando **llegaron** sus amigos.	*Paula was reading when her friends arrived.*
Cuando yo **entré**, todos **trabajaban**.	*When I came in, everyone was working.*
Cerré las ventanas porque **llovía**.	*I closed the windows because it was raining.*

G *Complete the following sentences, choosing either the imperfect or the preterit for each verb in parentheses. Each sentence has two verbs, one of which will be imperfect and the other preterit.*

MODELO   Mientras él ___*esperaba*___ el autobús, ___*empezó*___ a llover. (esperar, empezar)

1. _____ las once de la noche cuando ellos _____ para la discoteca. (ser, salir)

2. _____ tanta congestión en Internet que yo no _____ hacer la conexión. (hay, poder)

3. Elena _____ a Carlos mientras (ella) _____ arte en París. (conocer, estudiar)

4. Mientras tú _____ la película, nosotros _____ cinco millas. (ver, correr)

5. Felipe _____ mucho en el problema hasta que le _____ una solución. (pensar, venir)

6. Nosotros no _____ cuánto costaban los muebles hasta que el

   dependiente nos _____ el precio. (saber, decir)

7. _____ un fallo del sistema cuando tú _____ en línea. (hay, trabajar)

8. Vosotros _____ un paseo por el parque cuando alguien

   _____ un grito. (dar, dar)

9. El barrio donde Mercedes _____ _____ hermoso. (nacer, ser)

10. Nosotros los hinchas (*fans*) _____ muy entusiasmados hasta que

    el otro equipo _____ un gol. (estar, marcar)

11. El proyecto _____ difícil y complicado pero yo _____ realizarlo. (ser, lograr)

12. El gato _____ de la casa mientras Uds. _____. (huir, dormir)

13. Yo _____ en la facultad cuando se _____ la serie de conferencias. (enseñar, iniciar)

14. Su esposa _____ a luz (*give birth*) mientras Jorge _____. (dar, viajar)

15. El alumno no _____ atención hasta que la maestra lo

    _____. (prestar, reñir)

16. Yo _____ la cuenta aunque mis amigos todavía _____ su postre. (pagar, comer)

17. Hasta que Sara y Esteban _____ nosotros no _____ a nadie. (aparecer, conocer)

18. Roberto _____ el doctorado cuando _____ veinticinco años. (conseguir, tener)

19. Se _____ una gran oportunidad mientras ellos más la

    _____. (presentar, necesitar)

20. Cuando _____ las visitas los anfitriones (*hosts*) todavía

    _____ la comida. (llegar, preparar)

Continuing Past Action

Spanish uses the imperfect tense to refer to past actions that are seen as continuing at another point of time in the past. English uses a *had been doing something* construction for this function. The Spanish construction consists of the following elements.

- **¿cuánto tiempo hacía que** + verb in the imperfect?

  This construction is used to ask a question about how long something had been going on. The word **tiempo** can be omitted in the question.

¿Cuánto (tiempo) hacía que Ud. trabajaba en aquella oficina?	*How long had you been working in that office?*

- **hacía** + time expression + **que** + verb in the imperfect OR
  verb in the imperfect + **hacía** + time expression

  These constructions are used to tell how long something had been going on.

—**¿Cuánto tiempo hacía que asistías** a aquella universidad?	*"How long had you been attending that university?"*
—**Hacía un año que cursaba** informática allí.	*"I had been taking computer science there for a year."*
—**Cursaba** informática allí **hacía un año.**	*"I had been taking computer science there for a year."*

- **Desde** is added to specify the starting point of an action that began in the past and continues to another point in the past.

—**¿Desde cuándo vivías** al lado de los Paz?	*"Since when had you been living next door to the Pazes?"*
—**Éramos** vecinos **desde** septiembre.	*"We had been neighbors since September."*

  A verb in the imperfect tense + **desde hacía** + expression of time is also used to label an action that was continuing in the past when something else happened.

Eran casados **desde hacía** tres años cuando nació su hijo.	*They had been married for three years when their son was born.*

- The imperfect of **llevar** (or, in Latin America, of **tener** as well) with expressions of time is commonly used to express *had been*.

—¿Cuánto tiempo **llevabas** en esa compañía?	*"How long had you been at that company?"*
—**Llevaba un año** allí.	*"I had been there for one year."*
Llevábamos más de dos años en esta universidad.	*We had been at this university for more than two years.*
¿Tenías mucho tiempo en esta oficina?	*Had you been at this office for a long time?*

The imperfect in the constructions presented above frequently occurs in the same sentence with a preterit. The preterit expresses a point in past time up to which the action expressed by the imperfect had been continuing.

Tenía tres meses sin trabajar cuando por fin **le ofrecieron** un buen puesto.	*He hadn't worked in three months when finally he was offered a good position.*
Hacía un año que Luisa **estudiaba** informática cuando **decidió** inscribirse en la facultad de administración.	*Luisa had been studying computer science for a year when she decided to enroll in business school.*

End Point Specified for Past Action

Although the imperfect is usually used to express repeated actions in the past, when the end point of those actions is specified, the verb is in the preterit because the speaker's focus shifts to the completion of the actions. In the sentence below, no end point is specified.

Cuando yo **era** niño, **iba** al mar todos los veranos.	*When I was a child, I went to the seashore every summer.*

Notice the change in tense when an endpoint is specifically mentioned.

Hasta la edad de doce años, **fui** al mar todos los veranos.	*Until the age of twelve, I went to the seashore every summer.*

Differences in Meaning Between the Imperfect and the Preterit of Some Common Verbs

Sometimes English uses entirely different verbs to express the difference between the imperfect and the preterit of some Spanish verbs. For example, **tenía** means *I was in the process of having* or *I had*; **tuve** means *I began to have* or *I got, I received.*

Ella **tenía** muchas ideas.	*She had a lot of ideas. (They were in her head.)*
Ella **tuvo** una buena idea.	*She had a good idea. (It popped into her head.)*
Sabía su nombre.	*I knew his name.*
Supe su nombre.	*I found out his name.*
Conocíamos a Raquel.	*We knew Raquel.*
Conocimos a Raquel.	*We met Raquel.*
No podíamos salir por la nieve.	*We couldn't go out because of the snow. (It's not stated whether we went out or not, just that it was very difficult to go out.)*
No **pudimos** salir por la nieve.	*We couldn't go out because of the snow. (And we didn't go out.)*
Jaime **no quería** ir en taxi.	*Jaime didn't want to go by taxi. (It leaves open whether he went or not.)*
Jaime **no quiso** ir en taxi.	*Jaime didn't want (= refused) to go by taxi. (And he didn't go.)*

El cuadro **costaba** tanto que no lo compré.	*The painting **cost** so much that I didn't buy it.*
El cuadro **nos costó** treinta mil dólares.	*The painting **cost us** 30,000 dollars.*

Verbs of Perception

Verbs of mental activity and other verbs of perception can be used in either the preterit or the imperfect. However, the speaker's choice of tense determines the meaning of the sentence.

Pensé que él era colombiano.	*I thought that he was Colombian. (At that moment something made me think that he was Colombian.)*
Pensaba que él era colombiano.	*I thought that he was Colombian. (I used to think that he was Colombian.)*
Creí que no me entendían.	*I thought that they were not understanding me. (Something happened that made me think that.)*
Creía que no me entendían.	*I thought that they were not understanding me. (It was my ongoing impression.)*
Comprendió que yo no tenía interés.	*He understood that I had no interest. (He realized it at that moment.)*
Comprendía que yo no tenía interés.	*He understood that I had no interest. (He was under that impression because of what I was saying, doing, etc.)*
De repente **oímos** un ruido.	*Suddenly we heard a noise. (The noise began.)*
Oíamos mucho ruido.	*We heard a lot of noise. (There was a lot of noise going on.)*

Había/hubo and estaba/estuvo

The difference between **había** and **hubo** and between **estaba** and **estuvo** is especially difficult for English speakers.

Aquí **había** una fiesta.	*There was a party here. (It was going on here—the speaker may mention something that happened while the party was going on.)*
Aquí **hubo** una fiesta.	*There was a party here. (It took place and is finished.)*
En esa zona **había** muchas tormentas.	*In that region there were a lot of storms. (This describes the region in the past.)*
Hubo una tormenta ayer.	*There was a storm yesterday. (A completed event in the past.)*

En su casa casi no **había** muebles.	*There was almost no furniture in his house. (This describes the house in the past.)*
En su casa **hubo** un incendio.	*There was a fire in his house. (A completed event in the past.)*
¿Dónde **estabas** cuando llamé?	*Where were you when I called? (Where you were is a background to an event in the past.)*
Estuve diez horas en la oficina.	*I was in the office for ten hours. (The end of my time in the office is specified; my being there is seen as complete.)*
Estaban enfermos.	*They were sick. (A description in the past.)*
Estuvieron enfermos todo el mes.	*They were sick all month. (The endpoint of their illness is specified; their illness is seen as a completed event in the past.)*

H   *Translation. Express the following dialogues in Spanish.*

1. *How long had you (Uds.) been living in New York when you bought a condominium?*

   _____

   _____

2. *We had been living in the city for two years.*

   _____

3. *How long had you (tú) been studying Spanish in Madrid when you decided to return to your American (U.S.) university?*

   _____

   _____

4. *I had been there for six weeks.*

   _____

5. *How long had Julia been using her computer when she changed makes (brands)?*

   _____

   _____

6. *She had it for three years.*

   _____

7. *Since when had Jaime been working as a consultant?*

   _____

   _____

8. *Since last year when he got his MBA.*

_____

_____

| BUILDING SENTENCES | **Sentences with double object pronouns** |

In English, a direct object pronoun and an indirect object pronoun cannot occur together—the indirect object appears in a prepositional phrase beginning with *to* or *for* when a direct object is present.

> *I gave it **to him**.*

In Spanish, however, double object pronouns are very common.

With Spanish double object pronouns, the indirect object pronoun always precedes the direct object pronoun. Thus, indirect object pronouns **me** (*to/for me*), **te** (*to/for you,* informal singular), **nos** (*to/for us*), **os** (*to/for you,* informal plural) precede direct object pronouns **lo, la, los, las.**

—¿No tienes el libro de física?	*"Don't you have the physics book?"*
—Sí, **me lo** prestó Juan Carlos.	*"Yes, Juan Carlos lent **it to me**."*
—Perdí la dirección de Consuelo.	*"I lost Consuelo's address."*
—Yo la tengo en casa. **Te la** mando por correo electrónico.	*"I have it at home. I'll send **it to you** by e-mail."*
—Tengo las fotos de mi viaje.	*"I have the photos of my trip."*
—¿**Me las** puedes mostrar?	*"Can you show **them to me**?"*
—No entiendo los problemas de matemáticas.	*"I don't understand the math problems."*
—A ver si el profesor **nos los** explica.	*"Let's see whether the professor explains **them to us**."*

When one of the third-person indirect object pronouns, **le** (*to/for you* [formal singular], *to/for him/her*) or **les** (*to/for you* [formal plural], *to/for them*), precedes one of the direct object pronouns **lo, la, los, las,** it changes to **se.**

—Mis hijos quieren aquel videojuego.	*"My children want that video game."*
—¿**Se lo** vas a comprar? (**les** + **lo** → **se lo**)	*"Are you going to buy **it for them**?"*
—Éster y Julio quieren pedirte prestada tu maleta grande.	*"Éster and Julio want to borrow your big suitcase."*
—Yo **se la** presto con mucho gusto. (**les** + **la** → **se la**)	*"I'll gladly lend **it to them**."*
—José me dijo que le ibas a mandar los informes.	*"José told me you were going to send him the reports."*
—Ya **se los** mandé. (**le** + **los** → **se los**)	*"I already sent **them to him**."*
—Luisa necesita sus tarjetas de crédito.	*"Luisa needs her credit cards."*
—Mañana **se las** doy. (**le** + **las** → **se las**)	*"I'll give **them to her** tomorrow."*

Here are the possible combinations of double object pronouns in Spanish.

me lo	**me la**	**me los**	**me las**
te lo	**te la**	**te los**	**te las**
se lo	**se la**	**se los**	**se las**
nos lo	**nos la**	**nos los**	**nos las**
os lo	**os la**	**os los**	**os las**
se lo	**se la**	**se los**	**se las**

Double object pronouns, like single object pronouns, appear before the conjugated verb. They may also follow an infinitive, and when thus placed they are attached to it in writing. When two object pronouns are added to an infinitive, a written accent must be placed over the **a**, **e**, or **i** preceding the **r** of the infinitive.

—¿Vas a envi**á**r**selo**?   *"Are you going to send **it to him (to her, to them)**?"*

—Sí, **se lo** voy a enviar la semana que viene.   *"Yes, I'm going to send **it to him (to her, to them)** next week."*

—¿Quieres darles estas computadoras a los estudiantes?   *"Do you want to give these computers to the students?"*

—Cómo no. Debemos ofrec**é**r**selas**.   *"Of course. We should offer **them to them**."*

To focus on the identity of the referent of **se**, Spanish uses a phrase consisting of **a** + noun or pronoun.

—¿**Le** mandaste las tarjetas de memoria **a María**?   *"Did you send the memory cards **to María**?"*

—No, **a ella** no. **Se** las mandé **a Raquel**.   *"No, not **to her**. I sent them **to Raquel**."*

—Carlos y Rebeca querían ver tus fotos.   *"Carlos and Rebeca wanted to see your photos."*

—**Se** las mostré **a él**. **A ella se** las voy a mostrar hoy por la tarde.   *"I showed them **to him**. I'm going to show them **to her** this afternoon."*

The interrogatives **¿a quién?**, **¿a quiénes?** are also used with **se** when **se** is a replacement for **le** or **les** before a direct object pronoun.

—Necesito todos los apuntes de la clase de historia de los Estados Unidos.   *"I need all the notes from the United States history class."*

—¿**A quién se** los vas a pedir?   *"Whom are you going to ask for them?"*

Since the subject often follows the verb in Spanish, the presence or absence of the preposition **a** is what clarifies the role of an animate noun at the end of a sentence when the verb is in the third person.

¿Las fotos? Se las mostró **David**.   *The photos? David showed them to her.*
¿Las fotos? Se las mostró **a David**.   *The photos? She showed them to David.*

¿El dinero? Se lo devolvió **Luisa**.   *The money? Luisa returned it to him.*
¿El dinero? Se lo devolvió **a Luisa**.   *The money? He returned it to Luisa.*

I *Rewrite each sentence, changing the direct object nouns to pronouns.* **¡Ojo!** *Be sure to make necessary changes and watch out for the placement of object pronouns in the sentences.*

MODELO   Les dejó el recado. *Se lo dejó.*

1. Les expliqué las estrategias. _____

2. Le pidió el helado de mango. _____

3. Nos enseñaban el apartamento. _____

4. Me devuelve la tarjeta telefónica. _____

5. ¿Te ofrecieron el puesto de analista? _____

6. Os sirven las chuletas de cordero. _____

7. Le regalamos los pendientes de oro. _____

8. Le envío el mensaje electrónico. _____

9. Les mandó la tarjeta de crédito. _____

10. Nos recomiendan esta marca. _____

11. Les vendimos el televisor plasma. _____

12. Me dijo la palabra clave. _____

13. Te prestamos el quemador CD. _____

14. ¿Nos demostráis vuestro sitio Web? _____

15. Le dio los libros de texto. _____

16. Os suben vuestro equipaje. _____

17. Le trajisteis las camisas. _____

18. Les hice esos platos vegetarianos. _____

19. Le comentaban lo ocurrido. _____

20. Me entregó las llaves. _____

J *Express the following sentences in English.* **¡Ojo!** *Focus on the subject and indirect object in each pair of sentences.*

1. a. Se los dio Ricardo.

   _____

   b. Se los dio a Ricardo.

   _____

2. a. Se lo describían los consultores.

   _____

   b. Se lo describían a los consultores.

   _____

3. a. Se las repitió Ofelia.

   _____

   b. Se las repitió a Ofelia.

   _____

4. a. Se la pide Ud.

   _____

   b. Se la pide a Ud.

   _____

5. a. Se los iba a mandar Sarita.

   _____

   b. Se los iba a mandar a Sarita.

   _____

6. a. Se la quieren mostrar nuestros colegas.

   _____

   b. Se la quieren mostrar a nuestros colegas.

   _____

7. a. No pudo explicárselo el profesor.

   _____

   b. No pudo explicárselo al profesor.

   _____

8. a. Acaban de pedírselas estas abogadas.

   _____

   b. Acaban de pedírselas a estas abogadas.

   _____

K **Translation.** *Express the following dialogues in Spanish.*

1. *Can you (tú) lend me your digital camera?*

   _____

2. *I lent it to Esteban last week. You can ask him for it.*

   _____

3. *I bought this sweater to give to someone as a gift.*

   _____

4. *To whom do you want to give it?*

   _____

5. *We used to write them e-mails every day.*

_____

6. *Do you still send them to them so often?*

_____

7. *Did you (Uds.) make them dinner already?*

_____

8. *We're going to make it for them soon.*

_____

9. *Daniel wrote us that he was going to give his girlfriend a ring.*

_____

10. *Did he say when he intended to give it to her?*

_____

11. *Julia handed her thesis in to the professors the day before yesterday.*

_____

_____

12. *Didn't she have to hand it in to them last semester?*

_____

13. *How long had they been working for the company when the boss gave them a raise (el aumento de sueldo)?*

_____

_____

14. *They had been doing programming for six months when he gave it to them.*

_____

_____

The Past Participle;
The Present Perfect;
The Pluperfect

BUILDING SENTENCES

Uses of the past participle

Introduction to the Compound Tenses in Spanish

Compound tenses in Spanish consist of the conjugated form of the auxiliary verb **haber** (*to have*) plus the past participle, which is the form of the verb ending in **-do**. The past participle does not change for gender or number in the compound tenses.

The Past Participle

Most past participles are regular in Spanish. **-Ar** verbs change the **-ar** of the infinitive to **-ado**.

hablar	hablado	*spoken*
ganar	ganado	*earned, won*
ocupar	ocupado	*occupied*
enviar	enviado	*sent*

-Er verbs change the **-er** of the infinitive and **-ir** verbs change the **-ir** of the infinitive to **-ido**.

comer	comido	*eaten*
vender	vendido	*sold*
vivir	vivido	*lived*
dormir	dormido	*slept*

-Er and **-ir** verbs such as **caer**, **leer**, and **oír** whose stems end in a vowel add an accent mark over the **i** of the past participle ending **-ido**, just as they do over the **i** in the endings of the preterit.

caer	caído	*fallen*
creer	creído	*believed*
leer	leído	*read*
oír	oído	*heard*
poseer	poseído	*possessed*
traer	traído	*brought*

Some past participles are irregular. Most of them end in **-to**.

abrir	**abierto**	*opened*
cubrir	**cubierto**	*covered*
devolver	**devuelto**	*returned*
escribir	**escrito**	*written*
freír	**frito**	*fried*
imprimir	**impreso**	*printed*
morir	**muerto**	*dead*
poner	**puesto**	*put, placed*
resolver	**resuelto**	*resolved*
romper	**roto**	*broken, torn*
ver	**visto**	*seen*
volver	**vuelto**	*returned*

Two of the most common verbs have past participles ending in **-cho**.

decir	**dicho**	*said*
hacer	**hecho**	*done*

When a prefix is added to any of the verbs above, the past participle shows the same irregularities.

componer	**compuesto**	*composed*
descomponer	**descompuesto**	*broken, in disrepair*
describir	**descrito**	*described*
descubrir	**descubierto**	*discovered*
deshacer	**deshecho**	*undone*
imponer	**impuesto**	*imposed*
inscribir	**inscrito**	*registered, enrolled*
posponer	**pospuesto**	*postponed*
predecir	**predicho**	*predicted*
proponer	**propuesto**	*proposed, suggested*
prever	**previsto**	*foreseen*
rehacer	**rehecho**	*redone*
revolver	**revuelto**	*turned over*
satisfacer	**satisfecho**	*satisfied*

The past participles of **ser** and **ir** are **sido** and **ido**, respectively.

The Present Perfect Tense

The present perfect tense (English *I have done something.*) consists of the auxiliary verb **haber** + the past participle.

Study the conjugation of the present perfect of **hablar**, **comer**, and **escribir**.

hablar *to speak*	
he hablado	hemos hablado
has hablado	habéis hablado
ha hablado	han hablado

comer *to eat*	
he comido	hemos comido
has comido	habéis comido
ha comido	han comido

escribir *to write*	
he escrito	hemos escrito
has escrito	habéis escrito
ha escrito	han escrito

The present perfect of **hay** is **ha habido** *there has/have been.*

In the compound tenses, no words are placed between the auxiliary verb and the past participle. Thus, object pronouns are placed before the forms of **haber** in these tenses. In questions, subject pronouns or noun subjects are placed after the past participle when the word order is inverted. In the equivalent English questions, the subject *does* come between the auxiliary and the participle.

Los hemos llamado.	*We've called them.*
Nos han mandado el paquete.	*They've sent us the package.*
Se lo he explicado.	*I've explained it to them.*
¿Por qué **ha salido Juan?**	*Why has Juan gone out?*
¿Qué **han comprado ellos?**	*What have they bought?*
¿Ha llegado el asesor?	*Has the consultant arrived?*
¿No los has visto tú?	*Haven't you seen them?*

Uses of the Present Perfect

■ The Spanish present perfect corresponds to the English present perfect. Both languages use this compound tense to express a past action that has an effect on the present or that continues into the present.

Nadie ha llegado todavía.	*No one has arrived yet.*
¿Nunca has viajado por México?	*Have you ever traveled through Mexico?*
El mecánico ya ha reparado el carro.	*The mechanic has already fixed the car.*

■ Many Spanish speakers, especially in Spain, use the present perfect for recent events—events that have happened earlier in the day. English often uses the simple past in these cases.

No he desayunado esta mañana.	*I didn't have breakfast this morning.*
Hoy por la tarde han cerrado a las cinco.	*This afternoon they closed at five.*
El cartero ha venido a mediodía.	*The mailman came at noon.*
Los chicos han salido hace cinco minutos.	*The children left five minutes ago.*

In most parts of Latin America, the preterit is used in these cases.

No desayuné esta mañana.	*I didn't have breakfast this morning.*
Hoy por la tarde cerraron a las cinco.	*This afternoon they closed at five.*

El cartero vino a mediodía.   *The mailman came at noon.*
Los chicos salieron hace cinco minutos.   *The children left five minutes ago.*

■ Many Spanish speakers use the present perfect to emphasize the relationship of a past action to the present. In most of these cases, English prefers the simple past. This category overlaps with the present perfect to express recent events.

¿Quién te ha dicho que yo no iba   *Who told you that I wasn't coming?*
   a venir?

¿Has visto las noticias? Ha habido   *Did you see the news? There was an*
   un temblor.   *earthquake.*

A *Using the cue in parentheses, complete each verb phrase with either the missing form of the auxiliary verb* **haber** *or the past participle.*

1. _____ salido (nosotros)

2. han _____ (hablar)

3. _____ visto (Uds.)

4. habéis _____ (entender)

5. _____ vuelto (tú)

6. ha _____ (leer)

7. _____ aprendido (él)

8. ha _____ (decir)

9. _____ escogido (yo)

10. _____ hecho (Ud.)

11. han _____ (discutir)

12. has _____ (mirar)

13. he _____ (poner)

14. hemos _____ (escribir)

15. ha _____ (haber)

B *Write sentences in the present perfect, using the following strings of elements.*

MODELO   Rita / tomar / un café
           Rita ha tomado un café.

1. tú / hablar / por teléfono móvil

   _____

2. nuestro equipo / ganar / el partido

   _____

3. ellos / poner / la mesa

_____

4. Ud. / recibir / la correspondencia

_____

5. Gerardo / hacer / un login

_____

6. yo / leer / los titulares

_____

7. nuestra familia / vivir / bien

_____

8. Uds. / tener / mucha experiencia

_____

9. tú / descargar / el fichero

_____

10. vosotros / no comprender / el asunto

_____

11. nosotros / ser / muy felices

_____

12. nadie / decir / nada

_____

13. ¿quién / romper / la ventana?

_____

14. Nora y Daniela / ir / de compras

_____

15. ¿Ud. / oír / esta orquesta?

_____

16. yo / escribir / el informe

_____

17. nosotros / resolver / el conflicto

_____

18. ¿cómo / estar (Uds.)?

_____

19. la cocinera / freír / el pescado

_____

20. ellos / no querer molestar

_____

21. vosotros / imprimir / los papeles

_____

22. los electrodomésticos / funcionar / bien

_____

C *Rewrite each sentence, changing the verb from the present tense to the present perfect.*

MODELO   Demuestra los resultados.

   Ha demostrado los resultados. _____

1. Almuerzan en la cafetería.

_____

2. Llueve todo el día.

_____

3. Hacen construir una casa.

_____

4. Pierde el tren esta mañana.

_____

5. Hay mucha congestión en Internet.

_____

6. Este libro es un éxito de librería (*bestseller*).

_____

7. Vuelven del viaje de negocios.

_____

8. El director rueda la película en Texas.

_____

9. Los niños quieren ver los dibujos animados.

_____

10. Jorge consigue trabajar en la seguridad nacional y la ciberseguridad.

_____

_____

11. El armario huele mal.

_____

12. Los despierta.

_____

13. Te lo digo.

_____

14. Se las devolvemos.

_____

15. Prefieren dársela.

_____

16. No se lo puedo recomendar.

_____

17. ¿Tratas de enviárnoslos?

_____

18. Te la piensan regalar.

_____

19. Vuelve a pedírmelas.

_____

20. ¿Por qué necesitáis recordárselo?

_____

D   _Answer each question, writing the verb in the present perfect in your response._
Change each direct object noun to a pronoun and make all necessary changes.

MODELO   ¿Actualizas los datos? _Ya los he actualizado._

1. ¿Pruebas el guacamole? _____

2. ¿Empieza el programa de realidad? _____

3. ¿Uds. visitan esos sitios Web? _____

4. ¿Pedro rellena el formulario? _____

5. ¿La compañía lanza unos nuevos productos alimenticios?

_____

6. ¿Repites el plato (_have a second helping_)? _____

7. ¿Ellos emprenden una campaña publicitaria? _____

8. ¿Vas a comer comida rápida hoy? _____

9. ¿Rafael piensa estudiar ingeniería del medio ambiente? _____

10. ¿Uds. pueden realizar su proyecto? _____

11. ¿Vosotros tenéis que hacer vuestras investigaciones? _____

12. ¿Te muestran su nueva computadora personal? _____

13. ¿Les contamos a Uds. los chismes? _____

14. ¿El vendedor de coches le va a entregar la llave a Leo? _____

15. ¿Van a serviros las enchiladas? _____

16. ¿Quieres leer ese blog? _____

The Pluperfect Tense

The pluperfect tense (also called the past perfect) consists of the imperfect of the auxiliary verb **haber** and the past participle. In formation and function it is very much like the English pluperfect: *had done something.*

Study the conjugation of the pluperfect of **hablar**, **comer**, and **escribir**.

hablar *to speak*

había hablado	habíamos hablado
habías hablado	habíais hablado
había hablado	habían hablado

comer *to eat*

había comido	habíamos comido
habías comido	habíais comido
había comido	habían comido

escribir *to write*

había escrito	habíamos escrito
habías escrito	habíais escrito
había escrito	habían escrito

The pluperfect of **hay** is **había habido** *there had been.*

The pluperfect labels a past event that was completed before another past event occurred.

Cuando yo llegué, ella ya **había salido**.	*When I arrived, she had already left.*
He venido a verte porque me **habían dicho** que estabas enfermo.	*I've come to see you because they had told me that you were sick.*
¡Qué bien! Yo no sabía que Uds. **habían resuelto** el problema.	*Terrific! I didn't know that you had solved the problem.*
A las cinco, todos los empleados **habían terminado** su trabajo.	*At five, all the employees had finished their work.*

E *Write sentences with the cues given, using verbs in the pluperfect tense to say that things happened before the past events asked about. Change each direct object noun to a pronoun and make all necessary changes.*

MODELO   ¿Uds. llegaron de la costa el mes pasado? (hace un par de meses)

No, habíamos llegado de la costa hace un par de meses.

1. ¿Corriste en la carrera en julio? (abril)

   _____

2. ¿Uds. vieron al bebé por primera vez hace unos días? (hace un mes)

   _____

3. ¿Los Alonso hicieron la barbacoa el segundo fin de semana de mayo? (el primero)

   _____

4. ¿Abrieron la joyería la semana pasada? (hace tres semanas)

   _____

5. ¿Ud. volvió de vacaciones ayer? (anteayer)

   _____

6. ¿Diana y Alberto compraron su casa este año? (el año pasado)

   _____

7. ¿El novio de Inés le pidió la mano el día de su cumpleaños? (el Día de los Enamorados)

   _____

8. ¿Plácido celebró su cumpleaños el nueve de marzo? (el primero del mes)

   _____

9. ¿Llamaste a Éster para invitarla a la fiesta el jueves? (martes)

   _____

10. ¿Le disteis el carro a Elías en diciembre? (noviembre)

   _____

   _____

F *Create sentences from the following strings of elements, using the preterit in the **cuando** clause and the pluperfect in the main clause.*

MODELO   Marta / regresar del gimnasio / sus amigos / salir

Cuando Marta regresó del gimnasio, sus amigos ya habían salido.

1. tú / llamarnos / nosotros / ir de compras

   _____

2. yo / llegar al cine / Nicolás y Mari / ver la mitad de la película

   _____

   _____

3. los invitados / venir / Isabel / poner la mesa

_____

4. Paco / comenzar a trotar / los otros jugadores / correr cinco millas

_____

_____

5. Uds. / invitarme / yo / hacer planes para ese día

_____

6. nosotros / ir en lancha / dejar de llover

_____

7. vosotros / pasar la aspiradora / Susana / sacudir el polvo (*dust*)

_____

8. Toni / solucionar el problema por fin / Ud. / resolverlo

_____

9. Vicente / pedirle la cuenta al mesero / Enrique / pagarla

_____

10. yo / volver a la tienda de antigüedades (*antique store*) / alguien / comprar la estatua

_____

_____

BUILDING SENTENCES | **Uses of the past participle**

The Past Participle as an Adjective

Most past participles can be used as adjectives. They can modify nouns directly or serve as predicate adjectives. When a past participle is used as an adjective, it agrees in gender and number with the noun it modifies.

una novela mal **escrita**	*a poorly **written** novel*
unos edificios recién **construidos**	*recently **built** buildings*
un artículo muy **leído** y **comentado**	*a widely **read** and **commented upon** article*
el cielo **cubierto**	*the **overcast** sky*
cielos **despejados**	***clear** skies*
Trato **hecho**.	*It's a (**done**) deal.*
Luis tiene el brazo **roto**.	*Luis has a **broken** arm.*
Vimos unas aldeas **abandonadas**.	*We saw some **abandoned** villages.*
El contrato está **firmado**.	*The contract is **signed**.*
Sus padres estaban **preocupados**.	*His parents were **worried**.*
Mi computadora está **descompuesta**.	*My computer is **broken**.*
Las ventanas están **abiertas**.	*The windows are **open**.*

The Past Participle Used to Express Position

The past participle in Spanish is used to express position of the human body or of objects. English usually uses the *-ing* form for this function.

Estamos **sentados** en la primera fila.	*We're **sitting** in the first row.*
¿Por qué están Uds. **parados**?	*Why are you **standing**?*
Los feligreses estaban **arrodillados**.	*The congregants were **kneeling**.*
Lo vi **arrimado** a un árbol.	*I saw him **leaning** against a tree.*
¿Por qué estás **acostada**? ¿Estás enferma?	*Why are you **lying down**? Are you sick?*
Los chicos no están **levantados** todavía.	*The kids aren't **up** (= out of bed) yet.*

Absolute Use of the Participle

Past participles, especially in written Spanish, can be used as substitutes for clauses. This is possible in English too, but the English past participle is usually accompanied by the word *having*.

Aclarado el asunto, pudieron llegar a un acuerdo.	***The matter having been cleared up**, they were able to reach an agreement.*
Terminada la conferencia, los estudiantes se levantaron y se fueron.	***The lecture having ended**, the students got up and left.*
Entregado el informe de los asesores, los dirigentes empezaron a estudiarlo.	***The consultants' report having been submitted**, the directors began to study it.*

In everyday English, a clause in the pluperfect beginning with *once* is more common: *Once the matter had been cleared up, they were able to reach an agreement.*

Tener + Past Participle

Tener can be used with a past participle to emphasize the completion of an action, especially one that required considerable effort. In this construction, the past participle agrees in gender and number with the noun it refers to. This noun would be the direct object of the verb in the present perfect. Compare the following pairs of sentences.

He hecho la cena.	*I've made dinner.*
Tengo la cena **hecha**.	*I have dinner ready. (I have finished making dinner.)*
Hemos escrito todos nuestros informes.	*We have written all our reports.*
Tenemos escritos todos nuestros informes.	*We have completed the writing of all our reports.*
A ver si ya han reparado las computadoras.	*Let's see if they've already repaired the computers.*
A ver si ya **tienen reparadas** las computadoras.	*Let's see if they've already finished repairing the computers.*

G *Complete each phrase with an adjective derived from the past participle form of the verb in parentheses.*

MODELO el coche _descompuesto_ (descomponer)

1. a. la casa veraniega (*summer*) recientemente _____ (comprar)

   b. el apartamento recientemente _____ (alquilar)

   c. los condominios recientemente _____ (amueblar)

   d. las paredes recientemente _____ (pintar)

   e. el piso (*apartment,* Spain) recientemente _____ (vender)

   f. el centro comercial recientemente _____ (construir)

   g. las viviendas (*houses*) recientemente _____ (rehacer)

2. a. los datos electrónicamente _____ (entrar)

   b. la información electrónicamente _____ (introducir)

   c. las canciones electrónicamente _____ (bajar)

   d. el fichero electrónicamente _____ (cargar)

   e. los programas electrónicamente _____ (telecargar)

   f. los gráficos electrónicamente _____ (transmitir)

3. a. el pollo _____ (freír)

   b. los huevos _____ (cocer)

   c. el agua _____ (hervir)

   d. las hamburguesas _____ (asar)

   e. la carne muy _____ (hacer) (*too well done*)

   f. la carne poco _____ (hacer) (*underdone*)

4. a. un sitio Web frecuentemente _____ (ver)

   b. un sitio Web _____ (visitar) muy a menudo

   c. un sitio Web muy _____ (concurrir) (*visit*)

   d. un sitio Web fácilmente _____ (navegar)

   e. un sitio Web recientemente _____ (diseñar)

   f. un sitio Web inteligentemente _____ (crear)

5. a. las personas _____ (animar)

   b. las personas _____ (entusiasmar)

   c. las personas _____ (aburrir)

   d. las personas _____ (agradecer)

   e. las personas _____ (enfurecer)

   f. las personas _____ (casarse)

   g. las personas _____ (reunirse)

6. a. las palabras claramente _____ (decir)

   b. el correo electrónico claramente _____ (escribir)

   c. los pensamientos claramente _____ (expresar)

   d. los sonidos claramente _____ (pronunciar)

   e. la poesía claramente _____ (traducir)

   f. el susurro (*whisper*) claramente _____ (oír)

H *Modismos (Idioms). Using the expressions given, complete each sentence with the correct form of* **estar** *in the present tense plus the adjective that derives from the present participle.* **¡Ojo!** *Derive the adjective form from the verb if it is not already given.*

1. estar frito *to be done for, all washed up*

   Ella cree que (ella) _____ porque el jefe rechazó (*rejected*) todas sus ideas.

2. estar mojado hasta los huesos (*bones*) *to be soaking wet*

   Nosotros salimos sin paraguas y _____ hasta los huesos.

3. meterse en lo que no le importa *to meddle in things that don't concern someone*

   Como de costumbre él _____ en lo que no le importa.

4. dormirse en los laureles *to rest on one's laurels*

   Ellos han logrado mucho y ahora _____ en los laureles.

5. comerse de envidia *to be consumed by envy*

   Carolina _____ de envidia porque su ex-novio sale con otras chicas.

6. estar hecho una lástima *to be a sorry sight, in a sad state*

   Chicas, Uds. _____ una lástima. ¿Qué les pasa?

I *For each string of elements, write a sentence using the present perfect. Then write a sentence that shows the resulting condition of the sentence in the present perfect.* **¡Ojo!** *Remember that the adjectives derive from past participles and therefore must show agreement with the subjects.*

MODELO   ellos / abrir / el puerto

        Han abierto el puerto.

        El puerto está abierto.

1. yo / escribir / los poemas

   _____

   _____

2. Marcia / teñir / la tela

    _____

    _____

3. nosotros / cubrir / los gastos

    _____

    _____

4. la abuela / acostar / a sus nietos

    _____

    _____

5. Patricio / fotocopiar / las cartas

    _____

    _____

6. tú / hacer / las galletas

    _____

    _____

7. Ud. / apagar / el fuego

    _____

    _____

8. vosotros / perder / la plata

    _____

    _____

9. Uds. / tirar / la basura

    _____

    _____

10. alguien / estacionar / el coche

    _____

    _____

11. Perla / enloquecer / a sus amigas

    _____

    _____

12. ellos / atravesar / el puente

    _____

    _____

13. los soldados / caer

_____

_____

14. yo / resolver / el problema

_____

_____

15. nosotros / imprimir / la tesis

_____

_____

16. Lorenzo / romper / sus pantalones

_____

_____

17. el arquitecto / rehacer / estas casas

_____

_____

18. la directora / posponer / la reunión

_____

_____

19. la cocinera / freír / las croquetas

_____

_____

20. el dramaturgo / terminar / el guión (*script*)

_____

_____

J **Translation.** *Express the following sentences in Spanish.*

1. *We found out that you* (tú) *had already returned from your business trip.*

_____

2. *When the war broke out* (estallar) *in their country, the Reyes had already fled to the United States.*

_____

_____

3. *The successful novel having been written, the (female) author began to write the second one.*

_____

_____

4. *I've said the most important thing.*

_____

5. *The video camera? Eva has lent it to them.*

_____

6. *The guests are sitting at the table. The food and wine are served.*

_____

7. *Have you (Uds.) heard the news on the radio? There's been a seaquake* (el maremoto).

_____

8. *The money? I've asked Andrés for it, but he hasn't wanted to give it to me.*

_____

_____

9. *Have you (Ud.) packed (the suitcases)?*

_____

10. *Yes, the suitcases are packed.*

_____

11. *Have you (tú) plugged in* (enchufar) *the computer?*

_____

12. *No, it's not plugged in, because it's working on batteries.*

_____

9

The Imperative

Imperative sentences with object pronouns

The imperative, or command, forms in Spanish are used to tell someone to do something or not to do something.

There are imperative forms for **tú**, **Ud.**, **nosotros**, **vosotros**, and **Uds.** Most imperative forms involve a change in the vowel of the verb ending.

Formal Commands: Imperative Forms for **Ud.** and **Uds.**

Commands for **Ud.** and **Uds.** change the characteristic vowel of the conjugation. -**Ar** verbs change the endings of the present tense from -**a**, -**an** to -**e**, -**en** to form the commands. All stem changes occurring in statement forms appear in the command forms too.

STATEMENT FORM	COMMAND FORM
hablar	
(Ud.) habla	hable (Ud.)
(Uds.) hablan	hablen (Uds.)
regresar	
(Ud.) regresa	regrese (Ud.)
(Uds.) regresan	regresen (Uds.)
pensar	
(Ud.) piensa	piense (Ud.)
(Uds.) piensan	piensen (Uds.)
contar	
(Ud.) cuenta	cuente (Ud.)
(Uds.) cuentan	cuenten (Uds.)

For **Ud.** and **Uds.** commands, -**er** and -**ir** verbs change the endings of the present tense from -**e**, -**en** to -**a**, -**an**. All stem changes occurring in statement forms appear in the command forms too.

STATEMENT FORM	COMMAND FORM
comer	
(Ud.) come	coma (Ud.)
(Uds.) comen	coman (Uds.)
escribir	
(Ud.) escribe	escriba (Ud.)
(Uds.) escriben	escriban (Uds.)

STATEMENT FORM	COMMAND FORM
entender	
(Ud.) entiend**e**	entiend**a** (Ud.)
(Uds.) entiend**en**	entiend**an** (Uds.)
advertir	
(Ud.) adviert**e**	adviert**a** (Ud.)
(Uds.) adviert**en**	adviert**an** (Uds.)
pedir	
(Ud.) pid**e**	pid**a** (Ud.)
(Uds.) pid**en**	pid**an** (Uds.)
dormir	
(Ud.) duerm**e**	duerm**a** (Ud.)
(Uds.) duerm**en**	duerm**an** (Uds.)
volver	
(Ud.) vuelv**e**	vuelv**a** (Ud.)
(Uds.) vuelv**en**	vuelv**an** (Uds.)

In command forms, the subject pronouns **Ud.** and **Uds.** may follow the verb to add a polite note to the imperative, rather like English *please.*

Terminen Uds. este proyecto para la semana que viene.	*Please finish this project by next week.*
Trate Ud. de ayudarnos, entonces.	*Then please try to help us.*
No entren Uds. por esta puerta.	*Don't go in through this door, please.*

The corresponding negative commands are formed by placing **no** before the verb.

No coma en la sala.	*Don't eat in the living room.*
No interrumpa Ud.	*Please don't interrupt.*
No hablen Uds. ahora.	*Please don't talk now.*
No griten.	*Don't shout.*
No insistan Uds. en ir.	*Please don't insist on going.*

Imperative Forms for **nosotros**

The command forms for **nosotros** are formed in the same way as those for **Ud.** and **Uds.** For **-ar** verbs, the present tense ending **-amos** changes to **-emos**, and for **-er** and **-ir** verbs, the present tense endings **-emos** and **-imos** change to **-amos**.

STATEMENT FORM	COMMAND FORM	MEANING
habl**amos**	habl**emos**	*let's speak*
pens**amos**	pens**emos**	*let's think*
com**emos**	com**amos**	*let's eat*
volv**emos**	volv**amos**	*let's return*
escrib**imos**	escrib**amos**	*let's write*
abr**imos**	abr**amos**	*let's open*

-Ir verbs that have a vowel change in the stem of the third-person singular of the preterit have that same stem vowel change in the **nosotros** form of the imperative.

STATEMENT FORM	3RD-PERSON SING. PRETERIT	COMMAND FORM	MEANING
pedimos	pidió	pidamos	*let's ask for*
advertimos	advirtió	advirtamos	*let's warn*
dormimos	durmió	durmamos	*let's sleep*

The negative **nosotros** command is formed by placing **no** before the command form of the verb.

no hablemos	*let's not speak*
no comamos	*let's not eat*
no pidamos	*let's not ask for*

—**Entremos** en este restaurante.	*"Let's go into this restaurant."*
—No, **no comamos** aquí. Dicen que es muy malo. **Busquemos** otro restaurante.	*"No, let's not eat here. They say that it's very bad. Let's look for another restaurant."*

-Ar verbs ending in **-car**, **-gar**, and **-zar** have the same spelling changes in the **Ud.**, **Uds.**, and **nosotros** imperative that they have in the **yo** form of the preterit. Here is a chart of the changes.

INFINITIVE	Ud. COMMAND	Uds. COMMAND	nosotros COMMAND
buscar	bus**que**	bus**quen**	bus**quemos**
pagar	pa**gue**	pa**guen**	pa**guemos**
almorzar	almuer**ce**	almuer**cen**	almor**cemos**

-Er and **-ir** verbs ending in **-ger** or **-gir** change the final **g** of the stem to **j** before the imperative endings.

INFINITIVE	Ud. COMMAND	Uds. COMMAND	nosotros COMMAND
escoger	esco**ja**	esco**jan**	esco**jamos**
corregir	corri**ja**	corri**jan**	corri**jamos**

If the **yo** form of the present tense is irregular, that irregularity will show up in the **Ud.**, **Uds.**, and **nosotros** commands. The imperative endings are added to the stem of the **yo** form.

yo FORM	Ud. COMMAND	Uds. COMMAND	nosotros COMMAND
hago	**haga**	**hagan**	**hagamos**
pongo	**ponga**	**pongan**	**pongamos**
digo	**diga**	**digan**	**digamos**
ofrezco	**ofrezca**	**ofrezcan**	**ofrezcamos**
veo	**vea**	**vean**	**veamos**

Several verbs have irregular imperative stems.

INFINITIVE	**Ud.** COMMAND	**Uds.** COMMAND	**nosotros** COMMAND
ser	**sea**	**sean**	**seamos**
ir	**vaya**	**vayan**	**vayamos**
saber	**sepa**	**sepan**	**sepamos**

The **Ud.** command form of **dar** and the **Ud.** and **Uds.** command forms of **estar** have accent marks. These written accents serve to distinguish the imperative from unstressed words with the same spelling.

INFINITIVE	**Ud.** COMMAND	**Uds.** COMMAND	**nosotros** COMMAND
dar	**dé**	**den**	**demos**
estar	**esté**	**estén**	**estemos**

—**No hagamos** la cena todavía. Es temprano.   *"Let's not make dinner yet. It's early."*

—**Esperemos** a mamá. Ella llega a las siete.   *"Let's wait for Mom. She gets home at seven."*

—De acuerdo. Pero **pongamos** la mesa.   *"Okay. But let's set the table."*

—Sí, **comamos** todos juntos.   *"Yes, let's all eat together."*

—**Oiga**, necesitamos cajas de archivar.   *"Say (Listen), we need file boxes."*

—**Vaya** a Staples y **compre** diez cajas.   *"Go to Staples and buy ten boxes."*

—No, **vaya** Ud. mientras yo archivo estos documentos.   *"No, you go while I file these papers."*

In everyday speech, the **vamos a** + infinitive construction replaces the **nosotros** command.

nosotros COMMAND (FORMAL)	**nosotros** COMMAND (EVERYDAY SPANISH)	MEANING
Regresemos a casa.	**Vamos a regresar** a casa.	*Let's go home.*
Seamos pacientes.	**Vamos a ser** pacientes.	*Let's be patient.*
Almorcemos aquí.	**Vamos a almorzar** aquí.	*Let's have lunch here.*
Demos una vuelta.	**Vamos a dar** una vuelta.	*Let's take a walk.*

Thus, sentences that use the everyday Spanish **nosotros** command have two meanings.

Vamos a almorzar aquí.   *Let's have lunch here.* OR
    We are going to have lunch here.

However, the **no vamos a** + infinitive construction can only mean *we are not going to do something.* Thus, to express a negative **nosotros** command, you must use **no** + the **nosotros** command form.

No paguemos con tarjeta de crédito.   *Let's not pay with a credit card.*

No pidamos otro trago.   *Let's not order another drink.*

Similarly, while **vamos** is used for *let's go,* you must use **no vayamos** to express *let's not go.*

A *Write both an affirmative and a negative* **Ud.** *command for each item.*

MODELO   mandar el correo electrónico

_____*Mande el correo electrónico.*_____

_____*No mande el correo electrónico.*_____

1. arreglar el cuarto

_____

_____

2. cerrar la puerta

_____

_____

3. correr en el maratón

_____

_____

4. leer el artículo

_____

_____

5. contar lo que pasó

_____

_____

6. compartir los gastos

_____

_____

7. reñir al chico

_____

_____

8. seguir por el río

_____

_____

9. probar la sopa

_____

_____

10. encender la luz

   _____

   _____

11. ir con nosotros

   _____

   _____

12. buscar al perro

   _____

   _____

13. imprimir el informe

   _____

   _____

14. beber el jugo

   _____

   _____

15. despertar al niño

   _____

   _____

16. pagar la cuenta

   _____

   _____

17. ver ese programa

   _____

   _____

18. jugar al tenis

   _____

   _____

19. descargar el fichero

   _____

   _____

20. dar un paseo

   _____

   _____

B *Write the affirmative or the negative* **Uds.** *command indicated for each item.*

MODELOS tomar el autobús *Tomen el autobús.*

no tomar el autobús *No tomen el autobús.*

1. llevar los paquetes _____

2. aparcar en este parqueo _____

3. pedir el helado de coco _____

4. hacer una lista _____

5. organizar estos papeles _____

6. tocar jazz _____

7. no gastar tanto dinero _____

8. no decir tonterías _____

9. asistir al concierto _____

10. no rechazar su idea _____

11. no ser desagradables _____

12. empezar a programar _____

13. no volcar (*knock over*) el florero _____

14. llegar a las ocho _____

15. sonreír _____

16. conseguir los billetes _____

17. no tener miedo _____

18. no caer por la casa sin llamar _____

19. venir lo antes posible _____

20. introducir los datos _____

C *Write affirmative or negative* **nosotros** *commands in response to each of the following questions, using the cues given. Write each affirmative command in two ways.*

MODELOS ¿Quieres/Quiere nadar? (sí)

Sí, nademos.

Sí, vamos a nadar.

¿Quieres/Quiere nadar? (no)

No, no nademos.

1. ¿Quieres tomar algo? (sí)

_____

_____

2. ¿Quiere navegar en la Red? (sí)

   _____

   _____

3. ¿Quieres comer una hamburguesa? (sí)

   _____

   _____

4. ¿Quiere volver a ese balneario (*beach resort*)? (no)

   _____

5. ¿Quieres comenzar el proyecto? (sí)

   _____

   _____

6. ¿Quieres jugar al béisbol? (sí)

   _____

   _____

7. ¿Quiere oír música? (sí)

   _____

   _____

8. ¿Quieres salir al cine? (sí)

   _____

   _____

9. ¿Quiere hacer planes? (no)

   _____

10. ¿Quieres escoger un postre? (sí)

    _____

    _____

11. ¿Quieres ir al centro comercial? (no)

    _____

12. ¿Quiere dar una vuelta? (sí)

    _____

    _____

13. ¿Quieres reducir nuestros gastos? (sí)

    _____

    _____

14. ¿Quiere envolver el regalo? (no)

_____

15. ¿Quiere subir en el telesquí? (no)

_____

16. ¿Quieres traer una botella de vino? (sí)

_____

_____

17. ¿Quieres servir arroz con pollo? (no)

_____

18. ¿Quieres mecer al bebé? (no)

_____

19. ¿Quiere seguir por esta calle? (sí)

_____

_____

20. ¿Quieres conocer al nuevo asesor? (sí)

_____

_____

Informal Commands: Imperative Forms for **tú** and **vosotros**

For most verbs, the affirmative **tú** command is derived from the present indicative **tú** form minus the second-person ending -**s**.

STATEMENT FORM	**tú** COMMAND FORM
regresa**s**	regresa
cierra**s**	cierra
come**s**	come
vuelve**s**	vuelve
abre**s**	abre
pide**s**	pide
duerme**s**	duerme

Eight verbs have irregular affirmative **tú** command forms, all of which are one-syllable forms.

INFINITIVE	**tú** COMMAND
decir	**di**
hacer	**haz**

INFINITIVE	**tú** COMMAND
ir	**ve**
poner	**pon**
salir	**sal**
ser	**sé**
tener	**ten**
venir	**ven**

—**Sal** y **cierra** la puerta con llave.   *"Go out and lock the door."*
—**Ve** y **busca** la llave entonces.   *"Then go and look for the key."*

—**Pasa** la aspiradora y **saca** la basura.   *"Vacuum the house and take out the garbage."*

—Y tú, **pon** la ropa limpia en la cómoda.   *"And you, put the clean clothes in the chest of drawers."*

Note that the affirmative **tú** command forms for the verbs **ver** and **ir** are identical: **ve**. Context clarifies which one is meant.

Compounds of the above eight verbs have the same irregularity in their affirmative **tú** command forms. Note the use of accent marks on compound command forms ending in **n**.

INFINITIVE	**tú** COMMAND
rehacer	**rehaz**
suponer	**supón**
mantener	**mantén**

Negative **tú** command forms are not the same as the corresponding affirmative command forms. To form the negative **tú** command, add **-s** to the corresponding **Ud.** command and place **no** before the verb.

NEGATIVE **Ud.** COMMAND	NEGATIVE **tú** COMMAND	AFFIRMATIVE **tú** COMMAND
no hable	no hable**s**	habla
no cierre	no cierre**s**	cierra
no coma	no coma**s**	come
no escriba	no escriba**s**	escribe
no pida	no pida**s**	pide
no duerma	no duerma**s**	duerme
no **haga**	no **haga**s	**haz**
no **vaya**	no **vaya**s	ve
no **sea**	no **seas**	**sé**
no esté	no est**és**	está

No hables así con tu profesor.   *Don't speak like that to your teacher.*
No seas arrogante.   *Don't be arrogant.*
No estés inquieta.   *Don't be nervous.*

D *Write both affirmative and negative* **tú** *commands for each item.*

MODELO   preparar los tacos

Prepara los tacos.

No prepares los tacos.

1. escribir en la tarjeta de memoria

_____

_____

2. leer los cuentos

_____

_____

3. repetir (*to have a second helping*) el plato

_____

_____

4. hacer un clic en el icono

_____

_____

5. enviar un fax

_____

_____

6. colgar el cartel en esta pared

_____

_____

7. exigir más de ellos

_____

_____

8. poner un anuncio en el periódico

_____

_____

9. pedir un aumento de sueldo

_____

_____

10. decir que sí

_____

_____

11. ver el sitio Web

_____

_____

12. ser interesado

_____

_____

13. analizar la información

_____

_____

14. salir a pasear

_____

_____

15. ir a caballo

_____

_____

16. llegar temprano

_____

_____

17. venir al cibercafé

_____

_____

18. teñir la camisa

_____

_____

19. crear una base de datos

_____

_____

20. tener confianza en ellos

_____

_____

NEOLOGISMS computer terms

The need to create terms for the computer has influenced the Spanish language. As Spanish-speaking societies adopted the technology, many English words were brought into Spanish unchanged, while others were borrowed and completely or partially adapted to Spanish spelling.

Here are some commonly used verbs borrowed from English and adapted to the Spanish language with their synonyms in parentheses: **formatear, escanear, cliquear, linkear (enlazar), chatear (conversar, charlar, platicar), hackear** or **jaquear (piratear)**, and **crashear (chocar, colgar, quebrar, romper, estrellar, congelar)**. These new verbs created in Spanish are integrated into the **-ar** conjugation, with the **-ear** suffix.

Another way of creating new verbs is to use the verb **hacer** + an English noun: **hacer (un) clic, hacer un login/logon/logoff/download/backup/link**, etc. Spanish verbs such as **bajar, descargar**, and **subir** take on new meanings to accommodate the new functions: **bajar** and **descargar** *to download*, **subir** *to upload*.

For all verbs, the affirmative **vosotros** command is formed by replacing the **-r** ending of the infinitive with **-d**. All **vosotros** commands are regular.

INFINITIVE	**vosotros** COMMAND
habla**r**	habla**d**
pensa**r**	pensa**d**
come**r**	come**d**
volve**r**	volve**d**
escribi**r**	escribi**d**
pedi**r**	pedi**d**
dormi**r**	dormi**d**
relaja**rse**	relaja**os**
vesti**rse**	vest**íos**

To form the negative **vosotros** command, replace the ending **-emos** of **nosotros** command forms with **-éis**, and replace the ending **-amos** of **nosotros** command forms with the ending **-áis**. The word **no** stands before the verb form.

NEGATIVE **nosotros** COMMAND	NEGATIVE **vosotros** COMMAND
no habl**emos**	no habl**éis**
no pens**emos**	no pens**éis**
no est**emos**	no est**éis**
no com**amos**	no com**áis**
no volv**amos**	no volv**áis**
no escrib**amos**	no escrib**áis**
no pid**amos**	no pid**áis**
no advirt**amos**	no advirt**áis**
no durm**amos**	no durm**áis**
no busqu**emos**	no busqu**éis**
no pagu**emos**	no pagu**éis**

NEGATIVE **nosotros** COMMAND	NEGATIVE **vosotros** COMMAND
no corrij**amos**	no corrij**áis**
no hag**amos**	no hag**áis**
no ofrez**camos**	no ofrez**cáis**
no vay**amos**	no vay**áis**
no se**amos**	no se**áis**
no nos qued**emos**	no os qued**éis**

—Mamá, queremos ir al parque.
—Chicos, **no seáis** impacientes. **Tened** un poco de paciencia y **no hagáis** tanto ruido.

"Mom, we want to go to the park."
"Children, don't be impatient. Be a little patient and don't make so much noise."

E *Write both affirmative and negative* **vosotros** *commands for each item.*

MODELO   trotar hoy

     Trotad hoy.

     No trotéis hoy.

1. estudiar mercadeo

_____

_____

2. vender vuestro coche

_____

_____

3. abrir el baúl

_____

_____

4. recoger las uvas

_____

_____

5. ser agresivos

_____

_____

6. seguir nuestros consejos

_____

_____

7. hacer cola

   _____

   _____

8. venir en taxi

   _____

   _____

9. dormir la siesta

   _____

   _____

10. publicar vuestras memorias

    _____

    _____

11. irse mañana

    _____

    _____

12. casarse en julio

    _____

    _____

13. salir a bailar

    _____

    _____

14. aplazar (*postpone*) la reunión

    _____

    _____

15. medir las cortinas

    _____

    _____

16. oír las noticias

    _____

    _____

17. traer el cheque

    _____

    _____

18. buscar el cajero automático (*ATM*)

_____

_____

19. decir la clave personal (*PIN*)

_____

_____

20. quedarse hasta el sábado

_____

_____

Indirect Commands

Indirect commands are commands about the third person: *he, she, it,* and *they.* In English, indirect commands are formed with the verbs *let* or *have*: *Let him do it, Have them come in.*

Spanish indirect commands consist of **Que** + the **Ud.** or **Uds.** command form of the verb. Remember that **Ud.** and **Uds.** forms are third-person forms.

Que Juan te **ayude**.	*Let Juan help you.*
Que los programadores **terminen** el proyecto esta semana.	*Have the programmers finish the project this week.*
Que nadie **entre** antes de las ocho.	*Don't let anyone in before eight.*
Que los clientes **esperen** abajo.	*Have the customers wait downstairs.*
Que se lo **hagan** (a Ud.).	*Have them do it for you.*

F *Write indirect commands in which Jaime says* let *or* have *others do the things people want him to do.*

MODELO Juan dice que debes sacar la basura.

Yo no quiero. Que saque la basura él.

1. Anita dice que debes hacer los quehaceres.

_____

2. Paco y Javier dicen que debes comprar la cerveza.

_____

3. Consuelo dice que debes aprender a bailar salsa.

_____

4. Tu hermana dice que debes llevar a tu novia al cine más a menudo.

_____

5. Tu entrenador de baloncesto dice que debes practicar todos los días.

_____

6. Tus amigos dicen que debes buscar trabajo.

_____

7. Lorenzo dice que debes llamar a Pedro.

_____

8. Mario dice que debes ir a ver el partido de tenis.

_____

G **_Translation._** _Express the following sentences in English._

1. Disfruten Uds. esta estupenda exposición de arte.

_____

2. Que vean todos esta estupenda exposición de arte.

_____

3. Que vaya él por los cartuchos de tinta.

_____

4. Que envíe la secretaria los correos electrónicos ahora mismo.

_____

5. Que los clientes hagan cola en la taquilla.

_____

6. Que nadie interrumpa la reunión de los jefes de Estado.

_____

7. Que participen los demás en el evento.

_____

8. Que alguien nos advierta lo antes posible.

_____

Other Ways of Giving Commands

The infinitive of the verb, rather than the command form, is often used as an imperative in newspaper ads, recipes, instructions, and notices.

Interesados **mandar** curriculum vitae.	_Interested persons send your curriculum vitae._
Enviar historial a esta dirección electrónica.	_Send résumé to this e-mail address._
Pasar las chuletas por harina y **freírlas** en aceite hirviendo.	_Dip the chops in flour and fry them in boiling oil._
Doblar a la derecha y **pasar** bajo el puente.	_Turn right and go under the bridge._

Arrastrar y **soltar**.	*Drag and drop.*
Agregar compra, **ver** carrito, **pasar** a la caja.	*Add purchase, see cart, go to checkout.*
Destornillar los tornillos.	*Unscrew the screws.*

The infinitive rather than the command form is used with the following expressions that convey formality and politeness.

Favor de esperar aquí.	*Please wait here.*
Haga el favor de entregar el informe.	*Please hand in the report.*
Tengan la bondad de registrarse.	*Please register.*

H *Rewrite each sentence, changing the command forms to infinitives that will serve as imperatives.*

MODELO   Vengan a la apertura (*opening*) de la nueva tienda.

Venir a la apertura de la nueva tienda.

1. Sigan derecho.

   _____

2. No pisen el césped (*lawn*).

   _____

3. Utilicen nuestra banca electrónica (*online banking*).

   _____

4. Reserven sus billetes en línea.

   _____

5. Agreguen una cucharadita de canela (*teaspoonful of cinnamon*).

   _____

6. Abran una cuenta corriente (*checking account*).

   _____

7. Guarden las recetas en su PDA (*personal digital assistant*).

   _____

8. Para más información llamen al teléfono 182329.

   _____

9. Para mayores informes envíen un e-mail a esta dirección.

   _____

10. Calienten el guisado (*stew*) a fuego lento (*on a low flame*).

    _____

11. Abróchense el cinturón de seguridad.

_____

12. No toquen los cables de electricidad.

_____

13. Interesados pónganse en contacto con el director.

_____

14. Alójense en el Hotel Caribe.

_____

I *Rewrite each formal* **Ud.** *or* **Uds.** *command as an infinitive, using the expressions in parentheses. You are giving commands to people with whom you have a formal relationship.*

MODELO Archive los documentos. (Favor de)

Favor de archivar los documentos.

1. Vuelva más tarde. (Haga el favor de)

_____

2. Espérenos en la oficina. (Favor de)

_____

3. Siéntense en la sala. (Tengan la bondad de)

_____

4. Hágame una copia de seguridad. (Favor de)

_____

5. Pulse el botón. (Tenga la bondad de)

_____

6. Explíquenmelo. (Hagan el favor de)

_____

7. Reúnanse la semana próxima. (Favor de)

_____

8. No se meta en este asunto. (Haga el favor de)

_____

9. No se oponga al plan. (Favor de)

_____

10. No se lo digan a nadie. (Tengan la bondad de)

_____

| BUILDING SENTENCES | **Imperative sentences with object pronouns** |

The rules for the placement of object pronouns are different with imperatives than with other verb forms.

In negative commands, object pronouns are placed before the verb, just as they are with statement forms. This applies to both single and double object pronouns.

—Este libro no me interesa.
—**No lo lea**, entonces.

"I'm not interested in this book."
"Then don't read it."

—Estas acciones no nos parecen muy buenas.
—Entonces, **no las compren**.

"We don't think these stocks are very good."
"Then don't buy them."

—¿Te traigo la revista?
—No, gracias, **no me la traigas**.

"Shall I bring you the magazine?"
"No, thanks. Don't bring it to me."

—Este reloj no le va a gustar a Pablo.
—En ese caso, **no se lo regalemos**.

"Pablo won't like this watch."
"In that case, let's not give it (as a gift) to him."

—¿Les envío los documentos mañana?

—No, **no nos los envíe**.

"Shall I send you the documents tomorrow?"
"No, don't send them to us."

—Roberto no quiere prestarle su bicicleta a Memo.
—Bueno, **que no se la preste** entonces.

"Roberto doesn't want to lend his bicycle to Memo."
"Okay, then don't have him lend it to him."

J *Answer each question with a negative command. Change direct object nouns to pronouns and make all necessary changes in your answers.* **¡Ojo!** *Make sure to use the correct command forms for* **tú, Ud., Uds., nosotros,** *or* **vosotros.** *Some items will have more than one answer.*

MODELOS ¿Compro la mochila?

No, no la compres/compre.

¿Te llevo al centro?

No, no me lleves al centro.

¿Le entregamos el informe a José?

No, no se lo entreguen (Uds.)/entreguéis (vosotros)/

entreguemos (nosotros).

1. ¿Pulso el botón?

_____

2. ¿Pisamos el césped?

_____

3. ¿Hago la lista?

   _____

4. ¿Comemos las ensaladas?

   _____

5. ¿Te llamo mañana?

   _____

6. ¿Los ayudo (a Uds.) con los cajones?

   _____

7. ¿Traemos el café?

   _____

8. ¿Le regalamos la videocámara a José?

   _____

9. ¿Les mandamos los contratos a Uds.?

   _____

10. ¿Paseamos al perro?

   _____

11. ¿La buscamos (a Ud.) esta noche?

   _____

12. ¿Les enseño las fotos a nuestros amigos?

   _____

13. ¿Os cuento el secreto?

   _____

14. ¿Le solicito la beca a mi profesor?

   _____

15. ¿Os explicamos las ideas?

   _____

16. ¿Te doy tu regalo de cumpleaños ahora?

   _____

In affirmative commands, object pronouns follow the verb form and are attached to it in writing. A written accent is added on the vowel of the stressed syllable of the verb.

—¿Debo servir el pollo?   *"Shall I serve the chicken?"*
—Sí, **sírvelo**.   *"Yes, serve it."*

—¿Qué hago con esta ropa, señora?   *"What shall I do with this clothing, ma'am?"*
—**Lávela** y **plánchela**, por favor.   *"Please wash it and iron it."*

—¿Usted necesita estos informes, señor?   *"Do you need these reports, sir?"*
—Sí, **entréguemelos** en seguida.   *"Yes, submit them to me immediately."*

—¿Uds. saben lo que le pasó a Julia?   *"Do you know what happened to Julia?"*

—No, **cuéntanoslo.**   *"No, tell (it to) us."*

When the pronoun **se** is added to an affirmative **nosotros** command, the resulting double **s** is reduced to a single **s** in writing.

> **Mandemos + selo → Mandémoselo.**

When the pronoun **nos** is added to an affirmative **ustedes** command, a double **n** is written (and often pronounced in deliberate speech), thus distinguishing the **ustedes** command from the **usted** command. Compare the two forms below.

> **Enseñe + nos → Enséñenos Ud.**
> **Enseñen + nos → Enséñennos Uds.**

The imperative of **dar, dé,** often keeps its written accent when a single pronoun is attached, in spite of the fact that two-syllable words ending in a vowel and stressed on the first syllable don't have written accent marks: **Déme ese libro.** It must have the written accent when double object pronouns are attached to it in writing: **Démelo.**

K   *Answer each question with an affirmative command. Change nouns to direct object pronouns and make all necessary changes in your answers. ¡Ojo! Make sure to use the correct command forms for* **tú, Ud., Uds., nosotros,** *or* **vosotros.** *Some items will have more than one answer.*

MODELOS   ¿Descargo el archivo?

> *Sí, descárgalo/descárguelo.*

¿Te llevo al centro?

> *Sí, llévame al centro.*

¿Le entregamos el informe a José?

> *Sí, entréguenselo/entregádselo/entreguémoselo.*

1. ¿Escribo el mensaje electrónico?

---

2. ¿Cierro la cuenta?

---

3. ¿Alquilamos los apartamentos?

---

4. ¿Dirigimos la orquesta?

---

5. ¿Las recojo (a Uds.) en el museo?

   _____

6. ¿Les pagamos la cena a ellos?

   _____

7. ¿Te decimos lo que pasó?

   _____

8. ¿Le hago el sándwich a Isabel?

   _____

9. ¿Les devolvemos los libros a Uds.?

   _____

10. ¿Vestimos a los niños?

    _____

11. ¿Te recordamos la fecha?

    _____

12. ¿Le mostramos las pinturas a Ud.?

    _____

13. ¿Les sirvo los aperitivos a las visitas?

    _____

14. ¿Le pedimos un préstamo al director?

    _____

15. ¿Os espero en el bar?

    _____

16. ¿Te vendo el quemador de CD?

    _____

L   ***Translation.*** *Express the following commands in English. Then write the infinitive and the subject of the command form. Some items will have more than one answer.*

    MODELO   Démelo.   *Give it to me. (dar, Ud.)*

1. Ve y velo. _____

2. Muéstreselo. _____

3. Envíenselas. _____

4. Subídnoslos. _____

5. Dásela. _____

6. Tráigannosla. _____

7. No se los ocultes. _____

8. No me la diga. _____

9. Pidámoselos. _____

10. Háganselo. _____

M **Translation.** *Express the following sentences in Spanish, using the cues given.*

1. *The cell phone? Give it to me. (tú)*

   _____

2. *The computer? Show it to us. (Uds.)*

   _____

3. *The packages? Wrap them up for me. (Ud.)*

   _____

4. *Your questions? Ask him them. (vosotros)*

   _____

5. *The (piece of) news? Let's write it to her.*

   _____

6. *That brand? Let's not ask them for it.*

   _____

7. *If the meal is made, serve it to us. (tú)*

   _____

8. *If the report is printed, read it to them. (Ud.)*

   _____

9. *The tennis racket? Offer it to him. (Ud.)*

   _____

10. *Be patient. Don't go yet. (tú)*

    _____

The Future and the Conditional; The Future Perfect and the Conditional Perfect

BUILDING SENTENCES

Sentences expressing probability

The Future Tense

The future tense in Spanish is formed by adding a specific set of endings to the infinitive of the verb. The endings are the same for all **-ar**, **-er**, and **-ir** verbs.

Hablaré. *I will speak.*
Comeré. *I will eat.*
Escribiré. *I will write.*

hablar *to speak*

hablar**é**	hablar**emos**
hablar**ás**	hablar**éis**
hablar**á**	hablar**án**

comer *to eat*

comer**é**	comer**emos**
comer**ás**	comer**éis**
comer**á**	comer**án**

escribir *to write*

escribir**é**	escribir**emos**
escribir**ás**	escribir**éis**
escribir**á**	escribir**án**

Several verbs have modified infinitive forms in the future. These verbs have the same endings as the verbs in the charts above. The **yo** form is given as a model for the entire conjugation.

Some verbs have **-d-** in place of the infinitive vowel **-e-** or **-i-**.

INFINITIVE	FUTURE
poner	**pondré**
salir	**saldré**
tener	**tendré**
valer	**valdré**
venir	**vendré**

Some verbs lose the infinitive vowel **-e-**.

INFINITIVE	FUTURE
caber	**cabré**
haber	**habré**
poder	**podré**
querer	**querré**
saber	**sabré**

Note that the future of **hay**—a modified form from **haber**—is **habrá** (*there will be*).

Some verbs shorten the infinitive.

INFINITIVE	FUTURE
decir	**diré**
hacer	**haré**

-Ir verbs that have an accent mark in the infinitive—**oír**, **reír**, **sonreír**—lose that accent mark in the future tense form.

INFINITIVE	FUTURE
oír	**oiré**
reír	**reiré**
sonreír	**sonreiré**

Compounds of verbs that have modified infinitives in the future show the same shortened infinitives in the future.

INFINITIVE	FUTURE
componer	**compondré**
retener	**retendré**
prevenir	**prevendré**
contradecir	**contradiré**
satisfacer	**satisfaré**

A *Rewrite each sentence, changing the verb from present tense to future tense in order to tell what will happen.*

MODELO   Paso el día en la biblioteca.

   Pasaré el día en la biblioteca.

1. Compramos muchas cosas en una tienda virtual.

   _____

2. Cuentan con nosotros para llevarlo a cabo.

   _____

3. Aprendes los lenguajes de programación.

   _____

4. Nieva pasado mañana.

_____

5. ¿A qué hora vienen?

_____

6. Gabriela estudia enfermería pediátrica.

_____

7. No les digo nada.

_____

8. Tenéis mucho que hacer.

_____

9. Hay millones de navegantes en línea.

_____

10. Marcos efectúa grandes cambios.

_____

11. No pueden vernos hasta la semana entrante.

_____

12. Jaime hace el papel del protagonista.

_____

13. Están muy emocionados por la noticia.

_____

14. Oyes la música mejor desde esta fila.

_____

15. La situación va de mal en peor.

_____

16. Nos ponemos los zapatos.

_____

17. Caben quinientas personas en el salón de actos.

_____

18. Queremos pintar unos paisajes.

_____

19. Persiguen al culpable.

_____

20. Empezáis a acostumbraros al horario.

_____

LA LENGUA ESPAÑOLA   the future

The endings of the future tense in Spanish look very much like the forms of the auxiliary verb **haber** for good reason. In late spoken Latin, the original Latin future was replaced by a verb + infinitive construction consisting of the auxiliary verb **habere** + the infinitive. The meaning shifted from *I have to go/ I am to go* to *I will go*. As late as the seventeenth century, the ending could still be separated from the verb and an object pronoun could be inserted between them: **ver lo he** *I will see him*. In the modern language, this separation is impossible, and in modern Spanish you can only say **lo veré**.

The future tense is used to express future events, although in spoken Spanish the **ir a** + infinitive construction and the present tense compete with it and are probably more common.

Mañana **iré** al centro.	*Tomorrow I'll go downtown.*
Mañana **voy a ir** al centro.	*Tomorrow I'm going to go downtown.*
Mañana **voy** al centro.	*Tomorrow I'm going downtown.*

In English, we often use the future tense to ask for instructions. Spanish also uses the present tense for this function.

¿**Estaciono** aquí?	*Shall (should) I park here?*
¿Te **ayudo**?	*Shall (should) I help you?*
¿**Salimos** por aquella puerta?	*Shall (should) we go out through that door over there?*
¿**Preparamos** la cena?	*Shall (should) we prepare dinner?*

Both English and Spanish use the future tense in the main clause of sentences that express possible hypotheses. These conditional sentences consist of a **si**-clause (*if*-clause) and a main clause. Notice that the **si**-clause and the main clause can be inverted.

Vendremos si tenemos tiempo.	*We'll come if we have time.*
Si recibo el software hoy, te lo **prestaré**.	*If I get the software today, I'll lend it to you.*

B *Rewrite each sentence, changing the infinitive of the* **ir a** + infinitive *construction to a future tense verb to tell what will happen.*

MODELO   Jorge va a necesitar una nueva impresora.

   Jorge necesitará una nueva impresora.

1. Virginia va a cumplir veintitrés años el lunes.

   _____

2. Ellos van a ponernos al día.

   _____

3. Vamos a profundizar el tema.

   _____

4. Voy a hacer un login.

_____

5. Van a formatear el documento.

_____

6. ¿No va a caber más memoria en el ordenador?

_____

7. La boda va a ser en un hotel céntrico.

_____

8. Estos jóvenes van a tener mucho éxito.

_____

9. Va a llover toda la temporada.

_____

10. Va a haber un simulacro de incendio (*fire drill*) esta tarde.

_____

11. Su cumpleaños va a caer en un miércoles.

_____

12. Sus esfuerzos van a valer la pena.

_____

13. Van a salir ganando como siempre.

_____

14. Los cursos van a satisfacer los requisitos.

_____

15. ¿Nos los vais a traer?

_____

16. Vamos a querer dársela.

_____

17. Voy a poder informarte mañana.

_____

18. Van a venir lo antes posible.

_____

19. Voy a saberlo pronto.

_____

20. La vas a oír cantar en la comedia musical.

_____

The Future Perfect Tense

The future perfect tense in Spanish consists of the future of the auxiliary verb **haber** + the past participle. The future perfect expresses the idea *will have spoken, will have eaten, will have written.*

hablar *to speak*

habré hablado	habremos hablado
habrás hablado	habréis hablado
habrá hablado	habrán hablado

comer *to eat*

habré comido	habremos comido
habrás comido	habréis comido
habrá comido	habrán comido

escribir *to write*

habré escrito	habremos escrito
habrás escrito	habréis escrito
habrá escrito	habrán escrito

Note that the past participle does not change for gender or number in the compound tenses.

In both Spanish and English, the future perfect tense indicates an event that will be completed in the future before another event occurs or that will be completed before some point in the future.

Si Uds. llegan a las diez, la reunión ya **habrá empezado**.	*If you arrive at ten, the meeting will have already begun.*
¿**Habrá terminado** Ud. el proyecto para el jueves de la semana entrante?	*Will you have finished the project by Thursday of next week?*
Habremos vuelto antes del quince.	*We will have returned before the fifteenth.*

C *Write sentences using the following strings of elements. Use verbs in the future perfect to tell what will have happened by some point in the future.*

MODELO   ellos / abrir la tienda de ropa / para principios del año

   Ellos habrán abierto la tienda de ropa para principios del año.

1. los empleados / salir de la oficina / para la hora de la cena

   _____

2. Diana y yo / volver del museo / a eso de las cuatro

   _____

3. Rogelio/conseguir la maestría en comunicaciones/para fines del semestre

_____

_____

4. yo/hacérselo/para la semana que viene

_____

5. Uds./reservar los billetes electrónicos/antes de las vacaciones de verano

_____

_____

6. Ud./enviarles el correo/después de verlos

_____

7. tú/resolver el problema/antes de la reunión

_____

8. vosotros/dárnoslas/para mediados de enero

_____

9. nosotros/verlos/para el Día de la Independencia

_____

10. ellos/mandar los impuestos (_taxes_)/para el quince de abril

_____

The Conditional Tense

The conditional tense in Spanish is formed by adding the imperfect endings of **-er** and **-ir** verbs to the infinitive. These **-ía** endings are the same for all **-ar**, **-er**, and **-ir** verbs.

Hablaría.	_I would speak._
Comería.	_I would eat._
Escribiría.	_I would write._

hablar _to speak_

hablar**ía**	hablar**íamos**
hablar**ías**	hablar**íais**
hablar**ía**	hablar**ían**

comer _to eat_

comer**ía**	comer**íamos**
comer**ías**	comer**íais**
comer**ía**	comer**ían**

escribir *to write*

escribir**ía**	escribir**íamos**
escribir**ías**	escribir**íais**
escribir**ía**	escribir**ían**

Those verbs that have modified infinitive forms in the future also form the conditional from those shortened infinitives.

Some verbs have **-d-** in place of the infinitive vowel **-e-** or **-i-**.

INFINITIVE	CONDITIONAL
poner	**pondría**
salir	**saldría**
tener	**tendría**
valer	**valdría**
venir	**vendría**

Some verbs lose the infinitive vowel **-e-**.

INFINITIVE	CONDITIONAL
caber	**cabría**
haber	**habría**
poder	**podría**
querer	**querría**
saber	**sabría**

Note that the conditional of **hay**—modified from **haber**—is **habría** (*there would be*).

Some verbs shorten the infinitive.

INFINITIVE	CONDITIONAL
decir	**diría**
hacer	**haría**

-Ir verbs that have an accent mark in the infinitive lose that accent mark in the conditional tense form.

INFINITIVE	CONDITIONAL
oír	**oiría**
reír	**reiría**
sonreír	**sonreiría**

Compounds of verbs that have modified infinitives in the conditional form the conditional with the shortened infinitive as well.

INFINITIVE	CONDITIONAL
componer	**compondría**
retener	**retendría**
prevenir	**prevendría**
contradecir	**contradiría**
satisfacer	**satisfaría**

D *Complete each sentence with the correct conditional form of the verb in parentheses to tell what would happen. The sentences in parentheses explain why these things would happen.*

MODELO   (Tardan en llegar al aeropuerto.) Ellos _*correrían*_ a la puerta (*gate*). (correr)

1. (No has comido ni bebido en todo el día.) Tú _____ hambre y sed. (tener)

2. (Vemos a la recién nacida.) Nosotros la _____ en brazos. (tomar)

3. (Un excelente restaurante acaba de abrir.) Yo _____ probar la comida. (querer)

4. (La reunión es mañana pero nadie sabe a qué hora.) Ellos _____ de averiguarla. (tratar)

5. (Uds. están inquietos y agotados de mucho trabajar.) Uds. _____ música para relajarse. (oír)

6. (Hay que comprar muchas cosas.) Ud. _____ una lista. (hacer)

7. (Su novia está enojada.) Diego le _____ tres ramilletes de flores y dos cajas de bombones. (traer)

8. (La carne está sosa [*tasteless*].) La cocinera _____ sal. (añadir)

9. (Se niegan a devolverle su dinero.) Ella _____. (exigírselo)

10. (Vosotros sabéis algo importante que desconoce vuestro amigo.) Vosotros

    _____. (decírselo)

As in English, the conditional in Spanish is used in hypotheses, or statements about what would happen.

¿Qué **harías** tú en ese caso?	*What would you do in that case?*
Yo no **diría** eso.	*I wouldn't say that.*
Con un jefe como el tuyo, yo **buscaría** otro trabajo.	*With a boss like yours, I would look for another job.*

In most sentences where the conditional is used to express a hypothesis, there are two clauses. The main clause has a verb in the conditional, and the **si**-clause (*if*-clause) has a verb in the imperfect subjunctive. This type of conditional sentence expresses a *contrary-to-fact* condition. (This pattern is studied in greater depth in Chapter 12. See "Building Sentences: Conditional sentences," p. 222.)

Si Uds. me **explicaran** el problema, a lo mejor les **podría** ayudar.	*If you would explain the problem to me, maybe I would be able to help you.*

The conditional appears frequently in subordinate (dependent) clauses after main verbs of communication (e.g., **decir**, **escribir**) and knowledge or belief (**saber**, **creer**), when the main verb is in one of the past tenses. There is a correspondence of tenses in Spanish and English in such situations: *main clause in present/subordinate clause in future; main clause in past/subordinate clause in conditional.*

El profesor **dice** que mañana **habrá** examen.	*The teacher says there will be an exam tomorrow.*
El profesor **dijo** que mañana **habría** examen.	*The teacher said there would be an exam tomorrow.*
Carla **escribe** que **llegará** el domingo.	*Carla writes that she will arrive on Sunday.*
Carla **escribió** que **llegaría** el domingo.	*Carla wrote that she would arrive on Sunday.*
No **sabemos** si **aceptarán** la invitación.	*We don't know if they will accept the invitation.*
No **sabíamos** si **aceptarían** la invitación.	*We didn't know if they would accept the invitation.*
Creo que **vendrán**.	*I think they will come.*
Creía que **vendrían**.	*I thought they would come.*
Estoy seguro de que te lo **dirán**.	*I'm sure that they will tell you.*
Estaba seguro de que te lo **dirían**.	*I was sure that they would tell you.*

Note that English often uses the auxiliary verb *would* to express habitual or repeated action in the past. In this function, Spanish uses the imperfect tense, not the conditional.

Ella siempre me **mandaba** e-mails.	*She would always send me e-mails.*
Los sábados **íbamos** al cine.	*On Saturdays we would go to the movies.*

The conditional of some verbs is used to express polite requests, suggestions, or refusals. The English conditional is often used in the same way.

¿Me **podría** Ud. ayudar?	*Could you help me?*
¿Le **gustaría** salir un poco?	*Would you like to go out for a while?*
Lo siento, pero no le **sabría** decir.	*I'm sorry, but I don't know (the information you asked for).*

E   *Complete each sentence with the correct form of the verb in parentheses. Select the future or the conditional, depending on the tense of the verb that appears in the main clause.*

MODELOS   (llamar)   Él dice que nos <u>llamará</u>.

(llamar)   Él dijo que nos <u>llamaría</u>.

1. (venir)   Me escribieron que (ellos) _____ a pasar el fin de semana.

2. (caber)   ¿Sabes si _____ diez personas en la furgoneta (*van*)?

3. (hay)   Pensaba que _____ lugar para todos.

4. (aceptar)   Pedro les informó que (él) _____ el puesto de analista.

5. (saber)   Creíamos que Ud. _____ el código.

6. (comprar)   Estáis seguros que nosotros _____ el condominio.

7. (poder)   Dijiste que (tú) _____ entregármelo, ¿verdad?

8. (estar)   Les expliqué que nadie _____ para atenderlos.

9. (hacer)   El programador nos dice que (él) _____ el trabajo mañana.

10. (aterrizar)   No sabían si el avión _____ a la hora fijada (*scheduled time*).

11. (interesarle)   Gabriela nos dijo que _____ ver la película.

12. (encantarles)   Creen que a los chicos _____ los regalos de Navidad.

The Conditional Perfect Tense

The conditional perfect tense in Spanish consists of the conditional of the auxiliary verb **haber** + the past participle. The conditional perfect expresses the idea *would have spoken, would have eaten, would have written.*

hablar *to speak*

habría hablado	habríamos hablado
habrías hablado	habríais hablado
habría hablado	habrían hablado

comer *to eat*

habría comido	habríamos comido
habrías comido	habríais comido
habría comido	habrían comido

escribir *to write*

habría escrito	habríamos escrito
habrías escrito	habríais escrito
habría escrito	habrían escrito

The conditional perfect is used to designate an action or event that would have been completed in the past, given an expressed or implied condition.

Yo no **habría hecho** eso.	*I wouldn't have done that.*
Nadie le **habría entendido**.	*Nobody would have understood him.*
¿Le **habrías dicho** tú la verdad?	*Would you have told her the truth?*

In most sentences in which the conditional perfect is used to express a hypothesis about the past, there are two clauses. The main clause has a verb in the conditional perfect, and the **si**-clause (*if*-clause) has a verb in the pluperfect subjunctive. This type of conditional sentence expresses a *contrary-to-fact* condition. (This pattern is studied in greater depth in Chapter 12. See "Building Sentences: Conditional sentences," p. 222.)

Si Uds. me **hubieran explicado** el problema, a lo mejor les **habría podido** ayudar.	*If you had explained the problem to me, maybe I would have been able to help you.*

F Write sentences that express that people (the subjects in parentheses) would not have done things that others did do.

MODELO   Edita contó chismes. (Ud.)

Ud. no habría contado chismes.

1. Inés mintió. (tú)

   _____

2. Yo los invité a comer en un restaurante caro. (Ud.)

   _____

3. Cristóbal cayó en una trampa. (nosotros)

   _____

4. Tú dijiste algo sin querer. (ellos)

   _____

5. Uds. comieron comida basura (_junk food_). (yo)

   _____

6. Mari y Sofi pusieron al cantante por las nubes. (Uds.)

   _____

7. Nosotros repetimos el plato de carne. (vosotros)

   _____

8. Vosotros visteis el programa de realidad. (Isaac)

   _____

9. Yo les regalé a los novios esa cámara digital. (Daniela y Alfredo)

   _____

10. Maximiliano utilizó una chuleta (_cheat sheet_) en el examen. (tú)

   _____

BUILDING SENTENCES   **Sentences expressing probability**

The four tenses studied in this lesson—the future, the future perfect, the conditional, and the conditional perfect—can all be used to express probability or conjecture.

The Future of Probability

The future tense expresses probability or conjecture about the present. The future of probability is used in both statements and questions. Notice the various English translations it may have.

Tus padres **estarán** cansados después
　de su viaje.　　*Your parents must be tired after their trip.*

Será demasiado tarde ya.　　*It is probably too late already.*
Juan **querrá** estudiar hoy.　　*I guess Juan wants to study today.*
Tendrás hambre.　　*You must be hungry.*
Laura **sacará** buenas notas.　　*Laura probably gets good grades.*

¿Qué hora **será**?　　*I wonder what time it is.*
¿**Nevará** mañana?　　*Do you think it might snow tomorrow?*
¿Qué **pensarán** de nosotros?　　*I wonder what they think of us.*
¿Cómo **estará** Juana?　　*I wonder how Juana is.*
¿Quién **ganará**?　　*Who do you think will win?*

The construction using **deber de** in the present tense + the infinitive may be used to express probability or conjecture in present time. The preposition **de** may be omitted.

Deben (de) ser las dos. = **Serán las dos.**　　*It's probably two o'clock.*
Debe (de) tener suerte. = **Tendrá suerte.**　　*She must be lucky.*

G　*Rewrite each sentence to express probability or conjecture about the present. Remove the words or phrases that indicate probability or conjecture, and write the verbs in the future tense.*

MODELO　Probablemente son las diez.
　　Serán las diez.

1. Probablemente hay celos entre las cuñadas (*sisters-in-law*).

2. Me imagino que la noche cae pronto.

3. Supongo que los gemelos tienen veintiún años.

4. Probablemente quieren bailar el tango.

5. Me imagino que los aficionados están entusiasmados.

6. Supongo que su sortija de diamantes vale mucho.

7. Probablemente llueve mañana.

8. Me imagino que es la una y media.

H *Translation.* Write questions using the future tense to express probability in the present.

1. *I wonder when they're arriving.*

    _____

2. *I wonder what time it is.*

    _____

3. *Who do you think might know their telephone number?*

    _____

4. *I wonder where the meeting might be.*

    _____

5. *What do you think the weather might be like this week?*

    _____

6. *I wonder how they are.*

    _____

The Conditional of Probability

The conditional expresses probability or conjecture about the past. The conditional of probability is most commonly used about past conditions that would appear in the imperfect in statement form.

—¿Por qué no vino el señor Galíndez?	*"Why didn't Mr. Galíndez come?"*
—No sé. **Estaría** enfermo.	*"I don't know. Maybe he was sick."*

(Statement would be: El señor Galíndez no vino porque **estaba** enfermo.)

—¿A qué edad se mudó Javier a la capital?	*"At what age did Javier move to the capital?"*
—No estoy seguro. Él **tendría** unos quince años cuando se fue con su familia a Ciudad de México.	*"I'm not sure. He was probably about fifteen years old when he left with his family for Mexico City."*

(Statement would be: Javier **tenía** unos quince años cuando se mudó a la capital.)

—¿Los chicos regresaron muy tarde anoche?	*"Did the kids get back very late last night?"*
—Ya lo creo. **Serían** las dos y media o las tres cuando oí la puerta.	*"I should say so. It must have been two thirty or three when I heard the door."*

(Statement would be: **Eran** las dos y media o las tres cuando oí la puerta.)

—¿Por qué crees que no compraron aquel carro que tanto les gustaba?	*"Why do you think they didn't buy that car that they liked so much?"*
—¿Quién sabe? **Costaría** un dineral.	*"Who knows? It probably cost a fortune."*

(Statement would be: No compraron aquel carro porque **costaba** un dineral.)

The construction using **deber de** in the imperfect tense + the infinitive may be used to express probability or conjecture in past time. The preposition **de** may be omitted.

Debían (de) ser las diez. = **Serían las diez.**   *It was probably ten o'clock.*
Debía (de) tener razón. = **Tendría razón.**   *He was probably right.*

I *Rewrite each sentence to express probability or conjecture about the past.*
Remove the words or phrases that indicate probability or conjecture,
and write the verbs in the conditional tense.

MODELO   Probablemente eran las diez.

_____*Serían las diez.*_____

1. Probablemente había treinta invitados en la fiesta.

   _____

2. Supongo que era un verano muy caluroso.

   _____

3. Probablemente tenía veintinueve años.

   _____

4. Me imagino que las joyas costaban un ojo de la cara (*an arm and a leg*).

   _____

5. Probablemente estaban de viaje.

   _____

6. Supongo que hacía mucho frío.

   _____

7. Probablemente nevaba mucho en la sierra.

   _____

8. Me imagino que él estaba contentísimo.

   _____

J *Translation.* *Express the following dialogues in Spanish, using the conditional tense*
to express probability in the past.

1. *I wonder what time it was when they called us.*

   _____

2. *It was probably nine thirty.*

   _____

3. *Why do you think she was so tired?*

   _____

4. *It was probably because of the long and difficult flight.*

   _____

5. *I think there was probably a problem with his car.*

   _____

6. *Maybe it (the car) was broken.*

_____

The Future Perfect of Probability

The future perfect is used to express probability or conjecture about the past. It is very common in this function, and is used about actions or conditions that would appear in the preterit or present perfect in statement form.

—¿Quién le **habrá prohibido** ir?	*"I wonder who could have forbidden him to go."*
—**Habrá sido** su padre.	*"It was probably his father."*
—Parece que el perro no tiene mucha hambre.	*"It seems that the dog is not very hungry."*
—Le **habrán dado** de comer.	*"They must have fed him."*
—Mira, las calles están mojadas.	*"Look, the streets are wet."*
—**Habrá llovido** mientras estábamos en el cine.	*"I guess it must have rained while we were in the movie theater."*
—Mi computadora está funcionando.	*"My computer is working."*
—Raúl la **habrá arreglado**.	*"Raúl probably fixed it."*
—¿Por qué **habrá contestado** así?	*"Why do you think he answered like that?"*
—No **habrá entendido** lo que le preguntaron.	*"I guess he didn't understand what they asked him."*
—¡Qué contentos están esos hinchas!	*"How happy those fans are!"*
—Su equipo **habrá ganado** el partido.	*"I suppose their team won the game."*

The construction using **deber de** + the perfect infinitive (**haber** + past participle) can be used instead of the future perfect tense to express probability in past time. The preposition **de** may be omitted.

Carolina debe (de) haber salido.	*Carolina must have (probably) gone out.*
Deben (de) haberlo hecho.	*They must have (probably) done it.*

K *Rewrite each sentence to express probability or conjecture about the past. Remove the word* **probablemente** *and write the verbs in the future perfect tense. The sentences in parentheses explain why these things would have happened.*

MODELO   (Todos están inquietos.) Probablemente ocurrió algo desagradable.
Habrá ocurrido algo desagradable.
_____

1. (Los amigos están reñidos.) Probablemente riñeron por una tontería.

_____

2. (¡Qué linda capa de nieve!) Probablemente nevó toda la noche.

_____

3. (El perro vomita.) Probablemente el perro tragó la pelota.

_____

4. (El incendio no ha hecho mucho daño.) Probablemente los bomberos llegaron
   muy rápidamente para apagar el incendio.

_____

5. (La cocina huele mal.) Probablemente no sacaron la basura.

_____

6. (¡Qué montón de periódicos!) Probablemente Emilio no recicló los periódicos
   en seis meses.

_____

The Conditional Perfect of Probability

The conditional perfect may also be used to express probability or conjecture about the past. It may add a note of astonishment or bewilderment to the conjecture, especially in questions.

¿Y le **habrían creído**?	_And could they possibly have believed him?_
¿Tú **habrías dicho** tal cosa?	_Would you possibly have said such a thing?_
¿Quién lo **habría hecho**?	_Who could possibly have done it?_

L _Translation. Express the following sentences of probability or conjecture in Spanish._
**¡Ojo!** Pay special attention to the tenses of the verbs and to English cues such as the words
I wonder, probably, and possibly. There may be more than one way to express these
sentences.

1. _I wonder when they'll come to see us._

_____

2. _It was probably eleven o'clock when I arrived at the train station._

_____

3. _You (Uds.) must have (probably) seen them at the party._

_____

4. _The Ferrari probably cost them a fortune._

_____

5. _Unbelievable! He could not possibly have said such a terrible thing._

_____

6. _When we met Irene, she was probably about twenty-two years old._

_____

7. *I guess you (tú) must have sent me an e-mail while you were at the Internet café.*

_____

8. *I wonder what time it is.*

_____

9. *I wonder why Carlos might have left without letting us know.*

_____

10. *I guess something unexpected* (algo imprevisto) *must have happened.*

_____

11. *I guess everyone read that book.*

_____

12. *You (Uds.) probably feel like going to the movies.*

_____

13. *I suppose it's too late already.*

_____

14. *There are probably no more shows* (la función).

_____

The Subjunctive (Part I): The Present Subjunctive

The subjunctive is largely a mood used in subordinate clauses, clauses introduced by **que** that are part of a larger sentence. The subjunctive is used after main clauses expressing volition (the imposition of will to get someone to do something), emotion and value judgment (personal reaction to an event or condition), doubt and denial, and wishes, and is used to form most commands.

Regular Verbs in the Present Subjunctive

The present subjunctive is formed by changing the ending vowel **a** (and the **-o** of the **yo** form) of the present indicative to **e** in **-ar** verbs, and changing the ending vowels **e** and **i** (and the **-o** of the **yo** form) of the present indicative to **a** in **-er** and **-ir** verbs. **-Er** and **-ir** verbs have the same set of endings in the subjunctive. The verbs in the main clause of the examples below express volition: **querer** *to want*, **esperar** *to hope*, **preferir** *to prefer*. Note that in the present subjunctive, the **yo** form and the **él/ella/Ud.** form are identical.

firmar *to sign*

Quiere que firm**e** el contrato.	*He wants me to sign the contract.*
Quiere que firm**es** el contrato.	*He wants you to sign the contract.*
Quiere que firm**e** el contrato.	*He wants her to sign the contract.*
Quiere que firm**emos** el contrato.	*He wants us to sign the contract.*
Quiere que firm**éis** el contrato.	*He wants you to sign the contract.*
Quiere que firm**en** el contrato.	*He wants them to sign the contract.*

vender *to sell*

Espera que vend**a** la casa.	*She hopes I'll sell the house.*
Espera que vend**as** la casa.	*She hopes you'll sell the house.*
Espera que vend**a** la casa.	*She hopes he'll sell the house.*
Espera que vend**amos** la casa.	*She hopes we'll sell the house.*
Espera que vend**áis** la casa.	*She hopes you'll sell the house.*
Espera que vend**an** la casa.	*She hopes they'll sell the house.*

abrir *to open*

Prefieren que no **abra** las ventanas.	*They prefer I not open the windows.*
Prefieren que no **abras** las ventanas.	*They prefer you not open the windows.*
Prefieren que no **abra** las ventanas.	*They prefer she not open the windows.*
Prefieren que no **abramos** las ventanas.	*They prefer we not open the windows.*
Prefieren que no **abráis** las ventanas.	*They prefer you not open the windows.*
Prefieren que no **abran** las ventanas.	*They prefer they not open the windows.*

-Ar and **-er** verbs that have changes in the vowel of the stem in the present indicative have these same stem changes in the present subjunctive. The changes take place in those forms of the present subjunctive where the stem is stressed.

Queremos que lo **pienses** con calma.	*We want you to think it over at your leisure.*
No quiero que Uds. **vuelvan** tarde.	*I don't want you to return late.*
Espero que **podamos** ir.	*I hope we will be able to go.*
No quieren que **cerráis** la cuenta bancaria.	*They don't want you to close the bank account.*

-Ir verbs that have changes in the vowel of the stem in the present indicative have additional changes in the stem vowel of the present subjunctive. They have the same changes as in the present indicative but, in addition, show a change in the **nosotros** and **vosotros** forms of the present subjunctive. Verbs that have the stem change **e > ie** or **e > i** change their stem vowel from **e** to **i** in the **nosotros** and **vosotros** forms. The verbs **dormir** and **morir**, in addition to the stem change **o > ue** in those forms where the stem is stressed, also change their stem vowel from **o** to **u** in the **nosotros** and **vosotros** forms.

In the following charts, the subjunctive forms appear in clauses beginning with **que** as they do in Spanish speech and writing.

invertir *to invest*

PRESENT INDICATIVE		PRESENT SUBJUNCTIVE	
inv**ie**rto	invertimos	que inv**ie**rta	que inv**i**rtamos
inv**ie**rtes	invertís	que inv**ie**rtas	que inv**i**rtáis
inv**ie**rte	inv**ie**rten	que inv**ie**rta	que inv**ie**rtan

pedir *to ask for*

PRESENT INDICATIVE		PRESENT SUBJUNCTIVE	
pido	pedimos	que pida	que pidamos
pides	pedís	que pidas	que pidáis
pide	piden	que pida	que pidan

dormir *to sleep*

PRESENT INDICATIVE		PRESENT SUBJUNCTIVE	
d**ue**rmo	dormimos	que d**ue**rma	que d**u**rmamos
d**ue**rmes	dormís	que d**ue**rmas	que d**u**rmáis
d**ue**rme	d**ue**rmen	que d**ue**rma	que d**ue**rman

Irregular Verbs in the Present Subjunctive

Verbs that have an irregularity such as **g** in the **yo** form of the present indicative have that same irregularity in all persons of the present subjunctive. These irregularities occur only in **-er** and **-ir** verbs, and therefore all the present subjunctive forms have the expected vowel ending -a-.

yo	tú	él/ella/Ud.	nosotros	vosotros	ellos/ellas/Uds.
caer (caigo)					
que caiga	que caigas	que caiga	que caigamos	que caigáis	que caigan
decir (digo)					
que diga	que digas	que diga	que digamos	que digáis	que digan
hacer (hago)					
que haga	que hagas	que haga	que hagamos	que hagáis	que hagan
oír (oigo)					
que oiga	que oigas	que oiga	que oigamos	que oigáis	que oigan
poner (pongo)					
que ponga	que pongas	que ponga	que pongamos	que pongáis	que pongan
salir (salgo)					
que salga	que salgas	que salga	que salgamos	que salgáis	que salgan
tener (tengo)					
que tenga	que tengas	que tenga	que tengamos	que tengáis	que tengan
traer (traigo)					
que traiga	que traigas	que traiga	que traigamos	que traigáis	que traigan
venir (vengo)					
que venga	que vengas	que venga	que vengamos	que vengáis	que vengan

The present subjunctive forms of other verbs that are irregular in the **yo** form are shown in the chart that follows. The **que** has been omitted to save space.

yo	tú	él/ella/Ud.	nosotros	vosotros	ellos/ellas/Uds.
caber (quepo)					
quepa	quepas	quepa	quepamos	quepáis	quepan
conocer (conozco)					
conozca	conozcas	conozca	conozcamos	conozcáis	conozcan
nacer (nazco)					
nazca	nazcas	nazca	nazcamos	nazcáis	nazcan
ofrecer (ofrezco)					
ofrezca	ofrezcas	ofrezca	ofrezcamos	ofrezcáis	ofrezcan
parecer (parezco)					
parezca	parezcas	parezca	parezcamos	parezcáis	parezcan

yo	tú	él/ella/Ud.	nosotros	vosotros	ellos/ellas/Uds.
construir (construyo)					
construya	construyas	construya	construyamos	construyáis	construyan
destruir (destruyo)					
destruya	destruyas	destruya	destruyamos	destruyáis	destruyan
ver (veo)					
vea	veas	vea	veamos	veáis	vean

The verbs **haber, ir, saber,** and **ser** have irregular stems in the present subjunctive. However, they follow the pattern of regular **-er** and **-ir** verbs in the subjunctive and thus have the expected endings with **-a-**.

yo	tú	él/ella/Ud.	nosotros	vosotros	ellos/ellas/Uds.
haber					
haya	hayas	haya	hayamos	hayáis	hayan
ir					
vaya	vayas	vaya	vayamos	vayáis	vayan
saber					
sepa	sepas	sepa	sepamos	sepáis	sepan
ser					
sea	seas	sea	seamos	seáis	sean

Spelling Changes in the Present Subjunctive

Many verbs that are regular in the present subjunctive in speech have spelling changes according to the rules of Spanish orthography.

-Ar verbs whose stem ends in **c, g,** or **z** have the same spelling change in all forms of the present subjunctive that they do in the **yo** form of the preterit. (See Chapter 6, p. 93.)

c > qu
g > gu
z > c

yo	tú	él/ella/Ud.	nosotros	vosotros	ellos/ellas/Uds.
buscar (busqué)					
busque	busques	busque	busquemos	busquéis	busquen
pagar (pagué)					
pague	pagues	pague	paguemos	paguéis	paguen
cruzar (crucé)					
cruce	cruces	cruce	crucemos	crucéis	crucen

-**Er** and -**ir** verbs whose stems end in **g**, **gu**, or **c** have the same spelling change in all forms of the present subjunctive that they do in the **yo** form of the present indicative. (See Chapters 1 and 3.)

g > **j**
gu > **g**
c > **z**

yo	tú	él/ella/Ud.	nosotros	vosotros	ellos/ellas/Uds.
escoger (escojo)					
escoja	escojas	escoja	escojamos	escojáis	escojan
seguir (sigo)					
siga	sigas	siga	sigamos	sigáis	sigan
convencer (convenzo)					
convenza	convenzas	convenza	convenzamos	convenzáis	convenzan

NOTE
-**Ar** verbs whose stems end in **j** do not change **j** to **g** before **e**.

Trabajo los domingos.
Quieren que trabaje los domingos.

Note the use of accent marks in the present subjunctive forms of **dar** and **estar**.

yo	tú	él/ella/Ud.	nosotros	vosotros	ellos/ellas/Uds.
dar (doy)					
dé	des	dé	demos	deis	den
estar (estoy)					
esté	estés	esté	estemos	estéis	estén

Uses of the Subjunctive in Noun Clauses

A *noun clause* is a subordinate clause that functions as a noun, that is, it can serve as either the subject or the object of a verb. Noun clauses are introduced in Spanish by the conjunction **que**.

All the Spanish tenses studied so far belong to the *indicative mood*. Verbs in the *indicative mood* express events or states that are considered factual, definite, or part of the speaker's experience or of reality as perceived by the speaker. The following examples have dependent noun clauses in the indicative. They show events perceived as part of reality because they are the objects of verbs such as **saber**, **parecer**, **oír**, and **ver**.

Sé que Juan **vive** por aquí.	*I know that Juan lives around here.*
Me parece que la reunión **es** arriba.	*I think that the meeting is upstairs.*
Hemos oído que la empresa **tiene** problemas.	*We have heard that the firm has problems.*
Veo que los resultados **son** buenos.	*I see that the results are good.*

The subjunctive is used after main clauses expressing volition, emotion and value judgment, doubt and denial, and wishes.

Volition (Imposition of Will)

The present subjunctive is used in subordinate clauses appearing after main clauses that imply that someone wants someone to do something or that someone wants something to happen that is not yet part of reality or that person's experience. Verbs of wanting, hoping, insisting, demanding, needing, and advising are representative of this type of main clause.

Quiero que me **ayudes**.	*I want you to help me.*
Ella **espera** que le **den** el puesto.	*She hopes that she gets the job.*
Insisten en que **salgamos** ahora.	*They insist that we go out now.*
Exijo que **paguen** en seguida.	*I demand that they pay immediately.*
Necesitamos que nos **llames**.	*We need for you to call us.*
Aconsejan que **busques** otro trabajo.	*They advise you to look for another job.*

In the examples above, the subject is different in the two clauses. When the verbs of both clauses have the same subject, the subordinate clause appears as an infinitive.

Quiero ayudar a mis vecinos.	*I want to help my neighbors.*
Espera conseguir el puesto.	*She hopes to get the job.*
Insisten en salir ahora.	*They insist on going out now.*
Necesitamos llamarte.	*We need to call you.*

NOTES

1 · **Insistir** is always followed by **en**.

2 · Verbs such as **exigir** and **aconsejar** are often preceded by the indirect object pronoun that corresponds to the subject of the subordinate clause.

Les exijo que paguen en seguida.	*I demand that they pay immediately.*
Te aconsejan que busques otro trabajo.	*They advise you to look for another job.*

Other verbs expressing volition are **decir**, **pedir**, **proponer**, **recomendar**, **rogar**, **sugerir**, and **suplicar**. They, too, are often preceded by the indirect object pronoun corresponding to the subject of the subordinate clause.

¿Por qué **les** dices que no vengan?	*Why are you telling them not to come?*
Él siempre **nos** pide que le prestemos el carro.	*He always asks us to lend him the car.*
Te recomiendo que veas esa película.	*I recommend that you see that film.*
Les ruego que no fumen.	*I request that you do not smoke.*
Me proponen que trabajemos juntos.	*They're proposing that we work together.*

Note the difference in meaning between the indicative and the subjunctive after **decir** in the examples that follow.

Les digo que **van** mañana. (INDICATIVE)	*I'm telling them **that they're going** tomorrow.*
Les digo que **vayan** mañana. (SUBJUNCTIVE)	*I'm telling them **to go** tomorrow.*

Several words of related meaning (influencing the actions of others) are more commonly constructed with the infinitive than with the subjunctive. Here are the most common of these verbs.

> **dejar a uno hacer algo** *to let someone do something*
> **hacer a uno hacer algo** *to make someone do something*
> **impedirle a uno hacer algo** *to prevent/keep someone from doing something*
> **mandarle a uno hacer algo** *to order someone to do something*
> **ordenarle a uno hacer algo** *to order someone to do something*
> **permitirle a uno hacer algo** *to permit/allow someone to do something*
> **prohibirle a uno hacer algo** *to forbid someone to do something*

Note that **dejar** and **hacer** take direct objects; the other verbs take indirect objects.

Sus padres no **lo dejan salir**.	*His parents don't let him go out.*
Mi trabajo **me impide aceptar** tu invitación.	*My work keeps me from accepting your invitation.*
Le mandé poner la mesa.	*I ordered her to set the table.*
¿Por qué no **les permite colaborar** con Ud.?	*Why don't you allow them to work with you?*
Te **prohíbo hablarme** así.	*I forbid you to talk to me like that.*

However, the subjunctive may also be found with these verbs. Compare the following pairs of sentences. Note that when a subjunctive clause is used, the direct or indirect object pronoun may be omitted.

Sus padres no **lo dejan salir**. Sus padres no **dejan que él salga**. }	*His parents don't let him go out.*
Nunca **lo hacen hacer** la tarea. Nunca **hacen que haga** la tarea. }	*They never make him do his homework.*
Te **prohíbo hablarme** así. **Prohíbo que me hables** así. }	*I forbid you to talk to me like that.*

Some impersonal expressions (expressions beginning with **es** or expressions with no personal subject) also express influence and volition and are followed by the subjunctive.

> **Es necesario/preciso que** *It's necessary that*
> **Es esencial que** *It's essential that*
> **Es imprescindible que** *It's crucial that*
> **Es obligatorio que** *It's mandatory that*
> **Es importante que** *It's important that*
> **Es urgente que** *It's urgent that*
> **Hace falta que** *It's necessary that*
> **Urge que** *It's urgent that*

Es necesario que entreguemos el informe.	*It's necessary for us to submit the report.*
Es importante que lo **sepas**.	*It's important for you to know that.*
Es obligatorio que estudien física.	*It's mandatory for them to study physics.*
Hace falta que Ud. responda por e-mail.	*You must answer by e-mail.*

These expressions can be followed by the infinitive when no subject is specified for the second verb.

Es preciso estudiar mucho.	*It's necessary to study hard.*
Es importante tomarlo todo con calma.	*It's important to take things calmly.*
Urge llamar al médico.	*It's urgent that someone call the doctor.*

Emotion and Value Judgment

The subjunctive is used in subordinate clauses that are dependent on main clauses expressing an emotional reaction to the action of the subordinate clause or a value judgment about it. The main clause may consist of a conjugated verb, a third-person verb with an indirect object, or an impersonal expression.

Me alegro de que puedan venir.	*I'm glad you can come.*
Sienten que su equipo **pierda** el partido.	*They're sorry their team is losing the game.*
Nos da rabia que nunca **quieran** ayudar.	*It makes us angry that they never want to help.*
Estoy furioso que no me **hagan** caso.	*I'm furious that they don't pay attention to me.*
Tengo miedo de que no **vengan.**	*I'm afraid they won't come.*
Temo que no me **ofrezcan** el puesto.	*I fear they won't offer me the position.*
Me sorprende que no **sepas** su nombre.	*I'm surprised that you don't know his name.*
Me asusta que viva tan sola.	*It frightens me that she's living so alone.*
No nos gusta que se ofendan.	*We don't like them to get insulted.*
Es triste que tenga esa enfermedad.	*It's sad that he has that illness.*
Es bueno que llegues temprano.	*It's good that you arrive early.*
Es malo que nadie **coopere.**	*It's bad that nobody is cooperating.*
Es útil que repasemos nuestros apuntes.	*It's useful for us to review our notes.*
Está mal que no te lo **digan.**	*It's bad that they won't tell it to you.*
Es una lástima que se muden.	*It's a pity that you're moving away.*
¡Qué lástima que la guerra **continúe!**	*What a pity the war goes on!*
Más vale que lleguemos todos a la misma hora.	*It's better that we all arrive at the same time.*

Note that **sorprender, asustar,** and **gustar** are usually used with an indirect object pronoun.

Main clause verbs expressing emotion or value judgment may be followed by the infinitive when the subject of the verbs of both clauses is the same. Impersonal expressions may be followed by the infinitive when no subject is specified for the second verb.

Me alegro de verte.	*I'm glad to see you.*
Le da rabia tener que hacer esto.	*He's furious that he has to do this.*
Tienen miedo de resfriarse.	*They're afraid to catch cold.*
Me sorprende oír eso.	*I'm surprised to hear that.*
Es útil repasar los apuntes.	*Reviewing one's notes is useful.*
Está mal decírselo.	*It's bad to tell him (it).*

Doubt and Denial

The subjunctive is used in subordinate clauses that are dependent on main clauses expressing doubt or uncertainty about the action of the subordinate clause, or that deny its existence.

Dudo que le **den** el ascenso.	*I doubt that they'll give him the promotion.*
Es dudoso que se venda este producto.	*It's doubtful that this product will sell.*
No creo que el jefe **acepte** eso.	*I don't think the boss will accept that.*
No piensa que tengas razón.	*She doesn't think that you're right.*
No me parece que lo **sepa.**	*I don't think she knows it.*
Niego que digamos tales cosas.	*I deny that we say such things.*
No he dicho que él **sea** perezoso.	*I didn't say that he is lazy.*
No estamos seguros que haya reunión hoy.	*We are not sure that there is a meeting today.*
Es posible que ya **estén.**	*It's possible that they're here already.*
Es poco probable que se vayan hoy.	*It's improbable that they'll leave today.*
No es cierto que ese empleado **entienda** chino.	*It's not true that that employee understands Chinese.*
Tal vez / Quizás tenga lugar el viernes.	*Perhaps it will take place on Friday.*
No es que suban los precios.	*It's not that prices are rising.*

The opposite of expressions of doubt or denial are followed by the indicative.

No dudo que lo **van** a ascender.	*I don't doubt that they'll promote him.*
No es dudoso que se venderá este producto.	*It's not doubtful that this product will sell.*
Creo que el jefe **acepta** eso.	*I think the boss will accept that.*
Me parece que lo **sabe.**	*I think she knows it.*
No niego que decimos tales cosas.	*I don't deny that we say such things.*
He dicho que él **es** perezoso.	*I said that he is lazy.*
Estamos seguros que hay reunión hoy.	*We are sure that there is a meeting today.*
Es cierto que ese empleado **entiende** chino.	*It's true that that employee understands Chinese.*
Es que los precios **suben.**	*The fact is that prices are rising.*

However, **es probable que** and **es imposible que** are followed by the subjunctive.

Sometimes the indicative is used after **no creer que**, **no pensar que**, **tal vez**, and **quizás**. By choosing the indicative rather than the subjunctive, the speaker signals a greater degree of certainty about the action.

No creo que captes la idea.	*I don't think you get the idea.*
No creo que captas la idea.	*I **really** don't think you get the idea.*
Tal vez se queden.	*Maybe they will stay. (The speaker is uncertain.)*
Tal vez se quedan (OR **se quedarán**).	*Maybe they will stay. (The speaker thinks they probably will stay.)*

Wishes

The present subjunctive is used after **ojalá (que)** to express a wish.

Ojalá que consigamos pasajes en ese vuelo.	*I hope we get tickets on that flight.*
Ojalá tengamos éxito con este negocio.	*I hope we're successful with this business deal.*

LA LENGUA ESPAÑOLA   borrowings from Arabic

The Spanish word **ojalá** is one of the most striking borrowings from Arabic in Spanish. It derives from the Arabic phrase *inshallah,* meaning *would to Allah.* It has become a word in Spanish that expresses hopes and wishes.

The Arabs (**los musulmanes**) began their invasion of Spain from North Africa in 711. Their domination of a large part of the country decreased steadily due to the efforts of the Christian kingdoms to take back their land. This reconquest, **la Reconquista,** began with the Battle of Covadonga in 718 and ended with the taking of Granada and the definitive expulsion of the Arabs in 1492.

The Spanish lexicon has approximately 4,000 words borrowed from Arabic. Many words referred to facets of medieval life and have fallen out of use, but others form part of the basic vocabulary of the language, such as **el azúcar, la tarea, la zanahoria, el álgebra, el alcohol, el cero, el café**, and **hasta**.

A clause beginning with **Que** followed by a verb in the subjunctive can also be used to express wishes.

¡Que tengas mucha suerte!	*Best of luck to you!*
Que te vaya bien.	*All the best to you.*
Que duermas bien.	*Sleep well.*

A *Complete each dependent noun clause with either the present indicative or the present subjunctive of the verb in parentheses. ¡Ojo! Think about the meaning of the verb in the main clause to determine the tense or mood you will use in the dependent clause.*

MODELOS   (poder)   Creo que Jorge no __*puede*__ venir hoy.

(poder)   Dudo que Jorge __*pueda*__ venir hoy.

1. (tener)   Comprenden que nosotros _____ prisa hoy.

2. (hacer)   Quieren que Uds. _____ construir la casa.

3. (estar)   Sé que su coche _____ descompuesto.

4. (encargar)   Prefieren que yo me _____ del proyecto.

5. (conocer)   Tememos que tú no _____ a nadie en la ciudad.

6. (ser)   Nos parece que Sol _____ muy comprensiva.

7. (venir)   Han oído que Ud. _____ el jueves.

8. (salir)   Prohíben que el público _____ por esa puerta.

9. (discutir)   ¿Deseáis que nosotros _____ el tema?

10. (utilizar) Vemos que vosotros _____ un nuevo ordenador.

11. (decir)   No permiten que Carlos _____ palabrotas (*swear*).

12. (ir)   Pienso que _____ a hacer mal tiempo mañana.

13. (llegar)   ¿Necesitas que ellos _____ para principios del mes?

14. (ocupar)   Entienden que yo me _____ de los planes.

15. (rechazar) Aconsejan que tú no _____ la oferta.

B *Complete each sentence with the correct form of the present subjunctive of the verb in parentheses.*

MODELO   (tener) Te suplico que *tengas* cuidado.

1. (impedir)   Esperamos que él no _____ su progreso.

2. (ver)   Insisten en que tú los _____ lo antes posible.

3. (almorzar)   Siente que Uds. no _____ con ella hoy.

4. (ser)   Me alegro de que ellos _____ tan responsables y serios.

5. (traer)   ¿No te sorprende que ellos no nos _____ una botella de vino?

6. (poner)   Le exijo que me _____ al día.

7. (hay)   Dudan que _____ cartuchos de tinta (*ink cartridges*).

8. (pagar)   Te recomiendan que _____ la cuenta inmediatamente.

9. (estar)   Niegan que Jaime _____ metido en el asunto.

10. (aparecer) No creemos que él _____ por aquí hoy.

11. (ir)   Nos piden que _____ de compras con ellos.

12. (criticar) Te digo que no lo _____ más.

13. (jugar)   ¿Le proponéis que _____ al baloncesto en vuestro equipo?

14. (salir)   No dejan que María Elena _____ con ese tipo (*guy*).

15. (invertir) Quieren que nosotros _____ más dinero en su empresa.

16. (saber)   Me extraña que Memo no _____ ni jota (*knows nothing*) del lenguaje de computadora.

17. (dar)   Nos gusta que nuestro hotel _____ a la playa.

18. (oír)   Les ruego que _____ la música de este compositor.

19. (volver)   No pienso que ellas _____ antes del anochecer.

20. (seguir)   Sugieren que nosotros _____ la autopista.

C *Rewrite the following impersonal expressions, using the subjects in parentheses.* **¡Ojo!** *Be sure to conjugate the verbs using the present subjunctive.*

MODELO   Es necesario salir para el aeropuerto ahora mismo. (nosotros)

Es necesario que nosotros salgamos para el aeropuerto

ahora mismo.

1. Es importante seguir una dieta equilibrada. (ellos)

   _____

2. Es útil tener palanca (*pull, influence*). (Ud.)

   _____

3. Es mejor esperar un par de días. (yo)

   _____

4. Es preciso hacer clic en el enlace (*link*). (Uds.)

   _____

5. Es imprescindible entender la política exterior (*foreign policy*). (tú)

   _____

   _____

6. Urge enviar el correo electrónico. (él)

   _____

7. Es obligatorio asistir a la reunión. (nosotros)

   _____

8. Más vale ir a pie. (Uds.)

   _____

9. Hace falta descargar los documentos. (vosotros)

   _____

10. Es bueno vivir cómodamente. (nuestra familia)

    _____

11. Es inútil buscar su billetera. (Anita)

    _____

12. Es malo no devolver el dinero prestado. (Pedro)

    _____

D *Rewrite each sentence, using the cues in parentheses. Choose either the present subjunctive or the present indicative tense for the verb.*

MODELOS   Viven en Barcelona. (es verdad)

Es verdad que viven en Barcelona.

Viven en Barcelona. (no es verdad)

No es verdad que vivan en Barcelona.

1. Hay tantos adelantos (*advances*) tecnológicos. (es bueno)

2. Yo trabajo para una compañía de alta tecnología. (es cierto)

3. Tienen interés en el proyecto. (no es evidente)

4. El dueño de la empresa abre otras sucursales. (no es dudoso)

5. No conocemos bien el interior del país. (es que)

6. Los novios están enamorados. (es obvio)

7. Sois de origen irlandés. (no es seguro)

8. Nadie quiere ayudarlos. (es una lástima)

9. La cosa no sale bien. (está mal)

10. El huracán hace tanto daño. (es triste)

E *Write sentences using the following strings of elements. Choose either the present subjunctive or the present indicative tense for the verb. ¡Ojo! Make sure you know how many subjects there are.*

MODELOS   yo / esperar / visitar el museo

Espero visitar el museo.

yo / esperar / Patricia / visitar el museo

Espero que Patricia visite el museo.

1. nosotros / querer / nuestros hijos / ser felices

   _____

2. el programador / necesitar / bajar el programa

   _____

3. yo / alegrarse / hacer el patinaje sobre hielo (*ice skating*)

   _____

4. tú / aconsejarle / Francisca / servir entremeses

   _____

5. ellos / temer / hay piratas informáticos (*hackers*) en Internet

   _____

6. Ud. / duda / ellos / saber utilizar la hoja de cálculo (*spreadsheet*) electrónica

   _____

7. a Uds. / gustarles / Paco / estudiar urbanización

   _____

8. vosotros / desear / practicar deportes acuáticos

   _____

9. yo / no creer / Ramón / tener don de gentes (*charm, getting on well with people*)

   _____

10. ellos / no pensar / hacer pintar la casa este año

    _____

11. Uds. / tener miedo / un virus / infectar su computadora

    _____

12. tú / pedirle / la agencia virtual / mandarte dos billetes electrónicos de ida y vuelta (*round trip*)

    _____

    _____

13. ella / no dejar / hablar

    _____

14. ellas / sentir / nosotros / no verlas

    _____

15. Ud. / insistir en / llegar antes que nadie

    _____

F *Translation.* *Express the following sentences in Spanish.*

1. *We hope you* (Uds.) *will be able to attend the lecture tonight.*

    _____

2. *The report? It's crucial that you* (Ud.) *give it to them right now.*

    _____

3. *I'm glad that they are going on vacation with us.*

    _____

4. *It's necessary that we pack the suitcases the night before.*

    _____

5. *They advise him to ask his boss for a raise.*

    _____

6. *They've suggested that we look for that brand in department stores.*

    _____

7. *Isn't he afraid you're* (tú) *deleting all the files?*

    _____

8. *At the online store they tell us to put our purchases in the cart and go to the cashier* (la caja).

    _____

    _____

9. *It's important to enjoy life. Enjoy* (Uds.) *life!* [Use a clause beginning with **Que.**]

    _____

10. *I hope you* (tú) *succeed in life.*

    _____

Uses of the Subjunctive in Adjective Clauses

An adjective clause is a subordinate clause that describes a noun much as an adjective does. Adjective clauses are also called *relative clauses*.

Most adjective clauses appear in the indicative.

Él tiene un trabajo **que le gusta**.	*He's got a job that he likes.*
Tenemos una oficina **que es cómoda**.	*We have an office that's comfortable.*
Utilizo una computadora **que tiene mucha memoria**.	*I use a computer that has a lot of memory.*
Hay empresas aquí **que comercian con México**.	*There are firms here that trade with Mexico.*

However, if the noun of the main clause is not identified or is negated, then the verb of the adjective clause appears in the subjunctive.

Él quiere un trabajo **que le guste**.	*He wants a job that he will like.*
Necesitamos una oficina **que sea cómoda**.	*We need an office that's comfortable.*
Busco una computadora **que tenga mucha memoria**.	*I'm looking for a computer that has a lot of memory.*
No hay empresas aquí **que comercien con México**.	*There are no firms here that trade with Mexico.*

The subjunctive is therefore used after **no hay nada que**, **no hay nadie que**, and **no hay ningún/ninguna *X* que**.

No hay nada que me **interese**.	*There's nothing that interests me.*
No hay nadie aquí **que sepa** programar.	*There's no one here who knows how to program.*
No hay ningún banco que abra hoy.	*There's no bank that's open today.*

BUT

Hay algo que me **interesa**.	*There's something that interests me.*
Hay alguien aquí **que sabe** programar.	*There's someone here who knows how to program.*
Hay algún banco que abre hoy.	*There's some bank that's open today.*

However, the subjunctive is usually used after **hay algo/alguien/algún/alguna** in questions because the antecedent is not identified.

¿Hay algo que te **guste**?	*Is there something you like?*
¿Hay alguien aquí **que sepa** programar?	*Is there someone here who knows how to program?*
¿Hay algún banco que abra hoy?	*Is there any bank that's open today?*

G *Complete each sentence with the correct form of the verb in parentheses. Choose either the present indicative or the present subjunctive for the adjective clauses.*

1. (interesar) Roberto tiene un puesto que le _____.

2. (esforzar) No conozco a nadie que se _____ más.

3. (saber) ¿Hay alguien en la oficina que _____ reparar la máquina?

4. (tener) Necesitan unos analistas que _____ varios años de experiencia.

5. (ser) Quiere amigos que _____ leales y sensibles.

6. (dar) Viven en un apartamento que _____ al jardín público.

7. (crear) Quieren contratar al administrador de Web que _____ sitios muy eficaces.

8. (atraer)   ¿No hay nada que te _____?

9. (gustar)   No hay ningún plato en la carta que me _____.

10. (hacer)   Queremos ver una película que nos _____ reír.

11. (estar)   Buscan una casa que _____ cerca del centro.

12. (tener)   Tengo una videocámara digital que _____ muchos píxeles.

Uses of the Subjunctive in Adverb Clauses

An adverb clause is a subordinate clause that modifies a verb much as an adverb does.

Certain adverbial conjunctions (conjunctions that introduce an adverb clause) are always followed by the subjunctive.

> **a condición de que** *on the condition that*
> **a fin de que** *so that, in order that*
> **a menos de que** *unless*
> **antes de que** *before*
> **con tal de que** *provided that, as long as*
> **en caso de que** *in case*
> **para que** *so that, in order that*
> **sin que** *without*

The **de** that appears in several of the conjunctions listed above is often omitted in Latin America.

Te diré lo que pasó **con tal (de) que** no **se lo cuentes** a nadie.	*I'll tell you what happened as long as you don't tell it to anyone.*
Vamos a discutir el proyecto **antes (de) que lleguen** los asesores.	*Let's discuss the project before the consultants arrive.*
Voy a prender mi computadora **para que** Ud. **consulte** la hoja de cálculo.	*I'm going to turn on my computer so that you can consult the spreadsheet.*
No vale la pena reunirnos **a menos que** todo el mundo **lea** los artículos del folletín electrónico.	*It doesn't pay to have a meeting unless everyone reads the articles in the e-zine.*
Tu computadora no va a servir **sin que** le **pongas** este nuevo sistema operativo.	*Your computer won't be of any use without your installing this new operating system on it.*
En caso de que Ud. **tenga** que ponerse en contacto conmigo, te doy mi casilla electrónica.	*In case you have to contact me, I'll give you my e-mail address.*

If the subjects of both clauses are the same, the subordinate clause is usually replaced by an infinitive.

No puedo empezar a trabajar **sin depurar** este programa.	*I can't begin to work without debugging this program.*
¿Qué hago **para bajar** la base de datos?	*What do I do to download the database?*

No se vaya **antes de borrar** todos esos archivos.	*Don't leave without deleting all those files.*
No podrás hacerte asesor **a menos de tener** un buen ordenador portátil.	*You won't be able to become a consultant unless you have a good laptop computer.*

Adverbial Clauses of Time Followed by Indicative or Subjunctive

Adverbial clauses of time are introduced by the following conjunctions.

después (de) que *after*
cuando *when*
hasta que *until*
tan pronto (como) *as soon as*
en cuanto *as soon as*
luego que *as soon as*

When the verb of the main clause is in one of the past tenses or the present tense, these conjunctions are followed by the indicative. The past tense signals actions that have taken place and are part of the speaker's experience. The present tense signals habitual actions that are part of reality.

Esperé **hasta que llamaron**.	*I waited until they called.*
Empezamos **tan pronto como llegó** el jefe.	*We began as soon as the boss arrived.*
Siempre leo mi correo electrónico **cuando estoy** de viaje.	*I always read my e-mail when I am traveling.*

However, when the verb of the main clause is in the future or is a command, these conjunctions are followed by the subjunctive, because the action of the subordinate clause is neither part of reality nor part of the speaker's experience.

Avíseme **en cuanto lleguen** los contables.	*Let me know as soon as the accountants arrive.*
Iré a comprarme un traje **cuando haya** rebajas.	*I'll go to buy a suit when there are sales.*
Me quedaré **hasta que descargues** el programa.	*I'll stay until you download the program.*
Ud. se podrá ir **después de que yo vuelva**.	*You'll be able to leave after I get back.*

When the subjects of both clauses are the same, the infinitive is used after **hasta** and **después de**.

Me quedaré **hasta terminar**.	*I'll stay until I finish.*
Trabajaré **después de volver**.	*I'll work after returning.*

After **cuando**, **en cuanto**, and **tan pronto como**, a subordinate clause in the subjunctive may be used even when the subjects of both clauses are the same.

Te avisaré **en cuanto llegue**.	*I'll notify you as soon as I arrive.*
Saldré **cuando termine**.	*I'll go out when I finish.*

The **al** + infinitive construction can replace the subjunctive clause when the subjects of the two clauses are the same. **Al** + the infinitive is interpreted as having the same subject as the main verb of the sentence.

Te avisaré **al llegar**.	*I'll notify you **when I arrive**.*
Saldré **al terminar**.	*I'll go out **when I finish**.*

Other Adverbial Clauses in Which Indicative and Subjunctive Contrast

There are other conjunctions besides adverbial conjunctions of time that may introduce clauses in the indicative as well as the subjunctive. Such conjunctions are followed by the indicative when the action of the subordinate clause is considered a known or established fact, but they are followed by the subjunctive when the action of the subordinate clause is considered uncertain or indefinite.

These conjunctions include **como** *how,* **aunque** *although, even though,* **según** *according to,* **donde** *where,* **mientras** *while,* **de manera que** *so that,* and **de modo que** *so that.* When these dependent clauses are used with a subjunctive verb, the conjunction often has the English equivalent of *ever* attached to it, as in *whenever, however,* or *wherever.*

Hazlo **como** ella **dice**.	*Do it **how (the way)** she says.* (*I know the way she says.*)
Hazlo **como** ella **diga**.	*Do it **however** she says.* (*I don't know the way she says.*)
Aunque va Jorge, nosotros no vamos.	***Even though Jorge is going**, we're not going. (I know Jorge is going.)*
Aunque vaya Jorge, nosotros no vamos.	***Even though Jorge may go**, we're not going. (I don't know whether Jorge is going or not.)*
Pintaré la casa **según me mandan**.	*I'll paint the house **the way they tell me to**. (I know how they want me to paint it.)*
Pintaré la casa **según me manden**.	*I'll paint the house **however they tell me to**. (I don't yet know how they want me to paint it.)*
Iré **donde** Uds. **quieren**.	*I'll go **where** you want to go.* (*I know where you want to go.*)
Iré **donde** Uds. **quieran**.	*I'll go **wherever** you want to go.* (*I don't know yet where you want to go.*)
Te lo expliqué **de modo que lo comprendiste**.	*I explained it to you **so that you understood it**. (Your understanding is the result of the action.)*
Te lo explicaré **de modo que lo comprendas**.	*I'll explain it to you **so that you will understand it**. (Your understanding is the purpose of the action.)*

H *Complete each sentence with the correct form of the verb in parentheses. Choose either the present indicative or the present subjunctive for the adverbial clauses.*

1. Te voy a dar mi contraseña (*password*) para que me _____ el correo electrónico. (hojear *to glance at*)

2. Compraré el libro antes de que Ud. lo _____ de la biblioteca. (sacar)

3. No les daré más información hasta que me la _____. (pedir)

4. Siempre me reúno con mis amigos tan pronto como nosotros _____ de la oficina. (salir)

5. Irán a la estación de invierno (*ski resort*) para esquiar a menos que no

   _____ nieve. (hay)

6. Se servirá la comida después que yo _____ el vino. (traer)

7. No vamos a salir hasta que _____ a despejar. (comenzar)

8. Siempre como perros calientes y palomitas de maíz (*popcorn*) cuando nosotros

   _____ a los partidos de béisbol. (ir)

9. En caso de que tú _____ a Esteban, dile que me llame. (ver)

10. Les prestaré mi videocámara con tal que me la _____ para el sábado. (devolver)

11. No podrás seguir con tu trabajo sin que yo _____ este programa para hacer gráficos. (instalar)

12. Siempre vemos a nuestros amigos ingleses cuando ellos _____ a los Estados Unidos en mayo. (venir)

I *Translation. Express the following sentences in Spanish.*

1. *I don't think you (tú) want to see this film.*

   _____

2. *It's necessary that he send them an e-mail.*

   _____

3. *It's useful that we do our research on the Internet.*

   _____

4. *I'm glad that they're coming to see us this weekend.*

   _____

5. *We're looking for a house that has six bedrooms.*

   _____

6. *They need a director who knows the company very well.*

   _____

7. *I hope our team will win the game on Sunday.*

_____

8. *Have (tú) a good time!* [Use a clause beginning with **Que**.]

_____

9. *There's no sandwich on the menu that I like.*

_____

10. *Let's get the e-tickets as soon as I log in.*

_____

11. *I'll show you (tú) the travel Web site so that you can choose a tourist package.*

_____

_____

12. *Do you (Uds.) want to eat something before the play starts?*

_____

13. *We'll buy you (tú) a souvenir (recuerdo) when we get to Granada.* [Write in two ways.]

_____

_____

14. *It doesn't pay to organize a party unless all our friends can come.*

_____

_____

BUILDING SENTENCES | **Compound and complex sentences**

There are two types of conjunctions that join sentences together.

Coordinating conjunctions create compound sentences, sentences in which neither clause is subordinate to the other. Typical coordinating conjunctions are **y**, **pero**, and **o**.

Fui a su oficina **y** pedí una entrevista.	*I went to his office and asked for an interview.*
Nosotros salimos, **pero** ella se quedó en casa.	*We went out, but she stayed home.*

Compound sentences joined by **o** usually have an additional **o** before the first sentence.

O aprenderás a trabajar con los demás, **o** tendrás que renunciar.	*Either you will learn to work with the others or you will have to quit.*

If there is a negative in the first clause of a compound sentence, then **pero** changes to **sino que**.

No sólo sabe francés, **sino que** también habla español.	*He not only knows French, but speaks Spanish too.*
Él no miente, **sino que** dice disparates.	*He doesn't lie, but (rather) says silly things.*

Subordinating conjunctions embed a sentence within a larger sentence, and that embedded sentence is then dependent on or subordinate to the main clause. This is called a complex sentence. The most common subordinating conjunction in Spanish is **que**.

Que is followed by the indicative after verbs that emphasize the truth value of the subordinate clause, like **saber, afirmar, confirmar**, and **jurar**.

Sabemos que les gusta España.	*We know they like Spain.*
Confirmo que vendí mi casa.	*I am confirming that I sold my house.*
Juro que se lo devolví.	*I swear that I returned it to him.*

Subordinating conjunctions that express cause and result also introduce clauses in the indicative. One of the most common is **porque** *because*.

No podemos salir **porque** llueve.	*We can't go out because it's raining.*

Subordinating conjunctions that express result only—**así que, conque, de (tal) modo que, de (tal) manera que**, and **de (tal) forma que**—are followed by the indicative.

Me llamaron desde la oficina, **así que** me tuve que ir.	*They called me from the office, so I had to leave.*
Conque no se pusieron en contacto contigo.	*So they didn't get in touch with you.*

Most other subordinating conjunctions take the subjunctive in certain situations. The conjunctions **de modo que, de manera que**, and **de forma que** take the subjunctive when they express purpose, but the indicative when they express results. Notice that **tal** is dropped in these conjunctions when they express purpose.

Arregla la sala **de modo que podamos** recibir a nuestros invitados.	*Straighten up the living room so that we can receive our guests. (A purpose is stated; subjunctive is used.)*
Arreglamos la sala **de (tal) modo que pudimos** recibir a nuestros invitados.	*We straightened up the living room so that we could receive our guests. (A result is stated; indicative is used.)*

J *Join the following pairs of sentences with a conjunction to create a new sentence, choosing one of the coordinating or subordinating conjunctions that appear in parentheses.*

MODELO   Me llamaron. Fui a verlos. (sino que | y)

   Me llamaron y fui a verlos.

1. Yo la invité al concierto. Ella no pudo ir. (pero | que)

2. No puede tomar el seminario de ciencias políticas a las once. Cursa literatura mundial a la misma hora. (y | porque)

_____

_____

3. Llegas puntualmente. No te dejan entrar. (o | así que)

_____

4. Terminó de mandar el correo electrónico. Apagó la computadora. (porque | y)

_____

5. No lo encontramos ni en casa ni en la oficina. Lo llamamos por teléfono móvil. (así que | que)

_____

_____

6. Él no sólo se ocupa de los quehaceres domésticos. Hace la jardinería también. (pero | sino que)

_____

_____

7. Te afirmo. Son dignos de confianza (_trustworthy_). (que | de forma que)

_____

8. Ellos fueron corriendo. Ud. no consiguió alcanzarlos. (porque | de tal modo que)

_____

9. Pasaron por mí a las seis. Logramos llegar al aeropuerto con tiempo de sobra (_time to spare_). (de manera que | porque)

_____

_____

10. El avión iba a despegar. Los pasajeros se abrocharon el cinturón de seguridad (_seat belt_). (o | conque)

_____

_____

 Translation. _Express the following sentences in Spanish._

1. _She doesn't only sing, but she dances also._

_____

2. _Either we will call them on the phone today or we will talk to them when we see them._

_____

_____

3. *Are you (Ud.) confirming that you've received the e-tickets?*

   _____

4. *I swear that I am not guilty.*

   _____

5. *He's going to spend his vacation in San Francisco because his parents live there.*

   _____

   _____

6. *Turn on (tú) the computer so that I can see your Web site.*

   _____

7. *So nobody was there when they arrived.*

   _____

8. *They went to the movies, but we decided to rent a film.*

   _____

9. *We went to the department store so that we could buy them a housewarming gift (inaugurar la casa).*

   _____

   _____

10. *She logged on and went to her Web site first.*

    _____

11. *I know those files are formatted and stored already.*

    _____

12. *They want us to travel with them, but we find them very boring.*

    _____

The Subjunctive (Part II):
The Present Perfect Subjunctive;
The Imperfect Subjunctive;
The Pluperfect Subjunctive

BUILDING SENTENCES

Conditional sentences

The Present Perfect Subjunctive

The present perfect subjunctive consists of the present subjunctive of the auxiliary verb **haber** + the past participle. Remember that **haber** has an irregular subjunctive stem: **hay-**.

hablar *to speak*

que haya hablado	que hayamos hablado
que hayas hablado	que hayáis hablado
que haya hablado	que hayan hablado

comer *to eat*

que haya comido	que hayamos comido
que hayas comido	que hayáis comido
que haya comido	que hayan comido

vivir *to live*

que haya vivido	que hayamos vivido
que hayas vivido	que hayáis vivido
que haya vivido	que hayan vivido

hacer *to do, make*

que haya hecho	que hayamos hecho
que hayas hecho	que hayáis hecho
que haya hecho	que hayan hecho

The present perfect subjunctive is used in the same kinds of dependent clauses as the present subjunctive. It is used to indicate that the action of the dependent clause happens before the action of the main clause. Study the following contrasting pairs of sentences.

Espero que **llegue** para la una.	*I hope that he arrives by one o'clock.*
Espero que **haya llegado** para la una.	*I hope that he arrived by one o'clock.*
Es triste que **no puedas** ir.	*It's sad that you can't go.*
Es triste que **no hayas podido** ir.	*It's sad that you couldn't go.*
No creo que **vengan**.	*I don't think they'll come.*
No creo que **hayan venido**.	*I don't think they came.*
Dudamos que el equipo **gane**.	*We doubt that the team will win.*
Dudamos que el equipo **haya ganado**.	*We doubt that the team won.*

The present subjunctive can be translated as a present or future tense. The present perfect subjunctive can be translated by a variety of past tenses. Subordinate clauses in the subjunctive have fewer tense distinctions than main clauses.

A *Rewrite each sentence, using the cue in parentheses. Use the present perfect subjunctive tense for the verb in the dependent clause.*

MODELO   Imprimió los papeles. (no creo)

No creo que haya impreso los papeles.

1. Se divirtieron mucho. (es probable)

   _____

2. Antonio y Nora fueron novios. (dudo)

   _____

3. Yo se lo expliqué. (es útil)

   _____

4. Él mintió. (estamos furiosos)

   _____

5. No tuvieron una vida privada. (es una lástima)

   _____

6. Ud. no la vio. (me sorprende)

   _____

7. El avión despegó. (es posible)

   _____

8. Los rescatadores (*rescue workers*) los encontraron sanos y salvos. (es bueno)

   _____

9. Me dijeron eso. (niego)

   _____

10. Llegaron a casa achispados (*tipsy*). (no es cierto)

   _____

11. Hubo un fallo del sistema (*crash*). (es malo)

_____

12. Su gato murió. (sienten)

_____

13. Hicimos algo interesante. (espera)

_____

14. Tecleaste correctamente la palabra clave (*key word*). (es importante)

_____

15. No contribuyó nada a la caridad. (no nos gusta)

_____

B **Translation.** *Express the following sentences in Spanish.*

1. *I doubt that Rebeca found her gold earring.*

_____

2. *It's good that you (Uds.) solved your problem.*

_____

3. *We don't like that they dropped by* (caer por la casa) *without calling.*

_____

4. *It's useful that you (tú) downloaded the files.*

_____

5. *Are you (Ud.) surprised that they didn't offer Carlos a raise?*

_____

6. *I'm glad it turned out well for you (tú).*

_____

7. *It's not true that Isabel quit her job.*

_____

8. *He's furious that the dog tore the rug to pieces.*

_____

9. *They're sorry that things went from bad to worse* (ir de mal en peor).

_____

10. *It's probable that you (vosotros) already returned the umbrella to her.*

_____

The Imperfect Subjunctive

The imperfect subjunctive in Spanish serves as the past of the present subjunctive. It is formed the same way for all verbs: drop the -**ron** ending of the **ellos/ellas/Uds.** form of the preterit, and replace it with a series of endings in -**ra**.

hablar (3RD-PERSON PLURAL PRETERIT **hablaron**)

que habla**ra**	que hablá**ramos**
que habla**ras**	que habla**rais**
que habla**ra**	que habla**ran**

comer (3RD-PERSON PLURAL PRETERIT **comieron**)

que comi**era**	que comié**ramos**
que comi**eras**	que comi**erais**
que comi**era**	que comi**eran**

vivir (3RD-PERSON PLURAL PRETERIT **vivieron**)

que vivi**era**	que vivié**ramos**
que vivi**eras**	que vivi**erais**
que vivi**era**	que vivi**eran**

Any irregularity or vowel change in the stem of the third-person plural of the preterit occurs in all persons of the imperfect subjunctive, as in the following examples.

3RD-PERSON PLURAL PRETERIT	1ST-PERSON SINGULAR IMPERFECT SUBJUNCTIVE
pidieron	que yo **pidiera**
mintieron	que yo **mintiera**
durmieron	que yo **durmiera**
hicieron	que yo **hiciera**
pudieron	que yo **pudiera**
fueron	que yo **fuera**
dieron	que yo **diera**
trajeron	que yo **trajera**
riñeron	que yo **riñera**

An alternate set of endings in -**se** exists in the imperfect subjunctive. The -**se** endings are less frequent in speech and can convey a formal tone. They have the same functions as the -**ra** endings, with the exception that the -**se** form never replaces the conditional in conditional sentences.

hablar (3RD-PERSON PLURAL PRETERIT **hablaron**)

que habla**se**	que hablá**semos**
que habla**ses**	que habla**seis**
que habla**se**	que habla**sen**

comer (3RD-PERSON PLURAL PRETERIT **comieron**)

que comie**se**	que comié**semos**
que comie**ses**	que comie**seis**
que comie**se**	que comie**sen**

vivir (3RD-PERSON PLURAL PRETERIT **vivieron**)

que vivie**se**	que vivié**semos**
que vivie**ses**	que vivie**seis**
que vivie**se**	que vivie**sen**

The **yo** and **él/ella/Ud.** forms are identical in the imperfect subjunctive, as they are in the present subjunctive, and all the **nosotros** forms have a written accent mark on the vowel before the **-ramos** or **-semos** ending.

> **habláramos, comiéramos, viviéramos**
> **hablásemos, comiésemos, viviésemos**

The use of the imperfect subjunctive in subordinate clauses in Spanish is determined by the *sequence of tenses*. You have learned that the present subjunctive is used in subordinate clauses when the verb in the main clause is in the present, future, present perfect, or imperative. The imperfect subjunctive is used in subordinate clauses when the verb in the main clause is in the imperfect, preterit, past perfect, or conditional.

The types of main clauses that trigger the subjunctive are the same. Compare the following pairs of sentences.

Noun Clauses

No **quiero** que **salgas**.	*I don't want you to go out.*
No **quería** que **salieras**.	*I didn't want you to go out.*
Es importante que se lo **dé**.	*It's important for you to give it to him.*
Fue importante que se lo **diera**.	*It was important for you to give it to him.*
Aconséjele que **busque** otro puesto.	*Advise her to look for another job.*
Ud. le aconsejó que **buscara** otro puesto.	*You advised her to look for another job.*
Le **pediré** que me **pague**.	*I will ask him to pay me.*
Le **pedí** que me **pagara**.	*I asked him to pay me.*
Insiste en que Ud. se lo **diga**.	*She insists that you tell her.*
Insistió en que Ud. se lo **dijera**.	*She insisted that you tell her.*
No **cree** que lo **hagamos**.	*He doesn't think we'll do it.*
No **creía** que lo **hiciéramos**.	*He didn't think we'd do it.*
He dudado que lo **sepan**.	*I have doubted that they know it.*
Dudaba que lo **supieran**.	*I doubted that they knew it.*
Nos alegramos de que Uds. **se diviertan**.	*We're happy that you are having a good time.*
Nos alegrábamos de que Uds. **se divirtieran**.	*We were happy that you were having a good time.*

Note that the English equivalents of the verb in many Spanish subjunctive noun clauses are infinitives and therefore do not show the tense distinctions that are seen in Spanish.

Adjective Clauses

Buscan un condominio que **sea** céntrico.	*They're looking for a condominium that is centrally located.*
Buscaban un condominio que **fuera** céntrico.	*They were looking for a condominium that was centrally located.*
He buscado una cámara digital que **tenga** muchos píxeles.	*I've looked for a digital camera that has a lot of pixels.*
Había buscado una cámara digital que **tuviera** muchos píxeles.	*I had looked for a digital camera that had a lot of pixels.*
No hay ningún postre que le **apetezca**.	*There's no dessert that she feels like eating (that tempts her, appeals to her).*
No había ningún postre que le **apeteciera**.	*There was no dessert that she felt like eating (that tempted her, appealed to her).*
Necesitamos asesores que **conozcan** muy bien estas industrias.	*We need consultants who are very familiar with these industries.*
Necesitábamos asesores que **conocieran** muy bien estas industrias.	*We needed consultants who were very familiar with these industries.*

Adverb Clauses

No **darán** un paseo **a menos que deje** de llover.	*They won't go for a walk unless it stops raining.*
No **daban** un paseo **a menos que dejara** de llover.	*They weren't going for a walk unless it stopped raining.*
Los **veremos antes de que se vayan**.	*We'll see them before they leave.*
Los **vimos antes de que se fueran**.	*We saw them before they left.*
Le **he prestado** mi computadora portátil **para que pueda** enviar el e-mail.	*I've lent him my laptop so that he can send e-mail.*
Le **había prestado** mi computadora portátil **para que pudiera** enviar el e-mail.	*I had lent him my laptop so that he could send e-mail.*
Compra carne **en caso de que queramos** hacer hamburguesas.	*Buy meat in case we want to make hamburgers.*
Comprarías carne **en caso de que quisiéramos** hacer hamburguesas.	*You would buy meat in case we'd want to make hamburgers.*

In Spanish, the infinitive is usually used instead of the subjunctive when the subject of both verbs is the same, whether the sentence is in the present or a past tense.

Queremos verte.	*We want to see you.*
Queríamos verte.	*We wanted to see you.*

Compare the use of the subjunctive when the subjects of the verbs of both clauses are different.

Queremos que **ella te vea.**	*We want her to see you.*
Queríamos que **ella te viera.**	*We wanted her to see you.*

Special Uses of the Imperfect Subjunctive

The imperfect subjunctive is used after **ojalá (que)** to express a wish for something that will probably not happen (English *I wish that*).

Ojalá que pudieran comprender esto.	*I wish they could understand this.*
Ojalá discutieran menos.	*I wish they would argue less.*
Ojalá no trataras de persuadirlo.	*I wish you wouldn't try to convince him.*

The imperfect subjunctive of a few verbs (mostly **poder, querer,** and **deber**) is used in main clauses to make polite requests and to soften suggestions.

¿Pudieran Uds. volver mañana?	*Could you come back tomorrow?*
Quisiera ir con Ud.	*I'd like to go with you.*
Debieras tratarlo mejor.	*You ought to treat him better.*

The imperfect subjunctive is used after **como si** *as if* to express an action that happens at the same time as the action of the main clause.

Él actúa **como si fuera** abogado.	*He acts **as if he were** a lawyer.*
Hablan **como si** realmente **supieran** algo de lo ocurrido.	*They talk **as if they** actually **knew** something about what happened.*
Salió furtivamente **como si tuviera** miedo.	*She sneaked out **as if she were** afraid.*

C *Complete each sentence, using the correct imperfect subjunctive form of the verb in parentheses. Write each verb, using both imperfect subjunctive endings, -ra and -se.*

MODELO   Queríamos que ellos _fueran/fuesen_ al cine con nosotros. (ir)

1. Yo esperaba que tú _____ tus sueños. (realizar)

2. Le aconsejé que no _____ en los asuntos ajenos (*other people's*). (meterse)

3. Era probable que _____ buen tiempo toda la semana de nuestras vacaciones. (hacer)

4. Preferirían que Aurora _____ en informática. (especializarse)

5. Les dijimos que _____ con cuidado por aquel barrio. (andar)

6. Había dudado que treinta mil personas _____ en el estadio. (caber)

7. Nos gustaría que Uds. _____ el manual del usuario (*user*). (leer)

8. Me alegré de que vosotros lo _____ tan bien en el desfile. (pasar)

9. No fue posible que nosotros _____ antes de las once. (estar)

10. Era bueno que nosotros _____ los gastos. (reducir)

11. Era importante que yo _____ los datos actualizados. (entrar)

12. No creían que tú _____ tantos regalos. (traer)

13. Buscaba un puesto que le _____ mucha oportunidad. (dar)

14. Necesitaban un gerente de ventas (*sales manager*) que _____ el mercado. (conocer)

15. No había nadie que _____ más a su profesión. (dedicarse)

16. ¿No habías visto ningún traje que te _____? (gustar)

17. Le entregaría el informe para que él lo _____. (corregir)

18. Yo te acompañaría al centro comercial con tal de que nosotros no

    _____ antes de las dos. (ir)

19. Le habíamos traído las tarjetas de memoria sin que nos las

    _____. (pedir)

20. Tenían el celular en caso de que yo _____ ponerme en contacto con ellos. (querer)

D *Translation.* *Express the following sentences in Spanish.*

1. *We hoped you* (tú) *would bring your digital camera to the party.*

   _____

2. *I advised her to buy the white silk blouse.*

   _____

3. *There was nothing that excited them.*

   _____

4. *Mariana asked them to set the table.*

   _____

5. *They had sent us the videos without our paying for them.*

   _____

6. *We would prefer that you* (Ud.) *not tell it to them.*

   _____

7. *They wanted a computer that would work well.*

_____

8. *I carried my mobile phone everywhere so that my children could call me at any time.*

_____

_____

9. *I wish they were arriving today.*

_____

10. *She would like us to give (as a gift) her an iPod.*

_____

11. *I wish they would calm down.*

_____

12. *I wish you (tú) were staying.*

_____

The Pluperfect Subjunctive

The pluperfect subjunctive (or past perfect subjunctive) consists of the imperfect subjunctive of **haber** and the past participle. The imperfect subjunctive of **haber**, like that of all verbs, derives from the third-person plural form of the preterit: **hubieron**.

hablar *to speak*

que hubiera hablado	que hubiéramos hablado
que hubieras hablado	que hubierais hablado
que hubiera hablado	que hubieran hablado

comer *to eat*

que hubiera comido	que hubiéramos comido
que hubieras comido	que hubierais comido
que hubiera comido	que hubieran comido

vivir *to live*

que hubiera vivido	que hubiéramos vivido
que hubieras vivido	que hubierais vivido
que hubiera vivido	que hubieran vivido

hacer *to do, make*

que hubiera hecho	que hubiéramos hecho
que hubieras hecho	que hubierais hecho
que hubiera hecho	que hubieran hecho

The **-se** form of the imperfect subjunctive of **haber** can also be used to form the pluperfect subjunctive, but it is used less frequently, especially in speech.

hablar *to speak*

que hubiese hablado	que hubiésemos hablado
que hubieses hablado	que hubieseis hablado
que hubiese hablado	que hubiesen hablado

comer *to eat*

que hubiese comido	que hubiésemos comido
que hubieses comido	que hubieseis comido
que hubiese comido	que hubiesen comido

vivir *to live*

que hubiese vivido	que hubiésemos vivido
que hubieses vivido	que hubieseis vivido
que hubiese vivido	que hubiesen vivido

hacer *to do, make*

que hubiese hecho	que hubiésemos hecho
que hubieses hecho	que hubieseis hecho
que hubiese hecho	que hubiesen hecho

The primary function of the pluperfect subjunctive is parallel to that of the present perfect subjunctive: It indicates that the action of the subordinate clause happened before that of the main clause. Study the following contrasting pairs of sentences.

Esperábamos **que ellos vinieran**.	*We hoped that they were coming.*
Esperábamos **que ellos hubieran venido**.	*We hoped that they had come.*
Me alegré **de que lo supieras**.	*I was glad that you knew it.*
Me alegré **de que lo hubieras sabido**.	*I was glad that you had found it out.*
Me sorprendió **que la conocieras**.	*I was surprised that you knew her.*
Me sorprendió **que la hubieras conocido**.	*I was surprised that you had met her.*

The pluperfect subjunctive is used after **ojalá (que)** to express a contrary-to-fact wish in the past (English *I wish that had happened*). **Ojalá que** + the pluperfect subjunctive expresses a wish for something that can't happen.

Ojalá me lo **hubieras dicho**.	*I wish you had told me.*
Ojalá que no se hubieran divorciado.	*I wish they hadn't gotten divorced.*
Ojalá nuestra casa **hubiera tenido** una piscina.	*I wish our house had had a pool.*

The Present and Imperfect Subjunctives vs. the Perfect Subjunctives

It is important to understand the contrasts between the present and imperfect subjunctives, which express actions simultaneous with or subsequent to the action of the main clause, and the perfect subjunctives (present perfect and pluperfect subjunctives), which express actions happening before the action of the main clause.

No creo **que salgan**.	*I don't think they are going out.*
No creo **que hayan salido**.	*I don't think they went out.*
No creía **que salieran**.	*I didn't think they were going out.*
No creía **que hubieran salido**.	*I didn't think they had gone out.*

The pluperfect subjunctive is used after **como si** to express an action that hypothetically occurred prior to the action of the main clause.

Comes **como si no hubieras comido** en un mes.	*You're eating **as if you hadn't eaten** in a month.*
Cantó **como si hubiera cantado** toda su vida.	*She sang **as if she had sung** her whole life.*
Actuaban **como si** nada **hubiera pasado**.	*They acted **as if** nothing **had happened**.*

E   *Rewrite each sentence, using the cue in parentheses. Use the pluperfect subjunctive tense for the verb in the dependent clause.*

MODELO   Ellos habían llamado. (dudaba)

  Dudaba que ellos hubieran llamado.

1. Habíamos hecho un viaje a Santa Fe. (me alegré)

   _____

2. Nos habían puesto al día. (era importante)

   _____

3. Ella había hecho la comida. (esperábamos)

   _____

4. No se lo habías dicho a nadie. (nos extrañó)

   _____

5. Había pasado una cosa así. (fue imposible)

   _____

6. Habíais leído tantos libros. (nos gustó)

   _____

7. Ellos habían impreso los documentos. (fue probable)

_____

8. Lo habíamos sabido lo antes posible. (ojalá)

_____

9. La computadora había tenido un gusano (*worm*). (temían)

_____

10. Yo había conseguido unos billetes electrónicos tan baratos. (les sorprendió)

_____

_____

F   ***Translation.*** *Express the following sentences in Spanish.*

1. *It wasn't true that Angélica had broken up with her boyfriend.*

_____

2. *He denied that they had said swear words.*

_____

3. *She was glad that we had heard the CDs.*

_____

4. *He answered as if he hadn't understood the question.*

_____

5. *I wish you (Uds.) could have spent the whole summer with us.*

_____

6. *We were surprised that you (tú) hadn't attended the meeting.*

_____

7. *It was bad that it had rained before the race.*

_____

8. *It was possible they had tried to telephone us.*

_____

9. *Did they doubt that I had told them the truth?*

_____

10. *I didn't think that you (Ud.) had written to them yet.*

_____

BUILDING SENTENCES	**Conditional sentences**

One of the most frequent uses of the imperfect subjunctive and pluperfect subjunctive is to express conditions. There are two main types of conditions: *possible conditions* and *contrary-to-fact conditions*.

Possible Conditions

Sentences expressing possible conditions tell what will happen if something else happens. Both Spanish and English use the present in the **si**-clause (*if*-clause) and the future in the main clause to express possible conditions.

si-CLAUSE	MAIN CLAUSE	MEANING
Si sales,	**yo saldré** también.	*If you go out, I'll go out too.*
(present)	(future)	

Contrary-to-Fact Conditions

To express a condition that is contrary to a fact or to a situation in *present* time, Spanish uses the imperfect subjunctive in the **si**-clause and the conditional in the main clause.

si-CLAUSE	MAIN CLAUSE	MEANING
Si salieras,	**yo saldría** también.	*If you were going out, I'd go out too.*
(imperfect	(conditional)	
subjunctive)		

The sentence **Si salieras, yo saldría también** expresses a condition that is *contrary to fact*. The fact is that **tú no sales** and the result is that **yo no salgo**. The meaning is **(pero) si salieras** (*but if you were going out, which you're not*), **yo saldría** también (*I'd go out too.*)

Spanish expresses a condition that is contrary to a fact or situation in *past* time by using the past perfect subjunctive in the **si**-clause and the conditional perfect or the past perfect subjunctive in the main clause.

si-CLAUSE	MAIN CLAUSE	MEANING
Si hubieras salido,	**yo habría salido** también.	*If you had gone out, I would have*
(past perfect	(conditional perfect)	*gone out too.*
subjunctive)		
Si hubieras salido,	**yo hubiera salido** también.	*If you had gone out, I would have*
(past perfect	(past perfect subjunctive)	*gone out too.*
subjunctive)		

Additional examples of conditional sentences follow.

Sentences expressing possible conditions use the present and future tenses.

Si le **pides** ayuda, él te **ayudará**.	*If you ask him for help, he will help you.*
Les **contestaremos** si **se ponen** en contacto con nuestra empresa.	*We'll answer them if they contact our firm.*

Sentences expressing conditions that are contrary to present fact use the imperfect subjunctive and conditional tenses.

Si la empresa **mejorara** la calidad de sus productos, **vendería** mucho más en Europa.	*If the firm improved the quality of its products, it would sell a lot more in Europe.*
La gente **viviría** mejor si el gobierno **bajara** los impuestos.	*People would live better if the government would lower taxes.*

Sentences expressing conditions that are contrary to past fact use the past perfect subjunctive tense with either the conditional perfect or the past perfect subjunctive tense.

Si le **hubiera visto** la cara, la **habría reconocido**.	*If I had seen her face, I would have recognized her.*
La empresa mexicana nos **habría concedido** el contrato si nuestro representante **hubiera hablado** español.	*The Mexican firm would have given us the contract if our representative had spoken Spanish.*

G *Possible conditions.* *Complete each sentence with the correct forms of the verbs in parentheses, using present indicative and future tense forms. ¡Ojo! Choose the appropriate tense for the si-clause and for the main clause.*

MODELO   Si yo _tengo_ tiempo más tarde, _iré_ al cibercafé. (tener, ir)

1. Si yo _____ a Costa Rica, _____ ecoturismo.
   (ir, hacer)

2. Nosotros _____ esta noche si no _____ mucho.
   (salir, nevar)

3. Si Ud. me _____ el problema, _____ resolvérselo.
   (explicar, procurar)

4. Laura me _____ al concierto si _____ ir en carro.
   (llevar, decidir)

5. Si _____ posible, Ignacio nos _____ en contacto con ellos.
   (ser, poner)

6. Elena se _____ en el curso si no _____ cupo (*limited enrollment*). (matricular, hay)

7. Si Uds. _____ a eso de las cuatro, _____ a toda la familia.
   (venir, ver)

8. Si tú _____ ahora, no _____ hambre a la hora de la cena.
   (merendar, tener)

9. Yo _____ ayudarte si _____ las plantas. (querer, regar)

10. Si Uds. _____ por comprar la casa con piscina, _____ nadar todos los días. (optar, poder)

H *Contrary-to-fact conditions in present time.* *Complete each sentence with the correct forms of the verbs in parentheses, using imperfect subjunctive and conditional tense forms.* **¡Ojo!** *Choose the appropriate tense for the **si**-clause and for the main clause.*

MODELO   Si Paquita *obedeciera* a sus papás, ellos no la *reñirían*.
(obedecer, reñir)

1. Si tú _____ al cine, yo _____ contigo. (ir, ir)

2. ¿Nosotros _____ hacer más operaciones si _____ ese software? (poder, tener)

3. Si _____ más tiempo, ellos se _____ un mes entero en Sicilia. (hay, quedar)

4. Si Uds. no se _____ por toda cosita, _____ más felices. (preocupar, ser)

5. Ud. _____ más salidas (*opportunities*) si _____ bilingüe. (tener, ser)

6. Nosotros _____ el día en la playa si _____ calor y sol. (pasar, hacer)

7. Si ellos _____ la dieta, _____ peso. (seguir, perder)

8. Si tú les _____ disculpas (*apologize*), ellos te _____. (pedir, perdonar)

9. Guillermo no se _____ si _____ mucho café. (dormir, tomar)

10. Si tú me _____ flores, yo te _____ un beso. (traer, dar)

I *Contrary-to-fact conditions in past time.* *Complete each sentence with the correct forms of the verbs in parentheses, using past perfect subjunctive and conditional perfect forms.* **¡Ojo!** *Choose the appropriate tense for the **si**-clause and for the main clause. Write the verbs in the main clause in two ways.*

MODELO   Si él *hubiera hecho* el viaje a la Suiza, *habría/hubiera hecho* alpinismo. (hacer, hacer)

1. Si tú _____ por la Red,

_____ el sitio Web de mi compañia.
(navegar, ver)

2. Ud. _____ empleo al graduarse

si _____ informática. (conseguir, estudiar)

3. Si ellos no _____ el amor y el apoyo de su familia,

¿_____ tanto éxito? (recibir, tener)

4. Ese chico _____ buenas notas

si no _____ videojuegos todo el día. (sacar, jugar)

5. Si nosotros _____ nuestro correo electrónico,

   _____ lo de Julia. (leer, saber)

6. Si Uds. _____ en el extranjero,

   _____ de menos (*miss*) a su familia.
   (vivir, echar)

7. Yo te _____

   si tú _____ más puntualmente. (ver, volver)

8. Si vosotros _____ las rebajas de enero,

   _____ mucho dinero. (aprovechar, ahorrar)

9. Leo y Olivia no se _____

   si no _____ al baile. (conocer, ir)

10. Si no _____ un fallo del sistema, tú no

    _____ tu trabajo. (haber, perder)

11. Ellos _____ menos calor

    si _____ el aire acondicionado. (tener, prender)

12. Si tú no _____ de la arroba (@) en el e-mail,

    yo lo _____. (olvidarse, recibir)

J **Translation.** *Express the following sentences in Spanish.*

1. *If we see him at the game, we'll say hello to him for you (tú).*

   _____

2. *They would share the expenses if they could.*

   _____

3. *The company would have hired her if she had had five years of experience.*

   _____

   _____

4. *If it weren't raining, we'd take a walk.*

   _____

5. *If you (Ud.) had given me the contract, I would have signed it.*

   _____

6. *I'd wait for them if I didn't have to catch the six o'clock train.*

   _____

7. *They'll ski this weekend if the weather is good.*

   _____

8. *If our colleagues were more hardworking, we wouldn't have so much to do.*

9. *If you (tú) wanted to use the car, we'd lend it to you.*

10. *If she had asked them for an iPod, they would have given it (as a gift) to her.*

11. *I would have taken the red-eye* (el vuelo de medianoche) *from San Diego to New York if I had had to attend a meeting at 9:00 A.M.*

12. *If you (Uds.) shop online, you'll save time and money.*

13

Reflexive Verbs

Reflexive verbs constitute a large verb class in Spanish. Spanish reflexive verbs always appear with an object pronoun that refers to the subject. English reflexive verbs, a relatively small category, usually imply that the subject is doing something to himself, for example, *to hurt oneself, to cut oneself.*

The function of reflexive verbs is different in the two languages. Most Spanish reflexive verbs correspond to English intransitive verbs (verbs that do not have a direct object) or English verb phrases consisting of *to be* or *to get* + an adjective or past participle.

In verb lists and vocabulary, Spanish reflexive verbs appear with the reflexive pronoun **se** attached to the infinitive.

> **levantarse** *to get up*
> **peinarse** *to comb one's hair*
> **quemarse** *to get burned*
> **vestirse (e > i)** *to get dressed*

Formation of Reflexive Verbs

Study the conjugation of reflexive verbs in the different tenses. Note that the reflexive pronoun **se** changes to agree with the subject of the verb. The reflexive pronoun precedes the conjugated verb in the simple tenses; it precedes the auxiliary verb **haber** in the compound tenses; it precedes the verb **estar** or is attached to the present participle in writing in the progressive tenses (see Chapter 14, p. 249).

Present Tense

acostarse (o > ue) *to go to bed*

me acuesto	**nos** acostamos
te acuestas	**os** acostáis
se acuesta	**se** acuestan

Preterit

vestirse (e > i) *to get dressed*

me vestí	**nos** vestimos
te vestiste	**os** vestisteis
se vistió	**se** vistieron

Imperfect

levantarse *to get up*

me levant**aba**	**nos** levant**ábamos**
te levant**abas**	**os** levant**abais**
se levant**aba**	**se** levant**aban**

Future

alegrarse *to be glad/happy*

me alegrar**é**	**nos** alegrar**emos**
te alegrar**ás**	**os** alegrar**éis**
se alegrar**á**	**se** alegrar**án**

Conditional

entusiasmarse *to get excited*

me entusiasmar**ía**	**nos** entusiasmar**íamos**
te entusiasmar**ías**	**os** entusiasmar**íais**
se entusiasmar**ía**	**se** entusiasmar**ían**

Present Perfect

caerse *to fall down*

me he caído	**nos hemos** caído
te has caído	**os habéis** caído
se ha caído	**se han** caído

The agreement of the reflexive pronoun with the subject of the sentence takes place both when the pronoun is attached to the infinitive and when it precedes the conjugated verb. This is shown in the examples that follow, which include verb + infinitive constructions and verb + connector + infinitive constructions.

No quier**o** levantar**me**. No **me** quier**o** levantar.	*I don't want to get up.*
V**as** a alegrar**te**. **Te** v**as** a alegrar.	*You're going to be glad.*
Empez**aban** a entusiasmar**se**. **Se** empez**aban** a entusiasmar.	*They were beginning to get excited.*

Study the following chart to see the changes of the reflexive pronouns in all persons and in both possible positions.

sentarse *to sit down*

Quiero sentar**me**.	Queremos sentar**nos**.	**Me** quiero sentar.	**Nos** queremos sentar.
Quieres sentar**te**.	Queréis sentar**os**.	**Te** quieres sentar.	**Os** queréis sentar.
Quiere sentar**se**.	Quieren sentar**se**.	**Se** quiere sentar.	**Se** quieren sentar.

Reflexive and Nonreflexive Verb Pairs

Most reflexive verbs can also be used nonreflexively. When they are used without the reflexive pronouns, they are transitive verbs—verbs that are used with a direct object. Study the following pairs of sentences.

Yo **acuesto** <u>a los niños</u>.	*I put the children to bed.*
Yo **me acuesto**.	*I go to bed.*
Los chicos **lavan** <u>el carro</u>.	*The boys are washing the car.*
Los chicos **se lavan**.	*The boys are washing up.*
¿Por qué no **acercas** <u>una silla</u>?	*Why don't you bring over a chair?*
¿Por qué no **te acercas**?	*Why don't you move closer?*
La madre **peinó** <u>a su hijita</u>.	*The mother combed her little daughter's hair.*
La madre **se peinó**.	*The mother combed her (own) hair.*

Here are some common verbs referring to one's daily routine. The verbs in the left column are transitive and express an action that one person does to another, as in the first example of each pair above. The verbs in the right column are reflexive and correspond to intransitive verbs in English.

acostar (o > ue) *to put (someone) to bed*	**acostarse (o > ue)** *to go to bed*
afeitar *to shave (someone)*	**afeitarse** *to shave*
arreglar *to arrange, fix (something)*	**arreglarse** *to get ready* (fix hair, clothing, etc.)
bañar *to bathe (someone)*	**bañarse** *to bathe, take a bath*
cansar *to tire (someone)*	**cansarse** *to get tired*
colocar *to place, put (something)*	**colocarse** *to get a job*
cortar *to cut (something)*	**cortarse** *to cut oneself*
cuidar *to take care of (someone)*	**cuidarse** *to take care of oneself*
desnudar *to undress (someone)*	**desnudarse** *to get undressed*
despertar (e > ie) *to wake (someone) up*	**despertarse (e > ie)** *to wake up*
duchar *to give (someone) a shower*	**ducharse** *to take a shower*
enfermar *to sicken, get sick*	**enfermarse** *to get sick*
lastimar *to hurt (someone)*	**lastimarse** *to hurt oneself*
lavar *to wash (someone/something)*	**lavarse** *to wash up*
levantar *to raise, pick up; get (someone)*	**levantarse** *to get up out of bed*
maquillar *to put makeup on (someone)*	**maquillarse** *to put on makeup*
peinar *to comb (someone's) hair*	**peinarse** *to comb one's hair*
pintar *to paint (something)*	**pintarse** *to put on makeup*
probar (o > ue) *to try, taste (something)*	**probarse (o > ue)** *to try on*
relajar *to relax (someone)*	**relajarse** *to relax*
reunir (reúno) *to join, gather (someone or something)*	**reunirse (con)** *to get together (with)*
vestir (e > i) *to dress (someone)*	**vestirse (e > i)** *to dress, get dressed*

Verbs referring to feelings and emotions can also be either reflexive or nonreflexive (transitive). The verbs in the left column below are transitive and express an action that one person does to another. The verbs in the right column are reflexive and correspond to intransitive verbs in English. The English equivalents of these verbs of emotion and feeling often include *to be* or *to get* + the past participle.

aburrir *to bore (someone)*	**aburrirse** *to get/be bored*
alegrar *to make (someone) happy*	**alegrarse** *to be glad/happy*
animar *to cheer (someone) up, encourage (someone)*	**animarse** *to cheer up, take to heart, feel like doing something*
asustar *to frighten (someone)*	**asustarse** *to get scared*
calmar *to calm (someone) down*	**calmarse** *to calm down*
decidir *to decide (something)*	**decidirse a** *to make up one's mind*
divertir (e > ie) *to amuse (someone)*	**divertirse (e > ie)** *to have a good time*
emocionar *to move, touch, excite (someone)*	**emocionarse** *to be moved/touched, be/get excited*
enfadar *to make (someone) angry*	**enfadarse** *to get angry*
enojar *to make (someone) angry*	**enojarse** *to get angry*
entusiasmar *to excite, thrill, stir (someone)*	**entusiasmarse** *to get excited, feel thrilled*
exasperar *to exasperate, make (someone) lose patience*	**exasperarse** *to get exasperated, lose one's/his/her patience*
interesar *to interest (someone)*	**interesarse en** *to be interested in*
involucrar *to involve (someone)*	**involucrarse** *to be involved, be implicated*
irritar *to irritate (someone)*	**irritarse** *to get irritated*
marear *to make (someone) dizzy*	**marearse** *to get/feel dizzy*
molestar *to annoy, bother (someone)*	**molestarse** *to get annoyed*
ofender *to offend/insult/hurt (someone)*	**ofenderse** *to get offended/insulted; to feel hurt*
preocupar *to worry (someone)*	**preocuparse** *to worry*
sorprender *to surprise (someone)*	**sorprenderse** *to be surprised*
tranquilizar *to calm (someone) down, reassure*	**tranquilizarse** *to calm down, stop worrying*

Many verbs of motion follow the same pattern. They occur in pairs: nonreflexive verbs that express an action that one person does to another and reflexive verbs that correspond to intransitive verbs in English.

acercar *to bring (something) closer/over*	**acercarse (a)** *to come closer, approach*
alejar *to move (something) away*	**alejarse (de)** *to move away from*
caer *to fall* (usually figurative)	**caerse** *to fall down*
correr *to move (something)*	**correrse** *to move over, make room for*
detener *to stop, bring (something) to a halt*	**detenerse** *to stop, come to a halt*
instalar *to install (something)*	**instalarse** *to move in*
levantar *to lift (something)*	**levantarse** *to get up, rise*
mover (o > ue) *to move (something)* (put in motion)	**moverse (o > ue)** *to move, stir, budge*
pasear *to take (someone) for a walk, to walk*	**pasearse** *to stroll, go for a walk*
perder (e > ie) *to lose (something)*	**perderse (e > ie)** *to get lost*
sentar (e > ie) *to seat (someone)*	**sentarse (e > ie)** *to sit down*
tirar *to throw (something)*	**tirarse** *to jump, throw oneself; to lie down*
volcar (o > ue) *to knock (something) over*	**volcarse (o > ue)** *to get knocked over*

Some verbs change considerably in meaning when they become reflexive.

despedir (e > i) *to fire, dismiss*	**despedirse de** (e > i) *to say good-bye to*
dormir (o > ue) *to sleep*	**dormirse** (o > ue) *to fall asleep*
empeñar *to pawn*	**empeñarse** (en) *to insist (on), persist (in)*
ir *to go*	**irse** *to go away*
llevar *to carry, take*	**llevarse** *to take away;* **llevarse bien/mal con** *to get along / not get along with*
meter *to put in, insert*	**meterse** (en) *to meddle, butt in*
negar (e > ie) *to deny*	**negarse a** (e > ie) *to refuse to*
parar *to stop*	**pararse** *to stand up* (Spanish America)
parecer (**yo parezco**) *to seem*	**parecerse a** *to resemble*
quedar *to remain, be left*	**quedarse** *to stay, remain*
volver (o > ue) *to return*	**volverse** (o > ue) *to turn around*

There are some verbs that nearly always appear as reflexives, at least with the meanings given. Verbs marked with an asterisk have no nonreflexive form at all.

*acatarrarse *to catch a cold*
 acordarse (o > ue) (**de**) *to remember*
 apoderarse (**de**) *to take possession (of)*
 apresurarse de *to hurry*
 aprovecharse (**de**) *to take advantage (of)*
 apuntarse a/para *to register, sign up for*
*arrepentirse de (e > ie) *to regret, repent*
*atreverse a *to dare to do (something)*
 ausentarse *to be out/away*
 burlarse de *to laugh at, make fun of*
 casarse (**con**) *to get married (to)*
 comprometerse *to get engaged*
*desmayarse *to faint*
*divorciarse *to get divorced*
 echarse *to lie down*
 enamorarse (**de**) *to fall in love (with)*
 encararse con *to face, confront*
 enterarse (**de**) *to find out (about)*
*equivocarse *to make a mistake*
 escaparse *to escape*
 fiarse de *to trust*
 figurarse *to imagine*
 fijarse (**en**) *to notice*
 graduarse *to graduate*
 inclinarse *to bend over*
*jactarse de *to boast about*
 matricularse *to enroll, register*
 mudarse *to move* (change residence)
 ocuparse de *to take care of*
 olvidarse (**de**) *to forget*
 oponerse a *to oppose, be against*
 ponerse de pie *to stand up* (Spain)

portarse bien/mal *to behave well/badly*
*__quejarse de__ *to complain about*
recostarse (o > ue) *to lie down*
reírse (e > i) de *to laugh at*
*__resfriarse__ *to catch a cold*
sentirse (e > ie) *to feel*
*__suicidarse__ *to commit suicide*

Here are some expressions that use reflexive verbs.

darse cuenta (de) *to realize*
darse prisa *to hurry*
echarse a + infinitive *to begin to*
hacerse daño *to hurt oneself*
hacerse tarde *to get/grow late*
ponerse a + infinitive *to begin to*
ponerse de acuerdo *to agree, come to an agreement*
quedarse con *to keep, hold onto*
referirse (e > ie) a *to refer to*
servirse (e > i) de *to use*
tratarse de *to be about, be a question of*
valerse de *to use*

A *Complete each sentence with the correct form of the reflexive verb in parentheses for the tense indicated. ¡Ojo! Be sure the reflexive pronoun refers to the subject.*

Present

1. Yo _____ en forma. (ponerse)

2. Ud. _____ a las once. (acostarse)

3. Tú _____ en seguida. (dormirse)

4. Ella _____ elegantemente. (vestirse)

5. Ellos _____ temprano. (despertarse)

6. Nosotros _____. (relajarse)

Preterit

7. Ud. _____. (equivocarse)

8. Tú _____. (irse)

9. Yo _____. (tranquilizarse)

10. Uds. _____. (arrepentirse)

11. Él _____ de sus amigos. (despedirse)

12. Vosotros _____. (casarse)

Imperfect

13. Nosotros _____. (sorprenderse)

14. Ud. _____. (enamorarse)

15. Yo _____. (entusiasmarse)

16. Tú _____. (irse)

17. Ellos _____. (reunirse)

18. Silvia _____. (aburrirse)

Future

19. Yo _____. (decidirse)

20. Tú y yo _____ a su política. (oponerse)

21. Ellos _____. (detenerse)

22. Ricardo _____ bien. (sentirse)

23. Tú _____. (reírse)

24. Uds. _____ en la nueva casa. (instalarse)

Conditional

25. Tú _____ de todo. (acordarse)

26. Nosotras _____. (animarse)

27. Ud. _____. (correrse)

28. Yo _____ de su hacienda. (apoderarse)

29. Vosotros _____. (enfadarse)

30. Uds. _____ en forma. (mantenerse)

Present Perfect

31. Ellos _____. (sonreírse)

32. _____ tarde. (hacerse)

33. Uds. _____ patinando. (caerse)

34. Yo _____ del diccionario en línea. (servirse)

35. Tú _____ el pie. (romperse)

36. Nosotros _____ de pie. (ponerse)

B *Expand each reflexive sentence with the verb in parentheses. You will form* verb + infinitive *or* verb + connector + infinitive *constructions. Write each sentence in two ways.* **¡Ojo!** *Retain the original tense of the verb.*

MODELO   Ella se arregla. (pensar)

Piensa arreglarse.   Se piensa arreglar.

1. Él se colocó. (conseguir)

_____

2. Se interesan. (empezar a)

_____

3. Uds. se reúnen. (pensar)

_____

4. Te encararás con él. (tener que)

_____

5. No me involucraría en eso. (querer)

_____

6. Os preocupabais. (dejar de)

_____

7. Se divierte. (esperar)

_____

8. No nos decidiremos. (poder)

_____

9. Me paseaba. (ir a)

_____

10. Os vestís. (deber)

_____

11. Se quedaron. (preferir)

_____

12. Se cortaba. (temer)

_____

13. Te casas. (desear)

_____

14. Se duchó. (terminar de)

_____

C *Create sentences using the following strings of elements. Write all verbs in the preterit.*

MODELO   él / hacerse daño / jugando al fútbol americano

Se hizo daño jugando al fútbol americano.

1. yo / darse cuenta de / el problema

_____

2. Ud. / echarse a / correr

_____

3. nosotros / ponerse de acuerdo

_____

4. ellos / quedarse con / el dinero

_____

5. tú / no fiarse de / tus socios

_____

6. Uds. / darse prisa / al ver la hora

_____

7. tratarse de / un asunto muy importante

_____

8. ella / servirse de / unos libros de consulta

_____

9. ¿vosotros / atreverse a / hablarles de esa manera?

_____

10. él / ponerse a / reír

_____

D *Translation. Express the following sentences in Spanish.*

1. *Each time Javier shaves, he cuts himself.*

_____

2. *That's why he likes the barber to give him a shave.*

_____

3. *I bathe my children before I put them to bed. Then I go to bed.*

_____

4. *Today Marta and Daniela woke up at 7:30. They took a shower, dressed, put on makeup, and combed their hair.*

_____

_____

5. *I tell them not to worry. I want them to calm down and relax.*

_____

6. *He persisted in meddling in our business.*

_____

7. *Consuelo and Jaime graduated from college, fell in love, got engaged, and got married.*

_____

_____

8. *You (tú) caught a cold last week and you still feel bad?*

   _____

9. *She was approaching the house when she felt dizzy.*

   _____

10. *I regret being involved in their shady business* (negocio turbio).

    _____

11. *We'll register for the online business course.*

    _____

Reflexive Verbs with Reciprocal Meaning ("Each Other")

In the plural, reflexive verbs may convey a *reciprocal meaning* equivalent to English "each other."

Carlos y Eva **se quieren** mucho.	*Carlos and Eva love each other very much.*
Nos escribimos y **nos hablamos**.	*We write to each other and we talk to each other.*
Nos vemos mañana.	*We'll see each other tomorrow.*
¿Dónde **os conocisteis**?	*Where did you meet each other?*
¡Chicos! Pórtense bien. ¡No **se peguen**!	*Children! Behave yourselves. Don't hit each other!*

Spanish uses the phrase **el uno al otro** (or **uno a otro**) to emphasize or specify the meaning "each other." This phrase usually agrees with the gender and number of the people referred to: **el uno al otro / la una a la otra / los unos a los otros / las unas a las otras**.

Mis dos hermanos se ayudan **el uno al otro**.	*My two brothers help **each other**.*
Las chicas se miran **la una a la otra**.	*The girls look at **each other**.*

The reflexive pronoun is not used to express "each other" with prepositions other than **a**.

Lola y Paula compran muchos regalos **la una para la otra**.	*Lola and Paula buy many gifts for each other.*

E *Create sentences using the following strings of elements. Use the verbs reflexively to convey reciprocal meaning.*

   MODELO   tú y yo / hablar por teléfono

   _Tú y yo nos hablamos por teléfono._____

1. Claudia y yo / escribir mensajes electrónicos

   _____

2. Alejandro y Catalina / entender perfectamente

   _____

3. Miriám y Alejo / querer mucho

   _____

4. David y yo / ver muy a menudo

   _____

5. Diana y su hermana / ayudar mucho

   _____

6. Miguel y Beatriz / comprar regalos

   _____

7. Esteban y yo / decir muchas cosas

   _____

8. Ud. y yo / llegar a conocer bien

   _____

9. tú y yo / tutear (*address each other as* tú [informally])

   _____

With many verbs, especially—but not only—verbs of motion, the switch from non-reflexive to reflexive shows a subtle shade of meaning that stresses the participation of the subject or an emotional, subjective reaction of the speaker. It is often difficult to capture the difference in meaning in English without completely altering the sentence. The reflexive forms are most common in informal language.

El niño **bajó** de su silla.	*The child got down from his chair.* *(This is an objective statement.)*
¡El niño **se bajó** de la silla!	*The child got down off his chair!* *(Isn't that amazing?)*
Salí porque era tarde.	*I left because it was late.*
Me enojé y **me salí**.	*I got angry and walked out.*
Ven conmigo.	*Come with me.*
Vente conmigo.	*Come along with me.*
No lo **creemos**.	*We don't believe it.*
No **nos** lo **creemos**.	*We can't believe it.*
Murió el rosal.	*The rosebush died.*
Se murió su padre.	*His father died. (And it was a terrible blow.)*
¿Qué **traes**?	*What are you bringing?*
¿Qué **te traes** entre manos?	*What are you up to?*
Sé el vocabulario.	*I know the vocabulary.*
Me sé el vocabulario.	*I (have studied and) know the vocabulary really well.*

When English uses reflexive pronouns (*myself, yourself, himself, herself, ourselves, your-selves, themselves*), the pronouns emphasize the fact that the subject performs the action upon himself. Spanish expresses this with **solo** or **mismo**.

—¿Su hijo ya se viste **solo**?   *"Can your son dress himself already?"*
—No, tiene solamente dos años. Yo lo   *"No, he's only two. I dress him."*
   visto.

—¿Dejas que te peine tu hermana?   *"Do you allow your sister to comb your*
                                                                   hair?"
—No, yo **misma** me peino.   *"No, I comb my own hair."*

How to Say "Become" in Spanish

In order to construct sentences containing the idea of *become* in Spanish, you have to select the appropriate verb or verbal phrase for the particular context.

To express *become* + an adjective, **ponerse** is usually used, especially for physical or emotional changes where no effort is implied.

—Siempre **te pones rojo** cuando hablo   *"You always get red when I talk about*
   de María Elena.   *María Elena."*
—Y tú **te pones colorada** cuando yo   *"And you blush when I mention Carlos."*
   menciono a Carlos.

El jefe **se puso bravo** cuando oyó la noticia.   *The boss got angry when he heard the*
                                                                          news.
Cuando Laura descolgó el teléfono y oyó   *When Laura picked up the phone and*
   la voz de Pedro, **se puso pálida**.   *heard Pedro's voice, she turned pale.*

Volverse can also be used with adjectives to imply a sudden, involuntary change, often a more profound one than that indicated by **ponerse**.

Si las cosas siguen así, **me voy a volver loco**.   *If things keep up like this, I will go crazy.*
Este niño **se ha vuelto imposible**.   *This child has gotten impossible.*
Nuestro barrio **se ha vuelto peligroso**.   *Our neighborhood has gotten dangerous.*
Los políticos **se vuelven** cada vez **más**   *The politicians are becoming more and*
   arrogantes.   *more arrogant.*

To express *become* + a noun of profession or nationality, or an adjective indicating social or economic status, **hacerse** or **llegar a ser** is used. Both phrases imply effort on the part of the subject, with **hacerse** implying greater intent than **llegar a ser**. The phrase **pasar a ser** is used to stress the process of change rather than the effort required to bring it about.

Ese joven **se va a hacer rico**.   *That young man is going to get rich.*
Se dice que él **se hizo presidente de la**   *They say that he became president of the*
   República por fraude electoral.   *country by voter fraud.*
Alicia y yo **nos hicimos amigas**.   *Alicia and I became friends.*
Luis **llegó a ser director** de la empresa.   *Luis became head of the firm.*
Él **pasó a ser tutor** de los hijos de su   *He became the guardian of his cousin's*
   primo.   *children.*

However, when **hacerse** is followed by the definite article and an adjective, it means *to pretend to be, to act like.*

Cuando el profesor preguntó quién había escrito eso en la pizarra, Raúl **se hizo el desentendido**.	*When the teacher asked who had written that on the board, Raúl played dumb.*
Cuando le piden que ayude, **se hace la sorda**.	*When they ask her to help, she turns a deaf ear.*
Cuando vino la hora de ir a visitar a los vecinos, **me hice el dormido**.	*When the time came to go to visit the neighbors, I pretended to be asleep.*
No invitemos a Nicolás a la fiesta. Siempre **se hace el tonto** y molesta a los demás.	*Let's not invite Nicolás to the party. He always acts silly and annoys everyone.*

Quedarse can mean *to become*, especially with physical conditions.

Se quedó ciego a raíz del accidente.	*He went blind because of the accident.*
Si no bajas la radio, todos **nos vamos a quedar sordos**.	*If you don't turn down the radio, we're all going to go deaf.*

The phrases **convertirse (e > ie) en** and **transformarse en** are sometimes used to express the idea of *becoming*.

La industria petroquímica **se ha convertido en la base** de la economía de la región.	*The petrochemical industry has become the mainstay of the economy of the region.*
El sapo **se ha transformado en un príncipe**.	*The toad has been changed into a prince.*

The idea of *becoming* in Spanish is often expressed by a reflexive verb.

alegrarse *to become happy*
asustarse *to get scared*
cansarse *to get tired*
deprimirse *to get depressed*
emocionarse *to get excited*
enojarse *to get angry*
enredarse *to get entangled/involved*
entristecerse (yo entristezco) *to become sad*
entusiasmarse *to get excited*

Te cansas porque trabajas demasiado.	*You get tired because you work too much.*
Yo no tengo la culpa. **No se enojen** Uds. conmigo.	*I'm not to blame. Please don't get angry with me.*

Often the idea of *becoming* can be expressed by either a reflexive verb or by **hacerse/ponerse/volverse** + an adjective. The reflexive verb is more formal and literary.

enfurecerse (yo enfurezco) / **ponerse furioso** *to get furious*
enorgullecerse (yo enorgullezco) / **volverse (o > ue) orgulloso** *to become proud*
enriquecerse (yo enriquezco) / **hacerse rico** *to get rich*

El rey **se enfureció** cuando supo lo de la rebelión de sus súbditos.	*The king got furious when he learned of the rebellion of his subjects.*
Cuando se dio cuenta de que su hija había vuelto a las tres de la madrugada, su padre **se puso furioso**.	*When he realized that his daughter had come home at three in the morning, her father got furious.*
La dama **se enorgulleció** del éxito de sus fiestas.	*The lady prided herself on the success of her parties.*
Ahora que tiene dinero **se ha vuelto muy orgulloso**.	*Now that he has money, he has become very haughty.*
Venezuela **se enriqueció** con sus exportaciones de petróleo.	*Venezuela got rich with its oil exports.*
Javier **se hizo rico** invirtiendo dinero en la Bolsa norteamericana.	*Javier got rich by investing money in the U.S. stock market.*

For some adjectives, the idea of *becoming* can be expressed either by a nonreflexive verb or by **ponerse/hacerse/volverse** + an adjective. The single verb is usually more formal and literary, and it may also be more literal than the phrase with **ponerse/hacerse/volverse**.

enflaquecer (yo enflaquezco) / ponerse flaco *to get thin*
engordar / ponerse gordo *to get fat*
enloquecer (yo enloquezco) / volverse (o > ue) loco *to go crazy/mad*
enmudecer (yo enmudezco) / volverse (o > ue) mudo *to become silent/speechless*
enriquecerse (yo me enriquezco) / hacerse rico *to get rich*
ensordecer (yo ensordezco) / volverse (o > ue) sordo *to go deaf*
envejecer (yo envejezco) / ponerse viejo *to grow old*
palidecer (yo palidezco) / ponerse pálido *to turn pale*

No como pasteles porque no quiero **engordar**.	*I don't eat cake because I don't want to get fat.*
Si comes tantos dulces **te vas a poner gordo**.	*If you eat so many sweets, you're going to get fat.*
Al saber que todos sus hijos habían muerto en el terremoto, la mujer **enloqueció**.	*When she found out that all her children had died in the earthquake, the woman went mad.*
¿A Paco le prestaste veinte mil dólares? ¿Qué te pasa? **¿Te has vuelto loco?**	*You lent Paco twenty thousand dollars? What's wrong with you? Have you gone crazy?*
Es difícil **envejecer** solo.	*It's hard to grow old alone.*
Mi madre no quiere salir mucho. **Se está poniendo vieja**.	*My mother doesn't want to go out much. She's getting/feeling old.*

F *Translation.* *Express the following sentences in Spanish.* **¡Ojo!** *Remember that there is more than one way to express* become *in Spanish.*

1. The fans went crazy when they saw their favorite player.

   _____

2. Due to his good investments, he became rich.

   _____

3. Pablo and Amanda became friends.

   _____

4. The small town became a bustling (bulliciosa) *international capital.*

   _____

   _____

5. Paula is a timid girl who blushes frequently.

   _____

6. Jacobo was getting fat while his brother Cristóbal was getting thin.

   _____

   _____

7. They got angry when they saw that their dog had torn the rug.

   _____

   _____

G *Translation.* *Express the following sentences in Spanish, using reflexive verbs to tell how these people reacted to events.*

1. Aurelia got happy. _____

2. I got excited. _____

3. Carlos got offended. _____

4. Pilar and I were touched. _____

5. They got angry. _____

6. You (tú) were annoyed. _____

7. You (Uds.) were exasperated. _____

8. You (Ud.) got bored. _____

9. You (vosotros) got irritated. _____

10. They got scared. _____

11. He got sad. _____

12. We were surprised. _____

BUILDING SENTENCES	**Sentences with the reflexive pronoun as indirect object**

Certain reflexive verbs can appear with direct objects. In these cases the reflexive pronoun is an indirect object, not a direct object. The equivalent of the indirect object reflexive pronoun in English is usually a possessive adjective. Most of these verbs express actions that have an effect on articles of clothing or parts of the body.

Me pongo el chaleco.	*I put on my vest.*
Los niños se ponen los zapatos.	*The children put on their shoes.*

The reflexive pronoun in the examples above is closely related in function to the indirect object. If the indirect object reflexive pronoun is replaced by an indirect object referring to someone other than the subject, the relationship among the elements of the sentence changes.

Le pongo el chaleco.	*I help him on with his vest.*
A los niños les ponemos los zapatos.	*We put the children's shoes on.*

Study the following pairs of sentences. The first member of each pair has a reflexive pronoun to signal that the indirect object refers to the subject of the sentence.

Los chicos **se lavan la cara.**	*The children are washing their faces.*
A los chicos **les lavo la cara.**	*I am washing the children's faces.*
Mónica **se quitó el abrigo.**	*Mónica took off her coat.*
A Mónica **le quité el abrigo.**	*I helped Mónica off with her coat.*
Me voy a cortar el pelo.	*I'm going to get a haircut.*
Si quieres, **te corto el pelo.**	*If you want, I'll cut your hair.*

Here are some common reflexive verbs and expressions that use the same pattern as in the examples above.

ponerse + article of clothing *to put on*
quitarse + article of clothing *to take off*
romperse + article of clothing *to tear*

lavarse + part of the body *to wash*
quebrarse (e > ie) + part of the body *to break*
quemarse + part of the body *to burn*
romperse + part of the body *to break*

Here are some typical expressions using this pattern.

abrocharse la chaqueta / los zapatos / los cordones / el cinturón de seguridad
  to button one's jacket, tie one's shoes/shoelaces, buckle/fasten one's seat belt
amarrarse los zapatos / los cordones *to tie one's shoes/shoelaces*
atarse los zapatos / los cordones *to tie one's shoes/shoelaces*
cepillarse los dientes / el pelo *to brush one's teeth/hair*
cortarse el pelo *to get a haircut*
desabrocharse la chaqueta / los zapatos / los cordones / el cinturón de seguridad
  to unbutton one's jacket, untie one's shoes/shoelaces, unbuckle/unfasten one's seat belt
desamarrarse los zapatos / los cordones *to untie one's shoes/shoelaces*

desatarse los zapatos / los cordones *to untie one's shoes/shoelaces*
lastimarse el dedo *to hurt one's finger*
lavarse la cabeza *to wash one's hair*
limarse las uñas *to file one's nails*
limpiarse los dientes *to brush one's teeth*
maquillarse la cara *to put makeup on*
pintarse los labios *to put lipstick on*
secarse el pelo *to dry one's hair*
torcerse (o > ue) el tobillo *to twist one's ankle*

NOTE

Spanish uses a singular noun for articles of clothing and parts of the body, even with plural subjects, when each person has only one of the mentioned item. Only when each person has more than one of the mentioned item does Spanish use a plural noun.

Se quitaron **el gorro**. *They took off their caps.*
Se quitaron **los guantes**. *They took off their gloves.*

H *Rewrite each sentence, changing the direct object noun to a pronoun and making all necessary changes. ¡Ojo! Retain the original tense.*

MODELO Pedro se rompió la pierna. *Pedro se la rompió.*

1. Roberto se torció el tobillo. _____

2. Eva y Ana se lavarán la cabeza. _____

3. Te probabas la camisa. _____

4. Pablo se ha roto el dedo meñique (*little finger*).

_____

5. Me puse las medias. _____

6. Ud. se abrochó los zapatos. _____

7. Nos ponemos el suéter. _____

8. Os laváis las manos. _____

9. Iba a cortarme el pelo. _____

10. Acaba de lastimarse el codo. _____

11. Quiere pintarse los labios. _____

12. Necesitabas cepillarte el pelo. _____

13. Me he atado los cordones. _____

14. Se había limado las uñas. _____

15. Quiero que te seques el pelo. _____

16. Era necesario que nos abrocháramos el cinturón de seguridad.

_____

The Imperative of Reflexive Verbs

Reflexive pronouns follow the same rules in commands as direct and indirect object pronouns. To review the placement of object pronouns with the imperative, see Chapter 9.

In negative commands, reflexive pronouns appear in their usual position before the verb.

No **te** quiebres el pie.	*Don't break your foot.*
No **se** preocupe Ud.	*Don't worry.*
No **nos** reunamos con ellos.	*Let's not get together with them.*
No **se** asusten Uds.	*Don't get scared.*
No **os** enojéis.	*Don't get angry.*
No **te** quites el anorak.	*Don't take off your ski jacket.*
No **te lo** quites.	*Don't take it off.*
No **se** rompa los pantalones.	*Don't tear your pants.*
No **se los** rompa.	*Don't tear them.*

In affirmative commands, reflexive pronouns are attached to the command form and an accent mark is added over the stressed syllable except in **vosotros** commands and in some two-syllable forms.

Levántate y **vístete** inmediatamente.	*Get up and get dressed immediately.*
Diviértase Ud.	*Have a good time.*
Acérquense Uds.	*Come closer.*
Animémonos.	*Let's cheer up.*
Calmaos.[1]	*Calm down.*
Vete.	*Go away.*
Lávate la cabeza.	*Wash your hair.*
Lávatela.	*Wash it.*
Pruébese el traje.	*Try on the suit.*
Pruébeselo.	*Try it on.*

When the reflexive pronoun **nos** is added to a **nosotros** command form, the final **s** of the verb form drops.

Sentémonos en esta fila.	*Let's sit down in this row.*
Despidámonos de nuestros amigos.	*Let's say good-bye to our friends.*
Escribámonos todas las semanas.	*Let's write to each other every week.*
Pongámonos las botas.	*Let's put on our boots.*
Pongámonoslas.	*Let's put them on.*

As with other affirmative **nosotros** commands, the **vamos a** + infinitive construction often replaces the command form derived from the subjunctive.

Vamos a sentarnos en esta fila.	*Let's sit down in this row.*
Vamos a despedirnos de nuestros amigos.	*Let's say good-bye to our friends.*
Vamos a escribirnos todas las semanas.	*Let's write to each other every week.*
Vamos a ponérnoslas (**las** = **las botas**).	*Let's put them on.*

---

[1]The final **-d** of the imperative is dropped when **-os** is added, except in **idos** *go away.*

I **Translation.** *Express the following sentences in English. Write more than one translation for each sentence where possible. ¡**Ojo!** Focus on the indirect object pronoun and indirect object reflexive pronoun.*

1. Abrócheselo.

   _____

2. Pónganselas.

   _____

3. Lávasela.

   _____

4. Se los quitó.

   _____

5. Se la desabrocharon.

   _____

6. Va a cepillárselo.

   _____

7. Me las puse.

   _____

8. Debes limpiártelos.

   _____

J *Answer each question, using imperatives. Write an affirmative command and a negative command for each question. The cue in parentheses tells you whom to address. Change the direct object nouns to pronouns and make all necessary changes.*

MODELO   ¿Me quito los zapatos? (tú)

   Sí, quítatelos. _____

   No, no te los quites. _____

1. ¿Me pongo este traje de baño? (tú)

   _____

   _____

2. ¿Nos limpiamos los dientes? (Uds.)

   _____

   _____

3. ¿Me seco el pelo? (Ud.)

   _____

   _____

4. ¿Nos quitamos el suéter? (nosotras)

_____

_____

5. ¿Me pruebo las chaquetas de cuero? (tú)

_____

_____

6. ¿Nos lavamos las manos? (vosotros)

_____

_____

7. ¿Me corto el pelo? (Ud.)

_____

_____

8. ¿Nos desabrochamos los zapatos? (nosotros)

_____

_____

9. ¿Nos abrochamos el cinturón? (Uds.)

_____

_____

10. ¿Nos pintamos los labios? (vosotras)

_____

_____

K *Translation.* *Express the following sentences in Spanish.*

1. *I helped her on with her coat.*

_____

2. *He twisted his ankle during the football game.*

_____

3. *Let's move into the new house as soon as possible.*

_____

4. *Are you (tú) going to have your hair cut?*

_____

5. *Look! I had it cut yesterday.*

_____

6. *Should I try on this navy blue suit?*

_____

7. *Yes, try it on, and put on that gray one too.* (Ud.)

_____

8. *Let's calm down. Let's not worry.*

_____

9. *Here is your T-shirt. Put it on.* (tú)

_____

10. *You broke your foot. Don't break the other one!* (tú)

_____

11. *Dry them* (las lágrimas *tears*). (Ud.)

_____

12. *Dry them* (las lágrimas) *for her.* (Ud.)

_____

13. *Fasten (Buckle) your seat belts.* (Uds.)

_____

14. *Fasten your little girl's seat belt.* (Ud.)

_____

The Present Participle;
The Progressive Tenses

Formation of the Present Participle (Gerund)

The Spanish present participle, or *gerund*, ends in **-ndo** and is a form parallel in many of its uses to the English present participle, which ends in *-ing*.

-Ar verbs form the present participle by removing the **-ar** of the infinitive and adding **-ando**. **-Er** and **-ir** verbs replace the **-er** and **-ir** of the infinitive with **-iendo** to form the present participle. However, **-er** and **-ir** verbs whose stems end in a vowel replace the ending **-iendo** with **-yendo** to form the present participle.

INFINITIVE	PRESENT PARTICIPLE
tomar	tomando
aprender	aprendiendo
abrir	abriendo
caer	cayendo
creer	creyendo
leer	leyendo
traer	trayendo
oír	oyendo
construir	construyendo

Stem-changing **-ir** verbs have the same vowel in the stem of the present participle as in the **él/ella/Ud.** form of the preterit.

INFINITIVE	**yo** FORM PRESENT TENSE	**él/ella/Ud.** FORM PRETERIT	PRESENT PARTICIPLE
sentir	siento	sintió	sintiendo
pedir	pido	pidió	pidiendo
servir	sirvo	sirvió	sirviendo
dormir	duermo	durmió	durmiendo
morir	muero	murió	muriendo

-Ir verbs with irregular preterit stems show the vowel of that form in the present participle.

INFINITIVE	**yo** FORM PRESENT TENSE	**él/ella/Ud.** FORM PRETERIT	PRESENT PARTICIPLE
decir	digo	dijo	diciendo
venir	vengo	vino	viniendo

Poder and **ir** have irregular gerunds.

poder	**pudiendo**
ir	**yendo**

Object pronouns and reflexive pronouns are attached to the present participle in writing, and an accent mark is written over the **a** or **e** of the **-ndo** ending.

esperándolo
dándomelas
levantándose
viéndolos
trayéndosela
sintiéndose

The gerund often functions as an adverbial phrase or adverb clause beginning with *by, if, when, while,* or *because.*

Los niños aprenden mucho **escuchando** la conversación de los mayores.	*Children learn a lot by listening to the conversation of adults.*
Se acatarró **caminando** bajo la lluvia.	*He caught a cold while walking in the rain.*

With verbs of perception, such as **ver**, **mirar**, **oír**, and **escuchar**, either the infinitive or the gerund can be used, as in English.

Los oímos cantar. Los oímos cantando.	*We heard them sing/singing.*
Siempre la veo pasear a su perro. Siempre la veo paseando a su perro.	*I always see her walk/walking her dog.*

A   Create sentences using **pasar** + the present participle. Include the time cue in parentheses to tell how long people spent doing their activities.

MODELO   ella / trotar (treinta minutos)
          Pasó treinta minutos trotando.

1. yo / hacer ejercicio (una hora)

   _____

2. tú / vestirse (diez minutos)

   _____

3. Juan Carlos / navegar en la Red (dos horas)

   _____

4. ellos / pasearse (media hora)

_____

5. nosotros / divertirse (el día entero)

_____

6. Uds. / instalarse en el condominio (una semana)

_____

7. Ignacio / oír música (cuarenta y cinco minutos)

_____

8. vosotros / discutir (mucho tiempo)

_____

9. Marisol / probarse ropa (toda la tarde)

_____

10. tú / dormir la siesta (veinte minutos)

_____

11. Uds. / leer (toda la mañana)

_____

12. nosotros / ver tele (menos de una hora)

_____

B *Write sentences using the following strings of elements. Use verbs of perception, and write two sentences for each item—one using the infinitive, the other using the gerund. Use the preterit for all verbs.*

MODELO   él / oír cantar / a Juan Diego
        Él lo oyó cantar.   Él lo oyó cantando.

1. Uds. / ver bailar ballet / a Cristina

_____

2. tú / escuchar hablar / a los locutores

_____

3. nosotros / mirar actuar / a las actrices

_____

4. Ud. / oír llorar / al niño

_____

5. yo / ver correr / los miembros del equipo

_____

6. vosotros / observar hacer gimnasia / a la gimnasta

_____

_____

7. ellos / oír silbar (*whistle*) una melodía / a mí

_____

_____

8. él / ver cruzar la calle / a nosotros

_____

The Progressive Tenses

The progressive tenses consist of any tense of **estar** + the present participle.

TENSE NAME	EXAMPLE SENTENCE	ENGLISH TRANSLATION
PRESENT PROGRESSIVE	Estoy leyendo una novela.	*I am reading a novel.*
IMPERFECT PROGRESSIVE	Estaba leyendo una novela.	*I was reading a novel.*
PRETERIT PROGRESSIVE	Estuve leyendo una novela hasta las dos de la tarde.	*I was reading a novel until two in the afternoon.*
FUTURE PROGRESSIVE	Estaré leyendo una novela.	*I will be reading a novel.*
CONDITIONAL PROGRESSIVE	Estaría leyendo una novela.	*I would be reading a novel.*

The progressive forms of **estar**, **ir**, and **venir** are rarely used.

The present, imperfect, future, and conditional progressives all emphasize that the action is, was, will be, or would be in progress. The preterit progressive, a less common tense, usually appears in a sentence where the end of the action is specified and, like all preterits, implies a completed action. It conveys the idea of an action going on in the past that ended.

Estuvieron bailando en la discoteca hasta el amanecer.	*They were dancing in the discotheque until dawn.*
Estuvo corriendo hasta que comenzó a llover.	*He was running until it began to rain.*
Estuve formateando hasta que mi computadora crasheó.	*I was formatting until my computer crashed.*

The progressive tenses may convey the idea of a temporary action or an action that represents a change from what the speaker is used to.

Tenemos que entrar. **Está lloviendo.**	*We have to go in. It has started to rain.*
¿Qué es esto? ¿Miguel **está fumando**?	*What's this? Miguel has started to smoke?*

There is often not much difference in meaning between the simple imperfect and the imperfect progressive.

¿Qué me **decías**?	
¿Qué me **estabas diciendo**?	*What were you telling me?*

However, the simple imperfect conveys a habitual action in the past. The imperfect progressive may convey the idea of a recently begun action or strongly imply that the action was interrupted, but not that it was a habitual one.

Elisa **trabajaba** en el centro.	*Elisa used to work downtown.*
Elisa **estaba trabajando** en el centro.	*Elisa was working downtown.*

The future and conditional progressives may be used to express probability or conjecture. As with the simple future and conditional of probability, the future progressive expresses probability or conjecture about the present, the conditional progressive about the past.

¿Qué **estarán haciendo**?	*I wonder what they are doing.*
¿No quisieron salir? **Estarían estudiando.**	*They didn't want to go out? They were probably studying.*

The Spanish present progressive is never used to refer to future time like the English present progressive commonly is. Spanish uses either the simple present, the **ir a** + infinitive construction, or the future tense.

El avión sale a las tres.	
El avión va a salir a las tres.	*The plane is leaving at three.*
El avión saldrá a las tres.	

The sentence **El avión está saliendo** can only mean *The plane is leaving (right now).*

In the progressive tenses, object pronouns and reflexive pronouns either precede the form of **estar** or follow the present participle and are attached to it in writing, in which case an accent mark is added over the **a** or **e** of the present participle ending.

Los chicos **se están levantando.**	*The children are getting up.*
Los chicos **están levantándose.**	
¿El café? **Lo estoy haciendo.**	*The coffee? I'm making it.*
¿El café? **Estoy haciéndolo.**	

Other Verbs Used in Progressive Constructions

Verbs other than **estar** are also used in progressive constructions.

The verb **seguir** is used with the present participle to mean *to be still doing something, to keep on doing something.*

¿**Sigues tomando** clases de español?	*Are you still taking Spanish classes?*
Siguen viviendo en la casa de sus padres.	*They still live in their parents' house.*

Ir is used with the present participle to convey the idea of *gradually* or *little by little.*

Nuestra empresa **va prosperando.**	*Our firm is gradually prospering.*
El pueblo **fue creciendo** poco a poco.	*The town was growing little by little.*

Andar is used with the present participle to convey the idea of *going around doing something* and may imply aimlessness.

Anda pidiendo préstamos.	*He goes around asking for loans.*
Andan buscando casa.	*They are constantly house hunting.*

The **llevar** + **-ndo** construction expresses actions that began in the past and are continuing into the present. It is the equivalent of **hace** + time expression + **que**.

Llevo una semana redactando el informe. }
Hace una semana que redacto el informe. } *I've been writing up the report for a week.*

Verbs of motion such as **salir**, **entrar**, **subir**, and **bajar** can be used with present participles to specify how the motion was performed. English usually prefers to use a different verb for each type of motion, followed by an adverbial complement such as *out, in, into, up,* or *down*.

Salieron corriendo.	*They ran out.*
Un pájaro entró volando en la casa.	*A bird flew into the house.*
Subí la escalera cojeando.	*I limped up the stairs.*
El ascensor estaba descompuesto y por eso bajé caminando.	*The elevator wasn't working and that's why I walked down.*
Los niños bajaron la escalera saltando.	*The kids jumped down the stairs.*

C *Rewrite each sentence, changing the verb from the present indicative to the present progressive. Change direct object nouns to pronouns and make all necessary changes. Write each sentence in two ways. ¡Ojo! Focus on the placement of object pronouns and write accent marks as necessary.*

MODELO   Entra los datos.

Está entrándolos.   Los está entrando.

1. Alquila el video.

_____

2. Graban el programa.

_____

3. Te pruebas las sandalias.

_____

4. Les servimos las margaritas.

_____

5. Imprime los documentos.

_____

6. Le pongo el pañal (*diaper*) al bebé.

_____

7. Nos pedís el iPod.

_____

8. Leo el libro de cocina.

_____

9. Me escriben el correo electrónico.

_____

10. Os secáis las lágrimas (*tears*).

_____

11. Te rompes la camiseta.

_____

12. Enciende el fuego de campamento.

_____

13. Les consiguen los billetes.

_____

14. Se limpian los dientes.

_____

15. Nos comemos la torta de chocolate.

_____

D *Rewrite each sentence, changing the verb from the imperfect to the imperfect progressive. Change direct object nouns to pronouns and make all necessary changes. Write each sentence in two ways. ¡Ojo! Focus on the placement of object pronouns and write accent marks as necessary.*

MODELO   Escribían el informe.

   Estaban escribiéndolo.   Lo estaban escribiendo.

1. Descargaba los ficheros.

_____

2. Me vestía.

_____

3. Le quitábamos el abrigo.

_____

4. Te cortabas el pelo.

_____

5. Nos decían lo ocurrido.

_____

6. Compartíais las ganancias.

_____

7. Nos reuníamos.

_____

8. Le traía la correspondencia.

_____

9. Me mostraban las fotos.

_____

10. Se lavaba las manos.

_____

11. Me ponía en forma.

_____

12. Se reían a carcajadas (*split one's sides laughing*).

_____

E *Rewrite each sentence, changing the verb either from the future to the future progressive or from the conditional to the conditional progressive. Change direct object nouns to pronouns and make all necessary changes. Write each sentence in two ways.* **¡Ojo!** *Focus on the placement of object pronouns and write accent marks as necessary.*

MODELOS Preparé la cena.

    Estaré preparándola.   La estaré preparando.

Prepararía la cena.

    Estaría preparándola.   La estaría preparando.

1. Terminará la tesis.

_____

2. Cuidarían a sus sobrinos.

_____

3. Nos registraremos (*to register*) en el hotel.

_____

4. Se acostaría.

_____

5. Me dirían su plan.

_____

6. Les harías las chuletas de cordero.

_____

7. Le pondré la chaqueta.

_____

8. Se atarán los cordones.

_____

9. Te aburrirás.

_____

10. Le entregaréis las tarjetas de memoria.

_____

F *Rewrite each sentence, changing the verb from the preterit to the preterit progressive and incorporating the phrase in parentheses. Change direct object nouns to pronouns and make all necessary changes. Write each sentence in two ways. ¡Ojo! Focus on the placement of object pronouns and write accent marks as necessary.*

MODELO   Hice la comida (hasta que vinieron las visitas).

      Estuve haciéndola hasta que vinieron las visitas.

      La estuve haciendo hasta que vinieron las visitas.

1. Practiqué el béisbol (hasta las cinco).

_____

_____

2. Se arregló (hasta que él llegó a recogerla).

_____

_____

3. Se instalaron (hasta el sábado).

_____

_____

4. Nos paseamos (hasta el anochecer).

_____

_____

5. Te lavaste la cabeza (hasta que sonó el teléfono).

_____

_____

6. Se reunieron (hasta que la presidenta [*chairwoman*] levantó [*adjourned*] la reunión).

_____

_____

7. Se portó mal (hasta que sus papás le riñeron).

_____

_____

8. Le contó los chismes (hasta que su amiga no pudo más [*couldn't stand it anymore*]).

_____

_____

G *Rewrite each sentence, using the* **llevar** + **-ndo** *construction.*

MODELO   Hace una hora que hago las maletas.
            Llevo una hora haciendo las maletas.

1. Hace cuarenta minutos que navego en la Red.

_____

2. Hace tres horas que juegan al golf.

_____

3. Hace un par de días que se siente mal.

_____

4. Hace varios años que nos interesamos en el arte.

_____

5. Hace quince minutos que te limas las uñas.

_____

6. Hace media hora que os probáis esos pantalones.

_____

7. Hace mucho tiempo que me mantengo en forma.

_____

8. Hace una semana que se reúnen en el congreso.

_____

H *Translation. Express the following sentences in English.*

1. Patricia seguía trabajando en los suburbios cuando di con ella.

_____

2. La empresa iba aumentando sus precios para crear los sitios Web.

_____

3. Uds. subían la escalera corriendo.

_____

4. Bajaste la escalera bailando.

_____

5. Llevamos media hora escribiéndonos mensajes instantáneos.

_____

6. Se resfriaron bebiendo en los vasos ajenos.

_____

7. Pasaron el fin de semana divirtiéndose.

_____

8. Carmen se lastimó el dedo cortando el pan.

_____

I *Express the following sentences in Spanish. Use the progressive tenses where possible.*
¡Ojo! There might be more than one way to express some sentences.

1. *The chocolate ice cream? I'm serving it to them right now.*

_____

2. *Her coat? He's helping her on with it.*

_____

3. *They're combing their hair while we get dressed.*

_____

4. *The player tore his pants falling down.*

_____

5. *We were falling asleep when the phone rang.*

_____

6. *They're probably moving into their new house.*

_____

7. *I didn't see her dancing at the discotheque last night. I wonder what she was doing.*

_____

_____

8. *I hope you (tú) are getting ready so that we won't arrive late.*

_____

9. *Did you (Uds.) hear him coughing all night?*

_____

10. *We've been looking for a parking meter* (el parquímetro) *for twenty minutes.*

_____

11. *González was pitching very well until he twisted his ankle.*

_____

NEOLOGISMS baseball terms

Baseball has had an enormous impact on many Spanish American societies, and as the sport was adopted, a lexicon for baseball came into being. Many English words were adopted into the language and reshaped according to Spanish pronunciation and grammar, and existing Spanish words took on new meanings to express features of the sport.

Here are some verbs borrowed from English and adapted to the Spanish language with Spanish synonyms in parentheses: **pitchear (lanzar)**, **cachar** or **cachear** (**atrapar, coger, capturar**), **batear** and **jitear** (**palear**), **fildear**, and **embasar** *to put on base*. Note that these new verbs created in Spanish are integrated into the **-ar** conjugation, most of them with the **-ear** suffix.

BUILDING SENTENCES   **Word order in Spanish**

The basic Spanish word order pattern is like that of English: subject–verb–object.

> Claudia compró el carro.   *Claudia bought the car.*

A major difference between Spanish and English is that Spanish can omit the subject.

> —¿Qué hizo Claudia ayer?   *"What did Claudia do yesterday?"*
> —Compró el carro.   *"She bought the car."*

However, Spanish allows many variations in the basic word order that English does not. The two key aspects of Spanish word order are *focus* and *topicalization*. *Focus* refers to new information. *Topicalization* is the mechanism for setting up the topic of the sentence, or establishing what is being talked about. Both *focus* and *topicalization* entail changes in the basic word order pattern of subject–verb–object.

Focus

The final element of the sentence in Spanish is usually the one focused on, the one that conveys new information. Thus, when the subject of the verb adds new information, it is often moved from before the verb to after it. The Spanish response that follows shows a word order pattern of object–verb–subject.

> —¿Juan compró el carro?   *"Did Juan buy the car?"*
> —No, lo compró **Claudia**.   *"No, **Claudia** bought it."*

English does not change word order for focus. Instead, English speakers move the main stress of the sentence to the new piece of information. Compare the intonation and stress on *Claudia* in these two sentences.

> NEUTRAL STATEMENT   *Claudia bought the car.*
> NEW INFORMATION   *(Did Juan buy the car?) No, **Claudia** bought it.*

The element of a sentence that provides the information asked about in *information questions* usually appears at the end of the sentence that answers the question.

> —¿Cuándo compró Juan el carro?   *"When did John buy the car?"*
> —Lo compró **ayer**.   *"He bought it **yesterday**."*

Spanish speakers also put information that corrects an erroneous position expressed in a *yes/no question* at the end of the response.

—¿Juan compró el carro en esta ciudad?	*"Did Juan buy the car in this city?"*
—No, lo compró en **su ciudad natal**.	*"No, he bought it in **his home town**."*

Topicalization

The topic of a Spanish sentence is placed at the beginning of the sentence. For instance, when the topic of the sentence is the location of various events of a party, the location information is placed first in the sentence.

En el jardín sirvieron entremeses.	*They served hors d'oeuvres **in the garden**.*
En la sala conversaron.	*They talked **in the living room**.*
En el patio de atrás bailaron.	*There was dancing **on the patio in back of the house**.*
En el comedor sirvieron la comida.	*They served dinner **in the dining room**.*

The time for each of the party events could also be the topic, which would place the phrases of time at the beginning of the sentence and move the phrases of location to their normal position after the verb.

A las nueve sirvieron entremeses **en el jardín**.	*At nine they served hors d'oeuvres **in the garden**.*
A las diez bailaron **en el patio de atrás**.	*At ten there was dancing **on the patio in back of the house**.*
A las once y media sirvieron la comida **en el comedor**.	*At eleven thirty they served dinner **in the dining room**.*

However, if any of the sentences about the party is an answer to an *information question*, then the element that provides the new information sought by the question appears at the end of the sentence.

—¿Qué sirvieron en el jardín?	*"What did they serve in the garden?"*
—En el jardín sirvieron **entremeses**.	*"They served **hors d'oeuvres** in the garden."*
—¿Dónde sirvieron entremeses?	*"Where did they serve hors d'oeuvres?"*
—Sirvieron entremeses **en el jardín**.	*"They served hors d'oeuvres **in the garden**."*
—¿A qué hora sirvieron entremeses?	*"At what time did they serve hors d'oeuvres?"*
—Sirvieron entremeses **a las nueve**.	*"They served hors d'oeuvres **at nine**."*
—¿Quiénes sirvieron los entremeses?	*"Who served the hors d'oeuvres?"*
—Los sirvieron **los anfitriones**.	*"**The host and hostess** served them."*

A direct object noun can be topicalized by moving it to the beginning of the sentence and adding the direct object pronoun that refers to it before the verb. The idea conveyed is *as far as X is concerned.* . . . Note the *reduplicated* object pronouns that are mandatory when the direct object is moved to topic position.

El carro lo compró Juan.	*Juan bought the car. (Juan is the one who bought the car.)*
La computadora la usaba Lurdes.	*Lurdes was using the computer.*
Al embajador lo entrevistó el periodista.	*The journalist interviewed the ambassador.*
A sus nietos los acuesta la abuela.	*The grandmother is putting her grandchildren to bed.*
A la gerenta de publicidad la conocimos nosotros.	*We met the advertising manager.*

Topicalization of the direct object is especially common in correcting someone's impression. It adds specification.

—¿Sirvieron toda la comida en la casa?	*"Did they serve all the food in the house?"*
—No. **Los entremeses los** sirvieron en el jardín y **la cena la** sirvieron en el comedor.	*"No, they served the hors d'oeuvres in the garden and they served dinner in the dining room."*

Note that in the response for the example above, the phrases **en el jardín** and **en el comedor** add new information (focus) and are therefore placed at the end of their clauses. **Los entremeses** and **la cena** are the topics of their clauses, clarifying aspects of *la comida*, and are therefore placed at the beginning of their clauses.

J *Answer each yes/no question in the negative, using the new information in parentheses in your response. Change direct object nouns to pronouns and make all necessary changes. ¡Ojo! Remember that the final element of the sentence in Spanish is usually the one that conveys new information.*

MODELO   ¿Lola preparó la comida? (Diana)

  No, la preparó Diana.

1. ¿El equipo Azul ganó el campeonato? (el equipo Rojo)

   _____

2. ¿Rodrigo se torció el tobillo? (Raimundo)

   _____

3. ¿Ud. se quemó la mano? (mi amigo)

   _____

4. ¿Los analistas se reunieron? (los consultores)

   _____

5. ¿Abrirán una frutería en la esquina? (una pastelería)

   _____

6. ¿Ellos hacían preguntas? (nosotros)

   _____

7. ¿Verónica está probándose el vestido blanco? (Miriám)

   _____

8. ¿Esta sucursal busca dependientes? (la otra sucursal)

   _____

K *Rewrite each sentence, topicalizing the direct object noun and moving it to the beginning of the sentence. ¡Ojo! Remember to add the reduplicated direct object pronoun.*

   MODELO   Susana entregó el documento.

   El documento lo entregó Susana. _____

1. Sara cobró los cheques.

   _____

2. Antonio y yo hicimos la lista.

   _____

3. Tú preparabas el guacamole.

   _____

4. Inés ha cuidado a sus hermanitos.

   _____

5. Yo pagué las cuentas.

   _____

6. Ellos usarán mi cámara digital.

   _____

7. El enfermero tranquilizó a los pacientes nerviosos.

   _____

8. Andrés llevó a Lorena a un concierto.

   _____

9. Uds. han impreso el informe.

   _____

10. El dueño del negocio despidió al empleado insolente.

   _____

The Preposition **a** and Word Order

Since subjects frequently follow their verbs in Spanish, the preposition **a** helps you determine whether a noun that follows the verb is a subject or an object when that noun refers to a person. Compare the following pairs of sentences.

Le escribió Fernando.	*Fernando wrote to him.*
Le escribió **a** Fernando.	*He wrote to Fernando.*

In the first sentence above, **Fernando** is the subject of **escribió**. In the second, **Fernando** is the indirect object, labeled by the preposition **a** as referring to the same person as the indirect object pronoun **le**.

With direct objects, the personal **a** also helps to distinguish a direct object from a subject placed after the verb, but it is not the only distinguishing factor. The direct object pronoun is not used (except dialectally) when the direct object noun follows the verb.

Lo vio Fernando.	*Fernando saw him.*
Vio a Fernando.	*He saw Fernando.*

However, when the direct object is topicalized (moved to the beginning of the sentence), then the personal **a** does become the sole factor distinguishing the subject from the object.

Fernando lo vio.	*Fernando saw him.*
A Fernando lo vio.	*He saw Fernando.*

Thus, the word **a**—whether as a preposition marking the indirect object or a personal **a** marking the direct object—labels animate nouns as "oblique," the grammatical term for a noun playing a role other than that of subject in a sentence.

L *Translation. Express the following sentences in Spanish. ¡Ojo! There might be more than one way to express some sentences.*

1. *Victoria met him.* _____

2. *He met Victoria.* _____

3. *Isabel told it (lo) to her.* _____

4. *She told (it) to Isabel.* _____

5. *Jorge and Rita saw you (la).* _____

6. *You (Ud.) saw Jorge and Rita.* _____

7. *Martín showed them (las) to them.* _____

8. *They showed them to Martín.* _____

9. *Miguel read to her.* _____

10. *She read to Miguel.* _____

Passive Constructions; Reverse Construction Verbs

The Passive Voice

The passive voice in Spanish is similar in formation to the passive voice in English. It consists of a subject and a form of **ser** + the past participle. In the passive voice, the participle functions like an adjective and agrees with the subject in gender and number.

Aquella casa **fue construida** en el siglo XVIII.	*That house was built in the eighteenth century.*
Relaciones diplomáticas entre los dos países **serán establecidas**.	*Diplomatic relations between the two countries will be established.*

The function of the passive voice is to deemphasize the performer of the action and to shift the focus of the sentence to the action expressed by the verb and the direct object. To understand this, it is helpful to see passive sentences as deriving from active ones.

El duque **construyó** aquella casa en el siglo XVIII.	*The duke built that house in the eighteenth century.*
Los gobiernos **establecerán** relaciones diplomáticas entre los dos países.	*The governments will establish diplomatic relations between the two countries.*

In the sentences above, the subject is the performer of the action. When speakers wish to divert attention from the performer of the action, they remove it from the sentence, turn the direct object into the grammatical subject, and change the verb from active to passive.

The performer of the action may be added to a passive sentence in a phrase beginning with **por**. This is called the *agent*.

Aquella casa fue construida **por el duque** en el siglo XVIII.	*That house was built by the duke in the eighteenth century.*
Relaciones diplomáticas entre los dos países serán establecidas **por sus gobiernos**.	*Diplomatic relations between the two countries will be established by their governments.*

Both **ser** and **estar** can occur with the past participle in Spanish to form passive constructions: **ser** emphasizes the action of the verb, while **estar** focuses on the result of the action.

Las puertas **fueron abiertas.**

The doors were opened. (the passive expression of **Alguien abrió las puertas.***)*

Las puertas **estaban abiertas.**

The doors were open. (expresses the result of the action)

An agent phrase with **por** is not used with **estar** + the past participle.

English has various ways of deemphasizing the performer of the action. Compare the following sentences.

Articles were written.
One wrote articles.
They wrote articles.
You wrote articles.
We wrote articles.
People wrote articles.

The pronouns *they, you,* and *we* in the above sentences are general rather than specific in reference. They are therefore unstressed. All of the above sentences focus on the act of writing articles without focusing on who wrote them.

Although the passive voice in English is one of the most common ways of deemphasizing the performer of the action, in Spanish it is more characteristic of formal written language than of everyday speech.

A *Rewrite each sentence, changing it from active to passive. Retain the tense of the original sentence. ¡Ojo! Make sure that each verb agrees with its new subject.*

MODELO   El terremoto destruyó el pueblo entero.

   El pueblo entero fue destruido por el terremoto.

1. El técnico reparó la computadora.

   _____

2. Una empresa alemana abrirá una cadena de perfumerías.

   _____

3. El mesero derramó el vino.

   _____

4. Unos estudiantes de informática escriben la revista electrónica.

   _____

5. Este equipo de arquitectos hará los planes.

   _____

6. El electricista desenchufó (*unplugged*) los aparatos eléctricos.

   _____

7. Estos programadores instalarán el software.

_____

8. El director inglés rueda la película en Barcelona.

_____

9. El presidente ha dado la conferencia.

_____

10. Los soldados detuvieron a los terroristas.

_____

11. Una pastelera de la academia de artes culinarias hizo estas tortas.

_____

12. El periódico publicó una serie de artículos sobre la guerra.

_____

B *Rewrite each sentence, changing it from active to passive. Then derive a sentence from each one that shows the result of the action.*

MODELO El cocinero preparó los platos.

Los platos fueron preparados por el cocinero.

Los platos estaban preparados.

1. El asesor escribió el informe.

_____

_____

2. La directora suspendió la reunión.

_____

_____

3. Los voceros (*spokesmen*) pronunciaron los discursos.

_____

_____

4. El administrador de Web redactó las páginas Web.

_____

_____

5. La psicóloga resolvió los problemas.

_____

_____

6. El compositor francés compuso la sinfonía.

   _____

   _____

7. El jugador de béisbol rompió la ventana.

   _____

   _____

8. Los legisladores aprobaron la ley.

   _____

   _____

9. Los exploradores fundaron las colonias.

   _____

   _____

10. La enfermera cuidó a los pacientes.

    _____

    _____

C *Translation.* *Express the following sentences in Spanish.*

1. *The pizzas were home delivered* (a domicilio) *by the deliveryman* (el repartidor).

   _____

2. *The banks were closed by the managers.*

   _____

3. *The furniture was put in the living room by the movers* (cargadores).

   _____

4. *The walls were painted by our painter.*

   _____

5. *The car was rented by the tourists.*

   _____

6. *The car was rented.* [result of the action]

   _____

7. *The politicians of the two parties were interviewed by the press* (la prensa).

   _____

8. *The politicians were interviewed.* [result of the action]

   _____

9. *The gift was wrapped up by us.*

_____

10. *The gift was wrapped up.* [result of the action]

_____

11. *My friend got the tickets on the Internet.*

_____

12. *The tickets were bought.* [result of the action]

_____

Other Passive Constructions: The **se** Construction

Spanish uses a construction consisting of **se** + the verb in the third person to deemphasize the performer of the action. The noun that is logically the direct object of the verb becomes the grammatical subject of the sentence. The verb in this construction is either third-person singular or third-person plural, depending on whether the grammatical subject is singular or plural. No agent phrase can be used in this construction. In English, this **se** construction (**se** + verb) has many possible translations.

Singular Subjects

Se escucha el discurso del presidente.
People are listening to the president's speech.

Se va a construir un rascacielos en el centro.
They are going to build a skyscraper downtown.

Eso no se hace en nuestro país.
That's not done in our country.

Plural Subjects

Nunca **se limpian las calles** de esta ciudad.
The streets of this city are never cleaned.

Por fin **se solucionaron todos los problemas**.
All the problems were finally solved.

Todos estos platos se preparan con ají.
You prepare all these dishes with chile pepper.

An agent phrase with **por** is not used with the **se** construction.

D *Rewrite each sentence, using the* **se** *construction. Retain the tense of the original sentence.*

MODELO   El botones bajó el equipaje.

Se bajó el equipaje.

1. Nuestros amigos servían platos tejanomexicanos.

   _____

2. Esta florería vende flores exquisitas.

   _____

3. La compañía de alta tecnología necesita programadores.

   _____

4. Haremos tres copias del documento.

   _____

5. Realizaron el proyecto.

   _____

6. Estás organizando los archivos.

   _____

7. Hablan español en todas estas tiendas.

   _____

8. Leímos las obras clásicas.

   _____

9. Firmé el contrato.

   _____

10. Van a enviar el correo electrónico pronto.

    _____

11. No pueden hacer preguntas todavía.

    _____

12. Debes visitar ese sitio Web.

    _____

13. El panadero quemó el pan.

    _____

14. Necesitan almacenar los datos.

    _____

Intransitive verbs may also appear in the **se** construction. An intransitive verb in the **se** construction is always in the third-person singular. The English equivalents of these sentences may have nouns where Spanish has verbs in the **se** construction.

Intransitive Verbs

Se vive bien en este país.	*You live well in this country. (Life is good.)*
Por aquí no **se entra**.	*This is not the way in.*
¡Qué bien **se está** aquí!	*How comfortable one feels here.*

When an infinitive is the subject of a **se** construction, the verb is third-person singular.

Se debe comer frutas y legumbres frescas.	*You should eat fresh fruits and vegetables.*
Se puede subir al restaurante giratorio en aquel ascensor.	*One can go up to the revolving restaurant in that elevator.*
Se prohíbe tomar drogas.	*Taking drugs is forbidden.*

Transitive Verbs Used Intransitively

¡Qué bien **se come** en Italia!	*You eat so well in Italy! (How good the food is in Italy!)*
No **se cruza** aquí.	*You don't cross here.*
¡Qué rápido **se habla** en esta ciudad!	*How fast people talk in this city!*

Reflexive verbs cannot be used in the impersonal **se** construction. To express an impersonal subject, use **uno** (or **una** if the reference is specifically feminine) as the subject of the third-person singular form of the reflexive verb.

Uno se divierte mucho en Madrid.	*People have a great time in Madrid.*
Uno se acuesta más tarde durante las vacaciones.	*You go to bed later during vacation.*
A los doce años **una no debe maquillarse**.	*At twelve you shouldn't put on makeup.*

E   *Write sentences using the **se** construction with intransitive verbs.*

MODELO   Leemos en la biblioteca.

Se lee en la biblioteca.

1. Trabajan en equipo.

   _____

2. Navegamos en la Red.

   _____

3. Vives en una sociedad de información.

   _____

4. Compran y venden en un mercado global.

   _____

5. Puede hablar por teléfono móvil.

   _____

6. Deben llegar antes de las cuatro.

   _____

7. Entran por la puerta principal.

   _____

8. Salimos al jardín por aquí.

   _____

9. Suben en este elevador.

   _____

10. Bajas por la escalera trasera (*back*).

    _____

11. Charlan en el canal de conversación (*chat room*).

    _____

12. Buscamos el cajero automático (*ATM*).

    _____

Other ways of expressing the deemphasized performer of the action in Spanish are the following:

- **La gente** can serve as the subject, always with a third-person singular verb. This construction is especially common in the Caribbean.

La gente critica mucho a los políticos.	*People criticize politicians a lot.*
La gente sale mucho los domingos.	*People go out a lot on Sundays.*

- The third-person plural verb without an expressed subject can convey the impersonal subject, much like unstressed *they* in English.

Dicen que habrá una guerra.	*They say there will be a war.*
En esa tienda **cobran** demasiado.	*They charge too much in that store.*
Lo **entrevistaron** para ese puesto.	*They interviewed him for that position.* (*He was interviewed for that position.*)

- **Tú** can be used as an impersonal subject, much like unstressed *you* in English. This usage in Spanish is characteristic of informal speech.

Cuando **eres** pobre, todo es difícil.	*When you're poor, everything is difficult.*
Trabajas y **trabajas** y no **sales** adelante.	*You work and work and you don't get ahead.*

Other *se* Constructions

With many verbs, a **se** construction can be followed by an animate direct object that is preceded by the personal **a**. The verb is always in the third-person singular, whether the direct object is singular or plural.

Se mató a dos personas.	*Two people were killed.*

Such a construction removes the potential ambiguity of the more typical **se** construction when the subject is animate.

Se mataron dos personas.	*Two people killed themselves / got killed / were killed.*

Se mató a dos personas can only mean that the two people were killed by somebody else. Here are some additional examples.

Se liberó a los prisioneros.	*The prisoners were freed.*
Se detuvo a los terroristas.	*The terrorists were arrested.*
Se rescató al rehén.	*The hostage was ransomed.*
Se encarceló a los criminales.	*The criminals were jailed.*
Se destituyó a tres senadores.	*Three senators were removed from office.*

The direct objects in these sentences are replaced by **le, les**, not **lo, la, los, las**.

Se rescató al rehén. → **Se le rescató.**
Se encarceló a los criminales. → **Se les encarceló.**

F *Translation. Express the following sentences in Spanish, using passive constructions.*

1. *English is spoken here.*

   _____

2. *One should take the one o'clock train.*

   _____

3. *People worry too much.*

   _____

4. *You can live very well in this city.*

   _____

5. *The apartments are being shown between ten and six.*

   _____

6. *The employees were hired by the manager.*

   _____

7. *These products were made by an English company.*

   _____

8. *People wake up late on the weekend.*

_____

9. *How do you (How does one) say "the Web" in Spanish?*

_____

10. *You* [impersonal] *fasten your seat belt when you travel by car.*

_____

11. *Did the terrorists get killed?*

_____

12. *Yes, they got killed. And many others were jailed.*

_____

Reverse Construction Verbs

Some verbs in Spanish typically occur with an indirect object pronoun. **Gustar** *to like* is one of the most common of this class of verbs. In the English translations of sentences with such verbs, the Spanish subject usually corresponds to the English direct object. The English subject corresponds to the Spanish indirect object.

I like cookies.	I	like	cookies.
	SUBJECT	VERB	DIRECT OBJECT
Me gustan las galletas.	Me	gustan	las galletas.
	INDIRECT OBJECT	VERB	SUBJECT

I is the subject of the English sentence; **las galletas** is the subject of the Spanish sentence. *Cookies* is the direct object in the English sentence; **me** is the indirect object of the verb **gustan** in the Spanish sentence. It is useful to think of these verbs as *reverse construction verbs,* since the grammatical functions of the elements of the sentences are reversed.

Study the complete paradigm of **gustar** in the present tense. Note that the verb agrees with the subject of the Spanish sentence—**torta** or **galletas.**

Me gusta la torta. *I like the cake.*
Me gustan las galletas. *I like the cookies.*

Te gusta la torta. *You like the cake.*
Te gustan las galletas. *You like the cookies.*

Le gusta la torta. *He/She likes / You like the cake.*
Le gustan las galletas. *He/She likes / You like the cookies.*

Nos gusta la torta. *We like the cake.*
Nos gustan las galletas. *We like the cookies.*

Os gusta la torta. *You like the cake.*
Os gustan las galletas. *You like the cookies.*

Les gusta la torta. *You/They like the cake.*
Les gustan las galletas. *You/They like the cookies.*

When the grammatical subject of a verb like **gustar** is an infinitive, the verb is always in the third-person singular.

—**Me encanta patinar** sobre el hielo.   *"I love to ice skate."*
—A mí **me gusta** más **esquiar.**   *"I like skiing better."*

Here are some other verbs and verbal phrases that function like **gustar.**

agradarle a uno *to like something, find something pleasing*
caerle bien/mal a uno *to like/dislike (usually a person)*
convenirle a uno *to suit someone, be good for someone*
desagradarle a uno *to dislike something, find something unpleasant*
disgustarle a uno *to dislike something, find something unpleasant*
encantarle a uno *to love something*
entusiasmarle a uno *to be excited about something*
faltarle a uno *to be missing something, not have something; to be short* (money)
fascinarle a uno *to be fascinated (by something); to like*
hacerle falta a uno *to need something*
importarle a uno *to care about something; to mind; to matter*
interesarle a uno *to be interested in something*
quedarle a uno *to have something left*
sobrarle a uno *to have more than enough of something*
tocarle a uno *to be someone's turn*
urgirle a uno *to be urgent for someone to do something*

NOTE

The usual way to express *to like/dislike a person* in Spanish is **caerle bien/mal a uno.** **Gustarle a uno** often implies a romantic attraction when referring to people. **Gustar** may, however, be used to refer to a person as professional or to refer to children.

Me gusta aquella escritora.   *I like that writer.*
Nos gustan los hijos de los Peña.   *We like the Peñas' children.*

—¿**Te importa** acompañarme al museo?   *"Would you mind going to the museum with me?"*

—**Me encantaría. Me interesa** mucho el arte. *"I'd love to. I'm very interested in art."*

—Creo que **te convendría** salir un poco.   *"I think it would be good for you to go out a little."*

—Sé que **me hace falta,** pero **me sobra** trabajo. *"I know I need to, but I have too much work."*

—Parece que no **te entusiasma** mucho este juego. *"It seems that you're not very excited about this game."*

—Cada vez que **me toca a mí,** pierdo.   *"Every time it's my turn, I lose."*

When speakers want to focus on or contrast the indirect object pronouns, they add a phrase consisting of **a** + the corresponding stressed pronoun to the sentence. This prepositional phrase is also used for "short responses," that is, responses that are not complete sentences.

—¿Cuánto dinero nos queda?	*"How much money do we have left?"*
—A mí me quedan doscientos dólares. **¿Y a ti?**	*"I have two hundred dollars left. How about you?"*
—Chicos, ¿a quién le gusta la torta de chocolate?	*"Kids, who likes chocolate cake?"*
—**¡A mí! ¡A mí! ¡A mí!**	*"I do! I do! I do!"*

The phrase **¿Y a ti?** is short for **Y a ti, ¿cuánto dinero te queda?** The phrase **¡A mí!** is short for **A mí me gusta la torta de chocolate.**

G *Change the subject from singular to plural in each sentence. Retain the tense of the original sentence. **¡Ojo!** Remember to make all necessary changes.*

MODELO   Me gusta el libro.

Me gustan los libros.

1. Le gusta esta marca.

   _____

2. ¿Te interesa mi idea?

   _____

3. Nos encantó el concierto.

   _____

4. Me entusiasmaba su plan.

   _____

5. Les quedaba el examen oral.

   _____

6. Os fascinará el pianista.

   _____

7. Les agrada la exposición.

   _____

8. Nos ha caído bien ese profesor.

   _____

9. Le falta un dólar.

   _____

10. Me haría falta una tarjeta de memoria.

    _____

H *Expand each sentence by adding the* **ir a** + infinitive *construction.*

MODELO   Me gusta la película.

_____*Me va a gustar la película.*_____

1. No te conviene meterte (*meddle*) en sus asuntos.

   _____

2. No nos importa el qué dirán (*what others say*).

   _____

3. Me toca a mí hacer la compra.

   _____

4. Les sobra tiempo.

   _____

5. Le desagrada tu actitud.

   _____

6. Os disgustan sus costumbres.

   _____

7. Le interesan esas pinturas.

   _____

8. Te encantan los postres.

   _____

9. Nos urge contactarlos.

   _____

10. Me agrada pasar las vacaciones en Ibiza.

    _____

I **Translation.** *Express the following sentences in Spanish. Use reverse construction verbs.*

1. *Whose turn is it?*

   _____

2. *She likes these perfumes.*

   _____

3. *We were excited about the baseball game.*

   _____

4. *It will be good for them to wait.*

   _____

5. *Would you (Uds.)* be interested in it?

   _____

6. *She is not going to like them.* [Use **caer**.]

   _____

7. *Frankly, I don't care.*

   _____

8. *Would you (tú)* like to go out to eat?

   _____

9. *I would love it.*

   _____

10. *What do you (Ud.) need?*

    _____

11. *I don't need anything.*

    _____

12. *Do you (vosotros)* not have enough money?

    _____

13. *No, we have more than enough.*

    _____

14. *I would find them unpleasant.*

    _____

| BUILDING SENTENCES | **Se le construction for unplanned occurrences** |

The indirect object pronoun can be added to a **se** construction with certain verbs to express *unplanned occurrences*. These constructions focus on the object affected rather than on the person involved.

acabársele a uno *to run out of*
averiársele a uno *to get damaged, break down, fail*
caérsele a uno *to drop*
descomponérsele a uno *to have something break down*
ocurrírsele a uno *to dawn on, get the idea of*
olvidársele a uno *to forget*
perdérsele a uno *to lose*
quebrársele a uno *to break*
quedársele a uno *to leave something behind*
rompérsele a uno *to break*

—Veo que **se te rompieron** los anteojos.　　*"I see that you broke your glasses."*
—Sí, **se me cayeron** en la calle.　　*"Yes, I dropped them in the street."*

—¿Cómo **se les ocurrió** venir ayer?　　*"How did they get the idea to come yesterday?"*

—**Se les había olvidado** que la reunión es mañana.　　*"They had forgotten that the meeting is tomorrow."*

—**Se nos está acabando** la gasolina. Tenemos que comprar.　　*"We're running out of gas. We have to buy some."*
—Ay, **se me quedó** la tarjeta de crédito en casa.　　*"Oh, I left my credit card at home."*

Many other verbs can be used with this construction.

¡Cuidado! **Se te va a subir** la sopa.　　*Careful! Your soup is going to boil over.*
Se nos fue la chica au pair.　　*The au pair left us.*
Se me murió el perro.　　*My dog died.*

The equivalent of the English imperative of these verbs is an indirect command in Spanish.

¡**Que no se te caigan** los platos!　　*Don't drop the dishes!*
¡**Que no se les ocurra** hacer eso!　　*Don't even think about doing that!*

J　*Write sentences that express unplanned occurrences, using the following strings of elements. Use the preterit for all verbs.*

MODELO　　él / rompérsele / el tobillo

　　　　　Se le rompió el tobillo.

1. Ud. / perdérsele / los anteojos

　　_____

2. yo / ocurrírsele / una cosa increíble

　　_____

3. ellos / descomponérsele / el aire acondicionado

　　_____

4. ella / quebrársele / dos dedos

　　_____

5. tú / caérsele / los platos

　　_____

6. nosotros / quedársele en casa / la llave del coche

　　_____

7. Uds. / acabársele / la paciencia

　　_____

8. vosotros / olvidársele / hacer la llamada

_____

9. él / averiársele / los frenos del coche

_____

10. yo / olvidársele / mi clave personal (*PIN*)

_____

11. ellas / perdérsele / la libreta de cheques

_____

12. Ud. / acabársele / el jugo de naranja

_____

K *Translation.* *Express the following sentences in Spanish, using the* **se le** *construction for unplanned occurrences.*

1. *He left his cell phone at the office.*

_____

2. *It hasn't occurred to anyone yet?*

_____

3. *Their computer is breaking down.*

_____

4. *Have you* (tú) *forgotten that her birthday is tomorrow?*

_____

5. *Who left these gloves here?*

_____

6. *How did you* (Ud.) *break your foot?*

_____

7. *I broke it playing soccer.*

_____

8. *We're running out of bread.*

_____

9. *I dropped the vase* (el florero).

_____

10. *Did it break?*

_____

Oral Exercises

Go to www.audiostudyplayer.com to access the recordings for the following oral exercises, which correspond to the 15 chapters in this book. Most exercises contain eight items.

Chapter 1
The Present Tense of Regular Verbs

A *Restate each of the following sentences, changing the subject from* **yo** *to* **nosotros.**

MODELO   Llego el sábado. → Llegamos el sábado.

B *Restate each of the following sentences, changing the subject from* **tú** *to* **Uds.**

MODELO   Vives en el centro. → Viven en el centro.

C *Create sentences from the elements given to tell what these people are doing in the office.*

MODELO   Ud./escribir un informe → Ud. escribe un informe.

D *Respond to each of the following questions, telling how long these people have been doing things. Each question begins with* **¿Cuánto tiempo hace que...?** *Use* **hace** + *time expression* + **que** + *verb in the present tense in your response. The cue provides the time expression.*

MODELO   ¿Cuánto tiempo hace que Uds. estudian español?/dos años
→ Hace dos años que estudiamos español.

E *Create sentences using the subject* + *verb* + *direct object construction to tell what these people are doing.*

MODELO   yo/terminar el trabajo → Yo termino el trabajo.

F *Say that these people never do the things they are said to do. Use the negative word* **nunca** *in your responses.*

MODELO   Uds. siempre discuten. → ¡Qué va! Nunca discutimos.

G *When asked if anyone is doing something, respond that no one is doing anything. Use the negative words* **nadie** *and* **nada** *in your responses. Their affirmative counterparts* **alguien** *and* **algo** *are used in the questions.*

MODELO   ¿Alguien toma algo? → No, nadie toma nada.

Chapter 2
Stem-Changing Verbs; Special Verbs Ending in **-iar** and **-uar**

 Restate each of the following sentences, changing the subject from **nosotros** *to* **yo.**

MODELO   Queremos una computadora nueva. → Quiero una computadora nueva.

 Restate each of the following sentences, changing the subject from **Uds.** *to* **nosotros.**

MODELO   No pierden el tren. → No perdemos el tren.

 Add the verb in the cue to the original sentence to create a sentence with a verb + infinitive construction.

MODELO   Alejandro trabaja para esta empresa./pensar
              → Alejandro piensa trabajar para esta empresa.

 Respond to each of the following questions, saying that you think these people want to do the things asked about. Add the correct form of the verb **querer** *in your response.*

MODELO   ¿Pilar vuelve a Madrid? → No sé, pero creo que quiere volver a Madrid.

 Respond in the negative to each of the following questions. Use the personal **a** *before* **nadie** *in your response.*

MODELO   ¿A quién llamas? → No llamo a nadie.

 Use the elements given to create sentences with a subject, a verb, and a direct object noun. Add the personal **a** *where necessary.*

MODELOS   ellos/ver/la película → Ellos ven la película.
                 ellos/ver/el programador → Ellos ven al programador.

 What is Isabel doing today? Use the elements given to create sentences with a verb and a direct object noun. Add the personal **a** *where necessary.*

MODELO   comenzar/su proyecto → Comienza su proyecto.

Chapter 3
Irregular Verbs (Part I)

A *Restate each of the following sentences, changing the subject from* **nosotros** *to* **yo.**

MODELO   Hacemos un viaje de negocios. → Hago un viaje de negocios.

B *Restate each of the following sentences, changing the subject based on the cue.*

MODELO   Sales a las nueve y media./yo → Salgo a las nueve y media.

C *Create sentences about these people, using expressions with* **tener.**

MODELO   Juana/frío → Juana tiene frío.

D Restate each of the following sentences as a yes/no question. Change the intonation of the sentence from the falling intonation used at the end of a statement to the rising intonation used at the end of a yes/no question.

MODELO   Todavía no resuelven el problema. → ¿Todavía no resuelven el problema?

E Restate each of the following sentences, adding the tag in the cue to turn it into a question.

MODELO   Hace muy buen tiempo. / ¿no? → Hace muy buen tiempo, ¿no?

F State the question that would elicit each of the following statements. Remember that in Spanish, the intonation of information questions is the same as the intonation of statements: Intonation falls at the end of both types of sentences.

MODELO   Hoy es el veintisiete de enero. → ¿Cuál es la fecha de hoy?

Chapter 4
Irregular Verbs (Part II)

A Where are these people going today? Use the verb **ir** with the elements given in your responses.

MODELO   yo / el museo de arte → Yo voy al museo de arte.

B Restate the following sentences, using the **ir a** + infinitive construction to tell what people are going to do.

MODELO   Ud. vuelve al campo. → Ud. va a volver al campo.

C Create sentences from the elements given to say what people know. Select either **saber** or **conocer** as the verb.

MODELO   Consuelo / francés → Consuelo sabe francés.

D Restate each of the following sentences, adding the verb in the cue plus its connector to create a sentence with a verb + connector + infinitive construction. Choose among these connectors: **a**, **de**, **en**, **con**, and **que**.

MODELO   Cocinamos platos exóticos. / aprender
         → Aprendemos a cocinar platos exóticos.

E The Herrera sisters are young designers who want to open a boutique. Expand the original sentence with the verb in the cue to tell what they are going to do. Add connectors as needed. You will create either a verb + infinitive or a verb + connector + infinitive construction.

MODELO   Carmen y Paloma diseñan ropa de alta costura. / querer
         → Carmen y Paloma quieren diseñar ropa de alta costura.

F When your friend tells you what he does to lead a balanced and happy life, you agree that these are good ideas. Restate his ideas, using the **hay que** + infinitive construction.

MODELO   Hago ejercicio. → Ah sí, hay que hacer ejercicio.

G *Use the elements given to create sentences with* **hay** *or* **hay que**.

MODELOS   hay / sacar billetes en la taquilla → Hay que sacar billetes en la taquilla.

hay / billetes en la taquilla → Hay billetes en la taquilla.

Chapter 5
Ser and Estar

A *Respond to each of the following questions, saying that these people are not from the countries your friend thinks they are from. Use the verb* **ser** *and the cue in your responses.*

MODELO   Uds. son de México, ¿no? / Panamá

No, somos de Panamá.

B *Create sentences that tell the origin of these people. Use the verb* **ser** *and the cue in your responses.*

MODELO   yo / inglés → Yo soy de origen inglés.

C *Create sentences from the elements given, selecting either* **ser** *or* **estar** *as the verb, based on the cue. Remember to make adjective agreements as needed.*

MODELOS   Daniel y Carlota / simpático → Daniel y Carlota son simpáticos.

Paula y Alano / en el cibercafé → Paula y Alano están en el cibercafé.

D *Create sentences telling where these people are spending their vacation. Use the verb* **estar** *and the cue in your responses.*

MODELO   ellos / París → Ellos están en París.

E *Restate each of the following sentences as a yes/no question. All sentences consist of a subject, the verb* **ser** *or* **estar**, *and an adjective. Note that unlike English, Spanish places the subject at the end of the sentence.*

MODELO   Esa tienda por departamentos está abierta.

→ ¿Está abierta esa tienda por departamentos?

F *Answer each of the following questions, changing the direct object noun to a pronoun in your response.*

MODELO   ¿Uds. envuelven los paquetes? → Sí, los envolvemos.

G *Restate each of the following sentences, adding either the verb or the verb + connector in the cue. You will use either a verb + infinitive or a verb + connector + infinitive construction. Change the direct object noun to a pronoun, and state the expanded sentence in two ways.*

MODELO   Compran el coche. / ir a → Van a comprarlo. / Lo van a comprar.

Chapter 6
The Preterit

A *Restate each of the following sentences, changing the verb from the present tense to the preterit.*

MODELO   Comemos arroz con pollo. → Comimos arroz con pollo.

B *Answer each of the following questions, saying that people already did the things asked about. Use the preterit in your response. Change direct object nouns to pronouns.*

MODELO   ¿Mario va a conseguir los billetes? → Ya los consiguió.

C *Restate each of the following sentences, changing the verb from present tense to preterit.*

MODELO   Estoy en el cibercafé. → Estuve en el cibercafé.

D *Replace the indirect object pronoun in each of the following sentences with the cue.*

MODELO   Mateo y Emilia le enseñaron el centro histórico. / a ellos
              → Mateo y Emilia les enseñaron el centro histórico.

E *Expand each of the following sentences with the indirect object noun in the cue and its corresponding pronoun.*

MODELO   Ud. vendió su casa. / sus vecinos → Ud. les vendió su casa a sus vecinos.

F *Restate each of the following sentences, replacing the indirect object noun with the corresponding indirect object pronoun.*

MODELO   Ella dio los regalos a sus hijos. → Ella les dio los regalos.

Chapter 7
The Imperfect; The Imperfect vs. the Preterit

A *Restate each of the following sentences, changing the verb from present tense to imperfect.*

MODELO   Tú me esperas en la estación de tren.
              → Tú me esperabas en la estación de tren.

B *Restate each of the following sentences, replacing the weather or time expression in the first clause with the weather or time expression in the cue. Keep verbs in the first clause in the imperfect.*

MODELO   Hacía frío cuando yo salí. / nevar → Nevaba cuando yo salí.

C *Ask questions about how long these people had been doing things. Use ¿**Cuánto tiempo hacía que** + the verb in the imperfect.*

MODELO   Ud. / trabajar en esa empresa multinacional
              → ¿Cuánto tiempo hacía que Ud. trabajaba en esa empresa multinacional?

D *Use the cue to answer each of the following questions about who did something or for whom something was done. Each response will have double object pronouns.*

MODELO   ¿Quién te mandó el correo electrónico? / Bernardo → Me lo mandó Bernardo.

E *Answer each of the following questions in the preterit. Change the direct object noun to a pronoun, and make all necessary changes. Each response will have double object pronouns.*

MODELO   ¿Él te va a prestar las maletas? → Ya me las prestó.

F *Restate each of the following sentences to find out what people said. To show reported speech in the past, replace the present tense of **decir** in the first clause with the preterit, and replace the present tense verb in the second clause with the imperfect.*

MODELO   Laura dice que sale con Diego. → Laura dijo que salía con Diego.

G *What we were doing when he arrived. Restate each of the following sentences, replacing the verbal phrase in the second clause with the verbal phrase in the cue. Keep verbs in the second clause in the imperfect.*

MODELO   Cuando él llegó, jugábamos al tenis. / darle de comer al perro
→ Cuando él llegó, le dábamos de comer al perro.

Chapter 8
The Past Participle; The Present Perfect; The Pluperfect

A *Restate each of the following sentences in the present perfect to tell what has or has not happened.*

MODELO   Juliana celebra su cumpleaños. → Juliana ha celebrado su cumpleaños.

B *Answer each of the following questions, saying that people have done these things already. Use the present perfect in your response. Change direct object nouns to pronouns, and make all necessary changes.*

MODELO   ¿Vas a llamar a tus papás? → Ya los he llamado.

C *Restate each of the following sentences, saying that these things had or had not happened. Use the pluperfect (past perfect) in your response.*

MODELO   Tomé un curso a distancia. → Había tomado un curso a distancia.

D *Create phrases with the noun given and an adjective derived from the past participle of the verb in the cue.*

MODELO   las casas / construir → las casas construidas

E *The following questions are in the present perfect. Answer each one, using the past participle as an adjective.*

MODELO   ¿Han alquilado la casa? → Sí, la casa está alquilada.

F *What had happened when I returned from vacation. Restate each of the following sentences, replacing the elements in the second clause with the cue. Use the past perfect (pluperfect) in the main clause.*

MODELO   Cuando yo volví de las vacaciones / poco / cambiar
→ Cuando yo volví de las vacaciones, poco había cambiado.

Chapter 9
The Imperative

A *Answer each of the following questions with an affirmative* **Ud.** *command.*

MODELO   ¿Debo regresar ahora mismo? → Sí, regrese ahora mismo.

B *Use affirmative* **Uds.** *commands to tell people what office tasks they must do. Change direct object nouns to pronouns, and make all necessary changes.*

MODELO   ¿Hay que instalar el programa? → Sí, instálenlo.

C *Your friend asks you if she should do certain things. Use an affirmative* **tú** *command to tell her to do them.*

MODELO   ¿Debo tomar un curso en línea? → Claro. Toma un curso en línea.

D *Use a negative* **tú** *command to tell your friend he shouldn't do the things he says he's going to do.*

MODELO   Voy a vender el carro. → No vendas el carro.

E *Use a negative* **nosotros** *command to tell your friend you do not want to do the things she suggests. Change direct object nouns to pronouns, and make all necessary changes.*

MODELO   ¿Quieres ver el blog de la moda? → No, no lo veamos.

F *Use the* **vamos a** + *infinitive construction to tell your friend you would be happy to do the things he suggests. Change direct object nouns to pronouns, and make all necessary changes.*

MODELO   ¿Por qué no montamos en bicicleta?
              → Muy bien. Vamos a montar en bicicleta.

G *Answer each of the following questions with an affirmative or negative* **Ud.** *command. After each question, you will hear the cue:* **sí** *or* **no.** *Change direct object nouns to pronouns, and make all necessary changes.*

MODELOS   ¿Tengo que escribirle el correo electrónico a Miguel? / sí → Sí, escríbaselo.
              ¿Tengo que escribirle el correo electrónico a Miguel? / no
                → No, no se lo escriba.

Chapter 10
The Future and the Conditional;
The Future Perfect and the Conditional Perfect

A *Restate each of the following sentences, changing the infinitive of the* **ir a** + *infinitive construction to a future tense verb.*

MODELO   Vamos a poner fin al problema. → Pondremos fin al problema.

B *Restate each of the following sentences, changing the verb from the present tense to the future.*

MODELO   Saludamos a nuestros amigos. → Saludaremos a nuestros amigos.

C *Create sentences from the elements given to express things that will have happened by a certain time. Use the future perfect in your responses.*

MODELO   Uds. / salir / antes de las ocho → Uds. habrán salido antes de las ocho.

D *Create sentences that tell what people would do to maintain good health. Use the conditional in your responses.*

MODELO   él / comer comida sana → Él comería comida sana.

E *Restate each of the following sentences to find out what people said or wrote would happen. Change the verb in the main clause to the preterit, and change the verb in the subordinate clause to the conditional.*

MODELO   Dicen que hará mal tiempo. → Dijeron que haría mal tiempo.

F *Use the conditional perfect to say that people would not have done the following things.*

MODELO   Ud. les contó el secreto. / yo → Yo no les habría contado el secreto.

G *Restate each of the following sentences to express probability or conjecture about the present. Remove the words or phrases that indicate probability or conjecture, and express the verb in the future tense.*

MODELO   Supongo que ellos están contentos. → Ellos estarán contentos.

Chapter 11
The Subjunctive (Part I): The Present Subjunctive

A *Jaime hopes that certain things will happen. To find out what they are, restate each of the following sentences, adding **Espero que** as a new main clause. Change the verb in the dependent clause from present indicative to present subjunctive.*

MODELO   Isabel gana una beca. → Espero que Isabel gane una beca.

B *Restate each of the following sentences, using the phrase in the cue to add a new main clause. Change the verb in the dependent clause from present indicative to present subjunctive.*

MODELO   Uds. vienen este fin de semana. / me alegro de
         → Me alegro de que Uds. vengan este fin de semana.

C *Restate each of the following sentences, using the phrase in the cue to add a new main clause. Choose between the present indicative and the present subjunctive for the verb in the dependent clause.*

MODELO   Ellos trabajan los miércoles. / es necesario
         → Es necesario que ellos trabajen los miércoles.

D *Create sentences from the elements given. The main verb will be followed either by an infinitive or by a dependent clause. Use the present subjunctive as required.*

MODELOS   Yo quiero / aprender español → Yo quiero aprender español.
          Yo quiero / ellos / aprender español → Yo quiero que ellos aprendan español.

E *Use the conjunction in the cue to combine each pair of sentences into a single sentence.*

MODELO Llegó al parque. Empezó a trotar./y → Llegó al parque y empezó a trotar.

F *Use the conjunction in the cue to combine each pair of sentences into a single sentence. The subordinate clause will be in the present subjunctive.*

MODELO Mandarán a Daniel a Costa Rica. Él conoce el mercado cafetero./a fin de que
→ Mandarán a Daniel a Costa Rica a fin de que él conozca el mercado cafetero.

Chapter 12
The Subjunctive (Part II): The Present Perfect Subjunctive; The Imperfect Subjunctive; The Pluperfect Subjunctive

A *Restate each of the following sentences, telling how these people react to something that happened in the past. Use the cue in the main clause, and change the verb in the dependent clause to the present perfect subjunctive.*

MODELO Realizaste tu sueño./me alegro de
→ Me alegro de que hayas realizado tu sueño.

B *Restate each of the following sentences, telling how these people reacted to things that happened in the past. Use the cue as the main clause, and change the verb in the dependent clause to the imperfect subjunctive.*

MODELO Claudia y Juan nos invitaron a su fiesta./queríamos
→ Queríamos que Claudia y Juan nos invitaran a su fiesta.

C *The people mentioned are not professionals in their respective fields, but they talk as if they were. Use* **como si fuera** *to create a statement to that effect.*

MODELO Consuelo no es profesora. → Pero habla como si fuera profesora.

D *Restate each of the following sentences, using the cue as the main clause and the pluperfect subjunctive in the dependent clause.*

MODELO El avión había aterrizado./fue probable
→ Fue probable que el avión hubiera aterrizado.

E *Tell what will happen if Felipe arrives late. Restate each of the following sentences, replacing the main clause with the cue. You will use the future tense in the main clause.*

MODELO Si Felipe llega tarde/perder el avión → Si Felipe llega tarde, perderá el avión.

F *Tell what you would do if you had a fortune. Restate each of the following sentences, replacing the main clause with the cue. You will use the conditional tense in the main clause.*

MODELO Si yo tuviera una fortuna/ya no trabajar
→ Si yo tuviera una fortuna, ya no trabajaría.

G *Restate each of the following sentences to tell how some people would have reacted if they had heard the news. Change the subject according to the cue. Use the past perfect subjunctive in the **si**-clause, and use the conditional perfect in the main clause.*

MODELO   Si él hubiera oído la noticia, se habría alegrado. / yo
           → Si yo hubiera oído la noticia, me habría alegrado.

Chapter 13
Reflexive Verbs

A *Create sentences to tell when these people are doing their daily routine. Use reflexive verbs in your responses.*

MODELO   Manuel / levantarse a las siete → Manuel se levanta a las siete.

B *Expand each of the following sentences to state what people are going to do. Use the **ir a** + infinitive construction in your response.*

MODELO   Eduardo se queda en la ciudad. → Eduardo va a quedarse en la ciudad.

C *Create sentences from the elements given, using the reflexive to show reciprocal meaning.*

MODELO   Gabriela y Sofía / conocer muy bien → Gabriela y Sofía se conocen muy bien.

D *Answer each of the following questions, changing the direct object noun to a pronoun. Make all necessary changes in your response.*

MODELO   ¿Te lavaste la cabeza? → Sí, me la lavé.

E *Answer each of the following questions, using an affirmative **Ud.** or **Uds.** command in your response. Change direct object nouns to pronouns, and make all necessary changes.*

MODELOS   ¿Me pongo el abrigo? → Sí, póngaselo.
            ¿Nos ponemos el abrigo? → Sí, pónganselo.

F *Tell your friend not to do the things she asks you about. Use the negative **tú** command in your responses. Change direct object nouns to pronouns, and make all necessary changes.*

MODELO   ¿Debo cortarme el pelo? → No, no te lo cortes.

G *You agree with your friend's suggestions about the party you're attending. To tell him so, restate the following **nosotros** commands, using the **vamos a** + infinitive construction as **nosotros** command forms.*

MODELO   Vamos a divertirnos en la fiesta. → Ah sí, divirtámonos en la fiesta.

Chapter 14
The Present Participle; The Progressive Tenses

A *Respond to each of the following questions, telling how people spent the afternoon. Use the verb in the cue as a gerund in your response.*

MODELO   ¿Cómo pasaste la tarde? / leer un libro de historia
           → Pasé la tarde leyendo un libro de historia.

B *Answer each of the following questions in the affirmative, telling what people are doing right now. Use the present progressive in your response. Change direct object nouns to pronouns, and make all necessary changes.*

MODELO ¿Ud. se abrocha el cinturón de seguridad?
→ Sí, me lo estoy abrochando ahora mismo.

C *Your friend asks if people stopped doing certain things. You reply "no," they kept on doing them. Use the imperfect progressive with* **seguir** *in your responses. Change direct object nouns to pronouns, and make all necessary changes.*

MODELO ¿Sara dejó de descargar las canciones? → No, seguía descargándolas.

D *Respond to each of the following questions, using the* **llevar** + -**ndo** *construction and the time cue in your response. Note that the questions are asked using* **¿Cuánto tiempo hace que** + *verb in the present tense. (See Chapter 1, Exercise D.) Change direct object nouns to pronouns, and make all necessary changes.*

MODELO ¿Cuánto tiempo hace que ellos se reúnen? / dos horas
→ Llevan dos horas reuniéndose.

E *Create sentences from the elements given to tell what people were doing at the office this morning. Use the imperfect progressive in your responses.*

MODELO David y yo / trabajar en equipo
→ David y yo estábamos trabajando en equipo.

F *Restate each of the following sentences, changing the verb from the future tense to the future progressive. Change direct object nouns to pronouns, and make all necessary changes.*

MODELO Uds. harán ecoturismo. → Uds. estarán haciéndolo.

G *Respond in the negative to each of the following yes/no questions about dining out. Use the cue to add the correct information about the subject. Note that the word order pattern is object–verb–subject. Change direct object nouns to pronouns.*

MODELO ¿Rafael invitó a los amigos a cenar? / Jaime → No, los invitó a cenar Jaime.

Chapter 15
Passive Constructions; Reverse Construction Verbs

A *Restate each of the following sentences, changing from active to passive voice.*

MODELO Este arquitecto construyó el centro comercial.
→ El centro comercial fue construido por este arquitecto.

B *Create a sentence in the preterit from the elements given, using the* **se** *construction. The verb will be in the third-person singular or third-person plural.*

MODELO abrir / la zapatería → Se abrió la zapatería.

C *Restate each of the following sentences, using the* **se** *construction in the present tense.*

MODELO Hablamos inglés. → Se habla inglés.

D *Restate each of the following sentences, changing the subject from singular to plural.*

MODELO   Me gustó el concierto. → Me gustaron los conciertos.

E *Tell what these people like and dislike by answering each of the following questions. Use a reverse construction verb and the cue in your response.*

MODELO   ¿Qué le gusta a Rafael? / la alta tecnología → Le gusta la alta tecnología.

F *Create sentences in the preterit from the elements given, expressing an unplanned occurrence.*

MODELO   Uds. / / perdérsele el equipaje en el aeropuerto
              → Se les perdió el equipaje en el aeropuerto.

G *Restate each of the following sentences, using* **tocar** *as a reverse construction verb to tell who is doing what to prepare for the dinner party.*

MODELO   Tú preparas las tapas. → Te toca a ti preparar las tapas.

Answer Key

Chapter 1
The Present Tense of Regular Verbs

A 1. mando 2. estudia 3. tomamos 4. entran 5. escuchas 6. habláis 7. toca
8. llevo 9. navegan 10. regresan 11. alquila 12. miramos 13. llegan 14. trabaja
15. guardas 16. viajamos 17. enseña 18. estacionan 19. esperáis 20. charlan
21. paso 22. cambia 23. entrega 24. doblas 25. funciona 26. dura
27. desayunamos 28. necesita

B 1. a. Nosotros buscamos las llaves. b. Él busca su teléfono móvil. c. Uds. buscan la tienda
de ropa. 2. a. Yo compro unos libros de texto. b. Vosotros compráis un condominio.
c. Ud. compra zapatos de tenis. 3. a. Tú estudias informática. b. Ella estudia
programación. c. Tú y yo estudiamos mercadeo. 4. a. Uds. graban una película.
b. Ellas graban un programa de televisión. c. Él graba una canción francesa.
5. a. Ud. habla inglés. b. Vosotras habláis italiano. c. Ellos hablan chino. 6. a. Tú llevas
una maleta. b. Yo llevo mi portafolio. c. Uds. llevan el equipaje.

C 1. Alquiláis un coche. 2. Escuchan las noticias. 3. Tomáis café en Starbucks.
4. Telecargan los documentos. 5. Estacionáis detrás del banco. 6. Cambian de opinión.
7. Averiguan la información. 8. Mandáis el correo electrónico. 9. Pulsan el botón.
10. Llegáis a las siete.

D 1. Crean un sitio Web. 2. Regresan al anochecer. 3. Ganan una beca.
4. Aprovechan la oferta. 5. Arrastran el ratón. 6. Compran jeans. 7. Trabajan en
el centro. 8. Preparan los sándwiches. 9. Llevan una computadora portátil.
10. Desarrollan un plan.

E 1. Acepta 2. Averiguamos 3. Saco 4. Practican 5. firmas 6. preparáis 7. Escucha
8. Descarga 9. Marca 10. Crean 11. Celebra 12. Bailamos 13. Contestas 14. Trotan
15. Llevan

F 1. nosotros/nosotras 2. Uds./ellos/ellas 3. yo 4. Ud./él/ella 5. tú 6. Ud./él/ella
7. vosotros/vosotras 8. Uds./ellos/ellas 9. yo 10. tú 11. Ud./él/ella
12. nosotros/nosotras 13. yo 14. vosotros/vosotras 15. tú

G 1. comen 2. leo 3. asistimos 4. imprime 5. metes 6. discuten 7. vende 8. escribe
9. corréis 10. comparten 11. tose 12. beben 13. vivo 14. aprendemos 15. subís
16. comprenden 17. recibe 18. ocurre 19. creen 20. interrumpen 21. insistes
22. debes 23. transmite 24. resiste 25. abre

H 1. tú 2. Ud./él/ella 3. nosotros/nosotras 4. yo 5. Uds./ellos/ellas 6. vosotros/vosotras
7. nosotros/nosotras 8. Ud./él/ella 9. vosotros/vosotras 10. Uds./ellos/ellas 11. yo
12. tú 13. nosotros/nosotras 14. tú 15. Ud./él/ella

I 1. Discuto la idea con ellos. 2. Viven en esta vecindad. 3. Vende cosas en eBay.
4. Abrimos las maletas. 5. Bebéis vino con la carne. 6. Aprende latín y griego.
7. Suben en la escalera mecánica. 8. No comprendes la teoría. 9. Comparten una pizza.
10. Debe una fuerte cantidad de dinero. 11. Comemos de todo. 12. ¿Asistís al partido
de fútbol? 13. Leemos varias revistas electrónicas. 14. Prende las luces.
15. Escribes un artículo para el periódico.

J 1. sigues 2. escojo 3. exijo 4. construye 5. recojo 6. huyen 7. consiguen
8. corrige 9. cogéis 10. elige 11. destruye 12. protege 13. extinguimos 14. persigue
15. dirige 16. acogemos 17. surgen 18. distingo 19. diluyes 20. urge

K 1. ¿Cuánto tiempo hace que Carolina navega en la Red? Hace dos horas que navega
en la Red. Navega en la Red hace dos horas. 2. ¿Cuánto tiempo hace que estudias
administración de empresas? Hace un año que estudio administración de empresas.
Estudio administración de empresas hace un año. 3. ¿Cuánto tiempo hace que Uds. viven
en Londres? Hace cuatro años que vivimos en Londres. Vivimos en Londres hace cuatro
años. 4. ¿Cuánto tiempo hace que los Soriano viajan por Europa? Hace seis semanas
que viajan por Europa. Viajan por Europa hace seis semanas. 5. ¿Cuánto tiempo hace
que vosotros asistís a estas conferencias? Hace un par de meses que asistimos a estas
conferencias. Asistimos a estas conferencias hace un par de meses. 6. ¿Cuánto tiempo
hace que Ud. descarga los documentos? Hace media hora que descargo los documentos.
Descargo los documentos hace media hora. 7. ¿Cuánto tiempo hace que discutimos
los trámites? Hace una semana que discutimos los trámites. Discutimos los trámites hace
una semana. 8. ¿Cuánto tiempo hace que exijo la colaboración de todos? Hace varios
días que exige/exiges la colaboración de todos. Exige/exiges la colaboración de todos hace
varios días.

L 1. ¿Trabajas en la oficina mañana? 2. No, paso el día en casa. 3. ¿Asiste al concierto
esta noche? 4. Sí, y antes ceno con unos amigos. 5. ¿Cuánto tiempo hace que construyen
la casa? 6. Hace un año que construimos la casa. / Construimos la casa hace un año.
7. ¿Cuánto tiempo hace que están en los Estados Unidos? / ¿Cuánto tiempo llevan en los
Estados Unidos? / ¿Cuánto tiempo tienen en los Estados Unidos? 8. Hace quince años que
están aquí. / Llevan quince años aquí. / Tienen quince años aquí. 9. ¿Desde cuándo
prosigue (OR sigue con) sus estudios? 10. Curso (OR Tomo clases de) ingeniería desde
enero.

M 1. transitive 2. intransitive 3. transitive 4. transitive 5. transitive 6. intransitive
7. transitive 8. intransitive 9. transitive 10. transitive 11. transitive 12. intransitive
13. transitive 14. transitive 15. intransitive

N 1. Tú cantas afinadamente. 2. Los atletas corren en la carrera. 3. Pablo tose mucho.
4. ¿Uds. viven en las afueras? 5. Yo regreso la semana entrante. 6. El programa funciona
bien. 7. Nosotros subimos al tercer piso. 8. Los habitantes huyen del terremoto.
9. Yo troto por el parque. 10. El gerente trabaja de lunes a viernes. 11. ¿Vosotros llegáis
en tren? 12. Tú viajas por el sudoeste del país. 13. ¿Mercedes y Sofía estornudan por
su alergia? 14. Un conflicto surge entre los socios. 15. Ud. baja por la escalera.
16. Nosotros participamos en el foro de debate. 17. ¿Qué opinan Uds. de la facultad
de educación?

O 1. Roberto y yo ahorramos dinero. 2. Yo rijo la empresa. 3. Los jefes concluyen su conversación. 4. ¿Ud. consigue sus billetes electrónicos? 5. Tú guardas el secreto. 6. Uds. compran una cámara digital. 7. Vosotros imprimís el informe. 8. Beatriz y Alicia comparten la computadora. 9. Ud. lee la página Web. 10. Nosotras creamos unas carpetas. 11. Marco Antonio aprende las fechas de memoria. 12. ¿Vosotros marcáis el número de teléfono? 13. Yo consigo los boletos. 14. Los programadores instalan un programa de gráficas. 15. Tú recibes revistas de informática. 16. El director de la junta interrumpe la reunión.

P 1. Alberto y Daniela esperan un taxi. 2. ¿Ud. asiste al congreso? 3. Tú y yo escuchamos estos discos compactos. 4. La jefa renuncia a su puesto. 5. El ingeniero entra los datos. 6. Vosotras miráis los sitios Web. 7. Uds. salen del hotel. 8. Los jugadores pisan el césped. 9. Rafael y yo jugamos (al) fútbol. 10. Yo entro al / en el centro comercial. 11. Mi hermana sube su ropa al dormitorio. 12. Los vecinos comentan las noticias del barrio. 13. Los turistas visitan los monumentos. 14. ¿Vosotros aprobáis el plan económico? 15. ¿Tú buscas las llaves?

Q 1. Solicito este puesto. 2. Virginia mira su correo electrónico. 3. ¿Aprovechas las rebajas? 4. Asistimos a ese concierto. 5. Entran a/en la librería. 6. Entra datos. 7. Esteban renuncia al proyecto. 8. ¿Qué buscan?

R 1. No, no usamos una calculadora de bolsillo. 2. No, no habla por teléfono celular. 3. No, no echamos las cartas al buzón. 4. No, no prendo el ordenador. 5. No, no compartimos los gastos. 6. No, no transmiten el documental esta noche. 7. No, no corrijo las faltas en el manuscrito. 8. No, no renuncia a su puesto de contable. 9. No, no extinguen el fuego de campamento. 10. No, no influimos en la decisión.

S 1. No, no solicitamos nada. 2. No, no grita nadie. / No, nadie grita. 3. No, no salen a bailar nunca/jamás. / No, nunca/jamás salen a bailar. 4. No, no exijo nada. 5. No, no espero a nadie. 6. No, no lloran nunca/jamás. / No, nunca/jamás lloran. 7. No, no llega puntualmente nunca/jamás. / No, nunca/jamás llega puntualmente. 8. No, no montamos a caballo nunca/jamás. / No, nunca/jamás montamos a caballo. 9. No, no trasnochan nunca/jamás. / No, nunca/jamás trasnochan. 10. No, no llega tarde nunca/jamás. / No, nunca/jamás llega tarde.

T 1. ¿Ya no trasnochas? 2. No reparamos la computadora mucho / muchas veces / a menudo. 3. Jaime todavía no guarda los archivos. 4. Uds. nunca/jamás cenan antes de las ocho. / Uds. no cenan nunca/jamás antes de las ocho. 5. No miran nada. 6. Nadie aprovecha la oportunidad. 7. No pasa (OR ocurre) nada. 8. Yo no escojo (OR elijo) nada. 9. Muchas veces / A menudo navegamos en la Red. 10. A veces / Algunas veces miran (OR ven) los partidos de béisbol en la computadora. 11. Alguien te busca. 12. Ella nunca interrumpe a nadie.

Chapter 2
Stem-Changing Verbs; Special Verbs Ending in -iar and -uar

A 1. quiero 2. pensamos 3. comienza 4. entiendes 5. recomienda 6. pierden
7. encendéis 8. gobierna 9. desciendes 10. empiezo 11. cierran 12. Nieva
13. atravesamos 14. defienden 15. asciende 16. hiela 17. despierta 18. sientan

B 1. vuelven 2. encuentro 3. envolvemos 4. almuerzas 5. devuelve 6. cuesta
7. merendáis 8. demuestra 9. llueve 10. puede 11. probamos 12. recuerdan
13. huele 14. resuelvo 15. vuelan 16. muestra 17. acuestas 18. acordáis

C 1. Uds. juegan (al) béisbol. 2. Yo juego en un equipo de tenis. 3. Los jugadores juegan
limpio. 4. Él juega sucio. 5. Tú juegas (al) baloncesto. 6. Nosotros jugamos (al) fútbol
americano en otoño. 7. Vosotros jugáis (a los) juegos electrónicos. 8. Los campeones
juegan el partido el sábado.

D 1. siento 2. prefieres 3. divierten 4. refiere 5. hierve 6. mentimos 7. convierte
8. advierten

E 1. piden 2. sirve 3. visten 4. despido 5. sigues 6. reímos 7. impedís 8. sonríe
9. repite 10. medimos 11. consigo 12. persiguen

F 1. duermo 2. duermes 3. duermen 4. dormimos 5. duermen 6. duerme
7. duerme 8. duerme

G 1. confiamos 2. envían 3. continúas 4. gradúo 5. varían 6. resfría 7. insinuáis
8. fía 9. evaluamos 10. guía 11. efectúan 12. esquío 13. acentúas 14. vacían
15. actúa 16. espían 17. criáis 18. rocía

H 1. Logramos ahorrar mucho dinero. 2. No pueden averiguar nada. 3. Siento interrumpir
su conversación. 4. Suele llover por aquí en abril. 5. Consigue escribir el informe en
un solo día. 6. Hacen construir unos rascacielos. 7. ¿Teméis manejar en la autopista?
8. Procuras volver lo antes posible. 9. Quiero comprar un organizador personal.
10. Espera no perder el tren. 11. Prometen no mentir más. 12. Pienso aprovechar las
rebajas navideñas. 13. ¿Prefieres beber el vino tinto o el blanco? 14. Olvida pedir los
billetes electrónicos. 15. No recuerdan encender el lavaplatos. 16. Prohíben aparcar en
esta zona en hora punta. 17. Decidimos correr en el maratón. 18. Ese carro debe costar
una fortuna. 19. ¿Sabéis crear sitios Web? 20. Escojo enviar el paquete por
el FedEx.

I 1. Quiero navegar por Internet (OR por la Red). 2. Esperamos comenzar el proyecto
la semana que viene. 3. Puede leer su correo electrónico en el cibercafé. 4. ¿Piensan viajar
por avión o por tren? 5. Suelen pasar los fines de semana en Nueva York. 6. No debes
interrumpir la reunión. 7. Prefiere comprar ropa en las tiendas por departamentos.
8. ¿Sabéis descargar/bajar música?

J 1. X 2. A 3. X 4. a 5. al 6. a 7. X 8. A 9. a 10. X 11. a 12. a 13. X
14. a 15. X 16. a 17. a 18. a 19. X 20. a 21. X 22. al

K 1. ¿A quién quieres invitar al baile? 2. Piensan ver al ingeniero. 3. Isabel no ayuda
a nadie. 4. Espero a alguien. 5. La empresa debe contratar programadores. 6. ¿Conocen
a Roberto Murillo? 7. Buscamos a nuestro perro. 8. El restaurante necesita un cocinero.
9. ¿A cuántos jugadores de fútbol conoce? 10. No conozco a ninguno. / No conozco
a ningún jugador de fútbol. 11. Señor, ¿Ud. me busca? 12. No, señorita, no la busco.

Chapter 3
Irregular Verbs (Part I)

A 1. salimos, ponen   2. hace, tenemos   3. cae, hace   4. oyes, oigo   5. tengo, hago
6. vienen, caen   7. oyen, digo, oímos, dices   8. pones, traigo   9. venís, tenemos
10. sale, tiene   11. dicen, hace   12. cae, salgo   13. tiene, ponen   14. ponemos, vale
15. pongo, haces, valgo

B 1. Oigo hablar del nuevo centro comercial.   2. Vienen en taxi.   3. Tiene veintiséis años.
4. Pospongo la reunión un par de días.   5. Traemos dos botellas de vino a la fiesta.
6. ¿Quién dice tal cosa?   7. Salgo para la oficina temprano.   8. En otoño las hojas caen
de los árboles.   9. ¿Sales al cine esta noche?   10. No valgo para esas cosas.   11. Hago clic
al botón.   12. ¿Oye las noticias?

C 1. caer, cae   2. hacer, hago   3. venir, vienes   4. poner, ponen   5. tener, tiene
6. decir, dice   7. oír, oímos   8. salir, salís   9. traer, traigo   10. valer, vale   11. tener, tiene
12. hacer, hace

D 1. conozco   2. tuerce   3. vencen   4. permanecemos   5. introduzco   6. favorece
7. cuezo   8. conduces   9. obedecen   10. amanecéis   11. ofrezco   12. produce
13. agradezco   14. aparece   15. reduzco   16. traduzco   17. ejerce   18. resplandecen
19. reproduzco   20. establece

E 1. ¿Toca la flauta Miriam?   2. ¿Ellos traducen los informes?   3. ¿Hacen la cena Raquel
y Daniel?   4. Uds. oyen música clásica?   5. ¿Vienes en taxi tú?   6. ¿Pongo la mesa yo?
7. ¿Jorge conduce un coche deportivo?   8. ¿Hace una pregunta Ud.?   9. ¿Traemos la torta
Julia y yo?   10. ¿El cumpleaños de Miguel cae en viernes?

F 1. Miguel busca un sitio para aparcar, ¿no es cierto?   2. Uds. hacen una excursión el
domingo, ¿no?   3. Tú no conoces nuestro barrio, ¿verdad?   4. Pilar tiene confianza en
sí misma, ¿no es verdad?   5. Aquellos terrenos pertenecen a tu familia, ¿no?   6. Yo no
necesito pagar con contante, ¿verdad?   7. Nosotros debemos digitalizar los documentos,
¿no es cierto?   8. Ud. no consigue convencerlo, ¿verdad?

G 1. ¿Dónde / En qué ciudad viven?   2. ¿Cuántos hijos tiene(s)?   3. ¿Cuál es la capital de
Puerto Rico?   4. ¿Adónde van?   5. ¿Qué/Cuál libro lee(s)?   6. ¿Qué es la ofimática?
7. ¿A quién conocen/conocéis?   8. ¿Cómo salen las cosas?   9. ¿Para dónde salen?
10. ¿Por dónde camina?   11. ¿Qué es el comercio electrónico?   12. ¿Cuánto cuesta esta
cámara digital?   13. ¿Quiénes llegan?   14. ¿De quién son las tarjetas de memoria?
15. ¿A qué hora vuelve(s)?   16. ¿Cuál es la fecha de hoy?   17. ¿Con quién quiere Nicolás
bailar?   18. ¿Por qué no van/vais a la playa?   19. ¿Dónde / En qué avenida está el cibercafé?
20. ¿Cómo expresan sus ideas?   21. ¿Qué estudia Juan Ramón?   22. ¿Cuántas tarjetas
telefónicas compran?

H 1. ¿Cuándo / ¿Qué día tiene lugar la reunión?   2. ¿Qué necesitas comprar?   3. ¿Cuál marca
prefieres?   4. ¿Adónde vas esta noche?   5. ¿Qué estudia Elena?   6. ¿Con quién vas a la
fiesta?   7. ¿Trabajas el viernes?   8. ¿Haces ejercicio ahora?   9. ¿Mañana salimos de paseo?
10. ¿Conduces tú?   11. ¿A qué hora debemos ir?   12. ¿Vamos a estar de vuelta para las seis?

I 1. ¿De dónde vienen?   2. ¿Cuál es la capital de España?   3. ¿Con quién haces planes?
4. ¿En qué mes salen de viaje?   5. ¿Qué tiempo hace?   6. ¿Hace sol?   7. ¿Vale la pena?
8. ¿Por qué tiene tanta prisa?   9. ¿Qué es el telemercadeo?   10. ¿Hago clic / Cliqueo en
el enlace?

Chapter 4
Irregular Verbs (Part II)

A 1. va, ir   2. vemos, ver   3. doy, dar   4. cabe, caber   5. saben, saber   6. voy, ir
7. sabe, saber   8. quepo, caber   9. ve, ver   10. da, dar   11. Dan, dar   12. veo, ver
13. dais, dar   14. vas, ir   15. veis, ver   16. sé, saber   17. dais, dar   18. vais, ir
19. sabemos, saber   20. ves, ver   21. vamos, ir   22. Caben, caber

B 1. conoce, sé   2. conoces, conozco   3. sabe, sé   4. conoces, conozco, sé
5. conocen, conocemos   6. sabéis, conocemos   7. sabe, sabe   8. saben, saben

C 1. Hay una función el sábado a las dos.   2. Hay que hacer clic en el icono.   3. Hay que ser
un buen ciudadano.   4. No hay necesidad de quedarse.   5. Hay conferencias en la feria
del libro.   6. Hay una megatienda tecnológica en esta carretera.   7. Hay que pasar por
la aduana.   8. ¿Hay alguna dificultad en realizar el proyecto?   9. Hay que invertir en varias
industrias.   10. Hay que entrevistar a los candidatos.

D 1. de   2. con   3. que   4. a   5. en   6. a   7. en   8. a   9. con   10. de   11. que   12. de
13. a   14. a   15. en   16. a   17. en   18. en   19. por/en   20. de   21. por   22. de

E 1. X   2. en   3. X   4. a   5. en   6. X   7. de   8. X   9. a   10. X   11. X   12. con   13. por
14. en   15. de   16. a   17. X   18. en   19. de   20. a

F 1. Hay un teléfono celular en la mesa.   2. Hay que saber inglés en el mercado global.
3. Acaban de salir a cenar.   4. Sergio vuelve a llamar.   5. ¿Ud. empieza/comienza a escribir
el informe?   6. No conozco al nuevo programador.   7. ¿Saben su número de teléfono?
8. Sé descargar (OR bajar) los ficheros.   9. Quedamos/Consentimos en ir en carro.
10. Ana cuenta con ver a Federico en la fiesta.   11. Te esfuerzas por/en triunfar en la vida.
12. Me alegro de verlos.

Chapter 5
Ser and Estar

A 1. es   2. son   3. soy   4. son   5. somos   6. es   7. eres   8. es   9. sois   10. son

B 1. Yo soy de los Estados Unidos. Soy de origen inglés.   2. Matías es de Polonia. Es de origen
francés.   3. Tú eres de España. Eres de origen italiano.   4. Nosotros somos de Taiwán.
Somos de origen chino.   5. Ud. es de la India. Es de origen hindú.   6. Jacobo y Sara son
de Israel. Son de origen ruso.   7. Uds. son de Vietnám. Son de origen tailandés.
8. Vosotros sois de Australia. Sois de origen coreano.   9. María Luisa es de Chile. Es de
origen alemán.   10. Los Madero son de Francia. Son de origen kosovano.

C 1. estás   2. está   3. están   4. estoy   5. están   6. estamos   7. está   8. están   9. estáis
10. está

D 1. Los grandes almacenes están a la vuelta de la esquina.   2. El club de jazz está por esta
avenida.   3. El parqueo está detrás del teatro.   4. Los hoteles más lujosos están en frente
del jardín público.   5. La piscina del condominio de tiempo compartido está en el patio.
6. La estación de tren está en la zona oeste de la ciudad.   7. Los sillones están delante
de la ventana.   8. Los dormitorios están en el segundo piso.   9. La librería técnica está
a dos cuadras de aquí.   10. Los monumentos históricos están en la ciudad vieja.
11. La farmacia está al lado de la pizzería.   12. Los centros comerciales están en las afueras.

E　1. es　2. estamos　3. es　4. son　5. están　6. es　7. está　8. son　9. estoy　10. estáis
11. somos　12. soy　13. estás　14. sois　15. eres　16. está　17. somos　18. está　19. Son
20. ser　21. son　22. es　23. son　24. estar　25. estás　26. están

F　1. Yo soy ingeniero genético. ¿Cuál es tu/su profesión?　2. Son las siete y media de la
mañana. ¿Qué hora es?　3. El Cine Mediaplex está al lado de un bar. ¿Dónde está el Cine
Mediaplex?　4. Los mensajes electrónicos son para Eva. ¿Para quién son los mensajes
electrónicos?　5. Los aficionados de béisbol están entusiasmados y nerviosos. ¿Cómo están
los aficionados de béisbol?　6. Hoy es el veintitrés de junio. ¿Cuál es la fecha de hoy?
7. Estas llaves de coche son de Marcelo. ¿De quién son estas llaves de coche?　8. El euro está
a noventa centavos de dólar. ¿A cuánto está el euro?　9. Los gemelos de Hugo y Silvia son
consentidos y malcriados. ¿Cómo son los gemelos de Hugo y Silvia?　10. Nosotros somos
de Canadá. ¿De dónde son Uds.? (OR ¿Cuál es su nacionalidad?)

G　1. El coche está descompuesto. ¿Está descompuesto el coche?　2. Su ropa es elegante.
¿Es elegante su ropa?　3. Estos platos de comida fusión están ricos. ¿Están ricos estos platos
de comida fusión?　4. Las clases de finanzas son fáciles. ¿Son fáciles las clases de finanzas?
5. Los analistas son superinteligentes. ¿Son superinteligentes los analistas?　6. Su nuevo
abrigo es azul marino. ¿Es azul marino su nuevo abrigo?　7. El museo de arte está abierto.
¿Está abierto el museo de arte?　8. Los meseros están ocupados. ¿Están ocupados los
meseros?　9. La chica es simpática. ¿Es simpática la chica?　10. Las tiendas están cerradas.
¿Están cerradas las tiendas?　11. Aquellos hoteles son lujosos. ¿Son lujosos aquellos hoteles?
12. Los directores están reunidos. ¿Están reunidos los directores?　13. Su buzón de correo
electrónico está lleno. ¿Está lleno su buzón de correo electrónico?

H　1. Esteban es programador.　2. Están de vacaciones en este momento.　3. Son las nueve
y cuarto (OR quince).　4. El estreno de la película va a ser en Nueva York.　5. Alicia está
preocupada y cansada.　6. El programa es aburrido y los televidentes están aburridos.
7. Lo más interesante de la exposición (OR la exhibición) son los cuadros.　8. Julia es/está
casada con Miguel. Su hermana es/está divorciada.　9. ¿Están rotas las ventanas?
10. ¿Cómo son tus vecinos?　11. ¿Cómo están Uds.?　12. Son de origen inglés.
13. Los duraznos están verdes todavía.　14. Todas estas camisetas son de algodón.
15. Soy del sudoeste.

I　1. Sí, los uso.　2. Sí, la hago.　3. Sí, los toma.　4. Sí, las reparan.　5. Sí, las leen.
6. Sí, los entramos.　7. Sí, lo conocemos.　8. Sí, la aprovecho.　9. Sí, lo busca.
10. Sí, la felicitan.　11. Sí, las espero.　12. Sí, lo traemos.　13. Sí, los imprimen.
14. Sí, los oigo.　15. Sí, la conduzco.

J　1. Quiero comprarlo. Lo quiero comprar.　2. ¿Acabas de grabarla? ¿La acabas de grabar?
3. Vamos a analizarlos. Los vamos a analizar.　4. Ud. debe conocerla. Ud. la debe conocer.
5. ¿Comienzas a comprenderlas? ¿Las comienzas a comprender?　6. Los aficionados
piensan verlo. Los aficionados lo piensan ver.　7. Los usuarios no saben utilizarlas.
Los usuarios no las saben utilizar.　8. Ramón corre a buscarlos. Ramón los corre a buscar.
9. Aprendo a tocarlo. Lo aprendo a tocar.　10. Tratamos de ganarla. La tratamos de ganar.

K　1. ¿Pides el plato de carne como de costumbre?　2. Sí, si lo encuentro en la carta.
3. ¿Vas a esperarme? / ¿Me vas a esperar?　4. Sí, te veo después de la conferencia.
5. ¿Uds. quieren oír estas canciones?　6. No, acabamos de oírlas. / No, las acabamos
de oír.　7. ¿Daniela es la mejor bailarina?　8. Sí, lo es.　9. ¿Adónde lleva a los consultores
(OR asesores)?　10. Los llevo a conocer a la jefa.　11. Veo a Mauricio allí. ¿Lo ves?
12. A Laura la veo pero a Mauricio, no.

Chapter 6
The Preterit

A 1. Ud./él/ella, vender   2. yo, celebrar   3. nosotros/nosotras, imprimir   4. Uds./ellos/ellas, aprender   5. Ud./él/ella, patinar   6. vosotros/vosotras, vivir   7. nosotros/nosotras, correr   8. Uds./ellos/ellas, ahorrar   9. yo, aprender   10. tú, insistir   11. vosotros/vosotras, beber   12. vosotros/vosotras, saludar   13. Ud./él/ella, compartir   14. nosotros/nosotras, disfrutar   15. yo, escribir   16. tú, hablar   17. tú, romper   18. Uds./ellos/ellas, transmitir   19. Ud./él/ella, utilizar   20. yo, añadir

B 1. regresaste   2. asistí   3. corrimos   4. transmitieron   5. aceptó   6. recibisteis   7. aprendiste   8. discutimos   9. tosió   10. viajaron   11. abrí   12. tomaron   13. vendieron   14. insistió   15. alquilé   16. bebieron   17. rompió   18. viviste   19. compró   20. grabamos   21. dibujasteis   22. compartieron   23. comió   24. prendió

C 1. Volvieron   2. Pensé   3. Nos divertimos   4. perdió   5. Encontraste   6. probó   7. pidieron   8. Servisteis   9. Nevó   10. Entendí   11. se vistió   12. Tronó   13. Cerraron   14. llovió   15. riñeron   16. Medisteis   17. se convirtió   18. siguieron   19. sintió   20. se derritió   21. hirvió   22. Prefirieron   23. mintió   24. murió   25. durmieron

D 1. Ya lo marqué.   2. Ya jugué al béisbol.   3. Ya almorcé.   4. Ya navegué en la Red.   5. Ya lo aparqué.   6. Ya la aplacé.   7. Ya los conjugué.   8. Ya la expliqué.   9. Ya lo realicé.   10. Ya la entregué.   11. Ya adelgacé.   12. Ya lo toqué.   13. Ya lo practiqué.   14. Ya las fregué.   15. Ya los actualicé.   16. Ya los organicé.   17. Ya los colgué.   18. Ya lo agregué.   19. Ya la arranqué.   20. Ya las apagué.

E 1. Los muchachos tiñeron las camisetas de rojo.   2. La guerra destruyó el país.   3. Los consumidores no distinguieron entre los dos productos.   4. Ana consiguió la maestría en salud pública.   5. Unas empresas reconstruyeron los barrios bajos.   6. ¿Ud. oyó la noticia?   7. El soldado cayó en la batalla.   8. Los usuarios leyeron las páginas Web.   9. Los habitantes oprimidos huyeron de la dictadura.   10. ¿Por qué riñeron todo el día?   11. Uds. siguieron por la autopista.   12. Los hombres de negocios concluyeron la negociación del contrato.   13. La pastelera hiñó la masa.   14. Todo el mundo creyó sus relatos.

F 1. Ud./él/ella, hacer   2. Uds./ellos/ellas, poder   3. Ud./él/ella, ser AND ir   4. tú, decir   5. yo, estar   6. nosotros/nosotras, saber   7. Uds./ellos/ellas, producir   8. yo, ver   9. vosotros/vosotras, andar   10. yo, venir   11. nosotros/nosotras, querer   12. yo, ser AND ir   13. tú, tener   14. Uds./ellos/ellas, caber   15. Ud./él/ella, traer   16. yo, dar

G 1. Pusiste fin a la discusión.   2. Tuvieron mucho éxito con su compañía.   3. Hice clic al botón.   4. ¿Ud. vino en taxi?   5. No dijimos nada.   6. ¿Cómo lo supiste?   7. No pude entender su actitud.   8. Quisimos salir a comer.   9. Nos trajeron unos regalos.   10. Fui la directora del equipo.   11. Vio a Verónica en el cibercafé.   12. Hubo grandes ofertas en las tiendas.   13. El compositor compuso una canción.   14. Me dieron las gracias.   15. Fui de compras.   16. ¿Por qué intervinieron en el conflicto?   17. Conduje a setenta millas por hora.   18. ¿Qué les atrajo?   19. Tradujimos los documentos al inglés.   20. No cupo nadie más en el aula.

H 1. ¿Quién puso la mesa?   2. La puse yo.   3. ¿Qué hizo ayer?   4. Jugué al tenis y luego di un paseo.   5. ¿Adónde fuiste anoche?   6. Fui al cine.   7. ¿Viste a nuestros amigos?   8. No, llegué tarde y no pude encontrarlos.   9. ¿Sabe la dirección (OR casilla) electrónica de Susana?   10. Sí, la supe la semana pasada.

I 1. Tú les mostraste tu iPod.   2. Uds. me enviaron un e-mail.   3. Carolina le pidió un favor.
4. Yo les expliqué el concepto.   5. Ellos os hicieron una buena comida.   6. Nosotros le
dijimos el motivo.   7. Ud. les leyó las instrucciones.   8. Vosotros nos vendisteis el coche.
9. Carlos Manuel te recordó la fecha de la conferencia.   10. Yo les entregué los papeles.
11. Juan e Isabel le escondieron los regalos de cumpleaños.   12. Tú les ocultaste tu
desilusión.

J 1. Tú les escribiste unos mensajes electrónicos a los directores.   2. Él le contó el
argumento de la película a su amigo.   3. Uds. les enviaron unos paquetes a los soldados.
4. Nosotros le compramos el quitanieves al vecino.   5. La anfitriona les sirvió comida
italiana a los invitados.   6. Ud. le devolvió la calculadora de bolsillo a su amiga.
7. Los jefes le ofrecieron el puesto al programador.   8. Nuestro equipo le ganó el partido
al equipo suyo.   9. La niña les quitó los cubos a los otros niños.   10. Yo le mostré
mis maletas al guardia de seguridad.

K 1. I looked for the programmers everywhere.   2. The Red Sox won the World Series
from the Cardinals.   3. We returned the videos to the store employee.   4. The mother
told her children a fairy tale.   5. Did you send an e-mail to Pedro or did you call him?
6. Martita walked her dog in the park. There a big dog took her dog's toys away from him.

L 1. Le entregué el informe a mi jefe.   2. Mi jefe me solicitó el otro informe.   3. Adrián le
pidió prestado el carro a Jaime.   4. Jaime le dijo que sí.   5. El ladrón le robó al hombre su
reloj de oro.   6. El hombre le arrebató/arrancó el reloj al ladrón.   7. Les trajimos manzanas
y uvas a los niños.   8. Nos dieron las gracias. / Nos agradecieron.   9. ¿Le enseñaste/
mostraste tu nuevo vestido a Claudia?   10. Sí, y les enseñé/mostré el vestido a mis otras
amigas también.   11. La mesera le sirvió al cliente la torta de chocolate.   12. El cliente
le pidió un tenedor a la mesera.

Chapter 7
The Imperfect; The Imperfect vs. the Preterit

A 1. yo/Ud./él/ella   2. Uds./ellos/ellas   3. nosotros/nosotras   4. yo/Ud./él/ella
5. Uds./ellos/ellas   6. nosotros/nosotras   7. vosotros/vosotras   8. tú   9. vosotros/vosotras
10. yo/Ud./él/ella   11. tú   12. tú   13. Uds./ellos/ellas   14. yo/Ud./él/ella
15. nosotros/nosotras   16. Uds./ellos/ellas   17. nosotros/nosotras   18. vosotros/vosotras

B 1. trabajaban   2. leíamos   3. vivían   4. corría   5. jugaban   6. subían   7. estábamos
8. decíais   9. ponías   10. esperaba   11. rodaba   12. tenía   13. abría   14. hacían
15. tomabais   16. era   17. aprendía   18. escribías   19. hablaba   20. preferían
21. bebíais   22. salíamos   23. iba   24. veían   25. Nevaba   26. funcionaban

C 1. Quería acompañarlos.   2. Envolvían los paquetes.   3. ¿Qué decían Uds.?   4. Solía nevar
en enero.   5. Te divertías muchísimo.   6. Algo olía mal.   7. Pedía los billetes electrónicos
por computadora.   8. Íbamos a caballo en la hacienda.   9. Comenzaba a estudiar.
10. Volvían para las diez de la noche.   11. Les daba la bienvenida.   12. Se despertaban
tarde los fines de semana.   13. ¿Servías carne o pescado?   14. Soñaban con ser millonarios.
15. Fingía no entender el chiste.   16. Contaba con el apoyo de su familia.   17. No podían
tranquilizarse.   18. No entendía el por qué.   19. Eran muy serios.   20. Uds. se vestían
muy bien.   21. Concluían la presentación.   22. Tenía mucho interés en el proyecto.

D 1. Eran las diez y media cuando llegué a la oficina.   2. Hacía sol cuando comenzó el partido.
3. Era mediodía ya cuando vinieron.   4. Nevaba cuando salí para la pista de esquí.
5. Eran las siete treinta cuando despegó el avión.   6. Tronaba y había relámpagos cuando
aterrizamos.   7. Era la madrugada cuando sonó mi teléfono celular.   8. Llovía a cántaros
cuando los novios fueron a la iglesia.   9. Hacía muy buen tiempo cuando los recién casados
salieron de la iglesia.   10. Había montones de nieve en el parque cuando saqué a mi perro
a retozar.   11. Había tormenta cuando le devolvieron el coche de alquiler al agente.
12. Era ya tardísimo cuando los jóvenes se durmieron.   13. Estaba nublado y hacía viento
cuando llegamos a la cumbre de la montaña.   14. Eran las dos en punto cuando empezó
la función de la tarde.

E 1. Siempre les traía bombones a los abuelos.   2. De costumbre al terminar el trabajo los
compañeros tomaban una copa.   3. Todos los sábados Daniela salía con Federico a bailar.
4. A menudo Paco le pedía prestado el coche a su hermano.   5. Cada semana nadabas
en la piscina del gimnasio universitario.   6. Todos los inviernos íbamos a la sierra de
Guadarrama para esquiar.   7. Generalmente los chicos llegaban hambrientos a la casa.
8. Muchas veces pasábamos un par de horas en el centro comercial.   9. Veían a sus primos
italianos todos los veranos.   10. ¿Hacíais un viaje de negocios todos los meses?

F 1. Ignacio les informó que buscaba trabajo.   2. Laura anunció que iba a casarse.
3. Ellos insistieron en que sabían hacerlo.   4. Les escribí que hacía un viaje en mayo.
5. Nos avisaron que no podían llegar puntual a la cita.   6. Me advirtieron que el ordenador
estaba descompuesto.   7. Los jefes notificaron que despedían a muchos empleados.
8. Pedro y Consuelo me contaron que eran felices.

G 1. Eran, salieron   2. Había, pude   3. conoció, estudiaba   4. veías, corrimos
5. pensaba, vino   6. sabíamos, dijo   7. Hubo, trabajabas   8. dabais, dio   9. nació, era
10. estábamos, marcó   11. era, logré   12. huyó, dormían   13. enseñaba, inició
14. dio, viajaba   15. prestaba, riñó   16. pagué, comían   17. aparecieron, conocíamos
18. consiguió, tenía   19. presentó, necesitaban   20. llegaron, preparaban

H 1. ¿Cuánto (tiempo) hacía que vivían en Nueva York cuando compraron un condominio?
2. Hacía dos años que vivíamos en la ciudad.   3. ¿Cuánto (tiempo) hacía que estudiabas
español en Madrid cuando decidiste volver a tu universidad estadounidense?   4. Hacía seis
semanas que estaba allí.   5. ¿Cuánto (tiempo) hacía que Julia usaba su computadora
cuando cambió de marca?   6. Hacía tres años que la tenía.   7. ¿Desde cuándo trabajaba
Jaime de asesor?   8. Desde el año pasado cuando consiguió su maestría en administración
de empresas.

I 1. Se las expliqué.   2. Se lo pidió.   3. Nos lo enseñaban.   4. Me la devuelve.
5. ¿Te lo ofrecieron?   6. Os las sirven.   7. Se los regalamos.   8. Se lo envío.
9. Se la mandó.   10. Nos la recomiendan.   11. Se lo vendimos.   12. Me la dijo.
13. Te lo prestamos.   14. ¿Nos lo demostráis?   15. Se los dio.   16. Os lo suben.
17. Se las trajisteis.   18. Se los hice.   19. Se lo comentaban.   20. Me las entregó.

J 1. a. Ricardo gave them to you/him/her/them. b. You/He/She gave them to Ricardo.
2. a. The consultants described it to you/him/her/them. b. You/They described it to
the consultants. 3. a. Ofelia repeated them to you/him/her/them. b. You/He/She repeated
them to Ofelia. 4. a. You ask him/her/them for it. b. He/She asks you for it. 5. a. Sarita
was going to send them to you/him/her/them. b. I was / You were / He/She was going
to send them to Sarita. 6. a. Our colleagues want to show it to you/him/her/them.
b. You/They want to show it to our colleagues. 7. a. The professor wasn't able to explain
it to you/him/her/them. b. You weren't / He/She wasn't able to explain it to the professor.
8. a. These lawyers have just asked you/him/her/them for them. b. You/They have just
asked these lawyers for them.

K 1. ¿Puedes prestarme tu cámara digital? 2. Se la presté a Esteban la semana pasada.
Puedes pedírsela a él. 3. Compré este suéter para regalárselo a alguien. 4. ¿A quién
quieres dárselo? / ¿A quién se lo quieres dar? 5. Les escribíamos correos electrónicos
todos los días. 6. ¿Todavía se los mandan tan a menudo? 7. ¿Ya les hicieron la cena?
8. Vamos a hacérsela pronto. 9. Daniel nos escribió que iba a darle una sortija a su novia.
10. ¿Dijo cuándo pensaba dársela? / ¿Dijo cuándo se la pensaba dar? 11. Julia les entregó
su tesis a los profesores anteayer. 12. ¿No tenía que entregársela el semestre pasado?
13. ¿Cuánto (tiempo) hacía que trabajaban para la empresa cuando el jefe les dio un
aumento de sueldo? 14. Hacía seis meses que hacían programación / programaban cuando
se lo dio. / Hacían programación / Programaban hacía seis meses cuando se lo dio.

Chapter 8
The Past Participle; The Present Perfect; The Pluperfect

A 1. hemos 2. hablado 3. han 4. entendido 5. has 6. leído 7. ha 8. dicho
9. he 10. ha 11. discutido 12. mirado 13. puesto 14. escrito 15. habido

B 1. Tú has hablado por teléfono móvil. 2. Nuestro equipo ha ganado el partido.
3. Ellos han puesto la mesa. 4. Ud. ha recibido la correspondencia. 5. Gerardo ha hecho
un login. 6. Yo he leído los titulares. 7. Nuestra familia ha vivido bien. 8. Uds. han
tenido mucha experiencia. 9. Tú has descargado el fichero. 10. Vosotros no habéis
comprendido el asunto. 11. Nosotros hemos sido muy felices. 12. Nadie ha dicho nada.
13. ¿Quién ha roto la ventana? 14. Nora y Daniela han ido de compras. 15. ¿Ud. ha oído
esta orquesta? 16. Yo he escrito el informe. 17. Nosotros hemos resuelto el conflicto.
18. ¿Cómo han estado Uds.? 19. La cocinera ha frito el pescado. 20. Ellos no han querido
molestar. 21. Vosotros habéis impreso los papeles. 22. Los electrodomésticos han
funcionado bien.

C 1. Han almorzado en la cafetería. 2. Ha llovido todo el día. 3. Han hecho construir una
casa. 4. Ha perdido el tren esta mañana. 5. Ha habido mucha congestión en Internet.
6. Este libro ha sido un éxito de librería. 7. Han vuelto del viaje de negocios.
8. El director ha rodado la película en Texas. 9. Los niños han querido ver los dibujos
animados. 10. Jorge ha conseguido trabajar en la seguridad nacional y la ciberseguridad.
11. El armario ha olido mal. 12. Los ha despertado. 13. Te lo he dicho. 14. Se las hemos
devuelto. 15. Han preferido dársela. / Se la han preferido dar. 16. No se lo he podido
recomendar. / No he podido recomendárselo. 17. ¿Has tratado de enviárnoslos? /
¿Nos los has tratado de enviar? 18. Te la han pensado regalar. / Han pensado regalártela.
19. Ha vuelto a pedírmelas. / Me las ha vuelto a pedir. 20. ¿Por qué habéis necesitado
recordárselo? / ¿Por qué se lo habéis necesitado recordar?

D 1. Ya lo he probado.   2. Ya ha empezado.   3. Ya los hemos visitado.   4. Ya lo ha rellenado.   5. Ya los ha lanzado.   6. Ya lo he repetido.   7. Ya la han emprendido.   8. Ya la he comido.   9. Ya la ha estudiado.   10. Ya lo hemos realizado.   11. Ya las hemos hecho.   12. Ya me la han mostrado.   13. Ya nos los han contado.   14. Ya se la ha entregado.   15. Ya nos las han servido.   16. Ya lo he leído.

E 1. No, había corrido en la carrera en abril.   2. No, lo habíamos visto hace un mes.   3. No, la habían hecho el primer fin de semana de mayo.   4. No, la habían abierto hace tres semanas.   5. No, había vuelto de vacaciones anteayer.   6. No, la habían comprado el año pasado.   7. No, se la había pedido el Día de los Enamorados.   8. No, lo había celebrado el primero del mes.   9. No, la había llamado para invitarla a la fiesta el martes.   10. No, se lo habíamos dado en noviembre.

F 1. Cuando tú nos llamaste, nosotros ya habíamos ido de compras.   2. Cuando yo llegué al cine, Nicolás y Mari ya habían visto la mitad de la película.   3. Cuando los invitados vinieron, Isabel ya había puesto la mesa.   4. Cuando Paco comenzó a trotar, los otros jugadores ya habían corrido cinco millas.   5. Cuando Uds. me invitaron, yo ya había hecho planes para ese día.   6. Cuando nosotros fuimos en lancha, ya había dejado de llover.   7. Cuando vosotros pasasteis la aspiradora, Susana ya había sacudido el polvo.   8. Cuando Toni solucionó el problema por fin, Ud. ya lo había resuelto.   9. Cuando Vicente le pidió la cuenta al mesero, Enrique ya la había pagado.   10. Cuando yo volví a la tienda de antigüedades, alguien ya había comprado la estatua.

G 1. a. comprada b. alquilado c. amueblados d. pintadas e. vendido f. construido g. rehechas   2. a. entrados b. introducida c. bajadas d. cargado e. telecargados f. transmitidos   3. a. frito b. cocidos c. hervida d. asadas e. hecha f. hecha   4. a. visto b. visitado c. concurrido d. navegado e. diseñado f. creado   5. a. animadas b. entusiasmadas c. aburridas d. agradecidas e. enfurecidas f. casadas g. reunidas   6. a. dichas b. escrito c. expresados d. pronunciados e. traducida f. oído

H 1. está frita   2. estamos mojados   3. está metido   4. están dormidos   5. está comida   6. están hechas

I 1. Yo he escrito los poemas. Los poemas están escritos.   2. Marcia ha teñido la tela. La tela está teñida.   3. Nosotros hemos cubierto los gastos. Los gastos están cubiertos.   4. La abuela ha acostado a sus nietos. Sus nietos están acostados.   5. Patricio ha fotocopiado las cartas. Las cartas están fotocopiadas.   6. Tú has hecho las galletas. Las galletas están hechas.   7. Ud. ha apagado el fuego. El fuego está apagado.   8. Vosotros habéis perdido la plata. La plata está perdida.   9. Uds. han tirado la basura. La basura está tirada.   10. Alguien ha estacionado el coche. El coche está estacionado.   11. Perla ha enloquecido a sus amigas. Sus amigas están enloquecidas.   12. Ellos han atravesado el puente. El puente está atravesado.   13. Los soldados han caído. Los soldados están caídos.   14. Yo he resuelto el problema. El problema está resuelto.   15. Nosotros hemos impreso la tesis. La tesis está impresa.   16. Lorenzo ha roto sus pantalones. Sus pantalones están rotos.   17. El arquitecto ha rehecho estas casas. Estas casas están rehechas.   18. La directora ha pospuesto la reunión. La reunión está pospuesta.   19. La cocinera ha frito las croquetas. Las croquetas están fritas.   20. El dramaturgo ha terminado el guión. El guión está terminado.

J 1. Supimos que ya habías vuelto de tu viaje de negocios. 2. Cuando estalló la guerra en su país, los Reyes ya habían huido a los Estados Unidos. 3. Escrita la novela exitosa, la autora empezó a escribir la segunda. 4. He dicho lo más importante. / Tengo lo más importante dicho. 5. ¿La videocámara? Eva se la ha prestado. 6. Los invitados están sentados a la mesa. La comida y el vino están servidos. 7. ¿Han oído las noticias en la radio? Ha habido un maremoto. 8. ¿El dinero? Se lo he pedido a Andrés pero él no ha querido dármelo. 9. ¿Ha hecho las maletas? 10. Sí, las maletas están hechas. 11. ¿Has enchufado la computadora? 12. No, no está enchufada porque funciona con pilas.

Chapter 9
The Imperative

A 1. Arregle el cuarto. No arregle el cuarto. 2. Cierre la puerta. No cierre la puerta.
3. Corra en el maratón. No corra en el maratón. 4. Lea el artículo. No lea el artículo.
5. Cuente lo que pasó. No cuente lo que pasó. 6. Comparta los gastos. No comparta los gastos. 7. Riña al chico. No riña al chico. 8. Siga por el río. No siga por el río.
9. Pruebe la sopa. No pruebe la sopa. 10. Encienda la luz. No encienda la luz.
11. Vaya con nosotros. No vaya con nosotros. 12. Busque al perro. No busque al perro.
13. Imprima el informe. No imprima el informe. 14. Beba el jugo. No beba el jugo.
15. Despierte al niño. No despierte al niño. 16. Pague la cuenta. No pague la cuenta.
17. Vea ese programa. No vea ese programa. 18. Juegue al tenis. No juegue al tenis.
19. Descargue el fichero. No descargue el fichero. 20. Dé un paseo. No dé un paseo.

B 1. Lleven los paquetes. 2. Aparquen en este parqueo. 3. Pidan el helado de coco.
4. Hagan una lista. 5. Organicen estos papeles. 6. Toquen jazz. 7. No gasten tanto dinero. 8. No digan tonterías. 9. Asistan al concierto. 10. No rechacen su idea.
11. No sean desagradables. 12. Empiecen a programar. 13. No vuelquen el florero.
14. Lleguen a las ocho. 15. Sonrían. 16. Consigan los billetes. 17. No tengan miedo.
18. No caigan por la casa sin llamar. 19. Vengan lo antes posible. 20. Introduzcan los datos.

C 1. Sí, tomemos algo. Sí, vamos a tomar algo. 2. Sí, naveguemos en la Red. Sí, vamos a navegar en la Red. 3. Sí, comamos una hamburguesa. Sí, vamos a comer una hamburguesa.
4. No, no volvamos a ese balneario. 5. Sí, comencemos el proyecto. Sí, vamos a comenzar el proyecto. 6. Sí, juguemos al béisbol. Sí, vamos a jugar al béisbol. 7. Sí, oigamos música. Sí, vamos a oír música. 8. Sí, salgamos al cine. Sí, vamos a salir al cine.
9. No, no hagamos planes. 10. Sí, escojamos un postre. Sí, vamos a escoger un postre.
11. No, no vayamos al centro comercial. 12. Sí, demos una vuelta. Sí, vamos a dar una vuelta. 13. Sí, reduzcamos nuestros gastos. Sí, vamos a reducir nuestros gastos.
14. No, no envolvamos el regalo. 15. No, no subamos en el telesquí. 16. Sí, traigamos una botella de vino. Sí, vamos a traer una botella de vino. 17. No, no sirvamos arroz con pollo.
18. No, no mezamos al bebé. 19. Sí, sigamos por esta calle. Sí, vamos a seguir por esta calle. 20. Sí, conozcamos al nuevo asesor. Sí, vamos a conocer al nuevo asesor.

D 1. Escribe en la tarjeta de memoria. No escribas en la tarjeta de memoria. 2. Lee los cuentos. No leas los cuentos. 3. Repite el plato. No repitas el plato. 4. Haz un clic en el icono. No hagas un clic en el icono. 5. Envía un fax. No envíes un fax. 6. Cuelga el cartel en esta pared. No cuelgues el cartel en esta pared. 7. Exige más de ellos. No exijas más de ellos. 8. Pon un anuncio en el periódico. No pongas un anuncio en el periódico. 9. Pide un aumento de sueldo. No pidas un aumento de sueldo. 10. Di que sí. No digas que sí. 11. Ve el sitio Web. No veas el sitio Web. 12. Sé interesado. No seas interesado. 13. Analiza la información. No analices la información. 14. Sal a pasear. No salgas a pasear. 15. Ve a caballo. No vayas a caballo. 16. Llega temprano. No llegues temprano. 17. Ven al cibercafé. No vengas al cibercafé. 18. Tiñe la camisa. No tiñas la camisa. 19. Crea una base de datos. No crees una base de datos. 20. Ten confianza en ellos. No tengas confianza en ellos.

E 1. Estudiad mercadeo. No estudiéis mercadeo. 2. Vended vuestro coche. No vendáis vuestro coche. 3. Abrid el baúl. No abráis el baúl. 4. Recoged las uvas. No recojáis las uvas. 5. Sed agresivos. No seáis agresivos. 6. Seguid nuestros consejos. No sigáis nuestros consejos. 7. Haced cola. No hagáis cola. 8. Venid en taxi. No vengáis en taxi. 9. Dormid la siesta. No durmáis la siesta. 10. Publicad vuestras memorias. No publiquéis vuestras memorias. 11. Idos mañana. No os vayáis mañana. 12. Casaos en julio. No os caséis en julio. 13. Salid a bailar. No salgáis a bailar. 14. Aplazad la reunión. No aplacéis la reunión. 15. Medid las cortinas. No midáis las cortinas. 16. Oíd las noticias. No oigáis las noticias. 17. Traed el cheque. No traigáis el cheque. 18. Buscad el cajero automático. No busquéis el cajero automático. 19. Decid la clave personal. No digáis la clave personal. 20. Quedaos hasta el sábado. No os quedéis hasta el sábado.

F 1. Yo no quiero. Que haga los quehaceres ella. 2. Yo no quiero. Que compren la cerveza ellos. 3. Yo no quiero. Que aprenda a bailar salsa ella. 4. Yo no quiero. Que lleve a mi novia al cine más a menudo ella. 5. Yo no quiero. Que practique todos los días él. 6. Yo no quiero. Que busquen trabajo ellos. 7. Yo no quiero. Que lo llame él. 8. Yo no quiero. Que vaya él a ver el partido de tenis.

G 1. Enjoy this marvelous art exhibit. 2. Have everybody see this marvelous art exhibit. 3. Have him go to get the ink cartridges. 4. Have the secretary send the e-mails right now. 5. Have the customers line up at the box office. 6. Don't let anyone interrupt the meeting of the heads of state. 7. Let the rest participate in the event. 8. Have somebody notify us as soon as possible.

H 1. Seguir derecho. 2. No pisar el césped. 3. Utilizar nuestra banca electrónica. 4. Reservar sus billetes en línea. 5. Agregar una cucharadita de canela. 6. Abrir una cuenta corriente. 7. Guardar las recetas en su PDA. 8. Para más información llamar al teléfono 182329. 9. Para mayores informes enviar un e-mail a esta dirección. 10. Calentar el guisado a fuego lento. 11. Abrocharse el cinturón de seguridad. 12. No tocar los cables de electricidad. 13. Interesados ponerse en contacto con el director. 14. Alojarse en el Hotel Caribe.

I 1. Haga el favor de volver más tarde. 2. Favor de esperarnos en la oficina. 3. Tengan la bondad de sentarse en la sala. 4. Favor de hacerme una copia de seguridad. 5. Tenga la bondad de pulsar el botón. 6. Hagan el favor de explicármelo. 7. Favor de reunirse la semana próxima. 8. Haga el favor de no meterse en este asunto. 9. Favor de no oponerse al plan. 10. Tengan la bondad de no decírselo a nadie.

J 1. No, no lo pulses/pulse. 2. No, no lo pisen/piséis/pisemos. 3. No, no la hagas/haga.
4. No, no las coman/comáis/comamos. 5. No, no me llames mañana. 6. No, nos ayude
con los cajones. 7. No, no lo traigan/traigáis/traigamos. 8. No, no se la regalen/
regaléis/regalemos. 9. No, no nos los manden. 10. No, no lo paseen/paseéis/paseemos.
11. No, no me busquen esta noche. 12. No, no se las enseñes/enseñe. 13. No, no nos
lo cuentes. 14. No, no se la solicites/solicite. 15. No, no nos las expliquéis.
16. No, no me lo des ahora.

K 1. Sí, escríbelo/escríbalo. 2. Sí, ciérrala/ciérrela. 3. Sí, alquílenlos/alquiladlos/
alquilémoslos. 4. Sí, diríjanla/dirigidla/dirijámosla. 5. Sí, recógenos/recójanos
en el museo. 6. Sí, páguensela/pagádsela/paguémosela. 7. Sí, díganmelo.
8. Sí, házselo/hágaselo. 9. Sí, devuélvannoslos. 10. Sí, vístanlos/vestidlos/vistámoslos.
11. Sí, recuérdenmela/recordádmela. 12. Sí, muéstrenmelas. 13. Sí, sírveselos/sírvaselos.
14. Sí, pídanselo/pedídselo/pidámoselo. 15. Sí, espéranos en el bar. 16. Sí, véndemelo.

L 1. Go and see him/it. (ir, tú; ver, tú) 2. Show it to him/her/them. (mostrar, Ud.)
3. Send them to him/her/them. (enviar, Uds.) 4. Take them up for us. (subir, vosotros)
5. Give it to him/her/them. (dar, tú) 6. Bring it to us. (traer, Uds.) 7. Don't hide them
from him/her/them. (ocultar, tú) 8. Don't say it to me. (decir, Ud.) 9. Let's ask
him/her/them for them. / Let's order them from him/her/them. (pedir, nosotros)
10. Make/Do it for him/her/them. (hacer, Uds.)

M 1. ¿El teléfono celular? Dámelo. 2. ¿La computadora? Muéstrennosla. / Enséñennosla.
3. ¿Los paquetes? Envuélvamelos. 4. ¿Tus preguntas? Hacédselas. 5. ¿La noticia?
Escribámosela. / Vamos a escribírsela. 6. ¿Esa marca? No se la pidamos. 7. Si la comida
está hecha, sírvenosla. 8. Si el informe está impreso, léaselo. 9. ¿La raqueta de tenis?
Ofrézcasela. 10. Ten paciencia. No vayas todavía.

Chapter 10
The Future and the Conditional;
The Future Perfect and the Conditional Perfect

A 1. Compraremos muchas cosas en una tienda virtual. 2. Contarán con nosotros para
llevarlo a cabo. 3. Aprenderás los lenguajes de programación. 4. Nevará pasado mañana.
5. ¿A qué hora vendrán? 6. Gabriela estudiará enfermería pediátrica. 7. No les diré nada.
8. Tendréis mucho que hacer. 9. Habrá millones de navegantes en línea. 10. Marcos
efectuará grandes cambios. 11. No podrán vernos hasta la semana entrante.
12. Jaime hará el papel del protagonista. 13. Estarán muy emocionados por la noticia.
14. Oirás la música mejor desde esta fila. 15. La situación irá de mal en peor.
16. Nos pondremos los zapatos. 17. Cabrán quinientas personas en el salón de actos.
18. Querremos pintar unos paisajes. 19. Perseguirán al culpable. 20. Empezaréis
a acostumbraros al horario.

B 1. Virginia cumplirá veintitrés años el lunes.   2. Ellos nos pondrán al día.
3. Profundizaremos el tema.   4. Haré un login.   5. Formatearán el documento.
6. ¿No cabrá más memoria en el ordenador?   7. La boda será en un hotel céntrico.
8. Estos jóvenes tendrán mucho éxito.   9. Lloverá toda la temporada.   10. Habrá
un simulacro de incendio esta tarde.   11. Su cumpleaños caerá en un miércoles.
12. Sus esfuerzos valdrán la pena.   13. Saldrán ganando como siempre.
14. Los cursos satisfarán los requisitos.   15. ¿Nos los traeréis?   16. Querremos dársela.
17. Podré informarte mañana.   18. Vendrán lo antes posible.   19. Lo sabré pronto.
20. La oirás cantar en la comedia musical.

C 1. Los empleados habrán salido de la oficina para la hora de la cena.   2. Diana y yo
habremos vuelto del museo a eso de las cuatro.   3. Rogelio habrá conseguido la maestría en
comunicaciones para fines del semestre.   4. Yo se lo habré hecho para la semana que viene.
5. Uds. habrán reservado los billetes electrónicos antes de las vacaciones de verano.
6. Ud. les habrá enviado el correo después de verlos.   7. Tú habrás resuelto el problema
antes de la reunión.   8. Vosotros nos las habréis dado para mediados de enero.
9. Nosotros los habremos visto para el Día de la Independencia.   10. Ellos habrán
mandado los impuestos para el quince de abril.

D 1. tendrías 2. tomaríamos 3. querría 4. tratarían 5. oirían 6. haría 7. traería
8. añadiría 9. se lo exigiría 10. se lo diríais

E 1. vendrían 2. cabrán 3. habría 4. aceptaría 5. sabría 6. compraremos 7. podrías
8. estaría 9. hará 10. aterrizaría 11. le interesaría 12. les encantarán

F 1. Tú no habrías mentido.   2. Ud. no los habría invitado a comer en un restaurante caro.
3. Nosotros no habríamos caído en una trampa.   4. Ellos no habrían dicho nada sin querer.
5. Yo no habría comido comida basura.   6. Uds. no habrían puesto al cantante por las
nubes.   7. Vosotros no habríais repetido el plato de carne.   8. Isaac no habría visto
el programa de realidad.   9. Daniela y Alfredo no les habrían regalado a los novios esa
cámara digital.   10. Tú no habrías utilizado una chuleta en el examen.

G 1. Habrá celos entre las cuñadas.   2. La noche caerá pronto.   3. Los gemelos tendrán
veintiún años.   4. Querrán bailar el tango.   5. Los aficionados estarán entusiasmados.
6. Su sortija de diamantes valdrá mucho.   7. Lloverá mañana.   8. Será la una y media.

H 1. ¿Cuándo llegarán?   2. ¿Qué hora será?   3. ¿Quién sabrá su número de teléfono?
4. ¿Dónde será (OR tendrá lugar) la reunión?   5. ¿Qué tiempo hará esta semana?
6. ¿Cómo estarán?

I 1. Habría treinta invitados en la fiesta.   2. Sería un verano muy caluroso.   3. Tendría
veintinueve años.   4. Las joyas costarían un ojo de la cara.   5. Estarían de viaje.
6. Haría mucho frío.   7. Nevaría mucho en la sierra.   8. Él estaría contentísimo.

J 1. ¿Qué hora sería cuando nos llamaron?   2. Serían las nueve y media.   3. ¿Por qué estaría
tan cansada?   4. Sería por el vuelo largo y difícil.   5. Habría un problema con su carro.
6. Estaría descompuesto.

K 1. Habrán reñido por una tontería.   2. Habrá nevado toda la noche.   3. El perro habrá
tragado la pelota.   4. Los bomberos habrán llegado muy rápidamente para apagar el
incendio.   5. No habrán sacado la basura.   6. Emilio no habrá reciclado los periódicos
en seis meses.

L 1. ¿Cuándo vendrán a vernos? / ¿Cuándo deben (de) venir a vernos?   2. Serían las once cuando llegué a la estación de tren. / Debían (de) ser las once cuando llegué a la estación de tren.   3. Los habrán visto en la fiesta. / Deben (de) haberlos visto en la fiesta. 4. El Ferrari les habrá costado un dineral. / El Ferrari debe (de) haberles costado un dineral. / El Ferrari les costaría un dineral. / El Ferrari debía (de) costarles un dineral. 5. ¡Increíble! Él no habría dicho una cosa tan espantosa.   6. Cuando conocimos a Irene tendría unos veintidós años. / Cuando conocimos a Irene debía (de) tener unos veintidós años.   7. Me habrás mandado/enviado un e-mail mientras estabas en el cibercafé. / Debes (de) haberme mandado/enviado un e-mail mientras estabas en el cibercafé. 8. ¿Qué hora será?   9. ¿Por qué habrá salido Carlos sin avisarnos?   10. Habrá ocurrido algo imprevisto. / Debe (de) haber ocurrido algo imprevisto.   11. Todo el mundo habrá leído ese libro. / Todo el mundo debe (de) haber leído ese libro.   12. Tendrán ganas de ir al cine.   13. Será demasiado tarde ya.   14. Ya no habrá función.

Chapter 11
The Subjunctive (Part I): The Present Subjunctive

A 1. tenemos   2. hagan   3. está   4. encargue   5. conozcas   6. es   7. viene   8. salga 9. discutamos   10. utilizáis   11. diga   12. va   13. lleguen   14. ocupo   15. rechaces

B 1. impida   2. veas   3. almuercen   4. sean   5. traigan   6. ponga   7. haya   8. pagues 9. esté   10. aparezca   11. vayamos   12. critiques   13. juegue   14. salga   15. invirtamos 16. sepa   17. dé   18. oigan   19. vuelvan   20. sigamos

C 1. Es importante que ellos sigan una dieta equilibrada.   2. Es útil que Ud. tenga palanca. 3. Es mejor que yo espere un par de días.   4. Es preciso que Uds. hagan clic en el enlace. 5. Es imprescindible que tú entiendas la política exterior.   6. Urge que él envíe el correo electrónico.   7. Es obligatorio que nosotros asistamos a la reunión.   8. Más vale que Uds. vayan a pie.   9. Hace falta que vosotros descarguéis los documentos.   10. Es bueno que nuestra familia viva cómodamente.   11. Es inútil que Anita busque su billetera. 12. Es malo que Pedro no devuelva el dinero prestado.

D 1. Es bueno que haya tantos adelantos tecnológicos.   2. Es cierto que yo trabajo para una compañía de alta tecnología.   3. No es evidente que tengan interés en el proyecto. 4. No es dudoso que el dueño de la empresa abre otras sucursales.   5. Es que no conocemos bien el interior del país.   6. Es obvio que los novios están enamorados.   7. No es seguro que seáis de origen irlandés.   8. Es una lástima que nadie quiera ayudarlos.   9. Está mal que la cosa no salga bien.   10. Es triste que el huracán haga tanto daño.

E 1. Queremos que nuestros hijos sean felices.   2. El programador necesita bajar el programa. 3. Me alegro de hacer el patinaje sobre hielo.   4. Le aconsejas a Francisca que sirva entremeses.   5. Temen que haya piratas informáticos en Internet.   6. Duda que ellos sepan utilizar la hoja de cálculo electrónica.   7. Les gusta que Paco estudie urbanización. 8. Deseáis practicar deportes acuáticos.   9. No creo que Ramón tenga don de gentes. 10. No piensan hacer pintar la casa este año.   11. Tienen miedo de que un virus infecte su computadora.   12. Le pides a la agencia virtual que te mande dos billetes electrónicos de ida y vuelta.   13. No deja hablar.   14. Sienten que no las veamos.   15. Insiste en llegar antes que nadie.

F   1. Esperamos que Uds. puedan asistir a la conferencia esta noche.   2. ¿El informe? Es imprescindible que Ud. se lo dé ahora mismo.   3. Me alegro de que vayan de vacaciones con nosotros.   4. Es necesario / Es preciso / Hace falta que hagamos las maletas la noche anterior.   5. Le aconsejan que le pida a su jefe un aumento de sueldo.   6. Han sugerido que busquemos esa marca en los grandes almacenes.   7. ¿No tiene miedo de que / No teme que borres todos los archivos?   8. En la tienda virtual nos dicen que pongamos (OR coloquemos) nuestras compras en el carrito y que vayamos (OR pasemos) a la caja. 9. Es importante disfrutar (OR gozar) de la vida. ¡Que disfruten (OR gocen) de la vida! 10. Ojalá (que) / Espero que triunfes (OR tengas éxito) en la vida.

G   1. interesa   2. esfuerce   3. sepa   4. tengan   5. sean   6. da   7. crea   8. atraiga   9. guste 10. haga   11. esté   12. tiene

H   1. hojees   2. saque   3. pidan   4. salimos   5. haya   6. traiga   7. comience   8. vamos 9. veas   10. devuelvan   11. instale   12. vienen

I   1. No creo que quieras ver esta película.   2. Es necesario / Es preciso que les envíe un correo electrónico (OR un e-mail).   3. Es útil que hagamos nuestras investigaciones en la Red (OR por Internet).   4. Me alegro de que vengan a vernos este fin de semana. 5. Buscamos una casa que tenga seis dormitorios.   6. Necesitan un director que conozca la empresa muy bien.   7. Ojalá (que) / Espero que nuestro equipo gane el partido el domingo.   8. ¡Que te diviertas! (OR ¡Que lo pases bien!)   9. No hay ningún sándwich en la carta que me guste.   10. Consigamos los billetes electrónicos tan pronto como / en cuanto / luego que yo haga el login (OR la conexión).   11. Te muestro (OR Te mostraré OR Te voy a mostrar) el sitio Web de viajes para que / a fin de que puedas escoger un paquete turístico.   12. ¿Quieren comer algo antes de que comience la comedia (OR la obra de teatro)?   13. Te compraremos un recuerdo cuando lleguemos a Granada. / Te compraremos un recuerdo al llegar a Granada.   14. No vale la pena organizar una fiesta a menos que todos nuestros amigos puedan venir (OR ir).

J   1. Yo la invité al concierto pero ella no pudo ir.   2. No puede tomar el seminario de ciencias políticas a las once porque cursa literatura mundial a la misma hora.   3. O llegas puntualmente o no te dejan entrar.   4. Terminó de mandar el correo electrónico y apagó la computadora.   5. No lo encontramos ni en casa ni en la oficina así que lo llamamos por teléfono móvil.   6. Él no sólo se ocupa de los quehaceres domésticos sino que hace la jardinería también.   7. Te afirmo que son dignos de confianza.   8. Ellos fueron corriendo de tal modo que Ud. no consiguió alcanzarlos.   9. Pasaron por mí a las seis de manera que logramos llegar al aeropuerto con tiempo de sobra.   10. El avión iba a despegar conque los pasajeros se abrocharon el cinturón de seguridad.

K   1. Ella no sólo canta sino que baila también.   2. O los llamaremos por teléfono (OR O los telefonearemos) hoy o les hablaremos cuando los veamos.   3. ¿Ud. confirma que ha recibido los billetes electrónicos?   4. Juro que yo no tengo la culpa.   5. Él va a pasar las vacaciones en San Francisco porque sus padres viven allí.   6. Prende la computadora de modo que / de manera que / de forma que yo pueda ver tu sitio Web.   7. Así que / Conque / De tal modo que / De tal manera que / De tal forma que no había nadie cuando llegaron.   8. Ellos fueron al cine pero nosotros decidimos alquilar una película. 9. Fuimos a las grandes almacenes de modo que pudimos comprarles un regalo para inaugurar la casa.   10. Ella hizo el logon y fue a su sitio Web primero.   11. Sé que esos archivos ya están formateados y almacenados.   12. Ellos quieren que viajemos (OR hagamos un viaje) con ellos, pero los encontramos muy aburridos.

Chapter 12
The Subjunctive (Part II): The Present Perfect Subjunctive;
The Imperfect Subjunctive; The Pluperfect Subjunctive

A 1. Es probable que se hayan divertido mucho.   2. Dudo que Antonio y Nora hayan sido novios.   3. Es útil que yo se lo haya explicado.   4. Estamos furiosos que él haya mentido. 5. Es una lástima que no hayan tenido una vida privada.   6. Me sorprende que Ud. no la haya visto.   7. Es posible que el avión haya despegado.   8. Es bueno que los rescatadores los hayan encontrado sanos y salvos.   9. Niego que me hayan dicho eso.   10. No es cierto que hayan llegado a casa achispados.   11. Es malo que haya habido un fallo del sistema. 12. Sienten que su gato haya muerto.   13. Espera que hayamos hecho algo interesante. 14. Es importante que hayas tecleado correctamente la palabra clave.   15. No nos gusta que no haya contribuido nada a la caridad.

B 1. Dudo que Rebeca haya encontrado su pendiente de oro.   2. Es bueno que hayan resuelto su problema.   3. No nos gusta que hayan caído por la casa sin llamar.   4. Es útil que hayas descargado (OR bajado) los archivos.   5. ¿Le sorprende que no le hayan ofrecido a Carlos un aumento de sueldo?   6. Me alegro de que te haya salido bien.   7. No es cierto que Isabel haya renunciado a su puesto.   8. Está furioso que el perro haya hecho pedazos la alfombra. 9. Sienten que las cosas hayan ido de mal en peor.   10. Es probable que ya le hayáis devuelto el paraguas.

C 1. realizaras/realizases   2. se metiera/se metiese   3. hiciera/hiciese   4. se especializara/ se especializase   5. anduvieran/anduviesen   6. cupieran/cupiesen   7. leyeran/leyesen 8. pasarais/pasaseis   9. estuviéramos/estuviésemos   10. redujéramos/redujésemos 11. entrara/entrase   12. trajeras/trajeses   13. diera/diese   14. conociera/conociese 15. se dedicara/se dedicase   16. gustara/gustase   17. corrigiera/corrigiese 18. fuéramos/fuésemos   19. pidiera/pidiese   20. quisiera/quisiese

D 1. Esperábamos que trajeras tu cámara digital a la fiesta.   2. Le aconsejé que comprara la blusa blanca de seda.   3. No había nada que los entusiasmara.   4. Mariana les pidió que pusieran la mesa.   5. Nos habían mandado los videos sin que los pagáramos. 6. Preferiríamos que no se lo dijera.   7. Querían una computadora que funcionara bien. 8. Llevaba mi teléfono móvil por todas partes para que / a fin de que mis hijos pudieran llamarme a toda hora.   9. Ojalá llegaran hoy.   10. Le gustaría que le regaláramos un iPod. 11. Ojalá se tranquilizaran (OR se calmaran).   12. Ojalá te quedaras.

E 1. Me alegré de que hubiéramos hecho un viaje a Santa Fe.   2. Era importante que nos hubieran puesto al día.   3. Esperábamos que ella hubiera hecho la comida.   4. Nos extrañó que no se lo hubieras dicho a nadie.   5. Fue imposible que hubiera pasado una cosa así. 6. Nos gustó que hubierais leído tantos libros.   7. Fue probable que ellos hubieran impreso los documentos.   8. Ojalá (que) lo hubiéramos sabido lo antes posible.   9. Temían que la computadora hubiera tenido un gusano.   10. Les sorprendió que yo hubiera conseguido unos billetes electrónicos tan baratos.

F 1. No era cierto que Angélica hubiera roto con su novio.   2. Negó que ellos hubieran dicho palabrotas.   3. Se alegró de que hubiéramos oído los discos compactos.   4. Contestó como si no hubiera entendido la pregunta.   5. Ojalá hubieran podido pasar todo el verano con nosotros.   6. Nos sorprendió que no hubieras asistido a la reunión.   7. Era malo que hubiera llovido antes de la carrera.   8. Era posible que hubieran tratado de telefonearnos (OR llamarnos por teléfono).   9. ¿Dudaban que yo les hubiera dicho la verdad? 10. No creía que les hubiera escrito todavía.

G 1. voy, haré   2. saldremos, nieva   3. explica, procuraré   4. llevará, decide   5. es, pondrá
6. matriculará, hay   7. vienen, verán   8. meriendas, tendrás   9. querré, riegas   10. optan,
podrán

H 1. fueras, iría   2. podríamos, tuviéramos   3. hubiera, quedarían   4. preocuparan, serían
5. tendría, fuera   6. pasaríamos, hiciera   7. siguieran, perderían   8. pidieras, perdonarían
9. dormiría, tomara   10. trajeras, daría

I 1. hubieras navegado, habrías/hubieras visto   2. habría/hubiera conseguido, hubiera
estudiado   3. hubieran recibido, habrían/hubieran tenido   4. habría/hubiera sacado,
hubiera jugado   5. hubiéramos leído, habríamos/hubiéramos sabido   6. hubieran vivido,
habrían/hubieran echado   7. habría/hubiera visto, hubieras vuelto   8. hubierais
aprovechado, habríais/hubierais ahorrado   9. habrían/hubieran conocido, hubieran ido
10. hubiera habido, habrías/hubieras perdido   11. habrían/hubieran tenido, hubieran
prendido   12. te hubieras olvidado, habría/hubiera recibido

J 1. Si lo vemos en el partido, lo saludaremos por ti (OR de tu parte).   2. Compartirían los
gastos si pudieran.   3. La empresa la habría/hubiera contratado si ella hubiera tenido cinco
años de experiencia.   4. Si no lloviera, daríamos un paseo.   5. Si Ud. me hubiera dado el
contrato, yo lo habría/hubiera firmado.   6. Los esperaría si no tuviera que coger el tren
de las seis.   7. Esquiarán este fin de semana si hace buen tiempo.   8. Si nuestros colegas
fueran más trabajadores, nosotros no tendríamos tanto que hacer.   9. Si quisieras usar
el coche, te lo prestaríamos.   10. Si ella les hubiera pedido un iPod, ellos se lo
habrían/hubieran regalado.   11. Yo habría/hubiera tomado el vuelo de medianoche de San
Diego a Nueva York si hubiera tenido que asistir a una reunión a las nueve de la mañana.
12. Si Uds. compran (OR hacen las compras) en línea, ahorrarán tiempo y dinero.

Chapter 13
Reflexive Verbs

A 1. me pongo   2. se acuesta   3. te duermes   4. se viste   5. se despiertan   6. nos relajamos
7. se equivocó   8. te fuiste   9. me tranquilicé   10. se arrepintieron   11. se despidió
12. os casasteis   13. nos sorprendíamos   14. se enamoraba   15. me entusiasmaba
16. te ibas   17. se reunían   18. se aburría   19. me decidiré   20. nos opondremos
21. se detendrán   22. se sentirá   23. te reirás   24. se instalarán   25. te acordarías
26. nos animaríamos   27. se correría   28. me apoderaría   29. os enfadaríais
30. se mantendrían   31. se han sonreído   32. Se ha hecho   33. se han caído
34. me he servido   35. te has roto   36. nos hemos puesto

B 1. Consiguió colocarse. Se consiguió colocar.   2. Empiezan a interesarse. Se empiezan
a interesar.   3. Piensan reunirse. Se piensan reunir.   4. Tendrás que encararte con él.
Te tendrás que encarar con él.   5. No querría involucrarme en eso. No me querría
involucrar en eso.   6. Dejabais de preocuparos. Os dejabais de preocupar.
7. Espera divertirse. Se espera divertir.   8. No podremos decidirnos. No nos podremos
decidir.   9. Iba a pasearme. Me iba a pasear.   10. Debéis vestiros. Os debéis vestir.
11. Prefirieron quedarse. Se prefirieron quedar.   12. Temía cortarse. Se temía cortar.
13. Deseas casarte. Te deseas casar.   14. Terminó de ducharse. Se terminó de duchar.

C 1. Me di cuenta del problema.   2. Se echó a correr.   3. Nos pusimos de acuerdo.
4. Se quedaron con el dinero.   5. No te fiaste de tus socios.   6. Se dieron prisa al ver la
hora.   7. Se trató de un asunto muy importante.   8. Se sirvió de unos libros de consulta.
9. ¿Os atrevisteis a hablarles de esa manera?   10. Se puso a reír.

D 1. Cada vez que Javier se afeita se corta.　2. Por eso le gusta que el barbero lo afeite.
3. Yo baño a mis hijos antes de acostarlos. Luego yo me acuesto.　4. Hoy Marta y Daniela
se despertaron a las siete y media. Se ducharon, se vistieron, se maquillaron y se peinaron.
5. Les digo que no se preocupen. Quiero que se tranquilicen (OR se calmen) y que se relajen.
6. Se empeñaba en meterse en nuestros asuntos.　7. Consuelo y Jaime se graduaron en
la universidad, se enamoraron, se comprometieron y se casaron.　8. ¿Te acatarraste
(OR Te resfriaste) la semana pasada y todavía te sientes mal?　9. Se acercaba a la casa
cuando se mareó.　10. Me arrepiento de involucrarme en su negocio turbio.
11. Nos matricularemos (OR Nos apuntaremos) para el curso de administración en línea.

E 1. Claudia y yo nos escribimos mensajes electrónicos.　2. Alejandro y Catalina se entienden
perfectamente.　3. Miriám y Alejo se quieren mucho.　4. David y yo nos vemos muy
a menudo.　5. Diana y su hermana se ayudan mucho.　6. Miguel y Beatriz se compran
regalos.　7. Esteban y yo nos decimos muchas cosas.　8. Ud. y yo llegamos a conocernos
bien.　9. Tú y yo nos tuteamos.

F 1. Los aficionados se volvieron locos al ver a su jugador favorito.　2. Debido a sus buenas
inversiones, se hizo / llegó a ser rico.　3. Pablo y Amanda se hicieron / llegaron a ser
amigos.　4. El pequeño pueblo se convirtió en / se transformó en una bulliciosa capital
internacional.　5. Paula es una muchacha tímida que se pone roja/colorada con frecuencia.
6. Jacobo se ponía gordo / engordaba mientras su hermano Cristóbal se ponía flaco /
enflaquecía.　7. Se pusieron furiosos / Se enfurecieron al ver (OR cuando vieron) que
su perro había roto la alfombra.

G 1. Aurelia se alegró.　2. Yo me entusiasmé.　3. Carlos se ofendió.　4. Pilar y yo nos
emocionamos.　5. Ellos se enojaron / se enfadaron.　6. Tú te molestaste.　7. Uds. se
exasperaron.　8. Ud. se aburrió.　9. Vosotros os irritasteis.　10. Ellos se asustaron.
11. Él se entristeció.　12. Nosotros nos sorprendimos.

H 1. Roberto se lo torció.　2. Eva y Ana se la lavarán.　3. Te la probabas.　4. Pablo se lo
ha roto.　5. Me las puse.　6. Ud. se los abrochó.　7. Nos lo ponemos.　8. Os las laváis.
9. Iba a cortármelo. / Me lo iba a cortar.　10. Acaba de lastimárselo. / Se lo acaba de
lastimar.　11. Quiere pintárselos. / Se los quiere pintar.　12. Necesitabas cepillártelo. /
Te lo necesitabas cepillar.　13. Me los he atado.　14. Se las había limado.　15. Quiero que
te lo seques.　16. Era necesario que nos lo abrocháramos.

I 1. Fasten/Button/Tie it. / Fasten/Button/Tie it for him/her/them.　2. Put them on. /
Put them on for him/her/them.　3. Wash it for him/her/them.　4. You/He/She took them
off. / You/He/She took them off for him/her/you/them.　5. You/They unbuttoned/
unbuckled it. / You/They unbuttoned/unbuckled it for him/her/you/them.　6. He/She is /
You are going to brush it. / He/She is / You are going to brush it for him/her/you/them.
7. I put them on.　8. You should clean them.

J 1. Sí, póntelo. No, no te lo pongas.　2. Sí, límpienselos. No, no se los limpien.
3. Sí, séqueselo. No, no se lo seque.　4. Sí, quitémonoslo. No, no nos lo quitemos.
5. Sí, pruébatelas. No, no te las pruebes.　6. Sí, laváoslas. No, no os las lavéis.
7. Sí, córteselo. No, no se lo corte.　8. Sí, desabrochémonoslos. No, no nos los
desabrochemos.　9. Sí, abróchenselo. No, no se lo abrochen.　10. Sí, pintáoslos.
No, no os los pintéis.

K 1. Le puse el abrigo.   2. Él se torció el tobillo durante el partido de fútbol americano.
3. Instalémonos / Vamos a instalarnos en la casa nueva lo antes posible.   4. ¿Vas a cortarte
el pelo?   5. ¡Mira! Me lo corté ayer.   6. ¿Debo probarme este traje azul marino?
7. Sí, pruébeselo y póngase ese gris también.   8. Tranquilicémonos./Calmémonos. No nos
preocupemos.   9. Aquí tienes tu camiseta. Póntela.   10. Te quebraste / Te rompiste el pie.
¡No te quiebres / No te rompas el otro!   11. Séqueselas.   12. Séqueselas.   13. Abróchense
el cinturón de seguridad.   14. Abróchele el cinturón de seguridad a su hijita (OR niñita).

Chapter 14
The Present Participle; The Progressive Tenses

A 1. Pasé una hora haciendo ejercicio.   2. Pasaste diez minutos vistiéndote.   3. Pasó dos
horas navegando en la Red.   4. Pasaron media hora paseándose.   5. Pasamos el día entero
divirtiéndonos.   6. Pasaron una semana instalándose en el condominio.   7. Pasó cuarenta
y cinco minutos oyendo música.   8. Pasasteis mucho tiempo discutiendo.   9. Pasó toda
la tarde probándose ropa.   10. Pasaste veinte minutos durmiendo la siesta.   11. Pasaron
toda la mañana leyendo.   12. Pasamos menos de una hora viendo tele.

B 1. Uds. la vieron bailar ballet. Uds. la vieron bailando ballet.   2. Tú los escuchaste hablar.
Tú los escuchaste hablando.   3. Nosotros las miramos actuar. Nosotros las miramos
actuando.   4. Ud. lo oyó llorar. Ud. lo oyó llorando.   5. Yo los vi correr. Yo los vi
corriendo.   6. Vosotros la observasteis hacer gimnasia. Vosotros la observasteis haciendo
gimnasia.   7. Ellos me oyeron silbar una melodía. Ellos me oyeron silbando una melodía.
8. Él nos vio cruzar la calle. Él nos vio cruzando la calle.

C 1. Está alquilándolo. Lo está alquilando.   2. Están grabándolo. Lo están grabando.
3. Estás probándotelas. Te las estás probando.   4. Estamos sirviéndoselas. Se las estamos
sirviendo.   5. Está imprimiéndolos. Los está imprimiendo.   6. Estoy poniéndoselo.
Se lo estoy poniendo.   7. Estáis pidiéndonoslo. Nos lo estáis pidiendo.   8. Estoy leyéndolo.
Lo estoy leyendo.   9. Están escribiéndomelo. Me lo están escribiendo.   10. Estáis
secándooslas. Os las estáis secando.   11. Estás rompiéndotela. Te la estás rompiendo.
12. Está encendiéndolo. Lo está encendiendo.   13. Están consiguiéndoselos. Se los están
consiguiendo.   14. Están limpiándoselos. Se los están limpiando.   15. Estamos
comiéndonosla. Nos la estamos comiendo.

D 1. Estaba descargándolos. Los estaba descargando.   2. Estaba vistiéndome. Me estaba
vistiendo.   3. Estábamos quitándoselo. Se lo estábamos quitando.   4. Estabas cortándotelo.
Te lo estabas cortando.   5. Estaban diciéndonoslo. Nos lo estaban diciendo.   6. Estabais
compartiéndolas. Las estabais compartiendo.   7. Estábamos reuniéndonos. Nos estábamos
reuniendo.   8. Estaba trayéndosela. Se la estaba trayendo.   9. Estaban mostrándomelas.
Me las estaban mostrando.   10. Estaba lavándoselas. Se las estaba lavando.   11. Estaba
poniéndome en forma. Me estaba poniendo en forma.   12. Estaban riéndose a carcajadas.
Se estaban riendo a carcajadas.

E 1. Estará terminándola. La estará terminando.   2. Estarían cuidándolos. Los estaría
cuidando.   3. Estaremos registrándonos en el hotel. Nos estaremos registrando en el hotel.
4. Estaría acostándose. Se estaría acostando.   5. Estarían diciéndomelo. Me lo estarían
diciendo.   6. Estarías haciéndoselas. Se las estarías haciendo.   7. Estaré poniéndosela.
Se la estaré poniendo.   8. Estarán atándoselos. Se los estarán atando.   9. Estarás
aburriéndote. Te estarás aburriendo.   10. Estaréis entregándoselas. Se las estaréis
entregando.

F 1. Estuve practicándolo hasta las cinco. Lo estuve practicando hasta las cinco.
2. Estuvo arreglándose hasta que él llegó a recogerla. Se estuvo arreglando hasta que él llegó a recogerla. 3. Estuvieron instalándose hasta el sábado. Se estuvieron instalando hasta el sábado. 4. Estuvimos paseándonos hasta el anochecer. Nos estuvimos paseando hasta el anochecer. 5. Estuviste lavándotela hasta que sonó el teléfono. Te la estuviste lavando hasta que sonó el teléfono. 6. Estuvieron reuniéndose hasta que la presidenta levantó la reunión. Se estuvieron reuniendo hasta que la presidenta levantó la reunión. 7. Estuvo portándose mal hasta que sus papás le riñeron. Se estuvo portando mal hasta que sus papás le riñeron. 8. Estuvo contándoselos hasta que su amiga no pudo más. Se los estuvo contando hasta que su amiga no pudo más.

G 1. Llevo cuarenta minutos navegando en la Red. 2. Llevan tres horas jugando al golf.
3. Lleva un par de días sintiéndose mal. 4. Llevamos varios años interesándonos en el arte. 5. Llevas quince minutos limándote las uñas. 6. Lleváis media hora probándoos esos pantalones. 7. Llevo mucho tiempo manteniéndome en forma. 8. Llevan una semana reuniéndose en el congreso.

H 1. Patricia was still working in the suburbs when I ran into her. 2. The company was gradually raising its prices to create Web sites. 3. You were running up the stairs.
4. You danced down the stairs. 5. We've been writing instant messages to each other (OR We've been instant messaging to each other) for half an hour. 6. They caught a cold drinking from other people's glasses. 7. They spent the weekend having a good time.
8. Carmen hurt her finger cutting the bread.

I 1. ¿El helado de chocolate? Estoy sirviéndoselo / Se lo estoy sirviendo ahora mismo.
2. ¿Su abrigo? Él está poniéndoselo. / Él se lo está poniendo. 3. Ellos están peinándose / Ellos se están peinando mientras nosotros estamos vistiéndonos / nosotros nos estamos vistiendo. 4. El jugador se rompió los pantalones (OR el pantalón) cayéndose.
5. Estábamos durmiéndonos cuando sonó el teléfono. 6. Estarán instalándose en su casa nueva. 7. No la vi bailando en la discoteca anoche. ¿Qué estaría haciendo? 8. Espero que estés arreglándote / te estés arreglando para que no lleguemos tarde. 9. ¿Uds. lo oyeron tosiendo toda la noche? 10. Llevamos veinte minutos buscando un parquímetro.
11. González estuvo lanzando (OR pitcheando) muy bien hasta que se torció el tobillo.

J 1. No, lo ganó el equipo Rojo. 2. No, se lo torció Raimundo. 3. No, se la quemó mi amigo. 4. No, se reunieron los consultores. 5. No, abrirán en la esquina una pastelería.
6. No, las hacíamos nosotros. 7. No, está probándoselo Miriám. 8. No, los busca la otra sucursal.

K 1. Los cheques los cobró Sara. 2. La lista la hicimos Antonio y yo. 3. El guacamole lo preparabas tú. 4. A sus hermanitos los ha cuidado Inés. 5. Las cuentas las pagué yo.
6. Mi cámara digital la usarán ellos. 7. A los pacientes nerviosos los tranquilizó el enfermero. 8. A Lorena la llevó a un concierto Andrés. 9. El informe lo han impreso Uds. 10. Al empleado insolente lo despidió el dueño del negocio.

L 1. Victoria lo conoció. / Lo conoció Victoria. 2. Él conoció a Victoria. / A Victoria la conoció él. 3. Isabel se lo dijo. / Se lo dijo Isabel. 4. Ella se lo dijo a Isabel. 5. Jorge y Rita la vieron. / La vieron Jorge y Rita. 6. Ud. vio a Jorge y a Rita. / A Jorge y a Rita los vio Ud.
7. Martín se las mostró. / Se las mostró Martín. 8. Se las mostraron a Martín.
9. Miguel le leyó. / Le leyó Miguel. 10. Le leyó a Miguel.

Chapter 15
Passive Constructions; Reverse Construction Verbs

A   1. La computadora fue reparada por el técnico.   2. Una cadena de perfumerías será abierta por una empresa alemana.   3. El vino fue derramado por el mesero.   4. La revista electrónica es escrita por unos estudiantes de informática.   5. Los planes serán hechos por este equipo de arquitectos.   6. Los aparatos eléctricos fueron desenchufados por el electricista.   7. El software será instalado por estos programadores.   8. La película es rodada en Barcelona por el director inglés.   9. La conferencia ha sido dada por el presidente.   10. Los terroristas fueron detenidos por los soldados.   11. Estas tortas fueron hechas por una pastelera de la academia de artes culinarias.   12. Una serie de artículos sobre la guerra fue publicada por el periódico.

B   1. El informe fue escrito por el asesor. El informe estaba escrito.   2. La reunión fue suspendida por la directora. La reunión estaba suspendida.   3. Los discursos fueron pronunciados por los voceros. Los discursos estaban pronunciados.   4. Las páginas Web fueron redactadas por el administrador de Web. Las páginas Web estaban redactadas. 5. Los problemas fueron resueltos por la psicóloga. Los problemas estaban resueltos. 6. La sinfonía fue compuesta por el compositor francés. La sinfonía estaba compuesta. 7. La ventana fue rota por el jugador de béisbol. La ventana estaba rota.   8. La ley fue aprobada por los legisladores. La ley estaba aprobada.   9. Las colonias fueron fundadas por los exploradores. Las colonias estaban fundadas.   10. Los pacientes fueron cuidados por la enfermera. Los pacientes estaban cuidados.

C   1. Las pizzas fueron entregadas a domicilio por el repartidor.   2. Los bancos fueron cerrados por los gerentes.   3. Los muebles fueron puestos (OR colocados) en la sala por los cargadores.   4. Las paredes fueron pintadas por nuestro pintor.   5. El coche fue alquilado por los turistas.   6. El coche estaba alquilado.   7. Los políticos de los dos partidos fueron entrevistados por la prensa.   8. Los políticos estaban entrevistados.   9. El regalo fue envuelto por nosotros.   10. El regalo estaba envuelto.   11. Mi amigo/amiga consiguió los billetes en la Red (OR por Internet).   12. Los billetes estaban comprados.

D   1. Se servían platos tejanomexicanos.   2. Se venden flores exquisitas en esta florería. 3. Se necesitan programadores en esta compañía de alta tecnología.   4. Se harán tres copias del documento.   5. Se realizó el proyecto.   6. Se están organizando los archivos. 7. Se habla español en todas estas tiendas.   8. Se leyeron las obras clásicas.   9. Se firmó el contrato.   10. Se va a enviar el correo electrónico pronto.   11. No se puede hacer preguntas todavía.   12. Se debe visitar ese sitio Web.   13. Se quemó el pan. 14. Se necesita almacenar los datos.

E   1. Se trabaja en equipo.   2. Se navega en la Red.   3. Se vive en una sociedad de información.   4. Se compra y se vende en un mercado global.   5. Se puede hablar por teléfono móvil.   6. Se debe llegar antes de las cuatro.   7. Se entra por la puerta principal. 8. Se sale al jardín por aquí.   9. Se sube en este elevador.   10. Se baja por la escalera trasera.   11. Se charla en el canal de conversación.   12. Se busca el cajero automático.

F   1. Se habla inglés aquí.   2. Se debe tomar el tren de la una.   3. Uno se preocupa demasiado.   4. Se puede vivir muy bien en esta ciudad.   5. Se muestran (OR Se enseñan) los apartamentos entre las diez y las seis.   6. Los empleados fueron contratados por el gerente.   7. Estos productos fueron hechos por una empresa inglesa.   8. Uno se despierta tarde los fines de semana.   9. ¿Cómo se dice "the Web" en español?   10. Uno se abrocha el cinturón de seguridad cuando se viaja en coche.   11. ¿Se mató a los terroristas? 12. Sí, se les mató. Y se encarceló a muchos otros.

G 1. Le gustan estas marcas. 2. ¿Te interesan mis ideas? 3. Nos encantaron los conciertos. 4. Me entusiasmaban sus planes. 5. Les quedaban los exámenes orales. 6. Os fascinarán los pianistas. 7. Les agradan las exposiciones. 8. Nos han caído bien esos profesores. 9. Le faltan unos dólares. 10. Me harían falta unas tarjetas de memoria.

H 1. No te va a convenir meterte en sus asuntos. 2. No nos va a importar el qué dirán. 3. Me va a tocar a mí hacer la compra. 4. Les va a sobrar tiempo. 5. Le va a desagradar tu actitud. 6. Os van a disgustar sus costumbres. 7. Le van a interesar esas pinturas. 8. Te van a encantar los postres. 9. Nos va a urgir contactarlos. 10. Me va a agradar pasar las vacaciones en Ibiza.

I 1. ¿A quién le toca? 2. Le gustan estos perfumes. 3. Nos entusiasmó el partido de béisbol. 4. Les convendrá esperar. 5. ¿Les interesaría? 6. No le van a caer bien. / Le van a caer mal. 7. Francamente no me importa. 8. ¿Te gustaría salir a comer ? 9. Me encantaría. 10. ¿Qué le hace falta? 11. No me hace falta nada. 12. ¿Os falta dinero? 13. No, nos sobra. 14. Me desagradarían. / Me disgustarían.

J 1. Se le perdieron los anteojos. 2. Se me ocurrió una cosa increíble. 3. Se les descompuso el aire acondicionado. 4. Se le quebraron dos dedos. 5. Se te cayeron los platos. 6. Se nos quedó la llave del coche en casa. 7. Se les acabó la paciencia. 8. Se os olvidó hacer la llamada. 9. Se le averiaron los frenos del coche. 10. Se me olvidó mi clave personal. 11. Se les perdió la libreta de cheques. 12. Se le acabó el jugo de naranja.

K 1. Se le quedó su teléfono celular en la oficina. 2. ¿Todavía no se le ha ocurrido a nadie? 3. Se les está descomponiendo/averiando su computadora. 4. ¿Se te ha olvidado que su cumpleaños es mañana? 5. ¿A quién se le quedaron estos guantes aquí? 6. ¿Cómo se le quebró/rompió el pie? 7. Se me quebró/rompió jugando al fútbol. 8. Se nos está acabando el pan. 9. Se me cayó el florero. 10. ¿Se te rompió/quebró?

Oral Exercises

Chapter 1 The Present Tense of Regular Verbs

A 1. Terminamos el proyecto.
   2. Asistimos a un concierto.
   3. Viajamos a Inglaterra.
   4. Comprendemos el problema.
   5. Navegamos en la Red.
   6. Subimos la escalera.
   7. Comemos en este restaurante.
   8. Leemos una novela.

B 1. Aprenden las fechas de memoria.
   2. Compran una computadora.
   3. Eligen una película.
   4. Abren una tienda de ropa.
   5. Beben vino tinto con la comida.
   6. Siguen por esa carretera.
   7. Toman el tren de las once.
   8. Construyen una casa en la playa.

C 1. Yo mando correos electrónicos.
2. Laura habla por teléfono.
3. Uds. imprimen unos documentos.
4. Daniel repara su computadora.
5. Tú pagas las cuentas.
6. Pablo recibe a unos clientes.
7. Miguel y Rebeca crean un sitio Web.
8. Ud. y yo entramos datos.

D 1. Hace diez minutos que espero un taxi.
2. Hace siete meses que viven en San Francisco.
3. Hace un año que dirige la obra de teatro.
4. Hace diez años que enseño química.
5. Hace tres años que cocinan comida italiana.
6. Hace media hora que miramos televisión.
7. Hace veinte minutos que discuten el asunto.
8. Hace cuatro meses que toma clases de inglés.

E 1. Arturo estaciona el coche.
2. Nosotros rompemos la cita.
3. Sara y Jaime ahorran dinero.
4. Tú recibes un regalo de cumpleaños.
5. María Elena busca sus llaves.
6. Uds. sacan los billetes.
7. Ud. solicita el puesto.
8. Yo dirijo la empresa.

F 1. ¡Qué va! Nunca llora.
2. ¡Qué va! Nunca gritan.
3. ¡Qué va! Nunca llega tarde.
4. ¡Qué va! Nunca interrumpe.
5. ¡Qué va! Nunca rompe sus juguetes.
6. ¡Qué va! Nunca finge estar triste.
7. ¡Qué va! Nunca exijo lo imposible.
8. ¡Qué va! Nunca manejan rápidamente.

G 1. No, nadie escucha nada.
2. No, nadie come nada.
3. No, nadie recibe nada.
4. No, nadie vende nada.
5. No, nadie interrumpe nada.
6. No, nadie mira nada.
7. No, nadie exige nada.
8. No, nadie busca nada.

Chapter 2 Stem-Changing Verbs; Special Verbs Ending in **-iar** and **-uar**

A 1. Cierro la cuenta.
2. No entiendo sus ideas.
3. Vuelvo a la tienda por departamentos.
4. Empiezo el proyecto en mayo.
5. No encuentro los documentos.
6. Sirvo la cena a las ocho.
7. Nunca duermo la siesta.
8. Almuerzo en este restaurante.

B 1. Pensamos en la excursión.
2. Seguimos sus consejos.
3. Mostramos el sitio Web.
4. Lo sentimos mucho.
5. Jugamos al fútbol todas las tardes.
6. Resolvemos los problemas fácilmente.
7. Probamos todos los postres.
8. No mentimos nunca.

C 1. Marta espera conseguir una beca este año.
2. Los señores López no pueden volver hasta el viernes.
3. Yo sé crear una base de datos.
4. Ud. prefiere vivir en las afueras de la ciudad.
5. Roberto decide estudiar administración de empresas.
6. Tú no debes confiar en ese tipo.
7. Los jefes no necesitan despedir a nadie.
8. Mi marido y yo queremos disfrutar de la vida.

D 1. No sé, pero creo que quiere tocar el piano.
2. No sé, pero creo que quieren ascender a este gerente.
3. No sé, pero creo que quiere seguir con su equipo.
4. No sé, pero creo que quiere renunciar a su puesto.
5. No sé, pero creo que quiere rodar un video.
6. No sé, pero creo que quiere gobernar el país.
7. No sé, pero creo que quieren desarrollar nuevos proyectos.
8. No sé, pero creo que quiere construir edificios.

E 1. No busco a nadie.
2. No llevo a nadie.
3. No espero a nadie.
4. No visito a nadie.
5. No invito a nadie.
6. No escucho a nadie.
7. No veo a nadie.
8. No encuentro a nadie.

F 1. Uds. ayudan a sus papás.
2. Nosotros llevamos las maletas.
3. Yo recuerdo a la señorita Ramírez.
4. Tú no comprendes al profesor.
5. Él entiende el plan de negocios.
6. Ellos acuestan a sus hijos.
7. Ud. enciende la computadora.
8. Yo despierto al niño.

G 1. Estaciona el carro.
2. Viste a sus hijos.
3. Envuelve unos paquetes.
4. Juega al tenis con su marido.
5. Almuerza con su amiga Victoria.
6. Envía unos correos electrónicos.
7. Visita a sus padres.
8. Sirve una cena especial.

Chapter 3 Irregular Verbs (Part I)

A 1. Pongo fin a esa situación.
2. Salgo para el aeropuerto en seguida.
3. No conozco a ese arquitecto.
4. Siempre conduzco con cuidado.
5. Oigo hablar de eso.
6. Traigo dos botellas de vino tinto.
7. Traduzco el artículo al japonés.
8. Tengo ganas de ver una obra de teatro.

B 1. Venimos mañana en tren.
2. Oyes unos ruidos.
3. Caigo en el hielo.
4. Ofrecen un plan muy sencillo.
5. Dice la verdad.
6. Introduzco los datos.
7. No tienen razón en este caso.
8. No valgo para ese trabajo.

C 1. Tomás y yo tenemos hambre.
2. Ud. tiene sueño.
3. Tú tienes miedo.
4. Yo tengo éxito.
5. María y Paco tienen paciencia.
6. Viviana tiene celos.
7. Uds. tienen calor.
8. Ricardo tiene prisa.

D 1. ¿Piensan viajar en avión?
2. ¿Dicen que llueve esta noche?
3. ¿Hace la compra todos los días?
4. ¿No conocen a los programadores?
5. ¿Ponen películas extranjeras en este cine?
6. ¿El centro comercial abre a las diez?
7. ¿No quiere tomar las vacaciones en verano?
8. ¿Su cumpleaños cae en miércoles?

E 1. Aquella empresa crece muy rápidamente, ¿verdad?
2. No sabe reparar la máquina, ¿verdad?
3. Tienes que entregar el informe el lunes, ¿no es cierto?
4. Quieren vivir en el suroeste, ¿no es verdad?
5. Parece que el niño tiene mucho sueño, ¿no?
6. Ya no vienen con cuentos, ¿verdad?
7. Transmiten el programa a las diez, ¿no es cierto?
8. Haces clic a este botón, ¿no?

F 1. ¿Dónde tiene lugar la reunión?
2. ¿Quiénes llegan?
3. ¿Cuántos años tiene Lucía?
4. ¿Cuál es la capital de Colombia?
5. ¿A qué hora comienza la telenovela?
6. ¿Cuánto cuesta el coche?
7. ¿Cómo salen las cosas?
8. ¿De dónde vienen?
9. ¿De quién es esta casa?
10. ¿Qué tiempo hace hoy?

Chapter 4 Irregular Verbs (Part II)

A 1. Marco y yo vamos a la universidad.
2. Tú vas al centro comercial.
3. Uds. van de compras.
4. Susana va a un concierto.
5. Pablo va al dentista.
6. Alicia y Eduardo van de excursión.
7. Ud. va al cibercafé.
8. Carolina va a una tienda por departamentos.

B 1. Yo voy a dar un paseo por el parque.
2. Blanca va a merendar en un café.
3. Tú y yo vamos a conseguir los billetes de avión.
4. Tú vas a rodar una película.
5. Carlos y Eva van a venir por la tarde.
6. Ud. va a dormir la siesta.
7. Guillermo va a almorzar con sus colegas.
8. Uds. van a jugar al tenis.

C 1. Tú sabes a qué hora llegan los invitados.
   2. Yo conozco al profesor Durán.
   3. Rosario sabe hacer programación.
   4. Gerardo y Luisa conocen Costa Rica.
   5. Ud. conoce a mis cuñados.
   6. Nosotros sabemos el precio del condominio.
   7. Uds. saben lo del incendio.
   8. Guillermo sabe cuál es el problema.

D 1. Teresa sueña con hacer un viaje a la India.
   2. Los señores Bermúdez tienen que buscar casa.
   3. Va a llover todo el día.
   4. Acabo de dar con Martín y Lola.
   5. ¿Amenazas con renunciar a tu puesto?
   6. Uds. no tardan en entregar el informe.
   7. Los niños empiezan a tener sueño.
   8. Sergio trata de ahorrar lo más posible.

E 1. Las hermanas van a abrir una tienda en un barrio elegante.
   2. Piensan vender su ropa directamente a las clientes.
   3. Carmen sabe crear vestidos de fiesta.
   4. Paloma prefiere hacer ropa de moda deportiva.
   5. Tienen que contratar a tres modelos.
   6. Paloma empieza a poner un anuncio en los medios de comunicación.
   7. Las hermanas sueñan con tener éxito en su negocio.
   8. Se alegran de hacer una gran fiesta de apertura de su tienda.

F 1. Ah sí, hay que comer sano.
   2. Ah sí, hay que dormir ocho horas.
   3. Ah sí, hay que escuchar música.
   4. Ah sí, hay que pasar mucho tiempo con la familia.
   5. Ah sí, hay que salir con los amigos.
   6. Ah sí, hay que estar contento con la vida profesional.
   7. Ah sí, hay que disfrutar de la vida.
   8. Ah sí, hay que vivir con menos estrés.

G 1. Hay que pensar antes de actuar.
   2. Hay algunos problemas todavía.
   3. Hay clases de contabilidad en línea.
   4. Hay que cobrar el cheque lo antes posible.
   5. Hay que descargar los documentos.
   6. Hay una tienda de computadoras en esta calle.
   7. Hay que ver los diseños gráficos.
   8. Hay un tren a las tres de la tarde.

Chapter 5 Ser and Estar

A 1. No, es de Italia.
     2. No, son de Canadá.
     3. No, somos de los Estados Unidos.
     4. No, soy de Corea.
     5. No, es de Uruguay.
     6. No, son del Japón.
     7. No, es de la India.
     8. No, son de Polonia.

B 1. Tú eres de origen griego.
     2. Perla y César son de origen portugués.
     3. Juan es de origen irlandés.
     4. Elvira es de origen húngaro.
     5. Nosotros somos de origen cubano.
     6. Uds. son de origen árabe.
     7. Ud. es de origen español.
     8. Ellas son de origen tailandés.

C 1. Ester es inteligente.
     2. Andrés está hecho una sopa.
     3. Estas sinfonías son impresionantes.
     4. El hotel Cuatro Estaciones está a la vuelta de la esquina.
     5. Sara y Rebeca son encantadoras.
     6. David y yo estamos de vacaciones.
     7. El celular es de Antonio.
     8. Todos los directores están reunidos.
     9. El carro es azul oscuro.
   10. Estas blusas son de seda.
   11. Aurora y Julio están acatarrados.
   12. Manolo es periodista.

D 1. Yo estoy en Berlín.
     2. Juan Carlos está en Barcelona.
     3. Uds. están en Florencia.
     4. Eugenia está en Moscú.
     5. David y yo estamos en Londres.
     6. Tú estás en Viena.
     7. Ramón y Carlota están en Praga.
     8. Pablo está en Lisboa.

E 1. ¿Está terminado el proyecto?
     2. ¿Es encantadora su hermana?
     3. ¿Son orgánicos aquellos productos?
     4. ¿Son fáciles los exámenes?
     5. ¿Está servida la cena?
     6. ¿Está en la avenida de América el museo de historia?
     7. ¿Están escritos los informes?
     8. ¿Es aburrido ese programa?

F 1. Sí, la tengo.
2. Sí, los llamo.
3. Sí, lo entienden.
4. Sí, las busca.
5. Sí, lo hago.
6. Sí, lo baña.
7. Sí, las llevamos.
8. Sí, los ayudan.

G 1. Piensan llamarla./La piensan llamar.
2. Prefiero llevarlo./Lo prefiero llevar.
3. Quiere alquilarlo./Lo quiere alquilar.
4. Necesitamos firmarlos./Los necesitamos firmar.
5. Acaban de invitarlas./Las acaban de invitar.
6. Espero conocerlo./Lo espero conocer.
7. No deben perderlo./No lo deben perder.
8. No puedes visitarla./No la puedes visitar.

Chapter 6 The Preterit

A 1. Escucharon música.
2. Prendí la luz.
3. Subió a su cuarto.
4. No entendieron nada.
5. Esperamos el tren.
6. ¿En qué pensaste?
7. Estudié administración de empresas.
8. ¿Viviste en este barrio?
9. Almorcé con unos amigos.
10. No lo creyeron.

B 1. Ya las repitió.
2. Ya la sirvieron.
3. Ya lo despidió.
4. Ya las vistió.
5. Ya lo medimos.
6. Ya los siguieron.
7. Ya lo distribuyó.
8. Ya la construyó.

C 1. Fue abogado.
2. ¿Qué te dijeron?
3. Fuimos a la playa.
4. No pudo ir.
5. ¿No quisiste trotar?
6. Hice investigaciones.
7. Me diste un hermoso regalo.
8. Supimos qué pasó.
9. Vino tarde.
10. Traje flores.

D 1. Mateo y Emilia le enseñaron el centro histórico.
2. Mateo y Emilia me enseñaron el centro histórico.
3. Mateo y Emilia les enseñaron el centro histórico.
4. Mateo y Emilia nos enseñaron el centro histórico.
5. Mateo y Emilia te enseñaron el centro histórico.
6. Mateo y Emilia le enseñaron el centro histórico.
7. Mateo y Emilia le enseñaron el centro histórico.
8. Mateo y Emilia les enseñaron el centro histórico.

E 1. La clienta le enseñó la tarjeta de crédito a la dependienta.
2. Los estudiantes le entregaron el examen al profesor.
3. Yo les mandé un correo electrónico a mis primos.
4. El cocinero les sirvió el pescado a los invitados.
5. El jefe le ofreció el puesto a la señorita Vargas.
6. Los papás les contaron cuentos a sus hijos.
7. Él les mostró los edificios históricos a los turistas.
8. Ellos le dieron esos documentos al secretario.

F 1. Yo le solicité la beca.
2. Ud. les pidió el carro.
3. Nosotros le trajimos los discos compactos.
4. Él le leyó el cuento.
5. ¿Tú les dijiste el secreto?
6. Uds. no le enviaron la base de datos.
7. Ellos les mandaron los correos electrónicos.
8. Ella les ocultó su tristeza.

Chapter 7 The Imperfect; The Imperfect vs. the Preterit

A 1. Yo leía los periódicos en línea.
2. ¿Uds. volvían en coche o en tren?
3. ¿Tú pensabas viajar a Barcelona?
4. Ellos iban a ver esta exposición de arte.
5. Él no podía venir hasta el fin de semana.
6. Nosotros éramos amigos íntimos del gobernador.
7. Ella vivía en el barrio histórico de la ciudad.
8. Yo hacía cola en la taquilla para sacar entradas.
9. ¿Qué preferían Uds. hacer el domingo?
10. ¿Ud. no veía a ningún conocido en el grupo?
11. Llovía todos los días en primavera.
12. Yo estaba de acuerdo contigo.
13. No había manera de convencerlo.
14. Ellas querían aprovecharse de las ofertas.

B 1. Llovía cuando yo salí.
2. Eran las nueve de la noche cuando yo salí.
3. Estaba despejado cuando yo salí.
4. Era la una y media de la tarde cuando yo salí.
5. Hacía calor cuando yo salí.
6. Eran las siete de la mañana cuando yo salí.
7. Estaba nublado cuando yo salí.
8. Era mediodía cuando yo salí.

C 1. ¿Cuánto tiempo hacía que Uds. vivían en Sevilla?
2. ¿Cuánto tiempo hacía que Paco jugaba al golf?
3. ¿Cuánto tiempo hacía que Sofía y Javier estaban casados?
4. ¿Cuánto tiempo hacía que tú estudiabas administración de empresas?
5. ¿Cuánto tiempo hacía que Manuel y Clara eran novios?
6. ¿Cuánto tiempo hacía que Ud. esperaba el avión?
7. ¿Cuánto tiempo hacía que Alicia tocaba el piano?
8. ¿Cuánto tiempo hacía que nosotros buscábamos una casa en la playa?

D 1. Nos las enseñó el diseñador.
2. Se los di a mi compañero de cuarto.
3. Se lo dijeron a todos.
4. Se la pedí a mi mamá.
5. Me los hizo un carpintero.
6. Se los leyó su hermano mayor.
7. Se las compraron sus abuelos.
8. Se lo pagamos a nuestros hijos.

E 1. Ya se lo vendí.
2. Ya me los trajeron.
3. Ya se la regalé.
4. Ya se lo hizo.
5. Ya se las dimos.
6. Ya me lo contó.
7. Ya se las expliqué.
8. Ya se las enviaron.

F 1. Mario dijo que quería visitarnos.
2. Viviana y Juan dijeron que estaban contentos.
3. Mi amigo dijo que no podía ir conmigo.
4. Estrella dijo que iba a casarse con Mateo.
5. Miguel dijo que era feliz.
6. Jimena dijo que ya no fumaba.
7. Sus primos dijeron que venían en marzo.
8. Los niños dijeron que tenían hambre.

G 1. Cuando él llegó, navegábamos en la Red.
2. Cuando él llegó, veíamos una película.
3. Cuando él llegó, íbamos de compras.
4. Cuando él llegó, bailábamos salsa.
5. Cuando él llegó, tomábamos una copa.
6. Cuando él llegó, les servíamos el postre a los invitados.
7. Cuando él llegó, hacíamos planes para nuestro viaje.
8. Cuando él llegó, salíamos para el teatro.

Chapter 8 The Past Participle; The Present Perfect; The Pluperfect

A 1. Yo he hecho una excursión a la sierra.
2. Tú no has oído la buena noticia.
3. Nosotros nos hemos mudado al centro.
4. No ha ocurrido nada últimamente.
5. Los señores Álvarez han abierto una joyería.
6. Uds. se han divertido mucho.
7. Ha caído mucha nieve esta semana.
8. Ha habido mucho que hacer estos días.
9. La boda de Ana y Gerardo no ha tenido lugar todavía.
10. Antonio se ha graduado en la facultad de derecho.

B 1. Ya lo he colgado.
2. Ya lo han visto.
3. Ya la he puesto.
4. Ya se lo hemos leído.
5. Ya los ha impreso.
6. Ya se la ha devuelto.
7. Ya las he probado.
8. Ya se los hemos dado.

C 1. Había leído un libro de historia.
2. No habían vuelto todavía.
3. Te habías ido de viaje.
4. Había habido algunas dificultades.
5. Habíamos hecho nuestros planes.
6. Yo había traído la computadora.
7. Había comenzado a nevar fuerte.
8. No le habían dicho nada.

D 1. las flores abiertas
2. el agua hervida
3. los datos leídos
4. la reunión pospuesta
5. el pescado frito
6. los carros aparcados
7. las cosas perdidas
8. los estudiantes inscritos
9. los platos hechos
10. el programa transmitido
11. la vida examinada
12. las máquinas descompuestas

E 1. Sí, la cuenta está pagada.
2. Sí, los aparatos están encendidos.
3. Sí, el problema está solucionado.
4. Sí, las maletas están hechas.
5. Sí, los muebles están colocados.
6. Sí, las hojas están recogidas.
7. Sí, el almuerzo está servido.
8. Sí, los cheques están cobrados.

F   1. Cuando yo volví de las vacaciones, Paco y Luz habían llegado de Chile.
2. Cuando yo volví de las vacaciones, Elena había roto con su novio.
3. Cuando yo volví de las vacaciones, Jorge había renunciado a su puesto.
4. Cuando yo volví de las vacaciones, los Gutiérrez habían vendido su casa.
5. Cuando yo volví de las vacaciones, mis colegas habían comenzado un nuevo proyecto.
6. Cuando yo volví de las vacaciones, tú te habías ido a Australia.
7. Cuando yo volví de las vacaciones, Javier había terminado su tesis.
8. Cuando yo volví de las vacaciones, mi sobrina había nacido.

Chapter 9 The Imperative

A   1. Sí, deje un recado.
2. Sí, suba por la escalera.
3. Sí, salga ahora mismo.
4. Sí, venga con ellos.
5. Sí, haga ejercicio.
6. Sí, pida un préstamo.
7. Sí, vaya a ver esa película.
8. Sí, duerma ocho horas.

B   1. Sí, descárguenlos.
2. Sí, corríjanlas.
3. Sí, envíenselos.
4. Sí, imprímanlos.
5. Sí, háganla reparar.
6. Sí, explíquenselo.
7. Sí, introdúzcanlos.
8. Sí, muéstrensela.

C   1. Claro. Asiste a la conferencia.
2. Claro. Sal con Rafael.
3. Claro. Ve de vacaciones en agosto.
4. Claro. Sé más comprensiva.
5. Claro. Ten más paciencia.
6. Claro. Ven a verlos.
7. Claro. Juega al tenis el sábado.
8. Claro. Empieza a buscar trabajo.

D   1. No gastes una fortuna.
2. No renuncies a tu puesto.
3. No vayas a Tahití.
4. No compres una furgoneta.
5. No salgas con Valeria.
6. No llegues tarde a la fiesta.
7. No inviertas mucho dinero en esta compañía.
8. No juegues a las cartas.

E 1. No, no las llamemos.
2. No, no las probemos.
3. No, no vayamos a la tienda por departamentos.
4. No, no lo paseemos.
5. No, no asistamos a la conferencia.
6. No, no se los traigamos.
7. No, no se los enseñemos.
8. No, no se la hagamos.

F 1. Muy bien. Vamos a tomarlo.
2. Muy bien. Vamos a jugar al baloncesto.
3. Muy bien. Vamos a comerla.
4. Muy bien. Vamos a trotar en el parque.
5. Muy bien. Vamos a comprárselas.
6. Muy bien. Vamos a ir a la megatienda de computadoras.
7. Muy bien. Vamos a descargarlas.
8. Muy bien. Vamos a instalarlos.

G 1. Sí, désela.
2. No, no se lo explique.
3. Sí, muéstremelas.
4. No, no se los mande.
5. Sí, entrégueselos.
6. No, no se lo pida.
7. Sí, ofrézcaselo.
8. No, no se los preste.

Chapter 10 The Future and the Conditional; The Future Perfect and the Conditional Perfect

A 1. Tomaré fotos.
2. Saldrán a cenar.
3. ¿Harás la compra?
4. Irá a la tienda de cómputo.
5. No estaremos en casa.
6. Habrá mucho público en el teatro.
7. Todo saldrá bien.
8. Tendrán prisa por llegar.

B 1. Compartirás el apartamento.
2. Despertaré a los niños.
3. Lloverá toda la semana.
4. Vendrán el mes que viene.
5. ¿Querrás acompañarme?
6. No diremos nada más.
7. No podré ir todavía.
8. Su cumpleaños caerá en viernes.

C   1. Elena habrá regresado para el mes próximo.
        2. Nosotros habremos cenado para las nueve.
        3. La reunión habrá terminado antes de las tres.
        4. La librería habrá abierto para las diez.
        5. Yo habré vuelto para mediados del mes.
        6. Habrá nevado antes de enero.
        7. Pablo y Eva habrán llegado para el lunes.
        8. Tú habrás vendido el condominio para el verano.

D   1. Yo tomaría vitaminas.
        2. Nosotros haríamos ejercicio.
        3. Ellos beberían mucha agua.
        4. Tú dormirías ocho horas.
        5. Ella caminaría todos los días.
        6. Uds. saldrían al aire libre.
        7. Ud. mantendría un peso saludable.
        8. Él llevaría una vida relajada.

E   1. Nos escribió que vendría.
        2. Le expliqué que habría tiempo para todo.
        3. Te dijo que iría de viaje, ¿verdad?
        4. Me escribieron que volverían pronto.
        5. Les informó que no podría verlos.
        6. Nos dijeron que saldrían la semana entrante.
        7. Le informamos que la boda sería en enero.
        8. ¿Te dijeron que te invitarían a la fiesta?

F   1. Nosotros no habríamos dicho mentiras.
        2. Tú no habrías interrumpido al profesor.
        3. Lorenzo no se habría enojado al oír la noticia.
        4. Uds. no habrían conducido descuidadamente.
        5. Marco y Sofía no habrían caído en un error.
        6. Ud. no le habría dado consejos.
        7. Andrés y yo no nos habríamos molestado.
        8. Eugenia no se habría peleado con Paco.

G   1. Serán las tres.
        2. Ella tendrá treinta y dos años.
        3. Ellos querrán descansar.
        4. Lloverá mañana.
        5. Habrá problemas con el plan de negocios.
        6. Los pendientes costarán mucho dinero.
        7. Tú tendrás ganas de salir.
        8. Hará ochenta grados.

Chapter 11 The Subjunctive (Part I): The Present Subjunctive

A   1. Espero que mis colegas apoyen mi candidatura.
2. Espero que Rafael y Laura nos vengan a ver.
3. Espero que tú tengas éxito en tu nueva empresa.
4. Espero que Uds. no pierdan el avión.
5. Espero que nosotros disfrutemos de la vida.
6. Espero que Ud. salga a cenar con nosotros.
7. Espero que mi equipo gane el campeonato.
8. Espero que me den el puesto.

B   1. Quieren que ella les diga la verdad.
2. Insiste en que guardemos el secreto.
3. Necesitamos que él nos entregue el informe.
4. Tiene miedo de que las cosas no salgan bien.
5. Prefieren que vayas en coche.
6. Niego que hablemos mal de ellos.
7. Dudamos que Ud. empiece el proyecto esta semana.
8. Siente que yo no pueda acompañarlo.

C   1. Es posible que él no sepa lo que pasó.
2. Es cierto que ellos viven en este barrio.
3. No creo que tú tengas razón.
4. No dudamos que ella es trabajadora.
5. Es importante que Ud. actualice los datos.
6. Es bueno que él haga investigaciones ahora.
7. Saben que yo dirijo una empresa creciente.
8. Es una lástima que Uds. no encuentren su cámara.

D   1. Ellos esperan que él llegue pronto.
2. Ella teme perder el avión.
3. Nosotros insistimos en que tú vuelvas.
4. Tú sientes no poder llevarlas.
5. Uds. se alegran de que yo los visite.
6. Él prefiere ir al centro comercial hoy.
7. Yo necesito que ellos suban los muebles.
8. Ellas quieren que nosotros veamos la película.

E   1. Escribí el correo electrónico y lo mandé.
2. Salieron a las siete porque tenían que estar a las ocho.
3. Fuimos a verlos pero ya habían salido.
4. No sólo viaja a Inglaterra sino que también conocerá Italia.
5. No pudo llegar a tiempo porque había mucho tráfico.
6. Se sentaron a la mesa y comenzaron a comer.
7. Ella no compró galletas así que sólo sirvió fruta y queso.
8. La casa costaba tanto dinero de modo que nadie quiso comprarla.

F 1. Nosotros se lo diremos cuando él venga.
 2. Uds. entrarán en la casa en cuanto comience a nevar.
 3. Yo me quedaré en la oficina después de que tú te vayas.
 4. Ella recogerá a sus hijos tan pronto como ellos la llamen.
 5. Ellos usarán la impresora antes de que otras personas la necesiten.
 6. Él me prestará su celular para que yo haga una llamada.
 7. Te prestaremos el carro con tal de que nos lo traigas para el lunes.
 8. Ud. verá la película a menos que haya mucha cola en la taquilla.

Chapter 12 The Subjunctive (Part II): The Present Perfect Subjunctive; The Imperfect Subjunctive; The Pluperfect Subjunctive

A 1. Nos sorprende que Jaime haya dicho tonterías.
 2. Es una lástima que Ud. no haya hecho construir una casa.
 3. Es probable que Uds. hayan visto la exposición de arte.
 4. Esperamos que todo haya salido bien.
 5. Sientes que Felipe y Manolo no te hayan dado su apoyo.
 6. Es importante que Gabriela haya sacado buenas notas.
 7. No nos gusta que Mari Paz se haya ido sin despedirse de nosotros.
 8. No es cierto que hayamos estado enojados.

B 1. Ramón esperaba que el director le ofreciera el puesto.
 2. Hacía falta que nos reuniéramos todas las semanas.
 3. Nos alegrábamos de que nuestros hijos fueran felices.
 4. Nos sorprendió que el restaurante estuviera cerrado.
 5. No les gustaba que hiciera veinte grados todos los días.
 6. Era necesario que pusiera fin a esa terrible situación.
 7. Era imprescindible que Ud. llegara a la hora indicada.
 8. Insistieron en que trabajaras en su equipo.

C 1. Pero habla como si fuera abogado.
 2. Pero habla como si fuera actriz.
 3. Pero hablan como si fueran médicos.
 4. Pero habla como si fuera director ejecutivo.
 5. Pero hablan como si fueran enfermeros.
 6. Pero habla como si fuera ingeniero químico.
 7. Pero hablan como si fueran programadores.
 8. Pero habla como si fuera asesor estratégico.

D 1. Esperaban que tú los hubieras llamado.
 2. Ojalá yo la hubiera visto.
 3. No creía que Uds. hubieran oído la noticia.
 4. Les gustó que hubiéramos pasado las vacaciones con ellos.
 5. Nos sorprendió que él hubiera roto con su novia.
 6. Fue imposible que Ud. hubiera dicho algo tan feo.
 7. Dudábamos que ellos hubieran cambiado de idea.
 8. Temían que hubiera habido un terremoto muy fuerte.

E
1. Si Felipe llega tarde, nosotros no podremos hablar con él.
2. Si Felipe llega tarde, no verá a nadie.
3. Si Felipe llega tarde, no quedará nada de comida.
4. Si Felipe llega tarde, no oirá el concierto.
5. Si Felipe llega tarde, no terminará su trabajo.
6. Si Felipe llega tarde, sus colegas estarán enojados.
7. Si Felipe llega tarde, su esposa no lo esperará.
8. Si Felipe llega tarde, el director no le dará un ascenso.

F
1. Si yo tuviera una fortuna, iría en un vuelo a la luna.
2. Si yo tuviera una fortuna, donaría mucho dinero a las caridades.
3. Si yo tuviera una fortuna, invertiría plata en la Bolsa.
4. Si yo tuviera una fortuna, me compraría un Lamborghini.
5. Si yo tuviera una fortuna, me dedicaría a escribir novelas.
6. Si yo tuviera una fortuna, ayudaría a los niños necesitados.
7. Si yo tuviera una fortuna, me tumbaría en una playa tropical.
8. Si yo tuviera una fortuna, alquilaría un castillo en España.

G
1. Si tú hubieras oído la noticia, te habrías sorprendido.
2. Si Uds. hubieran oído la noticia, se habrían enojado.
3. Si nosotros hubiéramos oído la noticia, nos habríamos reído.
4. Si ellos hubieran oído la noticia, se habrían entusiasmado.
5. Si Raquel hubiera oído la noticia, se habría preocupado.
6. Si Ud. hubiera oído la noticia, se habría asustado.
7. Si Lupe y Pedro hubieran oído la noticia, se habrían molestado.
8. Si yo hubiera oído la noticia, me habría ofendido.

Chapter 13 Reflexive Verbs

A
1. Tú te despiertas a las ocho y media.
2. Beatriz y yo nos lavamos la cabeza a las diez menos cuarto.
3. Ud. se cepilla los dientes al levantarse.
4. Yo me visto después de desayunar.
5. Alberto y Esteban se afeitan antes de ducharse.
6. Uds. se secan el pelo después de lavárselo.
7. Alicia se maquilla la cara dos veces al día.
8. Pablo se acuesta a medianoche.

B
1. Yo voy a divertirme mucho en la reunión familiar.
2. Pedro va a probarse unos zapatos deportivos.
3. Camila y Leonardo van a casarse a mediados de mayo.
4. Tú vas a despedirte de tus amigos.
5. Los jefes van a reunirse en la sala de conferencias.
6. Uds. van a instalarse en la casa para el mes próximo.
7. Nosotros vamos a matricularnos este semestre.
8. Ud. va a graduarse después de aprobar los exámenes.

C 1. María y Marco se hablan por teléfono.
2. Tú y yo nos vemos todos los días.
3. Rafael y Miguel se mandan mensajes de texto.
4. Isabel y yo nos tuteamos.
5. Gerardo y Consuelo se quieren mucho.
6. Ud. y yo nos ayudamos en todo.
7. Juliana y Emilia se escriben con frecuencia.
8. Rosa y Carlos se entienden bien.

D 1. Sí, se lo cortó.
2. Sí, se los puso.
3. Sí, nos lo abrochamos.
4. Sí, se los cepillaron.
5. Sí, se lo quité.
6. Sí, se la lavaron.
7. Sí, me las rompí.
8. Sí, se la probó.

E 1. Sí, séqueselo.
2. Sí, abróchenselo.
3. Sí, láveselas.
4. Sí, quítenselas.
5. Sí, límpienselos.
6. Sí, límeselas.
7. Sí, pruébeselo.
8. Sí, píntenselos.

F 1. No, no te lo pongas.
2. No, no se lo cortes.
3. No, no te las pintes.
4. No, no se los limpies.
5. No, no se los desabroches.
6. No, no te los maquilles.
7. No, no te la pruebes.
8. No, no se los quites.

G 1. Ah sí, reunámonos con nuestros amigos.
2. Ah sí, sentémonos en el patio.
3. Ah sí, aprovechémonos de la ocasión.
4. Ah sí, acerquémonos a los músicos.
5. Ah sí, riámonos mucho.
6. Ah sí, despidámonos de los anfitriones.
7. Ah sí, vámonos ya.
8. Ah sí, démonos prisa.

Chapter 14 The Present Participle; The Progressive Tenses

A   1. Pasó la tarde haciendo funcionar su computadora.
     2. Pasamos la tarde arreglándonos para el cóctel.
     3. Pasó la tarde tocando el piano.
     4. Pasé la tarde enviando e-mails.
     5. Pasaron la tarde navegando en la Red.
     6. Pasé la tarde relajándome.
     7. Pasó la tarde escribiendo un cuento.
     8. Pasamos la tarde instalándonos en la nueva casa.

B   1. Sí, nos lo estamos poniendo ahora mismo.
     2. Sí, se está vistiendo ahora mismo.
     3. Sí, se los estoy cepillando ahora mismo.
     4. Sí, se están afeitando ahora mismo.
     5. Sí, me la estoy lavando ahora mismo.
     6. Sí, se está acostando ahora mismo.
     7. Sí, los estoy despertando ahora mismo.
     8. Sí, se los estoy quitando ahora mismo.

C   1. No, seguía viéndolo.
     2. No, seguía cortándoselo.
     3. No, seguíamos sirviéndosela.
     4. No, seguían preocupándose.
     5. No, seguía corriendo en el maratón.
     6. No, seguían dirigiéndola.
     7. No, seguía probándomela.
     8. No, seguían estudiándola.

D   1. Llevamos varios días buscándolo.
     2. Llevo veinte minutos bañándolo.
     3. Llevo quince minutos arreglándome.
     4. Lleva toda la vida quejándose.
     5. Llevan ocho años diseñándolos.
     6. Llevo poco tiempo escribiéndoselo.
     7. Llevamos casi quince años dedicándonos a la fotografía.
     8. Lleva mucho tiempo oyéndolos tocar.

E   1. Yo estaba navegando en la Red.
     2. Rosaura estaba creando una base de datos.
     3. Tú estabas leyendo los informes.
     4. Silvia estaba contestando el teléfono.
     5. Uds. estaban visitando unos sitios Web.
     6. Ud. estaba entrando datos.
     7. Daniel y Mario estaban reuniéndose con sus colegas.
     8. Sofía estaba recibiendo a unos clientes.

F 1. Tú estarás ocupándote de estos asuntos.
2. Ellos estarán poniéndose de acuerdo.
3. Yo estaré cuidándolos.
4. Nosotros estaremos sirviéndoselo.
5. Ella estará probándoselas.
6. Yo estaré lavándomela.
7. Él estará entusiasmándose con la buena noticia.
8. Ud. estará explicándonoslo.

G 1. No, lo eligieron Andrés y Beatriz.
2. No, la trajo la mesera.
3. No, la llevó al restaurante Pablo.
4. No, lo pidió Eduardo.
5. No, lo comimos nosotros.
6. No, lo bebió Octavio.
7. No, la pagó Jaime.
8. No, la dejé yo.

Chapter 15 Passive Constructions; Reverse Construction Verbs

A 1. Los programas fueron instalados por el técnico.
2. La base de datos fue creada por los asesores.
3. Las pastillas fueron recetadas por su médico.
4. Las ensaladas fueron preparadas por ese cocinero.
5. Otras sucursales fueron abiertas por la empresa.
6. El contrato fue firmado por los clientes.
7. La furgoneta fue alquilada por los turistas.
8. El proyecto fue realizado por estos hombres de negocios.

B 1. Se mandaron los mensajes de texto.
2. Se hizo el plan de negocios.
3. No se resolvieron los problemas.
4. Se marcó el número de teléfono.
5. Se consiguieron los billetes electrónicos.
6. Se produjeron manzanas.
7. Se compró un coche todo terreno.
8. No se cubrieron los gastos.

C 1. Se maneja con cuidado.
2. Se entra por aquella puerta.
3. Se vive felizmente.
4. Se llega a las siete.
5. Se necesita comprar jugo.
6. No se puede salir por aquí.
7. No se debe comer comida basura.
8. Se efectúan importantes cambios.

D 1. Le encantaron las obras de teatro.
    2. Nos cayeron bien esos señores.
    3. Les entusiasmaron nuestras ideas.
    4. Me interesaron las clases de arte.
    5. ¿No te fascinaron esas ciudades?
    6. Les desagradaron esos olores.
    7. No nos importaron sus opiniones.
    8. Le quedaron unos días de vacaciones.

E 1. Me interesa mucho la pintura de Velázquez.
    2. Le fascinan los mapas antiguos.
    3. Les entusiasma jugar al fútbol.
    4. Nos desagradan los malos modales.
    5. Me gusta su actitud optimista.
    6. Me importa más que nada mi familia.
    7. Nos disgusta oír los celulares por todas partes.
    8. Les falta capital para hacer crecer la compañía.
    9. Le hizo falta tener la mente abierta.
  10. Nos agradó la actitud positiva del equipo.

F 1. Se te quedó el celular en la oficina.
    2. Se les descompuso el carro en plena carretera.
    3. Se le olvidaron las tarjetas de crédito.
    4. Se nos cayeron los vasos.
    5. Se les ocurrieron unas ideas geniales.
    6. Se me acabó la paciencia de tanta espera.
    7. Se le rompió el meñique jugando al tenis.
    8. Se le quebró la voz de tanto hablar.

G 1. Les toca a ellos comprar los quesos.
    2. Le toca a Alejandro servir el vino.
    3. Les toca a Uds. poner la mesa.
    4. Le toca a Miriam arreglar las flores.
    5. Nos toca a nosotros traer los postres.
    6. Le toca a Roni cocinar el pescado.
    7. Me toca a mí encender las velas.
    8. Le toca a David cortar el pan.

Index